The Psychological Assessmer Reading

Children and some adults need to be assessed in their literacy skills to monitor their level of achievement. Assessors need to see if this level will meet their requirements in their educational setting or in their work environment, with a view to doing something about this achievement level should it fall below a certain criterion.

The Psychological Assessment of Reading is a comprehensive new handbook of literacy, including reviews of the latest and most helpful tests available. The book begins by examining the theoretical issues behind the assessment of reading, including dyslexia, screening, legal aspects, memory and visual problems and computer-based assessment. Assessment of reading for professional groups of teachers, educational psychologists and optometrists is focused on and discussed. There are also chapters covering the assessment of reading comprehension, spelling and written expression, reading skills in adults, and the acquired reading disorders. The final section independently reviews specific tests of literacy.

The Psychological Assessment of Reading offers guidance for all those involved in the assessment process. It outlines the pitfalls that have to be avoided and guidelines for good practice.

John R. Beech is a Senior Lecturer in Psychology at the University of Leicester, and co-editor of *Cognitive Approaches to Reading* (1987) with Ann Colley.
Chris Singleton is a Lecturer in Psychology at the University of Hull and editor of the *Journal of Research in Reading*.

Routledge Assessment Library
Series editors: John R. Beech and Leonora Harding

The *Routledge Assessment Library* is the definitive collection of reference books on assessment. Written by professionals from a wide range of different disciplines, the books are multi-disciplinary in their approach. Each contains a comprehensive discussion of all the important issues relating to assessment in the area specified, and a critical review of the main assessments in the field.

Assessment of the elderly
Edited by John R. Beech and Leonora Harding

Assessment in speech and language therapy
Edited by John Beech and Leonora Harding
with Diana Hilton-Jones

Assessment in neuropsychology
Edited by Leonora Harding and John R. Beech

The Psychological
Assessment of Reading

Edited by John R. Beech
and Chris Singleton

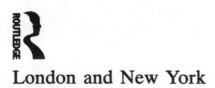

London and New York

First published 1997 by Routledge
11 New Fetter Lane, London EC4P 4EE

Simultaneously published in the USA and Canada
by Routledge
29 West 35th Street, New York, NY 10001

Typeset in Times by Florencetype Ltd, Stoodleigh, Devon
Printed and bound in Great Britain by Mackays of Chatham PLC,
Chatham, Kent

British Library Cataloguing in Publication Data
A catalogue record for this book is available from the British Library

Library of Congress Cataloguing in Publication Data
The psychological assessment of reading / edited by John R. Beech and
  Chris Singleton.
      p.   cm. – (Routledge assessment library)
    Includes bibliographical references and indexes.
    1. Reading–Ability testing. 2. Reading, Psychology of.
  I. Beech, John R. II. Singleton, Chris, 1944–   . III. Series.
  LB1050.46.P75   1997
  428.4'076–dc21   97–3684

ISBN 0–415–12858–7 (hbk)
ISBN 0–415–12859–5 (pbk)

Contents

Illustrations

Contributors

John R. Beech, Department of Psychology, University of Leicester, University Road, Leicester LE2 7RH.

Kate Cain, Laboratory of Experimental Psychology, University of Sussex, Brighton BN1 9QG.

Bruce J. W. Evans, Institute of Optometry, 56–62 Newington Causeway, London SE1 6DS.

John Friel, Kings Bench Walk Chamber (Lord Campbell of Alloway), Temple, London EC4Y 7DE.

Janice Kay, Department of Psychology, Washington Singer Laboratories, Exeter EX4 4QG.

David McLoughlin, Adult Dyslexia Centre, 5 Tavistock Place, London WC1H 9SN.

David V. Moseley, Department of Education, Fourth Floor, Ridley Building, Claremont Place, Newcastle upon Tyne NE1 7RU.

Jane V. Oakhill, Laboratory of Experimental Psychology, University of Sussex, Brighton BN1 9QG.

Peter D. Pumfrey, School of Education, University of Manchester, Oxford Road, Manchester M13 9PL.

John P. Rack, Centre for Reading and Language, Department of Psychology, University of York, York YO1 5DD.

Chris Singleton, Department of Psychology, University of Hull, Hull HU6 7RX.

Martin Turner, The Dyslexia Institute, 133 Gresham Road, Staines TW18 2AJ.

Denis Vincent, East London Assessment Group, University of East London, Longbridge Road, Dagenham, Essex RM8 2AS.

Series editors' preface

Assessment involves collecting information and making a judgement about someone in relation to a large group of people, usually matched in age. In carrying out such as assessment the professional believes that what they are doing is a necessary basis for deciding a particular course of action. This activity is considered to be mainly in the best interests of the person being assessed, but at times will also protect the interests of society, or an organisation. Whether or not one agrees with the concept of making an assessment, the practice continues in our society, even if it waxes and wanes in some professional sectors. Our own view is that assessment is here to stay and in many cases is beneficial to the individual.

It is important that the best available means of assessment are used by professional workers to provide an accurate body of knowledge on which to base decisions. Errors of diagnosis can sometimes have serious consequences. For instance, a violent prisoner might be released prematurely, a child might continue to be kept in a family where there is considerable risk of violence, and so on. Less dramatic situations would be ones in which a child is inaccurately assessed and is then put on a training programme that is not appropriate for his or her needs, or where an elderly person is inaccurately considered as unable to live in her own home and transferred to another environment. Given that many of these assessments are essential, improving their accuracy is a worthwhile goal. If this series of volumes is instrumental in improving accuracy to some degree, we will be very pleased.

As well as the problem of the inaccurate use of tests, breakdown of communication between professions can lead to wrong decisions and inappropriate therapy or placement plans. Any one client may be treated, assessed or discussed by a number of professionals with different training, areas of expertise, approaches to assessment and vocabulary. (The term 'client' itself suggests one particular approach to care.) This series is explicitly directed at the sharing of knowledge and the breaking down of barriers between professionals. We believe multidisciplinary cooperation and information exchange can only benefit the subjects of assessment. It should be borne in mind, however, that certain tests that have been reviewed in these volumes can only be applied by professionals with the appropriate qualifications. We continue to hope that there will be a certain amount of liberalisation of these strictures in the future in order to facilitate cooperation between professionals.

Our readership for these volumes is the professional workers who are involved with such groups, either directly as assessors or indirectly as those who use test results in their decision making. Students training for these professions, or professionals undergoing in-service training will also find them useful. We have, therefore, set our writers a very difficult task. Each contribution has to be easy to read, but at the same time has to provide information that the current professional worker will find useful when deciding on an assessment strategy. The writer might point to a new test that has been developed, or highlight the inadequacies of one being currently used. The chapters do describe the application of tests within a particular area, but they also provide a range of other useful information, for instance, check-lists, case studies, points to bear in mind with certain types of patient, and so on.

Most of the volumes contain a final section of reviews on the main tests currently applied in that area. Making choices about what to include has been difficult; but the final choice is based on extensive consultation with practising professionals and researchers. The end result should contain the tests used most frequently within an area. The problem is that there is usually a large variety of more minor tests, each of which is probably used by only a few workers. From this group we have chosen those tests which seem to contain a feature or application of outstanding interest, or those tests which we felt deserved wider use.

All the test reviews are written within a prearranged structure. Information is given about the purposes of the test, how to use it and an evaluation is also made. Some technical information is provided, such as the number of people who were tested in order to develop the test. Where available, the reliability and validity are supplied. The reliability shows the extent to which applying the same test again will give the same result. A low reliability indicates that assessment could be inaccurate as the outcome changes on successive occasions. The validity of the test shows how well the test is associated with similar tests measuring the same properties. The reader does not necessarily need any prior knowledge in order to understand these test reviews.

The present volume is mainly about the assessment of reading, but we also include a chapter on assessing spelling and written expression. The assessment of literacy is a very important field as so many individuals in our society suffer because they were not adequately assessed in their early years. They have missed out on what could have been appropriate training to enable them to become fluent readers in an important phase of their lives: their passage through secondary school. We hope that this volume will raise awareness of the issues involved and will be of specific help to specialists, teachers, and parents who are thinking about having their child assessed for reading difficulties.

Turning briefly to the contents of the present volume, it begins with an introduction that addresses the main issues in testing literacy, such as discussing whether it is valid to have a 'dyslexia' versus 'poor reader' separation. It describes the major ways of testing literacy, major concepts in psychometrics and possible developments in the field in the future. Chapters 2 and 3 examine testing from the perspectives of the teacher and the educational psychologist, respectively. Chapter 4 examines research into screening reading difficulties and its effectiveness. Chapters 5, 6 and 7 look at cognitive and perceptual problems that have been related to reading difficulties. Chapter 8 examines the problems involved in assessing emotional and motivational aspects of literacy performance. Chapter 9 is concerned with more advanced reading in which meaning from text is extracted. Chapter 10 is involved with testing written expression and spelling. Chapter 11 deals with how adults with reading problems are assessed for their literacy. Their problems can be more difficult to assess, and their sensitivities have to be handled carefully. Chapter 12 deals with the acquired dyslexias which are conditions caused by brain damage, usually stroke. These conditions are interesting because they impair certain functions but leave other functions intact and can tell us a great deal about how normal readers function. Chapter 13 is about the advantages of assessing literacy skills by means of computer. Finally, professionals at some time may find themselves in court over wrangles about their assessments. Chapter 14 is relevant within this context, as well as providing some cautions over what is appropriate.

Finally, we would like to thank Dr Viv Ward at Routledge for her encouragement and patient involvement with the project and the anonymous reviewers for their suggestions concerning the initial proposals. We would also like to thank all the contributors for their involvement in this volume.

John R. Beech and Leonora Harding
Series editors

1 The psychological assessment of reading
Theoretical issues and professional solutions

John R. Beech and Chris Singleton

Why do we need to assess literacy? Often because we, as professionals (either psychologists or specialist teachers), are called upon to do so. Usually it is because a child is experiencing (or is perceived by parents and/or teachers to be experiencing) some difficulties in learning to read, write or spell. We have to establish: (1) whether there really is a difficulty (not just an imagined problem); (2) the extent of the difficulty, should it exist; (3) the most likely cause, or causes, of the difficulty, and finally, (4) we are usually asked to recommend ways of putting things right. *Causes* are important, because they affect the recommendations one would make regarding appropriate help or support for the child. Many children with poor literacy skills are referred for assessment (whether privately or within the state system) on suspicion of dyslexia. Some are indeed found to have dyslexia, while others are often found to have been deprived of appropriate *teaching* (most commonly phonics tuition) or to lack the *practice* which is essential for basic literacy skills to become fluent. If the cause seems to be lack of appropriate teaching, simply recommending certain educational input may not be a sufficient remedy if the child's teacher does not have the appropriate skills or the child's school does not have the appropriate resources.

We could say initially that we need to assess children in order to monitor their level of achievement in literacy and we want to assess adults and adolescents because we need to see whether their achievement is sufficient to meet the requirements of whatever they are doing at work or in an educational setting. We assume here that assessment is in relation to the average literacy achievements of others of equivalent age. We might also implicitly assume that we are making the assessment in order to do something about it, if necessary.

Going deeper into this, we begin to get more controversial. Yes, we can monitor achievement in relation to others, but sometimes an assessor might say: 'I'm afraid that this level of achievement is to be expected given overall cognitive ability.' For example: 'This child's intelligence is predicting a level of performance in reading that is actually close to her actual level of reading.' This does not mean that we expect reading skill to be necessarily anchored firmly to expectation. For instance, a child on a par with expectation could probably still enhance reading skills. There may even be reciprocity so that improving reading skills gradually feeds back to improve intelligence (see Stanovich, 1986).

Returning to the adult or the adolescent, our problem is not just about potential cognitive processes in relation to literacy, but also about what we can do about it to compensate within an examination setting. Some might feel that it is a little late to tackle the problem in the examination room by allowing extra time, when the roots of the problem might have been tackled earlier. Another example might be that the adult is referred by the employer as the job requires an upgrade. Is the individual capable of handling more paperwork, perhaps taking down telephone messages, or entering information into a computer database? If not, could training be provided to improve the necessary skills?

These are some of the problems that permeate how we make an assessment in reading – and in writing as well. Assessment has grown in importance, due partly to the development of better techniques for assessment and to a change in political climate that requires more accountability. Not just politicians but parents are developing an increasing awareness of the issues involved. At the same time there has been a lot of publicity about the decline in standards in literacy. However, although there may be an impression of a decline, there is now little objective evidence for such a decline, simply because in the UK formal monitoring of standards was disbanded several years ago.

DYSLEXIA AND ASSOCIATED CONTROVERSIES

Many people still believe that it is not possible to make a reasonable assessment of reading until the child is about 8 years of age. The reason given is that children differ in their rate of progress in their early years and as they have only started to learn to read at about the age of 5 years, it is difficult to tell reliably whether children are seriously behind in their reading development. Nevertheless, testing is reliable enough for it to be possible to use the WORD reading and spelling tests in conjunction with the Wechsler Intelligence Scale for Children (WISC-III), to work out if there is a significant disparity between observed and expected WORD scores down to the age of 6 years. The likelihood of finding a discrepancy and its reliability in the early years is probably lower compared with later. However, a bright child who can hardly write anything coherently and who cannot read and understand simple sentences would probably be a good candidate for testing at the age of 6 or 7 years.

These tests are psychometric tests that cannot be undertaken by the teacher but only by an appropriately qualified psychologist. Most teachers at present would not make an assessment concerning whether the child is reading significantly below potential, only that reading performance was below the child's peers. (If they desired they could use an *open* test of intelligence, a test that is unrestricted in use, and calculate centile or standard score discrepancy.) This is currently an important distinction in mode of operation between psychologist and teacher. It is also part of the controversy surrounding intelligence testing referred to earlier.

The basis of the reading discrepancy approach is to produce regression equations on large samples of reading and Intelligence Quotient (IQ) scores. This enables a prediction from the regression line of what the expected reading level would be for a given level of intelligence, allowing for chronological age. The important assumption is that there is a good linear relationship, or correlation, between the two variables. One area of debate has been to argue that the correlation with reading is less for full-scale IQ than for verbal IQ. Full-scale IQ involves the assessment of verbal and non-verbal processes or abilities in equal measure. It would therefore be better to base these regression equations on verbal IQ alone. One slight problem with this suggestion is that the mental arithmetic component of verbal IQ can be affected by poor verbal memory in the WISC-III. Mental arithmetic requires an involvement in verbal working memory, which can be problematic in dyslexia.

Another problem is a practical one. In a city like Leicester, for example, it would be difficult for the educational authority, responsible for more than 300 schools, to make a mass assessment of reading potential based solely on verbal intelligence as a substantial part of the community is of Indian, Pakistani, African and Afro-Caribbean origin. A proportion of these children are using English as a second language and testing their verbal intelligence on an English verbal intelligence test may be under-estimating their intelligence. For example, Beech and Keys (in press) found that controlling for nonverbal IQ, there was a marked impairment in receptive oral vocabulary (a verbal IQ component) in a group of bilingual British Asian children of lower socioeconomic status aged 7-8 years compared with monolingual controls. This underestimate in verbal IQ would in turn reduce the proportion of such children who would be considered to be under-using their potential, because a lower predicted IQ in turn means a lower predicted potential in reading. An added complication is that the current data on the importance of phonology for early reading apply to an alphabetic language such as English in which letters approximately correspond to phonemes. This may not be so important in some other languages.

One alternative would be to produce special tests for each foreign language group, but this is also going to have the problem of being discriminatory. Clearly the issue has to be handled sensitively, but if one is too sensitive, many children may be forgoing appropriate skill learning.

If an education authority were to adopt the discrepancy approach there is the further problem that an application of an intelligence test, such as the WISC, has to be done individually by a qualified psychologist; this option is automatically ruled out for mass screening at present on the grounds of prohibitive cost.

The reading discrepancy approach can give rise to two different types of reading difficulty. First, there is the child with a specific reading difficulty, whose difficulties are confined to reading (and possibly other areas of literacy) but whose other skills and attainments are not significantly lower than expected. This is often referred to as 'dyslexia'.[1] In the context of reading, the term now generally refers to someone who from their full scale intelligence score is predicted to have a reading performance at a certain level, but who is statistically significantly behind this level of performance. Some authorities would argue that a 'discrepant' measure like this should be regarded as the defining characteristic of a *specific reading difficulty*, but not necessarily of *dyslexia*. There are many reasons why a child may be attaining in reading far lower than intelligence levels would predict. One reason might be that the child has not received appropriate teaching. If that were the sole reason for the child's difficulties one would not want to class this as a case of dyslexia, which usually implies a constitutional cause of some kind. Other authorities have sought to qualify a discrepancy approach by requiring several additional criteria, or impediments. However, to restrict the concept of 'dyslexia' to children who show no other difficulties (such as hearing problems) contradicts the fundamental concept of dyslexia being a *constitutional* condition. The same criticism may be levelled at those who in the past have adopted a view of dyslexia that has resulted in the condition being observed mainly among children from middle-class homes (see Critchley, 1970). This was an acknowledgement that there may be circumstances at home that may be responsible for a lack of literacy development. This is not necessarily to do with class, of course; it is thus difficult to make an assessment of this kind of influence. Similarly, a child may be emotionally affected in some way, perhaps manifesting substantial behavioural problems.

Another criterion used by some authors is that there has to be a minimum level of intelligence. For instance, Vellutino (1979) advocated an IQ more than 90 (the average, adjusting for age, is 100); Critchley refers to 'an adequate IQ'. However, given the use of the regression equation, one does come across children who have a lower IQ than 90, who still have a significant deficit in reading in relation to expectation. Realistically they should be referred to as having dyslexia. From the point of view of carrying out a research study on children with dyslexia one would normally use a cut-off point of something like 90. However, when testing an individual child for dyslexia, there should be no such limitation.

The second type of reading problem is often called 'poor reading', although in the past it has been referred to as 'reading backwardness'. This is usually where the child's intelligence is considerably below the norm. Using the same regression equation one would still be able to predict a certain level of reading performance. Because the child is at such a low level of IQ performance, the child is predicted to be low in reading as well. Thus this category of reader should be easily noticed in the class-room as reading performance would be poor on a standard reading test. The child with specific reading difficulties would not necessarily be noticed in the classroom, because the reading problem might be mild. However, in relation to potential it could be severe.

Do we treat the two types of children differently and should we treat them differently? The motivation of the teacher could be affected by this knowledge. One might think that learning is going to have to be at a slower pace for the poor reader. But this is not necessarily going to be the case. Yule *et al.* (1974) in a study of all the 9 and 10 year olds on the Isle of Wight found that children with specific reading difficulties actually made poorer progress. The main contrasts between the groups were that three-quarters of those with specific reading difficulties were boys and there were no organic disorders compared with 11% of the poor readers. There are interesting examples of children with low IQs who become very good read-ers, in the sense that their reading out loud becomes very accomplished.

Perhaps the major difference may be at the reading comprehension level. Brighter children with poor basic word reading skills often manage to compensate when reading text by making intelligent inferences about the gist of the text. They also use context more effectively, have a better knowledge of syntax and have a 'world knowledge' enabling them to make guesses that can compensate for specific word knowledge. By contrast, those who are less bright may have a better idea of word identification, but find it difficult to get to the appropriate meaning of the text. Another contrast is that those with specific reading difficulties tend to have prob-lems more concentrated in terms of phonological difficulties (Jorm *et al.*, 1986).

Some have argued against using the intelligence test altogether, espe-cially on the grounds that it is culturally biased. As far as assessing reading comprehension is concerned, some have advocated the use of listening comprehension as a simpler method of measuring the disparity between the potential to comprehend and actual level of comprehension by means of reading print. This is discussed further in Chpater 9 on reading compre-hension. Listening comprehension is obviously going to be useful to assess reading comprehension potential, but for tests of accuracy of reading print we are still left with full scale IQ as all that is available at present.

To be even handed, there are researchers (e.g. Siegel, 1992) who have argued that the discrepancy definition of reading problems is unnecessary as poor readers (whose reading is consistent with their IQ scores) are not differentiated from discrepant readers as both have problems in phonology and verbal memory and other aspects. (This is in contrast to Jorm *et al.* cited earlier (1986).) Another argument against the intelligence test is that it is increasingly being recognised that dyslexia is a constitutional condition that is generally inherited (but which may be due to birth difficulties).

There is no reason why it should not occur among children of below average IQ. It could also (and probably will) co-occur with other disabilities (e.g. hearing impairment). The conventional definition of dyslexia rules out such children. Perhaps one day a definition of 'genetic dyslexia' will be devised.

The practical problem is that even if there were no difference in the difficulties of the two different types of problem readers, it does not preclude the importance of finding children who are underachieving. There could be large numbers of children who are discrepant in their reading and who are not being identified as having problems as such because their absolute level of reading and spelling performance is superficially indicating that nothing is seriously amiss. The situation at the moment is that such children are only coming to light if their parents make a fuss. Many LEAs do not explicitly tie specific learning difficulties to a *statistically* significant discrepancy between reading quotient and IQ, but to some *arbitrary* threshold (e.g. reading age two years behind chronological age). Often the child lags behind, but not enough to trigger specialist help. Then the gap steadily widens until the threshold is crossed and specialist help is eventually provided (but disappointingly late).

Miles (1994) makes a wider criticism of the notion that readers with dyslexia and poor readers should be lumped together, maintaining that, by contrast, there should be a separation of reading from other allied difficulties. Many individuals with reading problems also suffer from other difficulties such as slowness of processing, numeracy difficulties and difficulty in writing ideas that can be expressed much more easily verbally. The dyslexic versus poor reader distinction may be too simplistic, when there could be far more significant distinctions to be made, possibly with implications for future prospects in training.

So far we have only discussed the involvement of the psychologist in making an assessment of literacy. There could be other professionals implicated in this who at present have hardly any involvement. For example, speech and language therapists and optometrists ought to be involved in assessment. There is now plenty of evidence for the importance of phonology in reading (see Chapter 6). Training children in establishing letter–sound connections can have positive benefits on their subsequent reading. Bradley and Bryant (1983) in a classic experiment trained children who were behind in phonology and showed that training such children in these skills, i.e. learning about letter–sound connections, significantly improved reading relative to other control groups. Many teachers would not be surprised in the least by these findings.

It could be helpful to involve speech and language therapists in assessments in phonology in relation to reading. There are simple initial tests that can be applied to see whether a referral would be useful. For instance, from about 6 or 7 years of age onwards a graded test of nonword reading could be a first filter to highlight children who are having problems with phonics. If it is clear that they have already been given extensive training in phonics by their teachers, they could be examined further by a speech and language therapist. This would be with a view to finding out if there is a problem with their underlying awareness of sound structure. If necessary, the therapist could be involved with appropriate intensive training to develop phonological and phonemic awareness further.

Chapter 5 by Bruce Evans covers visual problems in reading. One aspect related to reading is visual discomfort, for which at present we do not have very good ways of screening. However, it is potentially very important for the young child. It is clear that quite a number of children suffer from this problem (although we do not know how many) and it will inevitably affect their literacy acquisition from the beginning. When children are routinely screened in schools for eyesight, there is surely no reason why those who are also substantially behind in reading and spelling should not be given further tests for visual function that might relate to their current reading problems.

TYPES OR LEVELS OF DIAGNOSTIC LITERACY ASSESSMENT

The assessment of literacy is usually equated with giving the child or adult a series of isolated words and asking them to read them aloud. However, reading aloud single words is just one of several skills that are important. Some would argue that an even more important skill is reading comprehension. It is possible to have a reasonably good reading vocabulary and yet have a poor reading comprehension, even though one would understand the same passage if one simply listened to it.

Beginning with single word reading, this in itself is not sufficient to determine if a child has reading problems, but it is a good start. Such tests typically begin with highly frequent, regularly spelled, short words and gradually move to the opposite poles of these dimensions ending with low frequency, irregular and long words. The writing also begins in large print and ends in a smaller font. The value of the test is that it is taking away all contextual cues and leaves the reader only with the letters of the word that they have to read.

This type of test can provide clues to the child's approach to reading. Does the child seem to have a long pause before making a pronunciation, and are there 'regularisation' errors (e.g. 'dread' being read as 'dreed')? Does the child 'sound out', i.e. produce a whispered phonetic pronunciation (e.g. 'duh-ruh-ee-duh: dreed')? These could all be indications of the use of phonics. This is usually a good sign, as it indicates an alternative route to reading is being developed. But beware of its overuse, so that even very familiar words are given the same treatment. This condition is sometimes referred to as 'developmental surface dyslexia'. Although such reading can become relatively fast, reading letters or small letter clusters representing phonemes (these letters or letter clusters, e.g.

sh, are called 'graphemes'), then blending them to form words, is computationally a very demanding form of reading. The result is that such readers may rarely read for pleasure if they continue to do this for the majority of words (e.g. Hanley *et al.*, 1992).

Another test is a nonword test of reading. This is a more direct test of the use of the development of phonics in reading. The child is given a pronounceable nonword such as 'blenk' to read. This might be read by the use of letter–sound translation rules or by a mixture of analogy (with the words 'blank' or 'blend', perhaps) and phonics. Sometimes a child may be a poor reader, but be better developed in phonics. This could indicate a danger that phonics was being over-used in reading. The ideal is for a fast automatic response to familiar words.

A similar kind of test is one examining the efficiency of reading words that are regular and irregular in spelling. If there is a large disparity in performance, this can indicate that the child has an over-reliance on a phonic approach to reading. The irregular words are generating phonological codes that do not correspond to the correct pronunciation and therefore interfere with responses.

Another potential test of developmental surface dyslexia is to compare the reaction time to identify whether words which match vary according to length. This would normally be a laboratory-based task in which one is looking for an increased slope (the steepness of the angle of the line of best fit of the reaction times) as a function of word length relative to the slope of normal readers.

Little is known about what to do about an over-reliance on phonics. The first thing would be to try to produce an understanding of when it would be appropriate to use a phonics strategy, namely when a word is unfamiliar. However, fast automatised reading is far better for familiar words. For more inexperienced readers this might involve trying to work through a set of flash cards (containing individual words to be named aloud) against the clock. More experienced readers could be encouraged to speed read by tracing text with their fingers as quickly as possible.

Developmental phonological dyslexia is a condition when a child, or adult, is unable to read nonwords, or reads them with great difficulty. This inability does not present insuperable difficulties to learning to read, especially if the reader has someone to turn to who can supply the pronunciation of unfamiliar words (see the case studied by Campbell and Butterworth, 1985). From one perspective, many, if not most children with reading problems could be said to have developmental phonological dyslexia to varying degrees. They typically find it difficult to identify nonwords, but training in phonic skills can produce improvements in general reading performance (e.g. Adams, 1990). Therefore, poor nonword reading performance would normally be followed by the recommendation that the reader should be given training in phonics. This would not just be at a basic level of single letters to individual sounds, but would progress to more complicated grapheme–phoneme connections and further until pronounceable nonwords of sufficient length are tackled without difficulty. In this way, an efficient technique becomes available to help the reader over the hurdle of decoding difficult words. It has to be borne in mind that this technique will work better for regular words than for irregular ones. In addition, some children have such an impairment in their phonological processes that learning more than rudimentary grapheme–phoneme connections could be counter productive (Beech, 1994).

As the reader progresses, the reading comprehension test becomes increasingly important, as Jane Oakhill and Kate Cain (Chapter 9) demonstrate. In the early years a lot of emphasis is given to learning to read and write and become numerate. Gradually these same skills are used more and more to acquire information about the curriculum. If a child fails to progress in literacy in these early stages there is a double burden: trying to learn these basic skills and trying to keep up with the curriculum. Understandably they can fall further and further behind. This is where the reading comprehension test becomes so important, as it might indicate the extent to which the child can cope with the curriculum.

As mentioned before, the single word reading test is valuable for examining skills in reading in the absence of context. Sometimes readers do very poorly on the single word test, but do well on the reading comprehension test. Although such children will get by in reading materials within their curriculum, there could still be problems ahead in situations in which the precise meaning of the text is crucial. A critical point can be when reading examination questions and understanding precisely what is required. Examiners are often told to award no marks to candidates who have not answered the question. Therefore, being able to read accurately can be crucial at certain times, often in situations of maximum stress. Children and young people with dyslexia find multiple choice examinations particularly difficult. The questions typically require attention to the subtlety in the wording of the question and to the alternatives.

One aspect to look out for if conducting a comprehension test involving silent reading, as in the WORD test, is to watch the lips of the child while reading to see if they are moving. This might suggest that fast automatised access to the meaning of the passage is still some way off.

A final point to note about reading comprehension is that there is evidence that frequent reading is related to improved reading vocabulary. Stanovich and Cunningham (1992) have demonstrated that accuracy in the recognition of authors' names is related to reading performance. Like any skill, the more one uses it the better one becomes. It follows that a child with good reading comprehension has the facility to undertake a lot of reading. If this opportunity is used, reading skills should eventually be honed and accuracy in reading isolated words ought to improve as well.

Tests of reading speed are less common. There is a test of reading aloud accurately for one minute short, very common words. However, we do not know at this point how useful this is. At least it can show how automatised reading has become. It would probably be unwise to use it as evidence that a candidate needs extra time in examinations, as presumably slow reading can easily be faked. One problem with this test is that a line of words can be easily missed in the heat of the moment. The Neale Analysis test gives standardised measures of reading speed in terms of age equivalence up to 13 years of age (Neale, 1989).

The ideal test of reading speed and other allied elements would be to use eye monitoring equipment. This would allow an assessment of dysfunctional eye movements as well as scanning speed while reading, but this is not feasible for widespread use at the moment. David McLoughlin (Chapter 11) provides some norms of reading speeds for different types of text.

Finally there are tests of literacy related to writing, including spelling, that are covered by David Moseley (Chapter 10). There is perhaps not the same sense of urgency about problems in writing, and more particularly spelling, as there has been in the past. Massey and Elliott (1996) compared exam scripts from O level in 1980 with GCSE in 1994 and found significant declines in spelling, grammar, punctuation and powers of expression. For instance, exam scripts from 1994 had *three* times more spelling errors than those written in 1980. This could be due partly to significantly more candidates taking GCSEs, so it is difficult to make direct comparisons. In terms of priorities it is most important that the child approaching teenage years is able to read in order to acquire knowledge of school subjects. Being unable to spell correctly has not been considered to be so important. However, the importance of spelling is perhaps in the mind of the beholder. Poor spelling can be an impediment for job prospects. For instance, an employer does not want an employee to send out letters representing the organisation that appear 'illiterate'.

In the sphere of writing assessment, when the assessor is a psychologist the concern is most frequently with whether the writer is able to write normally under examination conditions. Poor spelling is often seen as an impediment to normal writing speed if the writer is having to stop at frequent intervals to review the correct spelling of words they are about to write. Content can also impede writing speed. Children whose spelling is poor often write in an immature manner because they are reluctant to use the vocabulary with which they can speak and understand but cannot spell correctly (e.g. 'big' versus 'enormous'). By having to continually stop and think about spelling when it should be automatic, the flow of thought is disrupted and writing thus becomes disjointed. When teachers are assessing children's (especially young children's) literacy development, they tend to be more concerned with legibility and whether the child can put down ideas and spoken thoughts accurately on paper.

As a footnote, it is important to observe whether the writer is using the appropriate tripod grip, holding the pen between the thumb and the first two fingers. An incorrect grip can lead to cramp or muscular fatigue, especially at crucial times in the examination room in later life. It is surprising how often a poor pen grip is overlooked in so many of our present reception classes. There are special triangular grips or triangular pencils which can be purchased to facilitate the tripod grip. (For detailed consideration of issues relating to assessment and teaching of handwriting see Alston, 1994, 1995, 1996; Alston and Taylor, 1985, 1987; Keily, 1996.)

PSYCHOMETRIC CONCEPTS

The first time we use a test we usually begin by looking at the test to give ourselves a rough idea of what the participant has to do. The next thing would be to examine the test manual to see how precisely the test is applied, how it is subsequently scored, and at what group the test is aimed. In the case of tests of reading and spelling, a major concern will be the age range of the test.

Another consideration is what information this test provides about the participant's skills. What is the rationale behind the test construction and what particular skills are being tested? Is there a sufficient range of skills being tested? For instance, a single word spelling test can inform about spelling vocabulary because it contains words that vary and are ordered in frequency of exposure and use. Thus, the inexperienced speller will only know how to spell words of a certain level of frequency of occurrence. However, does the test also inform about knowledge of those spellings that vary according to context (e.g. *weak* tea versus days of the *week*)?

Once satisfied at this level, check through the test's psychometric properties, which should be provided in the test manual. It is important not to skip this stage, even if the technical information may appear daunting at first. A good manual should provide information on reliability, validity and the distributions of the scores. It is less important to understand the statistical techniques that lie behind the actual test construction. The end result is that you will understand the test's purpose and have an impression of the extent to which you can trust its results. Do not be swayed too much by the tests used by other users. Form your own independent judgement.

One of the most important psychometric concepts is that of reliability. A measuring instrument should produce the same measurement on successive occasions. The extent of this consistency is known as the instrument's reliability. Reliability is going to depend to an extent on the stability of the underlying dimensions being tested, from one time to the next.

There are several kinds of reliability, all of which use the correlation statistic. This is a test of association in which a correlation of 1.0 indicates a maximum, or one-to-one, association and a correlation of zero indicates no relationship. Internal reliability or consistency measures the degree to which the scores on items correlate with other items. This is measured by computing how individual items correlate with the test as a whole. According to Kline (1990), internal consistency of a test should exceed 0.7. Stability measures (test-retest reliabilities) give correlations between successive testings, and equivalence measures provide the correlations in performance between different forms of the test.

Validity is another important concept that is really a matter of judgement. It goes to the heart of the matter as it queries what the test is actually measuring. For instance, is a test of reading comprehension really about the ability to extract information from print, is it about the accuracy of reading the individual words, or is it about both? Face validity refers to the test from the perspective of the person being tested. It is disconcerting for the testee if the tester appears to be applying tests that appear irrelevant to his or her particular problem. Content validity applies to validity as far as the professionals are concerned. Naturally, these two concepts overlap, but they differ insofar as content validity is about how well the test covers the breadth of the dimension under study. One concern here is whether the test items are sufficiently heterogeneous to measure the dimension.

Construct validity refers to the extent to which the test measures the theoretical construct underlying the test. Criterion-related validity is about the correlation between an assessment and an independent measure of a similar task. Concurrent validity refers to when the independent measure of the similar task is undertaken at the same time and is correlated with the test. Finally, predictive reliability is derived when the independent criterion test is carried out later. This would indicate the degree of association between the two tests and therefore the extent to which the assessment predicts performance of the future measure.

In the field of literacy testing face validity is usually high. Poor readers, for example, are asked to read aloud single words and to silently read passages of text. This is the kind of activity they do in everyday life when they experience difficulty in reading. When they are given tests that appear to be irrelevant, such as intelligence tests, the context of these needs to be explained.

Content validity can determine why one test is used in preference to another. Perhaps one relevant concern here is the age of the test; language use changes over time, so that some items may become inappropriate. A minority of professionals would criticise the content validity of using tests of single word reading because it is an unnatural test of reading, especially of children who are learning to read with the help of the context of pictures.

Comparing reliability and validity, reliability is necessary for validity, but not the other way round. It is possible to construct a test that is very reliable, but with no validity to the construction it is measuring. However, it is not possible to have a valid test that is at the same time low in reliability.

Finally, one has an outcome measure, such as a reading or spelling age equivalence, or a standard score. The standard score is in practice similar in distribution to the intelligence quotient, for which a score of 100 is the mean and the standard deviation is 15. They can have a mean of 50 and a standard deviation of 10, called T scores (e.g. as in the British Ability Scales). Technically, z scores are also 'standard scores'. Tables are available, even if not in that particular manual, in which the centile (or percentile) scores and confidence intervals can be checked. Centile scores have a range of zero to 100 and a mean of 50. Their main advantage is that a person's score can be viewed in relation to everyone else. A score on the 60th centile means that the individual is ranked in the 60th position out of 100 which is approximately equivalent to having 40 out of 100 individuals above that position in ranking. Another advantage is that they enable a comparison to be made across different test instruments that may themselves use different indices; for example, one might have an intelligence test (probably an IQ score), a reading test (a reading age) and a spelling test (perhaps a stanine score). Perhaps this Esperanto-like advantage should be used more often by all professionals involved in reading. Confidence intervals are an acknowledgement that there is imprecision in testing so that a standard score of 105, for example, provides a range in the tables between 100 and 110 where the true standard score lies on 95% of occasions. A more detailed account of the psychometric basis of testing may be found in Beech and Harding (1990).

ASSESSMENT AND THE CODE OF PRACTICE

One powerful reason why we need to assess reading and other literacy skills is that schools and teachers now have legal responsibilities concerning the identification of children with special educational needs, that will frequently require the use of appropriate tests of literacy as well as of other abilities. The 1996 Education Act places a statutory duty on LEAs and on the governing bodies of schools to do their best to ensure that the necessary provision is made for any pupil who has special educational needs, and in so doing to have regard to the Code of Practice on the Identification and Assessment of Special Educational Needs (DFE, 1994). In particular, the Code of Practice states that the governing body's report should state the number of pupils with special educational needs and demonstrate the effectiveness of the school's system for identification and assessment. The importance of early identification, assessment and provision for any child who may have special educational needs is strongly emphasised, and the use of appropriate screening or assessment tools is advocated by the Code. A staged model of assessment and intervention is recommended, with five stages being suggested – the first three stages being school-based, while the last two are LEA-based. The fundamental principle is that the school should take primary responsibility for identifying and making provision for children's special educational needs during the first three stages. This approach contrasts with that of the 1981 Education Act, which located such responsibility primarily with the LEA, which then made provision largely through the means of a Statement of Special Educational Needs, and which in turn entitled the school to additional resources in order to meet that particular child's needs. The Code of Practice, as it is now being applied, generally means that access to the statementing procedure and the resources which that can release only becomes possible when a child has passed through the school-based stages of assessment and intervention, and has been shown to require support that is beyond the capabilities of the school using its own expertise or resources.

In the wake of the Code it is therefore now incumbent upon schools and their teachers to have effective procedures for identifying and assessing all types of special educational needs. Among the various types of information relevant to these procedures, the use of standardised tests is advocated by the Code. In deciding whether or not to make a statutory assessment at Stage 4 of the Code, the LEA will require satisfactory evidence of the school's assessment of a child's learning difficulties at Stages 1–3. Although school attainment is an important factor here, it is not the only criterion by which special educational needs are to be judged. The Code recognises that a child may have a learning difficulty even though school attainment is at an average or apparently satisfactory level because the child's attainment may fall short of what is expected. The Code suggests that assessment using standardised tests may be particularly relevant in determining such cases. Where specific learning difficulties are concerned (e.g. dyslexia), there is an expectation expressed in the Code that the school will be able to show clear recorded evidence of lack of progress in reading and spelling, demonstrated by results of appropriately applied tests of reading and spelling, and that in its own attempts to address the problem a structured reading programme has been followed, based on diagnostic assessment of the child's reading performance.

In recent years there has been a spate of legal cases brought by parents against LEAs on the grounds that the LEA failed to provide adequately for the special educational needs of certain children (Callman, 1996). In such cases, most of which have been common law actions for negligence, much has hinged on the expert evidence presented to the courts by psychologists and others, and on the adequacy or otherwise of the information (including information from standardised assessment) which either side has relied on. It is quite likely that in future in educational legal cases reference will increasingly be made to the Code of Practice when trying to establish what might reasonably be expected of a school or LEA in identifying and making provision for pupils with special needs. However, it should be stressed that the wording of the 1996 Education Act is that LEAs and schools should 'have regard to' the provisions of the Code of Practice. Otton (1996) reminds us that where such an expression has been used in other statutes it has not been taken to mean 'obey', 'apply' or even 'follow', and that consequently the legal scope of the Code may require definition by the courts on a case-by-case basis. Clearly there is considerable room for discretion. Nevertheless, the Code is a reflection of the fact that we are now in a political, legal, educational and social climate in which there is increasing expectation that children's educational difficulties will be identified and addressed in the school as swiftly and as effectively as possible. More and more of the education budget is being devolved to schools, and parents will inevitably blame the school when they feel that their child is not making satisfactory progress. Schools will be compelled to keep records which demonstrate that children's progress is being properly monitored and that all reasonable steps are being taken to detect learning difficulties as early as possible. Since school attainment is not the only criterion in this matter, the use of standardised tests will become ever more important. Finally, the objective evidence provided by standardised tests could become enormously important to schools which find themselves in the position of having to defend legal actions. Regardless of one's attitudes towards the growth of the 'litigious society', the future for teachers and educational psychologists is likely to be one in which standardised tests of literacy skills become more, rather than less, important. That being the case, it is imperative that, as professionals, we endeavour to ensure that test (and testing) standards are upheld, that the tests we use are the best possible for the job and that they are applied in the most appropriate way.

ASSESSMENT OF BILINGUAL PUPILS

There can be little doubt that the assessment of bilingual pupils, and those for whom English is not their first language, creates major problems for any psychologist or teacher. Non-English-speaking children may acquire 'surface' language skills within about two years of attending school, but adequate written language skills may take up to another five years to develop (Cummins, 1984). There are obvious obstacles to learning for these children in many areas of the curriculum when the medium of instruction is English. However, it is particularly difficult for the teacher or psychologist to know whether such a pupil is progressing in literacy in English as well as could be expected. By law, the Standard Assessment Tests (SATs) must be administered to all UK children at age 7, other than those who have been in Britain for less than six months (Education Act 1996). Since the bilingual 7 year old's English skills are likely to be very limited, it is difficult to see how SATs can be fairly administered and sensibly interpreted in such cases. Unlike children at school in Wales, who may be SATs tested in spoken Welsh, children from other minority language groups are forced to cope in English. Perhaps surprisingly, research suggests that fully bilingual children are not generally impeded in education, and can actually display linguistic, cognitive and social advantages over monolingual children. This may be because bilingual children have to work much harder – linguistically, cognitively and socially – than monolingual children in order to cope in school. However, bilingualism must be additive and not subtractive for these advantages to appear; i.e. the second language and its culture must be added to the first, not detract from them (Cummins, 1984). Gregory and Kelly (1992) point out that the thinking behind the National Curriculum and the SATs is based on the erroneous assumption that developing proficiency in the first language will interfere with development in the second, and so the emphasis is on developing fluency in English as rapidly as possible – if necessary, at the expense of the first language. In the UK, therefore, advantages that might derive from being brought up in a multilinguistic subculture tend to be swiftly eroded by the insistence of the educational system that proficiency in English (and knowledge of the cultural concomitants of English) should be the paramount goal.

It has often been argued (e.g. Bryans, 1992; Gipps, 1990; Gregory and Kelly, 1992; Joyce, 1988) that all educational experiences and the forms of assessment which accompany such experiences are culture-bound and hence 'unfair' when used with children from cultural, ethnic or linguistic minority groups. Standardised tests of the type used by educational psychologists (especially intelligence tests) are those most frequently singled out for criticism in this respect (Cummins, 1984). Standardised assessment instruments are applicable to the population on which they have been standardised and norm-referenced tests tend to be biased in favour of the majority group within that population (Joyce, 1988). It can be seen, therefore, that cultural, ethnic or linguistic minority groups will usually be at a disadvantage in educational and psychological assessment. Nevertheless, the law in the United States and Britain, as in many other countries, requires that children with learning difficulties are assessed so that appropriate educational provision can be made for them. If such children are from ethnic linguistic groups, how are the psychologists or teachers who have responsibility for assessment to discharge their duty? Note that a child in Britain cannot be regarded as having a learning difficulty solely because the language or form of language of the home is different from the language in which he or she is being taught (Education Act 1996). Similar regulations apply in other countries, such as the United States and Canada. Hence we have a dilemma: when a child from a cultural, ethnic or linguistic minority background is failing at school there is a legal duty to make a proper assessment of that child's learning difficulties and to make appropriate provision, but the forms of assessment available in such cases will generally be inadequate. In this situation, some educational psychologists would go so far as to reject the use of standardised assessment altogether. Bryans (1992), for example, contends that 'psychometric standardised assessment with most non-indigenous, nonwhite groups is irrelevant and misleading and should be discontinued' (p. 144). Furthermore, Bryans goes on to ask: if standardised assessment has to be discarded for some pupils, then why not for all? In the end, this particular debate boils down to the issue of whether or not we want assessment, as far as possible, to have a reliable scientific basis, or whether we are prepared to abandon reliability totally just because at present our scientific tools are inadequate for some cases. The abandonment of all standardised testing would surely be a retrogressive step that would leave education increasingly vulnerable to political prejudice, and the future of individual pupils at the mercy of 'expert' opinion unsupported by empirical evidence.

We will not pretend that a resolution of these complex issues can be offered here. However, teachers and psychologists working in a multicultural and multilingual society cannot turn their backs on the problems. Joyce (1988) suggests that criterion-referenced tests are preferable, and that these should be specific to the child's own progress and not involve comparison with other pupils. However, even criterion-referenced assessment may also be criticised since the criterion itself is inevitably derived from some teacher expectation which is itself norm-related, although perhaps not explicitly so (Pumfrey, 1991). For example, in applying a criterion such as 'Is the child able to read 100 Key Words?' the teacher must have some normative expectations. Otherwise, it is impossible to decide whether or not action should be taken following the answer to the question. If the child failed to achieve the criterion but was only aged 5½ the teacher would probably not see the need to intervene, whereas if that same child passed the criterion the teacher would probably regard the child as quite advanced in literacy development terms. On the other hand, if the child in question was aged 7½ and failed to achieve the criterion, the teacher probably would want to instigate exceptional steps to try to remedy the situation. In other words, there is an assumption being made on the part of the teacher that the 'norm' for acquisition of this criterion is somewhere between 5 years 6 months and 7 years 6 months. If that 'norm' is based on one particular cultural or linguistic group it will not necessarily be accurate when applied to any other.

Common sense dictates that before assessing the pupil's needs the assessor should always have an understanding of the child's cultural and linguistic background and should combine that understanding with observation of their behaviour in the learning situation. One possible way of avoiding the bias that can occur when a norm-referenced assessment instrument is administered to different cultural and linguistic groups is to have a variety of norms based on different groups, although creating or locating an appropriate set of norms may be tricky. A major advantage of computerised assessment (see Chapter 13) is that as children are tested, the computer is able to collect data which may then be used to construct 'local' norms. Under these circumstances the assessor would not be forced to use the norms that accompany the test – which may have been based on some other and entirely inappropriate cultural or linguistic mix of children – but instead can use norms based on the particular group in question.

ASSESSMENT OF LITERACY IN HIGHER EDUCATION

Assessment of literacy skills in adults is complicated by a number of factors. Chief among these is the dearth of appropriate tests. The vast majority of tests of reading and spelling have been designed for use with people age 16 years and under. One notable exception is the WRAT-3 (Wide Range Achievement Test; see Wilkinson, 1993) which comprises sub-tests of single-word reading, spelling, and arithmetic. The norms are based on subjects in the United States, but in the absence of an equivalent British test it has become more widely used in the UK in the last few years. When carrying out assessment of students in higher education, testing of reading and spelling becomes even more problematic because of the lack of norms relating to this generally above average group. We do not know what are (or should be) acceptable limits of reading and spelling ability for undergraduates, and consequently a judgement of whether or not such individuals have a specific reading impairment which might be characteristic of dyslexia is highly uncertain.

Because of the lack of suitable tests (and perhaps also because most educational psychologists are more familiar with the assessment of children of 16 years and under) it is frequently found that psychologists administer to adults tests that were designed for use with children, a practice that is highly questionable (Singleton, 1994, 1995). Not only will the norms be inappropriate, but the content is likely to be as well. The Schonell Graded Word Reading Test (Schonell, 1950) and the Neale Analysis of Reading (Neale, 1989) are but two examples of tests which have been frequently misapplied in the past (Singleton, 1996), and there are some indications that the Wechsler WORD test is now being misused in this way (Singleton, in press). It may be argued that provided the raw scores rather than the norms are used, then administration of child tests to adults is acceptable. However, all tests tend to be relatively poor discriminators at their extremes (i.e. near the 'floor' and 'ceiling' of the test) and when a child's test is used with an older subject (particularly one of above average ability) the person is likely to be scoring close to the ceiling of the test. Any differences found are likely to be due to the reading of a relatively small number of words which the person may not have encountered before – for example, words such as 'somnambulist' (Schonell) and 'antithesis' (WORD). The Schonell test is also likely to be unreliable because of its antiquity: it is now almost half-a-century old. At its upper extremes it contains examples of words which will be exceptionally difficult for today's readers because they are now almost archaic (e.g. 'sepulchre' and 'sabre') as well as words that might have been regarded as difficult fifty years ago but which are fairly commonplace today (e.g. 'statistics' and 'miscellaneous'). The Neale test is typically used because it is a well-constructed test and because there is not a suitable adult prose reading test available. However, the ceiling on this test is a reading age of 13 years. There are many students who attain the ceiling of this test but who nevertheless have reading skills which are inadequate for study at higher education level, because the Neale test has no sensitivity in this range. When the Neale test is misapplied in this way, it may result in students being unfairly excluded from special help or provision to which they might otherwise be entitled.

Hence the use of tests that are out of date in either their content or their norms, or with subjects for whom they were never intended, is unacceptable practice. Until recently, however, there was no great demand for literacy tests for use with adults. Demand was largely confined to assessment of adult basic literacy or of literacy impairment in cases of neurological damage, for example, in brain injury or stroke. In the case of adult basic literacy the Adult Literacy and Basic Skills Test (ALBSU) has most commonly been employed, whereas in cases of neurological damage the NART (National Adult Reading Test; see Nelson and Willinson, 1991). In the last few years, however, the demand for assessment for suspected dyslexia among students at A level, as well as in further and higher education has escalated and in these cases neither the ALBSU test nor the NART is suitable. Many psychologists are using the WRAT at this level, but the lack of an appropriate prose-reading comprehension test is a serious limitation in the assessment process (Singleton, 1996). The situation has become acute in higher education, where applications for the Disabled Students Allowance (DSA) by students who have dyslexia have increased substantially since 1990. The DSA provides funds to enable the disabled student to purchase a computer and other technological aids for their studies, as well as possibly financing special tutorial help in study skills. More than half of all students in higher education now in receipt of the DSA are cases of dyslexia (Computer Centre for People with Disabilities, 1996). The cost of DSAs is also rising. The Department for Education and Employment reported a threefold increase in overall costs of the DSA during the two-year period up to 1994 (DFEE, 1995). Furthermore, the assessment of students suspected of having dyslexia has become critical not only because the award of a substantial allowance hangs on the outcome, but also because such students usually obtain special provision in examinations, such as additional time. A recent national survey reported that the incidence of dyslexia in higher education in the UK is in the region of 1.3%. Many universities are reporting between 75 and 200 students applying each year for dyslexia assessments, and issues such as the qualifications of assessors as well as the assessment materials and methods used have come under intense scrutiny (Singleton, in press). Although there are no figures to go on, concern has also been expressed about possible abuses of the assessment procedure in which students may attempt to 'fake' dyslexia in order to obtain a DSA. However, there are as yet no nationally agreed standards or safeguards, although the National Working Party on Dyslexia in Higher Education (Singleton, in press) is proposing some basic guidelines, including the use of appropriate tests by suitably qualified and experienced assessors. On the other hand, many high-ability students with dyslexia show extreme levels of 'compensation'. They have developed techniques for surmounting or circumventing many of their difficulties, often through immense personal effort, or they may camouflage their problems in various ways (McLoughlin *et al.*, 1994). Assessment in such cases is particularly tricky because the tests are insufficiently sensitive, and it may then be difficult for the students to obtain recognition of their dyslexia and access the support that they require and to which, arguably, they should be entitled. Unless there are agreed standards and appropriate tests, such a system (which has attractive financial and other benefits for students) will always be vulnerable to abuse by some and unfair to others.

THE FUTURE

The way that we currently assess literacy is the result of an evolution in testing techniques over the years. In some ways, because the production of test materials is haphazard and costly, there is a growing gap between the findings that pour out of the research journals and the assessment materials that are available to practitioners. In more recent times interest has also been taken in case studies of unusual reading and writing problems, and publishing outlets such as *Cognitive Neuropsychology* are now available for researchers to submit such findings. There is a growing demand for children and adults to be tested, so what would be a likely scenario in the future?

Suppose we were on an all-powerful committee. What would be our wish list? A major consideration would be the amount of money available. A minimum step would be to make it national practice for all classes to be given national reading and spelling tests in about February or March of each year. This would be in place of the present haphazard system of identification of reading problems. The information from these tests would be collated with two purposes in mind: first, to examine national standards of literacy with a view to maintaining, if not improving standards. Second, it would help the identification of poor readers who were falling behind. As our previous discussion has shown, it would not identify all children with dyslexia, or specific reading difficulties, as this necessitates some form of diagnostic assessment, usually involving intelligence testing.

The next filter, to identify those with dyslexia in the remaining 'normal' body, would be to apply a group intelligence test. However, this would be expensive both in cost and in time, unless the test materials were quick to apply and reliable. Unfortunately, these two qualities do not normally go hand-in-hand.

Mass screening for literacy, one might argue, could be useful on the grounds of economy and efficiency. Identification of problems as they are developing can mean the focused training of the necessary skills at the appropriate time. For instance, perhaps a child is missing some prerequisite skills that need to be gained before progress can be made. Consider the child approaching his or her teens who is confronted with an expanding syllabus and with an unidentified substantial reading problem. Many such children now face this problem. Even if their problem is identified at this point, there is not enough time available to acquire basic reading skills as well as cope with curriculum subjects. These literacy skills should have been learned much earlier. (For further consideration of screening, see Chapter 4.)

At present our educational system fails many children, leading to early truancy. Furthermore, there is a high incidence of reading problems in young offenders, with consequent economic costs to society. For the many who struggle on with their literacy problems, there is a lot of misery, embarrassment and frustration that could probably have been averted if there had been sufficient resources available at the right time.

Turning to the professional assessor, there is a case for using tailored testing techniques in the future. For instance, the testing session should be an identification of as many aspects as possible of the area of the problem. At present there seems to be too much of a tendency to give the same battery of tests to all those being assessed no matter what their particular problem. Instead, it would be more efficient to conduct faster (but still reliable) testing of a range of candidate problems, but then to go through a hypothesis testing sequence of tests, in the same way that doctors would undertake a diagnosis of their patients.

In the (more distant) future this might involve a computerised assessment of various faculties including eye movements, some kind of brain scan, perhaps a genetic analysis, sophisticated optical and hearing tests, cognitive reactions and tests of affect. This might be followed by detailed programmes of computerised (virtual?) training that are already known to overcome these problems. If all this seems highly unlikely now, just think how far we have come, and just what knowledge about reading we are now acquiring. (For further consideration of the potential for computer-based assessment methods, see Chapter 13.)

The classroom environment of the teacher has undergone many changes in recent years. Many teachers believe that they are now under a considerable amount of pressure due to the demands of the National Curriculum in the UK. This has meant that although there is now rudimentary testing of literacy in the new curriculum, time to hear children read (for example) has been squeezed because other subjects need to be covered as well.

Nevertheless, regular assessment is steadily becoming an integral part of even the primary school curriculum, and is widely seen as fundamental to the maintenance of educational standards and parental satisfaction. For example, in his report on the National Curriculum, Dearing (1993) quoted the Office for Standards in Education as saying:

> The assessment requirements of the National Curriculum have a vital role in raising the expectations of teachers, pupils and parents. In particular, assessment should ensure that individual learning is more clearly targeted and that shortcomings are quickly identified and remedied, thus contributing towards higher standards overall.
>
> (p.25)

Despite this, it is now possible for parents who think that their children are falling behind to pay for an assessment. If this shows that the child has a specific learning difficulty, it does not mean that the school is obliged to call in a psychologist for a Special Needs Assessment. However, teachers may feel pressurised into making a provision for the child that they believe is unnecessary or unjustified in financial terms, in relation to the problems they have to face elsewhere in the school. Not surprisingly, this can lead to resentment on the part of teachers and of parents who cannot afford such assessments.

On top of this, there has not really been much of an increase in resources, and as long as this continues it does not seem likely that there will be much scope for improvement in the classroom. In addition, in inner city schools in particular, problems of vandalism can be serious; thus computer use is restricted.

The mass screening we advocated (in our dreams) to identify poor readers and those with dyslexia needs to be undertaken in the classroom. Involvement of teachers in the administration of this would be important. Many teachers might argue that the present National Curriculum fulfils this need, so why carry out additional testing? At present the Curriculum's precision in assessment, by means of SATs, leaves a lot to be desired. It does not give accurate diagnostic information. Psychologists often discover a mismatch between what National Curriculum SATs results are saying about a child and the conclusions that may be drawn from psychometric test results from that child. Clearly, much more research is needed on this, but there is empirical evidence of poor reliability of SATs measures (Davies *et al.*, 1995; James and Conner, 1993; Pumfrey and Elliott, 1991). It is not simply that SATs are assessing different things from psychometric tests. Rather, it is an issue that directly concerns the reliability and validity of the SATs measures themselves, for they provide only the crudest categorisation of performance in various educational skills that are in fact highly complex.

Dreams are all very well, but what in the near future would be feasible in literacy assessment? First, there is still much scope for improvement in test constructions. Many tests are still inefficient to apply. For example, in the worst examples one applies a test in which there is a criterion of, say, six consecutive incorrect responses and on the sixth response the respondent gets the answer correct, so one has to continue; the test never seems to end and the grading of difficulty appears to be poor. It should be possible to get to the appropriate level of achievement on the tested dimension as swiftly as possible. Computerised testing can aid this, so that the selection of the next item is determined by the previous response.

Second, we should have better models concerning the types of literacy problems (or skill deficits) that we are looking for. This would be allied to appropriate training experiments that could teach these particular skills. Unfortunately, although there is much theoretical speculation in reading, a consensus is comparatively all too infrequent. This is probably confusing for practitioners, who in any case have their own models of what they are looking for. Miles (1994) offers the beginnings of a taxonomy for dyslexia that falls into seven categories, of which only one, that of phonological deficiency, has received overwhelming research interest and consensus. Some (e.g. Wilding, 1989) might argue in contrast that individuals cannot be fitted into categories, but this is not necessarily a helpful attitude as an atheoretical stance can imply no practical advice for training.

Third, there is a need for research money to be available to fund research into assessment. This is one area of research from which research councils in the UK have largely steered clear. There appears to be some prejudice against such research as it is considered to be practically oriented and scientifically dull. Research on assessment, especially that coupled with appropriate training, is costly and time consuming. At present, the funding is mainly coming from commercial agencies, although some enlightened education authorities have given some modest funding as well. This lack of funding means that in this country most of the major psychometric tools have to be imported into the UK and then standardised to UK samples.

NOTE

1 It is preferable to refer to dyslexia in this way than to refer to someone as being 'dyslexic'. In the USA in particular, there is strong criticism of this use as it infers that a person or child *is* this category rather than implying that they are human beings who happen to have a condition called 'dyslexia'. We now shy away from calling a person 'a cripple' or 'a spastic' as there was a time when these were also used as terms of abuse. Some would argue that, as in all things, there needs to be a middle path between causing offence on the one hand and creating stylistically awkward passages of prose on the other. For example, 'dyslexic' ought legitimately (and without offence) to be used adjectivally (as in 'dyslexic student'). Many individuals with dyslexia in the UK refer to themselves as 'dyslexic' and regard this particular debate as pointless.

REFERENCES

Adams, M.J. (1990). *Beginning to Read: Thinking and Learning about Print.* London: MIT Press.

ALBSU (1988). *Adult Literacy and Basic Skills Test.* London: Adult Literacy and Basic Skills Unit.

Alston, J. (1994). Written output and writing speeds. *Dyslexia Review*, 6, 6–12.

Alston, J. (1995). *Assessing and Promoting Writing Skills.* Tamworth: NASEN.

Alston, J. (1996). Assessing and promoting handwriting skills. In G. Reid (ed.) *Dimensions of Dyslexia*, Vol 2. Edinburgh: Moray House.

Alston, J. and Taylor, J. (1985). *The Handwriting File: Diagnosis and Remediation.* Wisbech: LDA.

Alston, J. and Taylor, J. (1987). *Handwriting File: Theory, Research and Practice.* London: Croom Helm.

Beech, J.R. (1994). Reading skills, strategies and their degree of tractability in dyslexia. In A. Fawcett and R. Nicolson (eds) *Dyslexia in Children: Multi-disciplinary Perspectives.* London: Harvester Wheatsheaf.

Beech, J.R. and Harding, L.M. (eds) (1990). *Testing People: a Practical Guide to Psychometrics.* London: Routledge.

Beech, J.R. and Keys, A. (in press). Reading, vocabulary and language preference in 7- to 8-year-old bilingual Asian children. *British Journal of Educational Psychology.*

Bradley, L. and Bryant, P.E. (1983). Categorizing sounds and learning to read: a causal connection. *Nature*, 301, 419–21.

Bryans, T. (1992). Educational psychologists working in a biased society. In S. Wolfendale, T. Bryans, M. Fox, A. Labram and A. Sigston (eds) *The Profession and Practice of Educational Psychology: Future Directions.* London: Cassell.

Callman, T. (1996). Negligent local education authorities? *Education, Public Law and the Individual*, 1, 3–6.

Campbell, R. and Butterworth, B. (1985). Phonological dyslexia and dysgraphia in a highly literate subject: a developmental case and associated deficits in phonemic processing and awareness. *Quarterly Journal of Experimental Psychology*, 37A, 435–75.

Computer Centre for People with Disabilities (1996). *Surveys into the Operation of the Disabled Students' Allowances.* London: University of Westminster Press.

Critchley, M. (1970). *The Dyslexic Child.* Springfield, Ill.: Thomas.

Cummins, J. (1984). *Bilingualism and Special Education Issues in Assessment and Pedagogy.* Clevedon: Multi-lingual Matters.

Davies, J., Brember, I. and Pumfrey, P. (1995). The first and second reading Standard Assessment Tasks at Key Stage 1: a comparison based on a five-school study. *Journal of Research in Reading*, 18, 1–9.

Dearing, R. (1993). *The National Curriculum and its Assessment.* London: School Curriculum and Assessment Authority.

DFE (1994). *Code of Practice on the Identification and Assessment of Special Educational Needs.* London: Department for Education.

DFEE (1995). *Further and Higher Education Review Programme: Interim Report, July 1995.* London: Department for Education and Employment.

Gipps, C. (1990). *Assessment – A Teacher's Guide to the Issues.* London: Hodder & Stoughton.

Gregory, E. and Kelly, C. (1992). Bilingualism and assessment. In G.M. Blenkin and A.V. Kelly (eds) *Assessment in Early Childhood Education.* London: Paul Chapman.

Hanley, J.R., Hastie, K. and Kay, J. (1992). Developmental surface dyslexia and dysgraphia: an orthographic processing impairment. *Quarterly Journal of Experimental Psychology*, 44A, 285–319.

James, M. and Conner, C. (1993). Are reliability and validity achievable in National Curriculum assessment? Some observations on moderation at Key Stage 1 in 1992. *The Curriculum Journal*, 4, 5–19.

Jorm, A.F., Share, D.L., Maclean, R. and Matthews, R. (1986). Cognitive factors at school entry predictive of specific reading retardation and general reading backwardness: a research note. *Journal of Child Psychology and Psychiatry*, 27, 45–65.

Joyce, J. (1988). The development of an anti-racist policy in Leeds. In S. Wolfendale, I. Lunt and T. Carroll (eds) *Educational Psychologists Working in Multi-cultural Communities*. Leicester: British Psychological Society Division of Educational and Child Psychology, Vol 5(2).

Keily, M. (1996). Handwriting – skills, strategies and success. In G. Reid (ed.) *Dimensions of Dyslexia*, Vol 2. Edinburgh: Moray House.

Kline, P. (1990). Selecting the best test. In J.R. Beech and L.M. Harding (eds). *Testing People: A Practical Guide to Psychometrics*. London: Routledge.

McLoughlin, D., Fitzgibbon, G. and Young, V. (1994). *Adult Dyslexia: Assessment, Counselling and Training*. London: Whurr.

Massey, A.J. and Elliott, C. (1996). *Aspects of writing in 16+ English examinations between 1980 and 1994*. Cambridge: University of Cambridge Local Examinations Syndicate.

Miles, T.R. (1994). A proposed taxonomy and some consequences. In A. Fawcett and R. Nicolson (eds) *Dyslexia in Children: Multidisciplinary Perspectives*. London: Harvester Wheatsheaf.

Neale, M.D. (1989). *Neale Analysis of Reading Ability. Revised Version*. Windsor, Berks: NFER-Nelson.

Nelson, H. and Willinson, J. (1991). *National Adult Reading Test. Second Edition*. Windsor, Berks: NFER-Nelson.

Otton, Rt Hon Lord Justice (1996). A view from the Bench: an overview of the Education Act 1993. *Education, Public Law and the Individual*, 1(1), 1–2.

Pumfrey, P.D. (1991). *Improving Children's Reading in the Ordinary School: Challenges And Responses*. London: Cassell.

Pumfrey, P.D. and Elliott, C.D. (1991). National reading standards and Standard Assessment Tasks: an educational house of cards. *Educational Psychology in Practice*, 7, 74–80.

Schonell, F.J. (1950). *The Graded Word Reading Test*. Edinburgh: Oliver & Boyd.

Siegel, L.S. (1992). An evaluation of the discrepancy definition of dyslexia. *Journal of Learning Disabilities*, 25, 618–29.

Singleton, C.H. (1994). Issues in the diagnosis and assessment of dyslexia in Higher Education. *Proceedings of the International Conference on Dyslexia in Higher Education*. Plymouth: University of Plymouth.

Singleton, C.H. (1995). Dyslexia in Higher Education. *Dyslexia Contact*, 14(2), 7–9.

Singleton, C.H. [chair] (1996). Dyslexia in higher education: issues for policy and practice. In C. Stephens (ed.) *Proceedings of the Conference on Dyslexic Students in Higher Education*. Huddersfield: Skill and the University of Huddersfield.

Singleton, C.H. (in press). *The Report of the National Working Party on Dyslexia in Higher Education*. Hull: The University of Hull.

Stanovich, K.E. (1986). Matthew effects in reading: some consequences of individual differences in the acquisition of literacy. *Reading Research Quarterly*, 21, 360–406.

Stanovich, K.E. and Cunningham, A.E. (1992). Studying the consequences of literacy within a literate society: the cognitive correlates of print exposure. *Memory and Cognition*, 20, 51–68.

Vellutino, F.R. (1979). *Dyslexia: Theory and Research*. Cambridge, Mass: MIT Press.

Wechsler, D. (1992). *Wechsler Intelligence Scale for Children. Third Edition*. London: Psychological Corporation.

Wilding, J. (1989). Developmental dyslexics do not fit into boxes: evidence from the case studies. *European Journal of Cognitive Psychology*, 1, 105–27.

Wilkinson, G.S. (1993). *WRAT-3: Wide Range Achievement Test*. Wilmington, Delaware: Jastak Wide Range.

Yule, W., Rutter, M., Berger, M. and Thompson, J. (1974). Over- and under-achievement in reading: distribution in the general population. *British Journal of Educational Psychology*, 44, 1–12.

2 Assessment by classroom teachers

Denis Vincent

INTRODUCTION

There continues to be a healthy commercial market in reading tests but the role of testing in education generally is increasingly being questioned. The advocates of testing reading therefore need to clarify good practice and to explain more effectively than hitherto how testing is part of the professional competence of a teacher of reading. The latter parts of this chapter will indeed seek to do precisely this by considering the way in which better use of tests can be made in schools for the following:

- screening;
- diagnostic assessment;
- assessing progress.

However, we need first to consider in more detail the nature of the tension between the long-established 'psychometric' models of testing reading and more recent counter-models which tend to distrust this technology and argue for broader 'edumetric' approaches which centre on teachers rather than tests. The final section returns to problematic matters by considering the popular practice of expressing performance in terms of reading 'ages'.

READING TESTS: AN UNFASHIONABLE CAUSE?

In 1983 I published, with colleagues, a review of all the published tests and materials available to teachers in the UK for assessing reading (Vincent *et al.*, 1983). Twelve years later, perusal of the catalogues of the main commercial publishers of educational tests shows that most tests reviewed in 1983 remain in print. Moreover, the subsequent addition of new materials has easily doubled the number of tests available for use in schools. Most of these are intended for use in the primary and middle years or with failing readers in secondary education. Most are for normative assessment of reading attainment although a significant number of published materials also have some form of diagnostic function. Oddly, this survival (flourishing, even) of commercially published reading tests takes place in parallel with the publication of a growing literature which is critical of the role of educational tests as part of national educational policy as well as in the teaching of reading. It has also continued at a time when teachers have actively boycotted tests for National Curriculum assessment. It appears that while there are public, academic and professional fora in which testing is heavily criticised, at a more local level it continues quietly and unobtrusively.

The published literature on educational assessment is approximately divided into two types of discourse. There is the technical or psychometric literature concerned with problems and issues which are internal to the project of educational measurement. These are predominantly quantitative in nature (e.g. Linn, 1989; Wood, 1991). In stark contrast, there is also much ideological commentary which is often critical of established assessment practices, notably the use of tests and quantification (e.g. Gipps, 1994) and which argues for greater use of qualitative methods of educational assessment (e.g. Adams and Burgess, 1989).

Qualitative reading assessment

The defining feature (and motive) of much qualitative assessment is that it should take any form *other than* a number or a score. The emphasis is upon the gathering of evidence about reading by accumulating portfolios, interviewing, observation and case study. The focus is on the way the individual reader responds to texts and upon affective as much as cognitive and linguistic characteristics of the reader. Assessments may take the form of a written commentary (The *Primary Language Record* developed by the Inner London Education Authority being a notable example) and this may include material from the pupil, parents and peers as well as the teacher. Use is also often made of some form of descriptive scale to express how far a reader has progressed or what level they have reached on a continuum. Such scales are strictly ordinal however, and differ from the interval scaling employed in standardised tests. The attainment targets and level descriptions used in the National Curriculum for English in England and Wales are a partial example which will be familiar to many readers. Coles and Jenkins (1996) and Harrison and Salinger (1996) present fuller discussion and further examples of this approach.

This movement, which might be described as 'edumetric' to distinguish it from the psychometric movement, owes its origins partly to dissatisfaction with objective standardised testing and to a desire to adopt a broader model which places a premium on the teacher's judgement and intuition, not the authority of the objective test. The introduction of a heavily assessed National Curriculum has stimulated an increase in critical and polemical writing. The underlying concern has been that a narrowly conceived test-based National Curriculum policy would form the basis for making questionable/unwarranted judgements or decisions of consequence about schools, teachers or pupils.

Such criticism has sometimes been generalised unfairly to the individual practice of classroom teachers. Teachers need to be pragmatic and balanced in their approach to assessment. Most of the evils attributed to standardised testing relate to the external imposition of these in ways which are detrimental to good practice. At classroom level assessment is managed and controlled by the teacher, not vice versa. There is thus scope and freedom to apply a range of methods. To exclude psychometric testing in this context seems every bit as 'deprofessionalising' as their external imposition might be.

The power of numbers

A central edumetric tenet is that assessment should be qualitative and based on professional judgement rather than external or objective measures. Vincent (1994), however, has argued that reluctance to use tests and quantification on the part of schools created an assessment vacuum which led to the imposition of a national assessment system. If teachers retreat even further from quantitative methods, then their control over the assessment of reading standards – and over their own professional destinies – will simply be further weakened. There is, therefore, good reason for using both qualitative and quantitative methods, teacher-based assessment *and* objective tests. Ways need to be found of balancing the two and communicating their results to parents and other audiences.

Much of what we know about the nature of reading comes from research which has been quantitative and often test-based. Researchers 'own', manage, analyse and interrogate their data in ways which provide potential models for managing assessment in school. The 'teacher as researcher' movement is now well established; Connor (1991) argues for primary teachers to adopt a 'research stance' in assessment. There is certainly a case for reading assessment to be viewed as a 'researcherly' activity. The examples given by Connor favour observational and qualitative methods and this is consistent with the general tendency for practitioner research to emphasise non-quantitative methodologies. However, the tools of quantitative data analysis are no longer the exclusive province of researchers with access to mainframe computers in universities.

The technology will, of course, need to evolve before it will be suitable for wide-scale use in schools. The scanning and semi-intelligent document reading technology (e.g. *Teleform*; *Formic*) currently being used by researchers and large public sector and commercial organisations will need to become more intelligent, much more stable and robust and less expensive. This could eventually automate much of the clerical work associated with running a school testing programme. It will also allow enterprising teachers to delve into their data in considerable detail.

MODELS OF PRACTICE

Testing as a technology: a two-dimensional model

The 'official' version of the psychometric testing of reading is one in which an assessor, using a set of standard published materials, closely follows a set of standard prescribed procedures in order to measure reading attainment and/or to diagnose difficulty. Having elicited reading performance under carefully controlled test conditions, the assessor observes and records what has been assessed, then interprets scores and other results, and finally makes decisions or reaches conclusions on the basis of the results. In this model the outcome of the testing and the conclusions that will be reached are taken to be functions of the reader who is being assessed and the design of the assessment materials and procedures. The individual who administers the assessments is essentially a skilled technician who would be 'interchangeable' with any other technician who happened to be available to carry out the assessments.

Of course, in this version of reading assessment it is recognised that some assessors may be more competent than others. Competence, however, is largely a matter of (1) practice and experience in using a particular instrument; (2) diligence in following the administration and scoring procedures; and (3) technical knowledge necessary to interpret the scores and results. In the official model the purposes and functions of assessment are very clearly defined, as are the criteria by which tests are selected for these applications.

National Curriculum assessment for England and Wales makes a similar set of assumptions: experts develop standard tasks and tests; teachers administer the test materials following prescribed routines so that classroom-to-classroom variations are avoided; children respond to tasks in varying (but anticipated) ways; teachers (or teams of external markers) score, rate or classify children's responses and allocate them to levels following a rubric which makes this entirely possible.

This model is concerned with using the right materials in the right way; good assessment is a matter of a teacher's technical knowledge and skill. The acquisition or extension of proficiency in assessment within this model is quite straightforward: beginners need to become familiar with the psychometric ground rules; experienced testers of reading need updates on the state of the art. This applies quite well to assessing children with reading difficulty. For example, *The Diagnostic Reading Pack* (Ames, 1984) is a useful introductory, self-instructional package of tests organised around a flow-chart structure. The original version of this was, with limited justification, entitled *Teach Yourself to Diagnose Reading Problems*. Similarly, for those seeking the 'state of the art' in diagnostic assessment, Goulandris and Snowling (1995) describe procedures for assessing and interpreting reading difficulty which are informed by psychological research in the field of word recognition. These authors generously provide examples of test items which can be used to carry out the assessments.

Such examples are entirely consistent with the claim that assessment is a professional skill which is characterised by its rigour. However, it must be asked how well, overall, does this model work?

In the world of classroom reality things do not run so smoothly. Teachers do not always follow prescribed test administration and marking procedures exactly. Such deviations may of course be quite unintentional, but sometimes they may be quite conscious decisions. For example, a teacher may decide to finish a test session prematurely because local circumstances dictate this. Clerical errors in marking and scoring tests surely occur and there are anecdotal accounts of incorrect test responses being credited as correct because the teacher 'knew' the child really intended a right answer/ response. There are no systematic studies of this phenomenon in the public domain so its extent remains a matter of speculation.

It is tempting to dismiss all this as no more than an aberration, to be avoided by better preparation and training and greater professional resolve to follow correct procedures. However, when it comes to the way in which tests are integrated into classroom practice and to the dynamics of their interpretation, the position is more complicated. Vinsonhaler *et al.* (1983) demonstrated that, when faced with real life assessment data, even expert reading 'clinicians' interpreted the same case study examples of children with reading problems differently. Gipps *et al.* (1983) provided some glimpses into the 'psychology' of testing in primary schools, revealing it to be a complex process, insofar as the way test results are used and interpreted is far from straightforward. Stierer (1986) argues that such evidence shows the technology of psychometric testing is fundamentally flawed and, by implication, should be abandoned.

Testing as a professional process: towards a three-dimensional model

An alternative but more challenging approach is to seek a reconciliation between the psychometric and the edumetric. Thus, reading assessment is viewed as a three-dimensional process in which the outcome of assessment depends not just on the nature of the assessment instruments and the constitution of the reader (as in the 'technical' model) but also on the identity, values and preferences of the individual assessor. This model accepts that not only is reading a complex behavioural process but so is that of assessing it. The *interaction* between the (more or less) free-standing technology of psychometrics with the assessment 'style' of the individual teacher is central. We know very little of how this works in practice. For example, the notion that there might be different styles of test use has been given little consideration either by test developers or in texts on educational assessment. Gipps *et al.* (1995) have presented data which strongly suggest that, in the context of Key Stage 1, National

Curriculum assessment teachers may adopt one or other of a number of different underlying models. Such variations have implications for the way tests and systems of testing are designed. If teachers are to become more effective users of tests to assess reading, the 'textbooks' on how to do this will eventually need some rewriting so that the two-dimensional technology is relocated in a framework of professional practice.

SCREENING

Many local education authorities have long-established policies of 'blanket' testing whole age groups to identify the children who need (or most need) special help with reading. The assumption behind any screening instrument is that it will detect the following:

- avoidable cases of potential reading difficulty;
- remediable cases of actual reading difficulty.

These two functions are complementary but require rather different types of tests. Screening for potential reading difficulty requires 'precursory' indicators of reading difficulty – 'at risk' factors. Screening to identify children who have already encountered difficulty involves testing reading itself. A suitable test for this allows the distribution of ability in a group of readers to be examined so that those who are furthest behind – the 'tail' of the attainment range – can be clearly identified.

Although both types of screening have traditionally been managed by LEAs, the effectiveness with which they have been implemented has been criticised (Gipps *et al.*, 1983). In fact, the trend towards less LEA central management of education implies much greater devolution of screening to individual schools. Indeed, it is also arguable that screening will work better when initiated and managed at school level. Teachers are less likely to feel that they are simply passive test givers and markers who just pass on the results upwards through the system.

This trend would mean that increasing numbers of schools would need to take informed decisions about the following:

- selecting the test(s);
- deciding when to screen;
- managing the data;
- acting on the results.

These issues have long exercised those responsible for setting up LEA systems. In many cases the options taken were probably compromises, particularly where teachers were dubious about testing and/or suspicious of the LEA's intentions. The tendency was to minimise the perceived intrusiveness of screening tests to secure schools' cooperation. This pressure should be much less where the decisions are made at school level.

Selection of test(s)

'At risk' screening

There have been numerous attempts to devise methods of predicting and anticipating the likelihood of reading failure (or learning failure more generally) among pre-readers. These have covered behavioural and emotional factors, generic learning skills and perceptual and linguistic factors thought to facilitate or hinder progress in learning to read. In a systematic review of fifity-eight research studies, Horn and Packard (1985) found that even the best early predictive measures were only moderately correlated (less than 0.6) with later reading achievement. It is thus not surprising that many early screening devices fail to pick up a substantial number of cases of subsequent reading failure (Lindsay and Wedell, 1982; Potton, 1983). Most screening tests now in print were constructed before research into the importance of early phonological development had been widely publicised. If the next generation of pre-reading screening devices succeeds in including phonological awareness alongside established predictors then their screening powers may well increase.

Screening for reading failure

A popular format for screening tests designed to pinpoint those who have begun to fail is a group sentence-completion test. Sentence-completion tests consist of lists of sentences (unconnected) in which a blank has to be filled by one of four possible words to complete the sentence meaningfully:

> This is an *inevitable/example/illusion/explanation* of a sentence-completion test question.

This is hardly an everyday reading experience. Such tests may work partly because *any* activity requiring decoding of printed text, however artificial, will prove a stumbling-block for weak/non-readers.

Young's *Group Reading Test* (Young, 1992), and the *Primary Reading Test* (France, 1981) are long-established examples although the more recent *Suffolk Reading Scale* (Hagley, 1986) is technically more sophisticated. Such tests 'do the job' quickly and cheaply. They are simple to construct because a large pool of trial sentences can be used to select those which offer a suitable gradient in difficulty. Tests composed of sentence completion items tend to be highly reliable: an important statistical characteristic which reduces the margin of error in identifying failing readers.

For some teachers it may not be enough that such tests work in practice. Psychometric efficiency is necessary but assessment practices in schools need also to be consistent with curricular values. There is thus a case for using tests, even for screening, which 'look' like reading, for example, by basing assessment on continuous prose (e.g. Level 1 of the *Edinburgh Reading Tests Series* or the NFER's *Reading Ability Series*).

The relatively demanding reading tasks these tests embody might seem out of place for screening groups of young children of unknown and varied levels of literacy. Might not the children we are most concerned about be overwhelmed by the complexity of what is asked of them? This does not always prove to be the case in practice. Vincent and de la Mare (1989) present the score distribution for 7 year olds who took part in the standardisation of a reading comprehension test based on two quite long narrative pieces. There was a pronounced left-hand tail in the score distribution – a desirable attribute for a screening instrument – with very few children (the unavoidable minimum) scoring at a level consistent with complete non-comprehension of the text. In fact, the NFER *Reading Ability Series* offers the choice of a simple twenty-five-question test of reading comprehension (Level A) or a simpler Test of Initial Literacy which might be used before deciding whether a child should attempt Level A.

Reading potential

For many years it was common for LEA screening to measure intelligence/IQ alongside reading. This practice, which is now probably less widespread, assumes that intelligence indicates reading potential and that a distinction should be made between poor readers who are nevertheless reading at their potential level and those who are retarded because their reading attainment is lower than their intelligence test score. These criteria continue to be applied by researchers although there are important theoretical arguments (e.g. Stanovich, 1992) which call into question the value of IQ tests as a basis for forming differential expectations about children's reading. For the clinician it will continue to be important to use intelligence/cognitive tests for clinically assessing children who present reading difficulties (e.g. Thomson, 1990). This is clearly important where there is a need to identify the extreme cases, for example, where high IQ is in contrast with very low reading or cases which are very low on both measures. There is also an accumulation of clinical evidence for the value of the main individual intelligence tests in identifying a characteristic profile for cases of specific reading difficulty/dyslexia.

What of the classroom teacher, who will be less frequently concerned with extreme cases and who may have access to group tests of verbal and nonverbal reasoning but not to individual intelligence tests? Further, many teachers will probably have been encouraged in their initial training to view intelligence testing as at best invalid and at worst harmful. Teachers certainly need to be alert to cases of reading difficulty and reading tests have a legitimate role in their identification. However, the primary concern is with reading, not with intelligence, and in many cases consideration of the role of intelligence can wait until it has been established that there is, in absolute terms, a reading problem. Such a policy will of course over-look cases of *relative* difficulty in reading: children with high general ability (and high potential for reading?) who manage only to attain average scores on reading tests.

Leaving aside the arguments about the precise meaning of such profiles, it is still questionable that 'blanket' group intelligence testing would be helpful in their identification. The verbal and nonverbal reasoning tests of intelligence available to teachers in schools have a very different pedigree from individual intelligence tests. The format of the verbal tests, in particular, derives fairly directly from that of the eleven-plus selection test. The purpose of such tests was to identify those most suited to selective secondary education. Their format may thus not be well suited to dealing with questions of potential/expected reading level among primary school pupils. Stanovich's (1992) recommendation that reading potential might better be measured via oral comprehension is an attractive one. Apart from picture-based tests such as the *British Picture Vocabulary Scales* (Dunn *et al.*, 1982) test, developers have yet to take up this challenge. In the absence of instruments which are purpose-designed one can only advo-cate the extant options with caution. The conclusion that although a child is reading as well as, or even slightly better than, their peers they should nevertheless be doing even better is not one which existing tests, of either reading or intelligence, could strongly inform.

When to screen

Screening needs to be done as early as possible. One positive outcome of National Curriculum assessment has been to establish that testing children at 7 years is by no means as harmful as some teachers had formerly assumed – this has perhaps cleared the way for considering 'baseline' test-ing at an even earlier stage in children's educational careers. Screening also needs to be recurrent. For instance, Wright *et al.* (1995) found that mem-bership of the group of children classified as dyslexic in the same cohort was subject to fluctuation over time. LEAs were constrained in the fre-quency with which they could carry out authority-wide screening because of their vulnerability to accusations of intrusiveness. School policies need not be so restricted. A comprehensive policy would include the following:

- screening, by a teacher-completed check-list or a test of pre-reading and early literacy skills very soon after entry to school;
- a follow-up test of reading later in the year;
- annual re-testing as part of monitoring progress.

This may be more than is always necessary but such a policy can be 'faded' in the light of experience so that, for example, annual testing becomes biennial.

Managing data

Before the advent of personal computers, LEAs rather than schools had the necessary technology to analyse the results of large-scale screening programmes. Once teachers had marked the tests, 'ownership' of the data passed to a centralised unit. This probably diluted the reality and significance of the exercise for many teachers, causing discontinuity between assessment policy and school level practice. The importance of being able to interrogate a set of test results and to make one's own decisions from the data should not be underestimated. The presence in schools of personal computers and, to some extent, suitable software to store, analyse, sort, sift and explore results allows teachers to retake control of 'their' data. This has symbolic, psychological and practical significance.

Acting on results: recognising the limits to testing

One of the most formidable difficulties facing the advocates of reading tests is the existence of a finely-honed rhetoric of resistance:

- The tests only told me what I already knew ...
- We *know* there is a problem but testing won't help us solve it ...
- We were no further on once we'd given the test ...
- The test didn't tell me what to do next ...
- You can't make a pig heavier by weighing it ...

The first two criticisms are less true than those who utter them usually realise: can one *know* the results of tests before they have been administered? The last three hinge on a specious premise that tests of reading attainment should provide solutions to the problems they identify, or confirm ('If you're so clever at *testing* reading how come you can't tell me how to *teach* it?'). Tests are designed to describe situations rather than to prescribe what should be done about them. The latter is the responsibility of the test user, not the test developer. Where a test of reading is a tool in the hand of a willing agent such objections are less likely to arise.

DIAGNOSIS

Diagnostic batteries: a history of innovation

There has been a succession of innovations in models, materials and methods intended to make some form of diagnostic assessment of reading difficulty. Some of these attracted considerable professional interest in their time (e.g. Frostig's *Developmental Test of Visual Perception*, the *Illinois Test of Psycholinguistic Abilities*, *The Aston Index*). Others, such as the *Boder Test of Reading–Spelling Patterns* were less well known to

UK teachers although they were certainly significant in the history of different approaches to diagnostic assessment. These titles are of historical interest only now. Miles and Miles (1990) and Pumfrey and Reason (1991) discuss theoretical difficulties associated with them.

Such tests seem to follow a common pattern: researchers develop a multi-trait model of reading/learning difficulty; they devise a test battery or system based on this model; the materials initially attract some professional interest; in the longer term the materials cease to be used.

Admittedly, some elaborate diagnostic test models such as Daniels and Diack's (1958) *The Standard Reading Tests* have remained 'to hand' in print for many years. These are a battery of sub-tests covering perceptual and linguistic processes as well as reading. Yet the majority of these are rarely used by teachers (although they have occasionally featured in research studies; e.g. Ellis, 1990). They survive in print only because they are published in book form with norm-referenced sub-tests which teachers continue to use even though they were standardised in the city of Nottingham around 1956.

Given their mixed fortunes, it can be asked whether these attempts were necessary milestones to be passed in the search for the 'true' diagnostic model or method – an expert system – which will really work and which is ready and waiting to be discovered.

Causes of reading failure

Diagnostic reading assessment models tend to be multi-faceted so that different patterns, categories or typologies of difficulty can be identified. However, it may be that all reading failure is due to the same cause, or, even if causes are different, the nature of the difficulty is the same for all readers. Thus, there would be nothing to 'diagnose' beyond the fact of poor reading itself; screening and diagnosis are the same thing here. Research into the phonological basis of reading difficulty provides a strong contender for this unitary thesis. In fact there is a diagnostic test, *Assessing Reading Difficulty* (Bradley, 1984), which deals directly with phonological skills. Yet, this particular test does not appear to be in very wide use. This may simply be due to the alleged lag between research and practice so that the research findings of the mid-1980s are only now being considered by teachers. This may also be an example of the difficulty in commercially marketing a test which does not give a reading age (even if it is not really designed for normative purposes). The notion of reading 'age' is discussed later in this chapter.

Alternatively, the causes of reading failure may be so diverse that diagnosis cannot be managed through a self-contained test package, i.e. all children are individuals and all diagnosis is particular to the case in hand. Although an oversimplification, this is a more 'teacherly' perspective. It respects individuality and values the teacher as a diagnostician rather than a 'psychometrician'. In reality, much diagnostic assessment which goes on in classrooms is in this mould. If the diversity thesis is correct, things could not be otherwise. However, this does not necessarily mean that it is always done well. This is an important but uncharted area of professional behaviour but such evidence as we have is not always reassuring. Bennett *et al.* (1984) noted that teachers could find it very difficult to 'stand back' to allow children time to reveal the nature of their difficulties. A possible example from oral reading is the pre-emptive correction or supplying of words when a child is hesitating or struggling.

An alternative framework

The challenge is to provide an explicit form and framework for such a model of diagnosis in reading. *Taking a Closer Look at Reading* (Scottish Council for Research in Education, 1995) is a recent example of an attempt to develop teachers as diagnosticians within the context of a National Curriculum and assessment policy. It presents teachers with a set of four broad areas of reading to investigate: attitude and motivation; decoding; pursuit of meaning; and awareness of the author's use of language. It suggests questions to ask the reader under each of these headings and makes sensible (if sometimes obvious) suggestions about further action. Six case examples of applying the framework to children's reading are provided.

Taking a Closer Look at Reading is clearly intended for teachers taking their first steps into diagnostic teaching and is concerned with a mainstream model of reading and its diagnosis. This is in contrast to most models of diagnostic assessment which are concerned with identifying specific deficits. How far this much broader framework will prove preferable to teachers working with poor readers is thus an interesting question.

Whither miscue analysis?

Miscue analysis once seemed like a major breakthrough in diagnostic reading assessment. It was based on the premise that reading involved the simultaneous use of a number of features of a text (for example, semantic and syntactic features) and that these provided the reader with 'cues' which readers used, with increasing economy, to construct the text. The misreadings, or 'miscues' a reader exhibited could thus be analysed diagnostically to determine which systems were being used by an individual reader. In this model, reading is an active quest for meaning and fluent reading is based on the overall text rather than the processing of individual words.

In fact, from quite early on in the history of its advocacy as a pedagogic method, there were reservations. Pumfrey (1985) noted that there was little direct evidence for its utility as a basis for intervention in individual

cases. Potter (1980) demonstrated that 'miscues' are not always inter-
pretable as evidence of a reader's use of context – a central feature of
the psycholinguistic 'guessing-game' model on which miscue analysis is
based.

The project of devising better ways of interpreting children's oral
reading errors is still a live one but some of the assumptions of miscue
analysis may need to be revised. A central assumption has been that fluent
readers use the information – cues – in text selectively and economically
to construct meaning, that this involves partial or minimal processing of
individual words and that intelligent use of contextual and semantic cues
is a mature reading strategy. It now appears that fluent readers do actually process the great majority of words in a text, albeit automatically and
rapidly. It is the poor readers, who are unable to do this with necessary
facility, who rely primarily upon context in reading. Although the underlying theory may therefore be open to question, miscue analysis should
not be entirely rejected. However, certain cautions must be exercised. For
example, the way a reader uses context needs to be interpreted carefully.
There is clearly a difference between a reader who is reliant upon context
and one who is sensitive to it and this distinction may not be entirely
clear in published guides to miscue analysis. Furthermore, the way in which
so-called grapho-phonic errors are classified would need to take greater
account of what is now known about the way word-recognition skills
develop (e.g. Ehri, 1995).

Arnold's (1992) *Diagnostic Reading Record* is probably the most convenient and accessible introduction to the technique of miscue analysis.
Although there must be reservations about its interpretive framework, in
many respects it remains a very usable means for teachers to engage with
individual readers in a structured way. In fact, it goes some way towards
meeting the reservations expressed above through its scoring method. This
classifies miscues which showed reliance on semantic sources only as negative, while those which showed the reader was also using grapho-phonic
information would be considered more positive. Even so, in general there
remains a major question as to what – if anything – there is to be diagnosed through miscue analysis.

Better models or better training?

Most commercially published diagnostic materials for reading are freely
available for teachers to purchase. Unlike many psychological tests, their
supply is not restricted to users who have been specially trained in their
use. The only notable exception is the Irlen screening procedure which can
only be used by teachers who have completed a training course. Otherwise,
it is assumed that even quite elaborate procedures may be assimilated and
applied correctly simply by reading an accompanying instruction manual.
Occasionally some self-training materials may be included – the revised

British edition of the *Neale Analysis of Reading Ability* (Neale *et al.*, 1988) includes a demonstration audio cassette – but few published diagnostic tests go as far as Ames (1984), mentioned earlier in this chapter.

Outside the mainstream of commercial publishing a rather different approach can sometimes be found in which support/advisory services in an LEA respond to a local need for materials *combined with* training. A good example of this is the *Reading Assessment for Teachers* materials – The 'RATpack' – produced for teachers in Wiltshire (Cooper *et al.*, n.d.). This consists of a set of materials covering a range of phonic skills, miscue analyses and emergent literacy skills. The assembly of materials is essentially pragmatic and fairly represents a professional consensus about what it is important to assess. It does however differ markedly from *Taking a Closer Look at Reading* (Scottish Council for Research in Education, 1995) in being concerned with specific skills and processes in quite a detailed way. What is noteworthy is that the RATpack is designed to be introduced via a six-session training programme. This is perhaps more important than the theoretical credentials of the materials themselves. The fact that a diagnostician has been trained to assess in a structured way and can use the procedures confidently may well have intrinsic benefits, regardless of the theoretical basis of the diagnostic model.

ASSESSING PROGRESS

The need to monitor

It has already been noted that there is an overlap between the functions of screening and longitudinal monitoring of progress which can effectively be 're-screening'. However, the monitoring of progress (and 'standards') is an important agendum in its own right. In its least controversial guise this is a matter of routine 'checking the gauge': teachers do need to reassure themselves that children are progressing normally and they certainly need to be the *first* to know if this is not the case. The occasional use of tests to this end is a matter of prudent professional 'housekeeping' (of course, testing would need to be set beside other sources of evidence that the teacher would draw upon). At an institutional level schools need to be able to satisfy themselves and their clientele that they are functioning well. Inspections and National Curriculum assessments do this but these are not under the control of schools or teachers themselves. Standardised testing is a relatively unintrusive 'early warning system' that can be established internally.

Test developers and publishers have put considerable effort into developing materials designed to meet precisely this need in the form of test 'series'. These contain a number of tests which follow a common format but are of increasing difficulty and standardised for successive age groups. The *Edinburgh Reading Test Series* was probably the first example of this approach in the UK. More recent examples are the NFER *Reading Ability Series*, *Effective Reading Tests* and, most recently, the *Reading Progress Tests*.

Norms for progress

A crucial feature of such tests is that the norms for each are comparable. For annual monitoring of successive intakes of a particular age group it may be sufficient to feel that one is using a test on each occasion which is appropriate for that age group. However, if a school wishes to examine the longitudinal progress of the *same* individuals or classes by comparing two or more successive sets of test results, then there are greater constraints. It will be important to ensure at each point both that (1) the content of what is assessed is the same, and (2) any norms applied are comparable and appropriate.

Test standardisation strategies

Regarding comparability of content and norms, it is instructive to compare the design of the *Effective Reading Tests* (ERT), first published in 1986, and the *Reading Progress Tests* series (RPT) which we are currently developing at the University of East London. The ERT series was designed in the mid-1980s as a group test of reading comprehension suited to a number of purposes and users, ranging from administrators requiring system-wide data to individual teachers who wished to look at reading comprehension in a more qualitative way within a class. It was then common (and may well still be) for LEAs to use tests to monitor trends across years. This required annual surveying of certain year group(s). This would normally be done at one or two age levels. Although in fact many children would take each test during their school careers, such 'cohort' data were probably of less interest than the results for children of the same age tested in different chronological years.

The ERT series was designed with such needs in mind and consists of six levels of tests which allow a choice of age groups to be assessed. The tests follow a common format and all items were written in conformity to a specified rationale. However, the correlations between tests at different levels, although substantial, were generally not as high as those for fully equivalent test forms. The priority in choosing the content and final item selection for each test in the series was that it should match its intended age range. This may have been optimised at the expense of some inter-level equivalence. Most of the tests in the series were standardised at the same time with closely comparable samples. This meant that where a child's performance on two or more levels of the series was to be assessed a fair degree of equivalence was ensured.

In the mid-1990s new pressures have emerged for schools to keep reading progress under closer review. The introduction of national testing and the move to publish results has led to a debate about the fairest way of judging the 'standards' reached by schools. Teachers are understandably concerned about the weight to be given to the amount of progress children make from a previous baseline. Indeed, even if such questions were not so prominent, it would seem to be a useful extension of practice for class teachers to be monitoring reading progress in these 'value-added' terms.

It was with this specific role in mind that the RPT, currently undergoing standardisation, was developed. This is also a series of reading comprehension tests but it was designed specifically for annually monitoring children's progress.

The prime intention was thus to develop a series of group tests which would allow teachers to evaluate reading progress against norms *for* progress. Most test series, including the ERT, allow progress to be assessed indirectly because the norms are 'cross-sectional'. This means that by including children of different ages in the test standardisation sample it is assumed that the differences in performance between any two age points in the sample reflect the amount of normal progress learners make *over time* between the two ages. This may be a serviceable assumption but 'difference' may not be synonymous with 'progress'. The most accurate norms for reading progress are those derived by actually measuring progress in the same children across one or more years. This could be done using the same test each time, although results might be distorted through the children's increased familiarity with the content of the test and there would also be the danger of a 'ceiling effect' upon the performance of older children.

An alternative is to use a series of tests which are similar in format and design but in which each test matches the ability of its target age group. Norms are established by arranging for the same children to take each test in the series at the desired intervals. Such norms are currently being obtained for the RPT series by re-testing the same sample of children at twelve-month intervals on successive versions of the tests. This provides direct progress norms. There is also scope, should it be needed, to differentiate progress norms according to previous attainment level. It remains to be seen whether the results of re-testing will necessitate this.

Time of year of standardisation and testing

Regardless of whether norms are cross-sectional or longitudinal, they will only accurately reflect children's attainment at the time of year at which they were obtained. This seemingly obvious point is too often overlooked by test users. The importance of any 'seasonal effects' is highlighted by longitudinal norms. For example, the amount of reading progress made between mid-July and the beginning of September is probably not as much as a comparable period starting in mid-January. Although such seasonal effects are occasionally uncovered by researchers engaged in longitudinal studies of cohorts of children, not enough is known about them. The problem for the practitioner is to know how significant such effects might be. The likely implications for the younger beginning reader are probably much greater than for the older primary school pupil. It will, however, be accepted in general that norms based on a test standardised late in the school year probably underestimate children's attainment if they are actually tested much earlier in the year. The counsel of perfection would be to use tests at the time of year at which they were originally standardised. This would mean the exclusion of some ancient tests, unfortunately still in use, for which no date of standardisation was reported.

Short-term progress norms

The RPT will be a group test of comprehension and will deal with progress over the relatively long period of a school year. Some teachers need to evaluate relatively short-term progress, for example, in the early stages of reading, or with backward readers receiving special help. So far, the only test published in the UK with longitudinal norms for this purpose is the *Individual Reading Analysis* (Vincent and de la Mare, 1990). This is an individual test of reading accuracy and comprehension with three equivalent forms. Each form was standardised on the same cohort of 1200 children at intervals of sixty-eight and ninety-four days and the published teacher's guide presents a number of alternative ways of evaluating progress. As with so much else in the testing of reading, it remains to be seen how in practice, over the years, teachers use this particular feature of the test.

Although the development of tests with genuinely longitudinal norms seems to be a highly desirable direction for reading test construction to take, it is an expensive option – the development of the *Individual Reading Analysis* required the recruitment and training of a national sample of over 300 teachers to carry out the testing. It is certainly unlikely that the number of reading tests with longitudinal norms will expand rapidly. A partial alternative solution is to place a test series on a common ability scale. A number of published tests (e.g. *The Reading Ability Series, The Effective Reading Tests*) have been calibrated by arranging for children in the standardisation sample to take a successive pair of tests. An 'ability' scale (see Pumfrey, 1987 and Choppin, 1979 for discussions of this form of scaling) is derived for each test. The individual test scales are then adjusted to align them to a common reference point. This means that a measure of ability obtained on one test is statistically comparable to an ability score on another test. Tests in a set scaled in this way are interchangeable and measure progress on a common scale. This means that a child who makes, say, five points of progress from test A to test B has

made as much progress as a child who improves by five points from tests
C to D. As with other normative scales, however, we cannot be sure that
the amount of progress children make is constant over any period during
the year.

Qualitative progress measures

So far we have concentrated upon normative evaluation of progress. As
with other aspects of reading assessment, other languages for describing
progress now compete with quantification. This trend began with criterion-
referenced testing: a movement to develop tests which measured the
content of learners' skills and knowledge rather than their ability relative
to a norm and to other learners. The way criterion-referenced tests were
interpreted in practice varied greatly (for a fuller review see Vincent 1985,
Chapter 8) and, for reading, this movement has failed to fulfil its promise.
The ideas have continued to be influential, however. The original 'statements of attainment' for reading in the English National Curriculum, and
to some extent the 'level descriptions' which replaced them in 1995 are
perhaps the most familiar example of a latter-day criterion-referenced
assessment system. The intention, which was to link an explicit account
of the content of learning to a numerical scale of ten (and subsequently
eight) points, was a worthy one.

The National Curriculum model of progression has been implemented
in increasingly ingenuous ways as the difficulty in criterion-referencing
any language skill became increasingly evident. The underlying problem
is the extent to which reading is to be regarded as a *psychological process*
– the view taken by most contributors to this volume – or a *curriculum
'subject'*. With the psychological model, our understanding of reading is
modified in the light of new knowledge but as a curriculum 'subject' its
definition can be changed because people *think* it should be changed. This
change may result from serious educational debate and reflection or it
may be made summarily at the whim of a government minister ('Children
ought to read Shakespeare . . .'). Psychologists who are concerned to get
at the truth about reading may be dismayed by such unscientific caprice.
On the other hand, teachers can hardly be expected to wait until there is
a psychological account of the many ways in which, once initial word-
recognition skills are learned, readers process and respond to texts. A
'hand-over' point from psychology to English as a curriculum subject has
to be agreed. Thus, attempts to describe reading development face a dual
challenge. They need to be consistent with empirical and theoretical
knowledge from disciplines such as psychology and linguistics while,
after the hand-over point, they must continue to provide a satisfactory
account of what counts as progress. Even if this is managed successfully
conceptually, practical means of applying the assessments will still have
to be devised.

THE PROBLEM OF A SCALE FOR READING

In practice the most common way in which progression in reading is expressed is in terms of an increase in Reading Age (RA). This has its origins in the earlier use of the concept of mental age as an index of intelligence generally. It is not possible to give a formal definition of what a reading age is because in practice different tests derive it in different ways. Most teachers and parents are no doubt content to assume that a reading age involves some kind of matching up of children's ages and scores with the implicit prescription that a child's reading age should at least equal their chronological age. However, there is a basic flaw in this analogy between chronological age and progression in reading.

Chronological age is only moderately related to reading ability. Thus, different ways of converting raw scores to 'ages' will give different results, even for the same test. For example, in the original version (no longer available) of the widely used *Neale Analysis of Reading Ability*, reading 'age' is the predicted chronological age for a given raw score. An identical procedure was used in the *New Reading Analysis* (Vincent and de la Mare, 1985). In fact, a more reliable method is to derive reading 'ages' by finding the predicted raw score from chronological age. Children's reading 'ages' are here the chronological age 'predictive of' their obtained raw score. This method was used in the *Individual Reading Analysis* (Vincent and de la Mare, 1990) which in other respects was very similar in content to the *New Reading Analysis*.

There are further ways in which reading ages have been derived for published tests, including the use of median ages or scores (rather than the means) and, more recently, methods which equate chronological age and scaled ability (e.g. The *Suffolk Reading Scale* (Hagley 1986); The *Neale Analysis of Reading Ability, Revised British Edition* (Neale *et al.*, 1988)).

Reading ages are popular because they are based on an intuitively appealing, but misleading, metaphor. The alternatives, of which standardised scores and percentiles are by far the most common, would be equally suitable for many purposes. Indeed, if the purpose of assessment is simply to identify the weakest readers in a group, this could be done by inspecting *raw* scores: there is no need for reference to reading age or, indeed, any other converted or scaled score. However, percentiles and standardised scores in most published reading tests are age-adjusted so that they compare children to their own chronological age group rather than locating them on a 'developmental' continuum.

Parents are often very concerned to know their children's reading ages, but it is surely time to find a better language for teachers to communicate with parents about their children's progress or difficulties in reading. The National Curriculum with its statements of attainment and subsequent level descriptions promised to be a new starting point for this. In practice, its use of a ten-level scale lacked the level of precision teachers required

– hence the subsequent introduction of supplementary reading and spelling tests to give finer within-level grades. Nevertheless, reading-test developers have yet to devise an entirely credible replacement for reading ages. For the time being it will be important for test users to be more aware of how, precisely, the reading ages they are obtaining, recording or reporting were derived by the test constructor.

CONCLUSION

This chapter has identified a number of ways in which tests for the classroom assessment of reading could or indeed should evolve (fuller management of quantitative data; improved ways of measuring progress; better ways of assessing reading potential and underachievement; more thoughtful interpretation of the reading age scale, etc.). The coverage has been by no means exhaustive but the discussion has underlined that while the 'technology' for testing reading is imperfect and does not amount to a ready-made 'expert system' it retains much potential for development as a useful part of the professional skill of the teacher of reading.

REFERENCES

Adams, E. and Burgess, T. (1989). *Teachers' Own Records: A System Promoting Professional Quality*. London: Routledge.
Ames, T. (1984). *The Diagnostic Reading Pack*. Slough: NFER-Nelson.
Arnold, H. (1992). *Diagnostic Reading Record*. Sevenoaks: Hodder & Stoughton.
Bennet, N., Deforges, C., Cockburn, A., and Wilkinson, B. (1984). *The Quality of Pupil Learning Experiences*. Hove: LEA.
Bradley, L (1984). *Assessing Reading Difficulties: A Diagnostic and Remedial Approach*. Slough: NFER-Nelson.
Choppin, B. (1979). Testing the questions: the Rasch model and item banking. In J. Raggett, C. Tutt and P. Raggett (eds) *Assessment and Testing of Reading: Problems and Practices*. London: Ward Lock Educational.
Coles, M. and Jenkins, R. (eds) (1996). *International Perspectives on Reading Assessment: Classroom innovations and Challenges*. London: Routledge.
Connor, C. (1991) *Assessment and Testing in the Primary School*. London: The Falmer Press.
Cooper, M., Parker, R. and Toombs, S. (n.d.). *Reading Assessment for Teachers, Tutor Notes (2nd edition) and Assessment Materials*. Swindon: Wiltshire County Council.
Daniels, J.C. and Diack, H. (1958). *The Standard Reading Tests*. St Albans: Granada Publishing.
Dunn, L.M., Dunn, L.M., Whetton, C. and Pintile, D. (1982) *British Picture Vocabulary Scales*. Slough: NFER-Nelson.
Ehri, L. (1995). Phases of development in learning to read words by sight. *Journal of Research in Reading*, 18(2), 118–27.
Ellis, N. (1990). Reading, phonological skills and short-term memory: interactive tributaries of development. *Journal of Research in Reading*, 13(2), 107–22
France, N. (1981). *The Primary Reading Test*. Slough: NFER-Nelson.
Gipps, C.V. (1994). *Beyond Testing: Towards a Theory of Educational Assessment*. London: The Falmer Press.

Gipps, C.V., Brown, M., McCallum, B. and McAllister, S. (1995). Intuition or Evidence? Buckingham: Open University Press.

Gipps, C.V., Steadman, S., Blackstone, T. and Stierer, B. (1983). *Testing Children: Standardised Testing in Schools and LEAs.* London: Heinemann.

Goulandris, N. and Snowling, M. (1995). Assessing reading skills. In E. Funnell and M. Stuart (eds) *Learning to Read: Psychology in the Classroom.* Oxford: Blackwell Publishers.

Hagley, F. (1986). *The Suffolk Reading Scale.* Slough: NFER-Nelson.

Harrison, C. and Salinger, T. (eds) (1996). *International Perspectives on Reading Assessment: Theory and Practice.* London: Routledge.

Horn, W.F. and Packard, T. (1985). Early identification of learning problems: a meta-analysis. *Journal of Educational Psychology*, 77(5), 597–607.

Lindsay G. A. and Wedell, K. (1982). The early identification of educationally 'at risk' children revisited. *Journal of Learning Disabilities*, 15(4), 212–17.

Linn, R.L. (ed.) (1989). *Educational Measurement* (3rd edn). Washington, DC: American Council on Education.

Miles, T.R. and Miles, E. (1990). *Dyslexia: A Hundred Years On.* Milton Keynes: Open University Press.

Neale, M.D., Christophers, U. and Whetton, C. (1988). *Neale Analysis of Reading Ability, Revised British Edition.* Slough: NFER-Nelson.

Potter, F. (1980). Miscue analysis: a cautionary note. *Journal of Research in Reading*, 3(2), 116–29

Potton, A. (1983). *Screening.* Basingstoke: Macmillan.

Pumfrey, P.D. (1985). *Reading: Tests and Assessment Techniques* (2nd edn). Sevenoaks: Hodder & Stoughton.

Pumfrey, P.D. (1987). Rasch scaling and reading tests. *Journal of Research in Reading*, 10(1), 75–86

Pumfrey, P.D. and Reason, R. (1991). *Specific Learning Difficulties (Dyslexia): Challenges and Response.* London: Routledge.

Stanovich, K. (1992). The theoretical and practical consequences of discrepancy definitions of dyslexia. In M. Snowling and M. Thomson (eds) *Dyslexia: Integrating Theory and Practice.* London: Whurr Publishers.

Stierer, B. (1986). The misuse of reading tests: malfunctioning technicians or a function of the technology. In D. Vincent, A. K. Pugh and G. Brooks (eds) *Assessing Reading: Proceedings of the UKRA Colloquium on the Testing & Assessment of Reading.* Basingstoke: Macmillan Education.

Thomson, M. (1990). *Developmental Dyslexia (3rd edn).* London: Whurr Publishers.

Vincent, D. (1985) *Reading Tests in the Classroom: An Introduction.* Slough: NFER-Nelson.

Vincent, D. (1994). The assessment of reading. In D. Wray and J. Medwell (eds) *Teaching Primary English: The State of the Art.* London: Routledge.

Vincent, D. and de la Mare, M. (1985). *The New Reading Analysis.* Slough: NFER-Nelson.

Vincent, D and de la Mare, M. (1989). *Effective Reading Tests Level 0, Teacher's Manual.* Slough: NFER-Nelson.

Vincent, D. and de la Mare, M. (1990). *The Individual Reading Analysis.* Slough: NFER-Nelson.

Vincent, D. Green, L., Francis, J and Powney, J. (1983). *Review of Reading Tests.* Slough: NFER-Nelson.

Vinsonhaler, J., Weinshank, A.B., Wagner, C.C. and Polin, R.M. (1983). Diagnosing children with educational problems: characteristics of reading and learning disabilities specialists and classroom teachers. *Reading Research Quarterly*, 3(18), 134–64.

Wood, R. (1991) *Assessment and Testing: A Survey of Research*. Cambridge: Cambridge University Press.
Wright, S.F., Fields, H. and Newman, S.P. (1995). Dyslexia: stability of definition over a five-year period. *Journal of Research in Reading*, 19(1) (in press).
Young, D. (1992). *Group Reading Test* (3rd edn). London: Hodder & Stoughton Educational.

OTHER TEST REFERENCES

Edinburgh Reading Test Series, London: Hodder & Stoughton Educational, 1977.
Effective Reading Tests, Slough: NFER-Nelson, 1986, 1989.
Reading Ability Series, Slough: NFER-Nelson, 1988.
Reading Progress Test Series, London: Hodder & Stoughton, 1996
Taking a Closer Look at Reading, Edinburgh: Scottish Council for Research in Education, 1995.

3 Assessment by educational psychologists

Martin Turner

INTRODUCTION: WHY TEST?

Since the first reading test was devised by P.B. Ballard in 1914, a widespread gradual introduction of tests has accompanied educational psychology. Their utility has won them a position more secure than that of any other contribution. Though psychologists have had fluctuating attitudes towards tests through the decades of this century, the present resurgence of interest in accountability seems, once again, to be restoring testing and its methods to a high public standing. This is a matter of regret for some, who look to far horizons when forms of teacher assessment will have displaced all other kinds (Gipps, 1994). But the profession of educational psychology has always been closely associated with idealism, as is apparent in its treatment at the hands of its first scholarly historian (Wooldridge, 1994).

It is not the intention of this chapter to review all useful current reading tests; the field is not lacking in reviews of this kind (Pumfrey, 1985; Turner, 1993; Vincent *et al.*, 1983). Rather, a variety of assessment purposes, of the kind that fall to the educational psychologist, will be considered. Tests have at least six distinctive purposes which it may be helpful to consider. These are as follows:

- The demonstration of progress
- Monitoring of reading standards
- The evaluation of outcomes
- Planning of instruction
- Assessment of the failing reader
- Identification of higher-level reading difficulties.

Perhaps greatest interest attaches to the diagnostic evaluation of the failing reader, and this will receive detailed consideration. But other purposes make different yet equally legitimate demands on the psychologist and pose technical challenges of a worthwhile kind. These demands often occur at points at which some objective check on reality has become desirable. In what follows, it will be helpful to keep in mind the empirical dimensions of reading: *accuracy, fluency* and *comprehension*. Much of what follows will be concerned with observation and measurement of reading within the paradigm of science.

READING: THE COMPONENTS AND THE ENSEMBLE

Much confusion about the teaching and learning of reading seems to be due to the long sequence of incremental improvements that takes place throughout an individual's life and the apparent discontinuity between activities at different stages. The concept of 'stages' has been effectively used by Jeanne Chall (1983) to reconcile those whose experience is mainly limited to a single stage. However, the implicit metaphor – of *developmental* stages – may mislead as to the inevitability of progress: 'reading is not a skill which spontaneously develops' (Beech, 1987, p. 188).

Investigators have commonly agreed on three empirical dimensions of reading skill: accuracy, fluency and comprehension. In a logical extension of this analysis, it has been proposed that if R (reading), D (decoding) and C (comprehension) are variables that range from 0 to 1, then

$$R = D \times C$$

(Gough and Tunmer, 1986; Hoover and Tunmer, 1993). The multiplicative relationship in this formula allows that reading is a *product* of decoding and comprehension; either of the components, if restricted, must in turn limit the scope of the other. Higher ('top-down') and lower ('bottom-up') processes are accorded equal importance in this view. However, that phonemic awareness and alphabetic coding skills are the main factors in initial and subsequent acquisition of reading skills is the conclusion, with which few would now disagree, of an influential review of this extensive field (Vellutino, 1991).

Scientific, as opposed to folk, agreement is also firm on other points. Without a fair degree of fluent decoding, comprehension – which depends critically on sentence structure – is compromised. Perfetti (1985) has proposed that attentional and other resources tied up in non-fluent decoding prevent the reader from attending to the meaning of print (verbal efficiency theory). Word recognition, so to speak, is the engine that drives the reading process. Moreover, though intuitively we seem to read *words*, in actuality it is *letters* (two or three at a time) that are fixated and recognized as spelling patterns (Adams, 1990, 1994); the text as a whole is subject to heavy, not light, sampling.

There are thus the makings of a broad framework within which both the teaching and the learning of reading can be accommodated. Letters and words are taught first, with more emphasis on sounds (phonology) and spelling patterns (orthography) than has been usual; then sentences and larger units can be interpreted and the meaning of the text as a whole modelled.

One way of referring to this framework is as a *component skills approach* (e.g. Beech, 1989; Carr and Levy, 1990; Frederiksen, 1982; Hoover and Tunmer, 1993). The fact that adults seem to expect children to pass rapidly through earlier, code-learning stages means that assessment is often a matter of presenting them with a complex task and demanding good integration of component skills. Yet individuals who have dyslexia in particular show persistent difficulties with foundation skills of establishing mappings between letters (and letter groups) and their sounds and often need vastly elaborated teaching before such units are consolidated.

In a sense, all structures for teaching literacy are arbitrary – but some are less arbitrary than others. Perhaps the most elaborately developed teaching sequence is that found in the Dyslexia Institute Language Programme (Walker and Brooks, 1993). A letter-order approach for teaching has evolved and has been exemplified with every known instance of a particular pattern or rule, complete with detailed word lists and well-tried methodologies for teaching. Associated teaching systems, similar in approach and only a little less elaborate, are too numerous to discuss here.

This is not, however, a rationale for teaching all children a sequence of subskills, even if an ideal sequence could be established. All children do not need this level of detail and the implementation of an ambitious programme would in many cases delay the goal of successful reading. Moreover,

> there may be no one organization of these multiple skills that charac-terizes good versus poor readers ... skill may include organizational flexibility, not some fixed equation whereby the various skill components always operate in the same fashion ... it may be important to analyze each child's particular strengths and weaknesses. While poor readers as a *group* have massive cognitive deficits, individual poor readers have very mixed profiles. We speculate that educational practices working on profile information may be more beneficial than practices based on group deficits.
>
> (Levy and Hinchley, 1990).

But conversely it seems that the need for structured literacy teaching, which increases with the severity of remedial need, may be the result of *lack* of such structure in initial teaching.

PURPOSE-APPROPRIATE ASSESSMENT

The assessment task, accordingly, takes very different shape in relation to the different stages at which children may be struggling. Even pupils who have considerable reading skill but remain retarded in relation to age and ability may have continuing difficulty with phonological processing;

low-level letter-identification errors are sometimes apparent even in more advanced readers.

It is necessary to adapt assessment methodology to many different purposes. Further, it should be accepted that the determination of a suitable teaching programme is not the entire aim of an assessment. A historically meaningful account of a pattern of reading failure is often an important part of the explanation. Since old and new reading behaviours co-exist in the same individual, and assessment readily becomes an exercise in educational archaeology, the longer-term influence of technical problems in reading can be demonstrated. Early instructional approaches, too, carrying as they do implicit messages about reading, seem to tune habits and strategies in young children – for instance, guessing – in ways that are very persistent. It is one purpose of an individual assessment to unravel the external, as well as the inherent, influences that have created, and may maintain, a reading problem.

DEMONSTRATING PROGRESS

It is not only unsuccessful readers who need assessment. The reading attainment of the unexceptional majority stands in need of regular and routine review. (The different question of actual monitoring of standards is discussed in the next section.) Here, any school or institution is well advised to stick to the same instrument, since fluctuating standards from year to year are best interpreted within a constant metric.

In Britain, evaluation of reading progress is usually attempted at the end of Key Stages. This new nomenclature describes the first two to three years of infant education as Key Stage 1; the ensuing four years of junior education as Key Stage 2; the first three years of secondary schooling as Key Stage 3, and the final two exam-oriented years of statutory education as Key Stage 4.

Test publishers have for many years provided instruments appropriate to the kinds of skill development of these different age groups. For instance, top infants are frequently given tests of *cloze procedure* where pupils 'fill in the blanks'. The Suffolk Test (Hagley, 1987) is among the best of the newer group tests and is timed (20 minutes). Sentence completion requires the child to work through a series of similar items in which a gap in a sentence must be filled from a choice of several alternative words. The selection is by underlining or circling, so the measurement of reading is not contaminated by the measurement of writing (a child may be poor at one and good at the other). Parallel forms enable progress to be measured – or cheating avoided! – through the whole primary age range. The *Macmillan Group Reading Test* (Macmillan Education, 1985) is another good recent group reading test of the sentence completion type. The earlier items are enhanced, for younger children, by picture cues (as in paired associate learning). Reading ages may be achieved from 6:3 to 13:3.

From Key Stage 2 and onwards through most of the years of statutory schooling, reading is conveniently measured by means of a group-administered test of reading *comprehension*, such as that included in the Richmond Tests (Hieronymus *et al.*, 1988). The Reading Comprehension test requires multiple-choice (no writing) responses to comprehension questions about several complex passages. Even at 15 years 8 months, 57 points of raw score give 60 points (70–130) of standard score, a fine power of discrimination. However, the test at Level 6 occupies nine pages of the pupil booklet, and 55 minutes of testing time may be thought to be something of a luxury.

National Curriculum Assessment still has to justify the large expenditures, expectation-arousing publicity and vast disruption that have attended it through five years of experimentation. Only personal intervention by the Secretary of State sufficed to retain the supposedly criterion-referenced Ten-level Scale in Sir Ron Dearing's final report (Dearing, 1993b). Meanwhile, conventional normative psychometric tests of reading are able to assert their authority over 'Standard Assessment Tasks' when the two methods give different results (Davies *et al.*, 1995).

THE MONITORING OF NATIONAL READING STANDARDS

The post-war period saw great public commitment to the cause of progress in reading standards, which was not to be revived until an adverse report in 1972 by Start and Wells of the NFER. In addition to the Watts-Vernon (WV) Test, which had been used between 1952 and 1964, the NS (National Survey) Test 6, also of the sentence-completion type, was given to an all-age sample of 1470 school pupils. It was found that, though reading standards had risen steadily (using carefully compared samples on the same tests) between 1948 and 1964, in the six years to 1970 they had fallen slightly (Watts-Vernon) or stood still (NS6):

> As measured by the WV test, there is a high probability that the reading comprehension standard of juniors had declined somewhat since 1964, and on the combined bases of both WV and NS6 tests, the mean scores of juniors and seniors had undergone no significant rise or fall since 1960–1. The almost linear increase in reading comprehension that existed from 1948 to 1964 has not been maintained.
>
> (Start and Wells, 1972, p. 67)

As a result of public concern following this report, the Bullock Committee was set up to enquire into reading methods and standards (DES, 1975). Another reasonably serious and objective account of reading standards appeared in 1978 when HMI reported on primary education in England (DES, 1978). This relied on comparisons between NS6 test results and found that the 1970 data had been an inconsequential interruption in a steady upward trend. Survey results on the reading attainment of some

5000 11 year olds were added to and compared with previous national survey data. Confidence was restored (DES, 1978).

Following Bullock and hints in earlier surveys about test ageing and the desirability of a 'rolling technique in testing', the Assessment of Performance Unit (APU) was set up in 1975: it published, in 1981, survey results obtained from 10,000 11 year olds in a 1979 survey (DES/APU, 1981). The whole methodology had changed. A series of ten booklets was prepared to permit investigation into higher-order reading skills of interpretation, description and explanation, attitudes to reading and reading for different purposes (to gain an overall impression, to select relevant information, to expand on previous information, to follow a sequence of instructions). Criteria for reading backwardness were, at the behest of Bullock, softened (Start and Wells had found 8.5% of 11 year olds with reading ages on NS6 below 7 years). Rasch scaling was introduced (a technical advance). A minimum obeisance to continuity was made: the NS6 test was given, for the last time, to a subset of 824 pupils – standards had, slightly but not significantly, fallen.

In 1988 the APU published the results of its 'language monitoring' since 1979, a series of five annual surveys into reading at ages 11 and 15. Unnormed raw data was reported within 'percentage bands' (upper, mid, lower) for questions answered in response to the booklets. There was emphasis on boy/girl and regional differences. This publication saw the appearance of a sentence which ranks as one of the most quoted of any government document:

> The incidence of illiteracy among school pupils in the age groups assessed is very low, in the sense that relatively few are unable to decode words that they are familiar with.
>
> (DES/APU, 1988, p. 7)

(i.e. that are within their oral vocabulary). Further,

> The first point to note is that very few pupils aged 11 are unable to read in the sense that they are unable to decode written language. The results of the surveys show that only one pupil in 100 responded with a success rate of 10 percent or less to questions asked about what they had read.
>
> (DES/APU, 1988, p.7)

This picture is certainly strange to anyone who works in a typical comprehensive school. In one South London comprehensive, 25% of pupils regularly arrive with a reading age of below 9 – and 10% below 8 – years. In another, East London comprehensive, roughly half the intake would be able to read only at a level below 9 years.

Official national monitoring of reading subsequently ceased. Nevertheless, HMI and other publications continued, through the 1970s, to demonstrate a responsible, factual, even reassuringly dull and dry approach to educational standards. High standards were in general to be preferred to low ones, but by the 1980s there was a new mood. Some signs of this could be observed in the 1990 HMI report, *The Teaching and Learning of Language and Literacy*. A new ideology had clearly taken hold. Reading schemes were adversely compared with 'books of quality'.

> Standards of reading are generally good and continue to improve. . . .
> [But where] . . . undue prominence [is given to reading and writing]
> . . . standards may be good but on a very narrow front.
>
> (HMI, 1990, p.7)

Meanwhile a few LEAs, though no more than half, had steadily been collecting test data on all their children over the decade. Some had been aggregating reading data over much longer periods and making use of computers to analyse the trends. In most cases the results were not made public. Following the chance discovery that several large authorities had testing programmes which showed a steady decline through the latter half of the 1980s, a specially convened conference of educational psychologists agreed that in the public interest the position should be made known (Turner, 1990a).

The resulting public controversy lasted well over a year and gave considerable impetus to the current efforts at educational reform. However, reforms in the UK that are intended to make schools more independent have been equivocal in impact; reforms that are intended to control curriculum and testing have been rendered counterproductive and unpopular by excessive regulation.

Some of the devices which operate at the apex of the pyramid of public education may be observed in the deliberations of the Parliamentary Select Committee on primary reading standards (Education, Science and Arts Committee, 1991). The members of this committee concerned themselves, succinctly, with two questions: Have reading standards declined? and: What is the state of reading teaching? But these were just the concerns which had already been addressed by two official reports into the alleged decline in standards (Cato and Whetton, 1991; HMI, 1991). The MPs stated that 'the scope of the enquiry has been restricted to the two reports'. As an exercise in disclosure, therefore, the Committee's report covered no new ground.

The committee took a positive approach with regard to teacher training ('more time should be given' and more opportunity to specialize) and good practice (encouraging 'teachers to use these centres of excellence to observe work of high quality'). Parental involvement, book variety and nursery provision were similarly commended. 'It is important to keep a sense of proportion,' said the members of the parliamentary committee. 'The various methods of teaching phonics should be evaluated' (again); 'we wholeheartedly agree . . . that "we have not got a crisis" '; and 'we have not found evidence to support this view', the one which had 'attributed the apparent decline in standards ... to the growth of 'real books' methods of teaching reading'.

Apparent decline? 'We therefore conclude that the claim that reading standards have fallen in recent years has not been proved beyond reasonable doubt.' Grounds for reasonable doubt, of course, were in plentiful supply. NFER statisticians apparently led the committee to believe that standardised scores and percentiles were 'different statistical reporting methods' such that 'there will necessarily be difficulty in combining the data'. (The two are direct equivalents.) These experts had been delegated – by Secretary of State MacGregor to the DES to SEAC to NFER – the painful task of analysing at second- or third-hand incomplete data reluctantly supplied by a minority of local education authorities. The data were, in an important sense, objective. However, the supplementary verbal accounts, including interpretations, given by education authorities were wide open to special pleading, bias and motivated reticence. The NFER authors conceded quite plainly that

> the survey could not establish reasons for any changes in reading standards since no relevant measures were sought.
>
> (Cato and Whetton, 1991, p. 11)

Yet suspect as the views of LEAs might be, few as were the number offering reasons for decline, far though such explanation fell beyond the scope of the NFER enquiry, the authors reached for the forbidden apple: 'In no case was a decline in reading standards associated with methods of teaching reading' (ibid., p. 69).

This sentence was no mere slip: it followed pages about modern methods, redefinitions of reading, the beauties of the National Curriculum and the general dubiousness and undesirability of testing. The sentence was elevated into a 'conclusion'. It was noticed gratefully by the *Times Educational Supplement* on 14 December 1990. It acquired enhanced importance as one of the report's 'three main points' in a summary drafted at the time by SEAC. It guided the thinking of the committee who were content, even so, with the Scottish verdict of Not Proven. The short, damaging sentence was picked up even by prominent educational psychologists to offset any useful contribution made by the British Psychological Society,[1] extracted carefully and quoted in the first direct editorial comment by competent psychologists on the events of the year (Gray and Lindsay, 1991, p. 78).

For the NFER analysts there would have been an 'association with methods of teaching reading' only if sizeable numbers of LEAs had come forward, announced significant downward trends in measured reading attainment, implicated widespread dereliction in the teaching of reading and accepted full responsibility. Such a development would undoubtedly have inspired interest.

In the only useful scientific test of the decline in measured reading attainment, a subsequent NFER report (Gorman and Fernandes, 1992) found just such a decline: between two and three points of standard score, equivalent to about four to six months of progress for an average child. This finding, which fell within a decimal point or two of that originally claimed, emerged from the best kind of enquiry: the readministration, under carefully controlled conditions, of tests from the new Reading Ability series, to a second sample in 1991 closely matched with the standardization sample of 1987. The conclusion merited two sentences in a recent review of the post-war period (Brooks *et al.*, 1995).

THE EVALUATION OF OUTCOMES

For purposes of research, smaller numbers of the pupils whose progress is to be evaluated may be offset by more precise quality specifications in tests used. An important requirement is for stable units of measurement. Just as in the US 'grade' age is supposed to be a generally understandable concept, so in the UK a reading 'age' is a common currency which apparently bridges the gap between measurement that is normative (comparing the child with his or her contemporaries) and measurement that is criterion referenced (relative to a given standard). Unfortunately this convention has little value, since it is based on the unit of a 'month', and a month of reading progress at age 6 to 7 years is vastly different from a month at 13 to 14 years, as any table of norms shows. For serious measurement purposes, the standard score is always best; at communicating to lay persons without excessive explanation, the percentile is probably most effective.

It is a matter for regret that many published reports, citing reading test data, continue to refer to age equivalents, in spite of the inherent limitations and measurement shortcomings in doing so. Any supposed benefit in communicating with a lay audience should be weighed against the fact that the sense of understanding thus created is partly illusory.

Moreover, researchers often demonstrate an inexplicable preference for antique tests. One traditional test whose use can no longer be recommended is the Schonell (Tests A and B). Evidence has accumulated over fifteen years – see Vernon's and Young's comments in the manuals for their respective tests (Vernon, 1977; Young, 1976) – that Schonell's spelling standards have either slipped most remarkably, or his test construction methodology, nowhere described, leaves a lot to be desired, or both. This is not to impugn the validity of the test: all spelling tests correlate extremely highly – typically 0.9 or above – and measure incremental spelling ability simply and directly. But the norms given by Schonell are quite inappropriate today, if they ever were appropriate. In the secondary years the spelling ages obtained on the Schonell and Vernon tests come adrift by a year at age 11 and 2.5 years at nearly 16; tests from three different decades chart the erosion of this important ability.

The benefits of using standardised tests are obvious: such instruments compare children precisely with their contemporaries. If for any reason such benefits are to be forgone, raw scores on tests are adequate for many evaluative purposes. But with older, technically limited tests, raw scores in any case may be the only kind that there are.

A further technical feature of modern tests which offers opportunities to the researcher is interval scaling. In an interval scale the difference between, say, 45 and 65 points means the same thing as another difference between 20 and 40 points. Such a feature can be very useful. The Yale team pursuing the Connecticut longitudinal study into incidence and definitions of dyslexia was recently able to demonstrate qualitatively similar learning increments for disabled and retarded groups by fitting to the data a model incorporating quadratic growth curves (Shaywitz *et al.*, in press, pp. 18–19). This was possible because of the Rasch scaling employed in the construction of the tests. Researchers used two tests, Reading and Mathematics, from the Woodcock–Johnson Psycho-Educational Battery (Revised) (WJ-R; see Woodcock and Johnson, 1989, 1990).

PLANNING OR FINE-TUNING INSTRUCTION

Reading attainment may be assessed for the purpose of planning teaching. Though still 'a check on reality', the *formative* purpose is the main one. Such a reading test, often called criterion referenced, often has, in relation to a particular programme, the nature of a *placement test*. It identifies, in other words, the starting point in a teaching programme justified by a pupil's present knowledge.

Leaving aside historical descriptions, developmental explanations, normative comparisons and statistical exceptions, two important dilemmas remain. The first of these is *stability*. A child may demonstrate competence today against a particular criterion (for instance, the short vowel *e* in *cvc* words), but this subskill may not be securely consolidated and successful performance on this test of competence may be misleading. This is the reason why specialist teachers, beginning to implement a detailed literacy programme, prefer to start the child among alphabetic skills which it might appear that he or she has already mastered. Criteria for mastery need to be kept stringent.

The second dilemma is that of agreeing the *curriculum sequence* in which, it is hypothesised, the child's progress belongs.

> Criterion-referenced diagnostic reading tests are designed to analyze systematically an individual's strengths and weaknesses without comparing that individual to others. ... [But] different authors view reading in different ways and see the sequence of development of reading skills differently.
>
> (Salvia and Ysseldyke, 1985, p. 414)

We have noted that teaching programmes vary according to the version of English structure which each adopts. Some are rudimentary, others elaborate. All are in a sense arbitrary, though sensitivity to the structure and *learnability* of written English distinguishes among them.

A recent implementation of this combination of criterion-referenced diagnostic methodology and teaching plan formulation is *Autoskill Reading*.[2] Based on a rationale of component skills training, this computer-mediated programme has received very favourable evaluations in the US, Canada and Havering, England. A task analysis identifies the small steps in which phonic decoding consists in the earliest stages. A 'placement test' locates the child's starting point within the programme, which keeps complete records and gives immediate, relevant feedback; stringent criteria for mastery are applied. Learning progresses in a logical sequence through one-, two-, three-, and four-letter nonsense syllables (e.g. *gug*) and words, to phrases, sentences and paragraphs. At the same time the pupil moves from perceptual (sound and shape) matching of letters to oral and silent reading. Later, comprehension and retention are probed through question-and-answer format. This approach is conventional: only in the fine detail of consonant and vowel structure is this programme likely to differ from others. Yet a typical finding is that primary and secondary pupils in outer London make gains of a 'month' of reading age for every 75 minutes spent on the programme (Foot, 1994).

DIAGNOSTIC ASSESSMENT OF THE FAILING READER

The diagnostic exercise is not limited to one with immediate implications for action; information about general abilities, severity of difficulty and learning strategies will also have implications for the teaching approach. The child's failure to progress may be *expected*, in that disappointing reading progress may be in line with the child's abilities and other accomplishments, for instance, in spoken language and other school learning; or it may be *unexpected*, when diagnosis will make use of information about family history, individual development (for instance, of speech), and any information-processing anomalies, such as in phonological skills or speed of processing. In the latter case, in which a dyslexia diagnosis is a serious possibility, the reading assessment is only one element in the diagnostic repertoire. This is because dyslexia is seen as an information-processing difficulty with generalised effects that may precede and, for instance, in cases of remediated or compensated dyslexia, succeed the learning of literacy. Other elements will include cognitive testing of information skills and verbal, nonverbal reasoning and visuospatial abilities. General ability testing, though for some years retreated from by educational psychologists, performs a role as the *general cognitive survey* by means of which pupils may be screened for many other kinds of problems. IQ, the midpoint of a cognitive profile, has a role as the first point of reference for the regression matrix by means of which *exceptionalities* (statistically unexpected contrasts in cognitive development or educational attainment) may be identified (Turner, 1997).

A description of wider scale cognitive testing remains outside the scope of this chapter. The use of conventional reading tests, moreover, may require little more than a mention. In general these are of three kinds, depending on the kinds of skills to be expected from a description of reading skills in terms of *accuracy*, *fluency* and *comprehension*.

In the earliest stages, when all-important word recognition skills are being established, tests of single-word reading are most relevant. Both the British and the Differential Ability Scales (BAS: see Elliott *et al.*, 1979, 1983; DAS: see Elliott, 1990) contain integral, co-normed word-recognition tests, in the case of the DAS with norms extending throughout the age range of the test (i.e. to 17:11). BAS-II, published in late 1996, has built on the impressive technical features, including the wide normative range, of the DAS. The Wide Range Achievement Test (WRAT-3; see Wilkinson, 1993) offers a Rasch-scaled word-recognition screening test normed up to 75 years. The Wechsler Objective Reading Dimension (WORD; see Rust *et al.*, 1993) offers recent UK norms for a test of word recognition, Basic Reading, which includes some early items dealing with sound-symbol skills.

In the next phase of sentence integration, simple passages and short sentences are appropriate. Although the Salford (Bookbinder, 1976) sentence-reading test is now too old to be accurate for today's children, it may be useful if used consistently, that is for within-child and within-school comparisons of progress. The silent sentence cloze tests, mentioned above, may be used with individuals. The *Macmillan Individual Reading Analysis* (Vincent and de la Mare, 1990) consists of page-length illustrations with small quantities of not-too-intimidating text. There is a comprehension, as well as an accuracy, scale. Though the test offers age equivalent scores only, form Z may be used with standard scores provided independently by Sawyer and Potter (1994).

Finally, integrated reading and comprehension of text is normally sampled by passage-reading tests of which the revised Neale (Neale, 1989) is best known in the UK. Another, technically less complete, test is the *New Macmillan Reading Analysis* (Vincent and de la Mare, 1985). For older, more advanced pupils, the group reading tests EH1 and EH2 (NFER, 1975), tests respectively of sentence completion (therefore mainly vocabulary) and passage comprehension, are still appropriate. A more modern, individually administered battery which includes an excellent measure of passage comprehension is the *Woodcock Reading Mastery Tests – Revised* (Woodcock, 1987), also reviewed in this volume.

Turning to the hinterland between orthodox tests of attainment and tests of cognitive processing, we come to a group of procedures which are essentially *diagnostic*. Often less developed from a psychometric point of view, these may be viewed as informal procedures, suggestive rather than definitive. Of these, the most generous assortment is contained in PALPA – *Psycholinguistic Assessments Of Language Processing In Aphasia* (Kay *et al.*, 1992). Based on *dual route theory* and essentially a cognitive neuropsychological assessment tool, the collection includes a whole volume of stimulus lists for use with reading and spelling. Such norms as there are derive from adult patients and their spouses. Especially useful are lists in which words with regular (*luck, pump*) and irregular (*cough, mortgage*) spelling patterns are read (Test 35); and others in which word-reading skills are contrasted as between high (*potato*) and low (*folly*) imageability words, controlled for high (*plane*) and low (*pact*) frequency (Test 31). In a variant of the Boder Test methodology (Boder and Jarrico, 1982) words which the subject can read but not spell (and perhaps vice versa) can be identified by means of overlapping lists. Results may be expressed in the form of differential error rates.

Word lists with a different purpose have been provided by Aaron and Joshi (Aaron, 1994; Aaron and Joshi, 1992). Two sets of words for reading aloud, easier and harder, are given, consisting of function and content words matched for letter length and frequency. Eye-movement studies have shown that all readers fixate slightly longer on content than on function words; this is because content words disproportionately carry the information in a sentence, whereas function words enact the sentence structure itself (Just and Carpenter, 1987). Dyslexic readers make more errors on function words (*also, once, ever*), as well as reading them more slowly than content words (*book, bird, gold*). This enables an interesting internal contrast to be made of potential diagnostic significance.

Probably the most important discrepancy analysis for evaluation of phonological reading deficits is that between word and nonword reading. In the UK the best-known set of nonwords, both for pronunciation and decoding, is that of Snowling, now published as *The Graded Nonword Reading Test* (Snowling, Stothard and McLean 1996).

However, at least two US tests are available which offer co-normed tests of word and nonword reading: *Woodcock–Johnson (Revised)* (WJ-R; see Woodcock and Johnson, 1989, 1990) and, by one of the same authors, the *Woodcock Reading Mastery Tests – Revised* (Woodcock, 1987), already mentioned above. Although no apparatus is provided for the comparative statistical evaluation of word and nonword reading, the standard error for each test allows some estimation of the significance of any disparity.

ADVANCED READING SKILLS

Accurate word recognition does not diminish in importance as the reading task becomes more advanced. A student of A level English, reading *Twelfth Night* in class, came to the lines in Act 2 Scene 5 (lines 126 ff.) where Malvolio is hoaxed by the letter he is reading, supposedly from his mistress, Olivia, while the true authors survey the effects of their mischief from the box-tree. After reading *consonancy* as *constancy* (l. 126), and *surly* as *surely* (l. 145), she read as follows: 'Remember who *condemned* thy yellow stockings, and wished to see thee ever cross-gartered' (ll. 148–9), substituting *condemned* for *commended*. Clearly, this risks the main meaning in a scene crucial to the plot of the play.[3]

Interpretation on the basis of patchy information derived from such misreadings is evidently an uncertain business. But advanced skills of comprehension may co-exist with persistently faulty decoding technique in individuals with dyslexia. Thus a three-level profile on the *Woodcock Reading Mastery Tests – Revised* (WRMT-R) characterises dyslexia: comprehension is typically better than word recognition, and recognition of words is better than decoding of nonwords. (This profile is illustrated with respect to a case, ED, in Turner, 1995). Separate measures of these three skill dimensions are provided within the WRMT-R.

If this profile is characteristic of dyslexia, the reverse problem, that of adequate decoding but poor comprehension, is described by Aaron and Joshi (1992) as *non-specific reading disability*. In this country, a familiar complaint, often made by secondary teachers of subjects other than English about pupils who have not understood their reading homework, is that they have a 'reading problem'. Poor comprehension skills are most often to blame. It is estimated that at least 10% of pupils have significantly poorer ability to comprehend than to decode text (Oakhill and Yuill, 1991; Stothard, 1994).

However, the problem is remediable. Oakhill and Yuill report impressive gains in measured comprehension from direct teaching of the skills involved, notably inference (Oakhill and Yuill, 1991). Metacomprehension skills – monitoring by the reader of his or her comprehension – can be taught successfully, as can many related skills and strategies: the area receives thorough coverage in Carnine *et al.* (1990), Part 4.

At Oxford University, Bradley found spelling, among other measures, to be a good guide to written language difficulties. Bradley's students typically complained of slow reading, expressive difficulties in writing, poor spelling and failure to reflect in writing their full verbal abilities. A group of twenty-two students with such difficulties had made a mean of 12.59 errors on the Schonell spelling test, compared with a mean of 2.56 for fifty-two controls. Bradley found that some needed to read written exam questions seven times. Comprehension problems, too, were rife (Bradley, 1993).

In conclusion, we have now addressed some of the varied uses of reading tests with both normal and exceptional readers. Normally developing reading skills and abilities can be appropriately monitored in relation to each stage of learning. The monitoring of reading standards, too, both local and national, may best be performed by the well-understood technologies of psychometric assessment. Reading problems and their components can be identified at all levels of ability by judicious selection among the variety of possible assessment techniques.

The desire to have the whole reading-for-meaning process humming along like a Rolls Royce Silver Cloud overlooks the contribution made by thousands of tiny parts, all of which must be working perfectly to support the overall effect of nonchalant ease. In most cases, respecting the principle that, if you wish to increase ability A, don't teach B, reading problems can be remedied by relatively straightforward direct instruction in the missing skills. Efforts to avoid this simple conclusion can seem bizarre. For instance, Scheirer and Kraut (1979) found overwhelming evidence for the futility of attempting to improve reading indirectly by massaging self-esteem. Conversely, the evidence (Chapman *et al.*, 1990) that reading failure can have an enormous negative impact on academic self-concept seems incontrovertible.

NOTES

1 To the effect that the SAT has the 'attribute of the elastic ruler' (BPS, 1991).
2 Developed in Canada with financial assistance from the Ministry of Education in Ontario, it has been anglicised and introduced, with training, by the Literacy Development Company Ltd, 8 Thorndales, Brentwood, Essex CM14 5DE; tel. 01277 229093.
3 I am indebted to Jennifer Chew for these actual misreadings by one of her A level students.

REFERENCES

Aaron, P.G. (1994). Differential diagnosis of reading disabilities. In G. Hales (ed.) *Dyslexia Matters*. London: Whurr.
Aaron, P.G. and Joshi, R.M. (1992). *Reading Problems: Consultation and Remediation*. New York: Guilford Press.
Adams, M.J. (1990). *Beginning to Read: Thinking and Learning about Print*. Boston: MIT Press.
Adams, M.J. (1994). Learning to read: modelling the reader versus modelling the learner. In C. Hulme and M. Snowling (eds) *Reading Development and Dyslexia*. London: Whurr.
Beech, J.R. (1987). Early reading development. In J.R. Beech and A.M. Colley (eds) *Cognitive Approaches to Reading*. Chichester, Sussex: Wiley.
Beech, J.R. (1989). The componential approach to learning reading skills. In A.M. Colley and J.R. Beech (eds) *Acquisition and Performance of Cognitive Skills*. Chichester, Sussex: Wiley.
Boder, E. and Jarrico, S. (1982). *The Boder Test of Reading–Spelling Patterns: A Diagnostic Screening Test for Subtypes of Reading Disability*. New York: Harcourt Brace Jovanovitch, The Psychological Corporation.
Bookbinder, G.E. (1976). *Salford Sentence Reading Test*. Sevenoaks, Kent: Hodder & Stoughton.
Bradley, L. (1993). Paper presented to a meeting on Speed of Processing at the Royal Society, October.
British Psychological Society (BPS) (1991). Reading standards: evidence to the Select Committee on Education, Science and Arts from the British Psychological Society. Leicester: British Psychological Society: Division of Educational and Child Psychology *Newsletter*, June, pp. 11–18.
Brooks, G., Foxman, D. and Gorman, T. (1995). *Standards in Literacy and Numeracy: 1948–1994*. London: National Commission on Education (Paul Hamlyn Foundation), June.

Carnine, D., Silbert, J. and Kameenui, E.J. (1990). *Direct Reading Instruction* (2nd edn). Toronto, Ontario: Merrill.

Carr, T.H. and Levy, B.A. (eds) (1990). *Reading and its Development: Component Skills Approaches*. New York: Academic Press.

Cato, V. and Whetton, C. (1991). *An Enquiry into LEA Evidence on Standards of Reading of Seven Year Old Children: A Report by the National Foundation for Educational Research*. HMSO: Department of Education and Science, January.

Chall, J. (1983). *Stages of Reading Development*. New York: McGraw Hill.

Chapman, J.W., Lambourne, R. and Silva, P.A. (1990). Some antecedents of academic self-concept: a longitudinal study. *British Journal of Educational Psychology* Vol. 60, 142–52.

Davies, J., Brember, I. and Pumfrey, P.D. (1995). The first and second Standard Assessment Tasks at Key Stage 1: A comparison based on a five-school study. *Journal of Research in Reading* 18(1), 1–9.

Dearing, R. (1993a). *The National Curriculum and its Assessment: An Interim Report*. York: National Curriculum Council; and London: School Examinations and Assessment Council, July.

Dearing, R. (1993b). *The National Curriculum and its Assessment: Final Report*. London: School Curriculum and Assessment Authority, December.

Department of Education and Science (DES) (1966). *Progress In Reading 1948–1964* (Education Pamphlet no. 50). London: HMSO.

DES (1975). *A Language for Life* (Bullock Report). London: HMSO.

DES (1978). *Primary Education in England: A Survey by HM Inspectors of Schools*. London: HMSO.

DES/APU (1981). *Language Performance in Schools: Primary Survey Report No. 1*. London: HMSO.

DES/APU (1988). *Language Performance in Schools: Review of APU Language Monitoring 1979–1983*. London: HMSO.

Education, Science and Arts Committee, Session 1990–91 (1991). *Third Report: Standards of Reading in Primary Schools*, Vols 1 (Report together with Proceedings of the Committee) and 2 (Minutes of Evidence and Appendices). London: HMSO, 8 May.

Elliott, C.D. (1990). *Differential Ability Scales*. New York: Harcourt Brace Jovanovitch, The Psychological Corporation.

Elliott, C.D., Murray, D.J. and Pearson, L.S. (1979, 1983). *The British Ability Scales*. Windsor, Berks: NFER-Nelson.

Foot, R.S. (1994). *Basic Skills Training Materials for Reading and Maths*. Brentwood, Essex: Literacy Development Company Ltd.

Frederiksen, J.R. (1982). A componential theory of reading skills and their interactions. In R.J. Sternberg (ed.) *Advances in the Psychology of Intelligence* Vol 1. Hillsdale, NJ: Erlbaum.

Gipps, C. (1994) *Beyond Testing: Towards a Theory of Educational Assessment*. Basingstoke, Hants: Falmer Press.

Gorman, T. and Fernandes, C. (1992). *Reading In Recession*. Windsor, Berks: National Foundation for Educational Research, February.

Gough, P.B. and Tunmer, W.E. (1986). Decoding, reading and reading disability. *Remedial and Special Education*, 7, 6–10.

Gray, P. and Lindsay, G. (1991). What price success? Appraising research in field settings. *Educational and Child Psychology*, Vol 8, No. 1. Leicester: British Psychological Society, May.

Hagley, F. (1987). *Suffolk Reading Scale*. Windsor, Berks: NFER-Nelson.

Her Majesty's Inspectorate (HMI) (1990). *Aspects of Primary Education, The Teaching and Learning of Language and Literacy*. London: HMSO.

HMI (1991). *The Teaching and Learning of Reading in Primary Schools*. London: HMSO, January.

Hieronymus, A.N., Lindquist, E.F. and France, N. (1988). *Richmond Tests of Basic Skills (RTBS)*, (2nd edn). Windsor, Berks: NFER-Nelson.

Hoover, W.A. and Tunmer, W.E. (1993). The components of reading. In G.B. Thompson, W.E. Tunmer, and T. Nicholson (eds) *Reading Acquisition Processes*. Clevedon, Avon: Multilingual Matters Ltd.

Just, M.A. and Carpenter, P.A. (1987). *The Psychology of Reading and Language Comprehension*. Boston: Allyn & Bacon.

Kay, J., Lesser, R. and Coltheart, M. (1992). *PALPA: Psycholinguistic Assessments of Language Processing in Aphasia*. Hove, Sussex: Lawrence Erlbaum Associates.

Levy, B.A. and Hinchley, J. (1990) Individual and developmental differences in the acquisition of reading skills. In T.H. Carr and B.A. Levy (eds) *Reading and its Development: Component Skills Approaches*. New York: Academic Press.

Macmillan Education (1985). *Macmillan Group Reading Test*. Basingstoke, Hants: MacMillan Education. Now distributed by: Windsor, Berks: NFER-Nelson.

National Foundation For Educational Research (NFER) (1975). *Reading Tests EH1 and EH2*. Windsor, Berks: NFER-Nelson.

Neale, M.D. (1989). *Neale Analysis of Reading Ability – Revised (NARA-R)* (British edn revised by U. Christophers and C. Whetton). Windsor, Berks: NFER-Nelson.

Oakhill, J. and Yuill, N. (1991). The remediation of reading comprehension difficulties. In M.J. Snowling and M.E. Thomson (eds) *Dyslexia: Integrating Theory and Practice*. London: Whurr.

Perfetti, C. (1985). *Reading Ability*. New York: Oxford University Press.

Pumfrey, P. (1985). *Reading Tests and Assessment Techniques*, (2nd edn). London: Hodder & Stoughton.

Rust, J., Golombok, S. and Trickey, G. (1993). *WORD: Wechsler Objective Reading Dimension*. Sidcup, Kent: Harcourt Brace Jovanovitch, The Psychological Corporation.

Salvia, J. and Ysseldyke, J.E. (1985). *Assessment in Special and Remedial Education* (3rd edn). Boston: Houghton Mifflin.

Sawyer, C. and Potter, V. (1994). Estimating standardised scores for MIRA. *Educational Psychology in Practice*, 10(1), 46–7.

Scheirer, M.A. and Kraut, R.E. (1979). Increasing educational achievement via self-concept change. *Review of Educational Research*, 49(1), 131–50.

Shaywitz, S.E., Fletcher, J.M. and Shaywitz, B.A. (in press). A conceptual model and definition of dyslexia: findings emerging from the Connecticut longitudinal study. In J.H. Beitchman, N. Cohen, M.M. Konstantarias, and R. Tannock, (eds) *Language, Learning and Behaviour Disorders*. New York: Cambridge University Press.

Snowling, M.J., Stothard, S.E. and McLean, J. (1996). *The Graded Nonword Reading Test*. Bury St Edmunds: Thames Valley Test Company.

Start, K.B. and Wells, B.K. (1972). *The Trend of Reading Standards*. Windsor, Berks: National Foundation for Educational Research.

Stothard, S. (1994). The nature and treatment of reading comprehension difficulties in children. In C. Hulme and M. Snowling (eds) *Reading Development and Dyslexia*. London: Whurr.

Turner, M. (1990a). A closed book? *Times Educational Supplement*, 20 July.

Turner, M. (1990b). *Sponsored Reading Failure*. Warlingham Park School, Warlingham, Surrey: IPSET.

Turner, M. (1993). Testing times (two-part review of tests of literacy). Part 1, *Special Children*, No. 65, pp. 12–16, April; Part 2, *Special Children*, No. 66, pp. 12–14, May.

Turner, M. (1995). Assessing reading: layers and levels. *Dyslexia Review*, 7(1), 15–19.

Turner, M. (1997). *Psychological Assessment of Dyslexia*. London: Whurr.

Vellutino, F.R. (1991). Introduction to three studies on reading acquisition: convergent findings on theoretical foundations of code-oriented versus whole language approaches to reading instruction. *Journal of Educational Psychology*, 83, 437–43.

Vernon, P.E. (1977). *Graded Word Spelling Test*. Sevenoaks, Kent: Hodder & Stoughton.

Vincent, D. and de la Mare, M. (1985) *New MacMillan Reading Analysis (NMRA)*. Basingstoke, Hants: Macmillan Education. Now distributed as the *New Reading Analysis (NRA)* by: Windsor, Berks: NFER-Nelson.

Vincent, D. and de la Mare, M. (1990). *Macmillan Individual Reading Analysis (MIRA)*. Basingstoke, Hants: Macmillan Education. Now distributed as the *Individual Reading Analysis (IRA)* by: Windsor, Berks: NFER-Nelson.

Vincent, D., Green, L., Francis, J. and Powney, J. (1983). *A Review of Reading Tests*. Windsor, Berks: NFER-Nelson.

Walker, J. and Brooks, L. (1993). *Dyslexia Institute Literacy Programme*. London: James & James.

Wilkinson, G.S. (1993) *The Wide Range Achievement Test* (3rd edn) (WRAT-3). Wilmington, Delaware: Wide Range.

Woodcock, R.W. (1987) *Woodcock Reading Mastery Tests – Revised (WRMT-R)*. Circle Pines, Minnesota: American Guidance Service.

Woodcock, R.W. and Johnson, M.B. (1989, 1990). *Woodcock–Johnson Psycho-Educational Battery – Revised (WJ-R)*. Allen, Texas: DLM.

Wooldridge, A. (1994). *Measuring the Mind: Education and Psychology in England c. 1860–c. 1990*. Cambridge: Cambridge University Press.

Young, D. (1976) *Spelling and Reading Tests (SPAR)*. Sevenoaks, Kent: Hodder & Stoughton.

4   Screening early literacy

Chris Singleton

Prediction is the most obvious hallmark of a successful science.
(Alan Clarke, Presidential Address to the
British Psychological Society, 1978)

The popularity of educational screening tests in the UK has diminished
of late. During the 1970s screening – especially for the identification of
children who were failing, or likely to fail, in reading – was being strongly
advocated by authorities within psychology, education and government.
As a result, the technique became widespread in schools and local education authorities in the late 1970s and during a large part of the 1980s.
Since then, screening as a method for the early identification of reading
difficulties and other special educational needs has waned, partly for political and economic reasons, but mainly because of a growing dissatisfaction
with the original conception of screening as a 'rough-and-ready' approach,
and the consequent failure to resolve the *practicality–accuracy dilemma*.
To be useful, screening tests have to be reasonably accurate. But to be
accurate, tests have to be fairly complex, and complex assessment procedures contradict the fundamental notion that screening should be simple
and easy to deliver.

   This chapter will begin with a critical review of methods and issues in
screening. The principal focus will be on *predictive* screening which is
carried out early in schooling, in contrast to either *attainment* screening
which is usually carried out later in schooling, or medical and developmental screening (which could fall into both predictive and attainment
types) normally carried out before the child goes to school. The reasons
for this focus are simple. Because of the inherent instability of human
development, our capacity to predict its course is admittedly limited.
Nevertheless, the educational benefits to be derived from even modestly
accurate prediction make it a goal well worth striving for. Successful
predictive screening thus represents an enduring scientific challenge to
researchers in both psychology and education, and our progress in this
regard over the past two decades will be evaluated. To seek to identify,
at an early age, those children who are likely to experience difficulties in

learning to read, so that teaching can be adapted to their individual needs and thus prevent failure, is a commendable objective. The chapter will go on to explore the reasons for the decline in the screening approach and consider possible solutions to the intrinsic dilemma concerning the practicality of screening instruments and their accuracy. Finally, the prospects for more effective screening using new techniques will be examined, particularly in the light of a recent resurgence of interest in the screening approach – albeit in the guise of baseline assessment.

SCREENING

The purpose of screening is the identification of a subgroup from within a larger group or population. The original meaning of the term 'screening' was to sieve materials such as coal through a coarse mesh (or 'screen') in order to eliminate unwanted matter such as stones or dust. Such a method, although by no means perfect, had the advantage of being speedy and more economical than having the materials sorted by hand. Screening, therefore, was an acceptable but essentially rough-and-ready approach, and the term has partly (but not entirely) retained this nuance. In its metaphorical sense, the term then became popular in medicine, referring first to procedures for identifying in the general population those suffering from a particular disorder (e.g. screening for tubercular lesions by X-ray examination of the lungs) and later to procedures for identifying individuals believed to be *at risk of* certain disorders (e.g. genetic screening). It is interesting, however, that in the medical context the idea of screening being a rough-and-ready solution to identification has steadily given way to expectations that screening will have quite high degrees of accuracy and reliability. In recent years, there have been concerns expressed about accuracy of various medical screening techniques – for example, those used in screening for breast or cervical cancer – and, in particular, about the large number of false negatives, i.e. cases where screening has not revealed a risk but in which cancer was subsequently found (Laming, 1995; Sharp, 1987; Wald *et al.*, 1991). Such concerns, of course, reflect the awareness that the consequences of false negatives in medical screening are likely to be serious. A further consideration is the high cost of medical intervention and the fact that it is rarely advisable if administered to a patient who does not actually require it.

Both in psychology and education, 'screening' now has a connotation somewhere between the original meaning of the term (a rough-and-ready selection process), and the sense which it has acquired in medicine (where reasonably high levels of accuracy are now expected). Sometimes, however, commentators seem to be unsure about exactly where, between those two extremes, educational screening properly lies. The consequences of inaccuracy in educational screening might not be as grave as in medical screening, but they are considerably more important than leaving a piece of rock in a bag of coal. If a child who does have a real learning difficulty is shown by a screening procedure to be 'not at risk' (i.e. a 'false negative') it is unlikely that the child will receive the proper help which is needed. Moreover, the teachers may quite understandably believe that the child's poor reading attainment and other problems are the result of lack of effort rather than, say, any underlying limitations in core cognitive skills, and admonish the child accordingly. Under these circumstances, the child may well become discouraged and lose motivation and confidence. Hence the child's problems could become compounded by the outcome of an inaccurate screening process.

However, in addition to being reasonably accurate, screening instruments are often required to meet certain *practical* requirements. According to Wolfendale and Bryans (1979), these are:

• Tests should not be lengthy or elaborate.
• The collected data should be readily and routinely available within the school.
• The data should be related to the goals and processes of the school.
• The teaching methods to be used following identification should be clearly thought out.

Satz and Fletcher (1988) commented: 'True screening is rapid and cost effective and does not require professional interpretation.' It should come as no surprise that there is a trade-off between the two requirements for ease of administration and accuracy of results. Relatively coarse procedures are not, in general, very accurate, and rarely are accurate procedures simple or easy to administer. The principal task confronting anyone attempting to create a screening device for use in education, therefore, is to find a satisfactory compromise between *practicality* and *accuracy*.

When educationists and psychologists have talked about screening it has not always been clear which type of screening is being discussed. Screening may be broadly divided into two types: *classificatory* screening and *predictive* screening. The latter has sometimes been referred to as 'speculative screening' (Potton, 1983). In classificatory screening an existing condition or difficulty is identified, while in predictive screening a condition or difficulty which has yet to become apparent is predicted from its antecedents. Further distinctions may be drawn between *attainment* screening and *criterion-referenced* screening. Attainment screening (sometimes referred to as 'survey screening') usually involves the administration of standardised tests to large numbers of children, so that the whole range of attainment is covered, whereas in criterion-referenced screening the intention is only to identify individuals whose performance falls above or below certain criteria. Attainment screening may have additional objectives to those of criterion-referenced screening, such as the general monitoring of educational standards over time within a defined area, but if the *only* purpose is to monitor standards, the process cannot legitimately be called screening.

The emergence of the screening approach

The distinction between classification and prediction began to emerge in UK education in the 1960s as school doctors were charged with the responsibility for early detection of physical, mental and emotional handicaps. At this time 'risk registers' for developmental and educational handicap were being widely advocated and although reservations were expressed about the long-term efficacy of such registers, epidemiological research showed that certain carefully selected factors, such as abnormal birth, birth weight or gestation, could provide a satisfactory basis for a general prediction of educational difficulties. The early identification of risk, particularly if refined by progressive examinations of motor, mental and sensory development, could therefore be of considerable importance in the efficient allocation of resources to children with special educational needs. The National Child Development Study (Davie *et al.*, 1972) found that social and biological factors such as social class, birth order, family size, and birth weight all had statistically separate effects on reading attainment. In particular, the difference between children from Social Class I and II and those from Social Class V was equivalent to seventeen months of reading age at age 7.

In 1972 the Report of the UK Government's Advisory Committee on Handicapped Children, entitled *Children with Specific Reading Difficulties* (Tizard, 1972), advocated the use of *predictive* screening methods to identify children with constitutional or developmental defects who are likely to experience subsequent difficulties in learning to read. However, the report stopped short of recognising the term 'developmental dyslexia' as a suitable label for neurological or constitutional conditions affecting the acquisition of reading skills. Instead, the Committee preferred the use of the term 'specific reading difficulties' (based on discrepancy between overall ability and attainment in reading). The report also goes on to recommend the use of *classificatory* screening at the appropriate time:

> at some stage a systematic screening of all children will also be necessary. The end of the infant stage would be a good time for this: at the age of 7–8 children should be sufficiently advanced in their reading for meaningful results to be obtained from the screening process; and it would be a suitably early stage to begin remedial treatment for disabilities which are revealed.
>
> (para 13)

During the late 1970s and into the 1980s, screening tests were increasingly employed by schools and local education authorities in the UK (Lindsay, 1984; Pearson and Lindsay, 1986; Potton, 1983). Lindsay (1988) estimated that by the mid-1980s in excess of 70% of LEAs had adopted some sort of early screening procedure. The principal stimulus for this can be identified in the staunch advocacy of the screening approach in the government report *A Language for Life* (Bullock, 1975). The Bullock Report recommended that problems with reading and language, instead of being assessed at age 7 or 8, should instead be recognised and addressed much earlier, at age 5 or 6, before the child is burdened with a sense of failure. Nevertheless, age 7 remained the most popular age for screening, perhaps partly because reading has always been the most popular screening measure, and partly because 7 is about the earliest age at which one can use group testing. A survey of local education authorities in England and Wales found that 41% carried out screening when children were seven years of age, and only 16% screened 6 year olds and 23% screened 5 year olds (Cornwall and Spicer, 1982). Gipps *et al.* (1983) discovered that the majority of LEAs were still using screening as a means of detecting children who were failing rather than for predicting failure before it happened.

The Bullock Report highlighted the distinction between classificatory and predictive screening for reading failure, and asserted that both should have a role in good educational practice. The conclusion was that although early identification screening is not without its disadvantages, it is nevertheless to be encouraged because of the benefits in facilitating early intervention. The report's Principal Recommendation Number 9 stated: 'LEAs and schools should introduce early screening procedures to prevent cumulative language and reading failure and to guarantee individual diagnosis and treatment' (p. 514). In the vast majority of cases, screening procedures used by local education authorities in the UK during the 1970s and 1980s were locally developed by teachers, advisers and educational psychologists. In general, they were either measures of developmental and/or learning readiness, usually involving an observational check-list which is completed by the teacher during the child's first year in school, or criterion-referenced tests to assess skills and attainment in basic subjects such as reading and number. The survey by Cornwall and Spicer (1982) found that 53% of local education authorities had made use of such 'home grown' products for screening. This enthusiasm for early screening must be seen against a background of research and educational thinking in which there was a principal focus on the theme of social and educational deprivation. The National Child Development Study (Davie *et al.*, 1972) had been of seminal importance. It had revealed that as children develop, the gap in attainment between children from deprived or disadvantaged backgrounds and other children steadily widens. At that time there was a tremendous amount of educational and psychological interest on both sides of the Atlantic in the efficacy of early intervention programmes (for review and critique see Clarke, 1978; Clarke and Clarke, 1976). In keeping with this, the clear intention of the Bullock Report was that the action to be taken after screening should be preventive. In theory, therefore, classificatory attainment screening should reveal those children who are already failing, and criterion-referenced predictive screening should identify children who are likely to be at risk. If both procedures are judiciously applied, then the children who most require help should be found as early as possible.

THE ACCURACY OF EDUCATIONAL SCREENING INSTRUMENTS

In theory, screening tests should meet the fundamental requirements of all psychological assessment instruments, in the sense that they should be objective and standardised measures of behaviour, the reliability and validity of which must be assured. They should also be norm-referenced or criterion-referenced in a manner which satisfactorily meets psychometric criteria. Over and above such preliminaries, however, the paramount question must be: how accurate are they at predicting?

Psychologists and educationists have long recognised the danger of screening results shaping or reinforcing teachers' expectation of pupils. In particular, any screening device will produce a proportion of children who are incorrectly classified. Such misclassification of children may lead to inappropriate action and unrealistic presumptions on the part of the teacher. The danger, of course, is that the true predictive accuracy of a screening device may not be properly known because the results of screening invite action on the part of teachers, and any intervention is likely to have some effect on the phenomena being predicted. Consequently, before any screening device should be accepted for general use, its accuracy should be properly established by means of a prospective validation study, which should be carried out in the absence of intervention. In education, however, rarely have these principles been applied, and all too often screening tests have been championed solely on the twin virtues of faith and face validity.

Correlation and discriminant function analysis are the two statistical techniques most frequently used to evaluate screening instruments. The correlation coefficient indicates how well the screening device predicts the criterion across all possible cutting points of the distributions while at the same time taking account of the common variance between them (Lichtenstein, 1981). It therefore may be said to represent the *predictive validity* of the screening instrument, since it covers the predictive efficacy of the test for the whole group, including high and intermediate scorers as well as the low scorers who will typically be of greatest practical interest. If the sample size is large then relatively low correlation coefficients will achieve statistical significance. Not all test users may appreciate this, and may believe that a given test is more efficient than it really is.

By contrast, discriminant function analysis must also take into account the number of incorrect categorisations of subjects, and hence gives a measure of *predictive accuracy*, usually expressed as a percentage. When *all* the results are reported, this is generally an extremely efficient way to judge the efficacy of a prediction tool. However, what often happens is that only *overall* prediction rates are reported, and these can be extremely high due to the fact that good prediction of a large grouping has occurred. This good prediction of the large group – say, children without reading difficulties – may outweigh a poor prediction rate of the smaller group – say, children with reading difficulties – and thus an overall high prediction rate can be reported, which is misleading. Proper prediction of group membership (e.g. an 'at risk' group and a 'not at risk' group) must include four reported rates for a proper evaluation to take place, i.e. *true positives* (those who are subsequently found to be at risk and who were predicted as at risk); *true negatives* (those who are subsequently found to be not at risk and who were predicted as not at risk); *false positives* (those who are subsequently found to be not at risk and who were predicted as at risk); and *false negatives* (those who are subsequently found to be at risk and who were predicted as not at risk). This categorisation is depicted as follows:

Found to be at risk?

		Yes	No
Predicted to be at risk?	Yes	True positive	False positive
	No	False negative	True negative

For those individuals who are in the false negative category this is likely to have serious implications for their education. The consequence for individuals who are classed as false positive is likely to be less serious – they may only have unnecessarily experienced extra tuition. However, the implications for the teacher and the school may well be different. Both false positives and false negatives can represent an unnecessary resource burden on the education system. In the case of false positives, extra provision may have been made when it was not required, but in the case of false negatives, the effects of failure to recognise a difficulty and the consequent requirement for intensive and more expensive remediation later in schooling may be a greater resource burden in the longer term. False negatives are also more likely to be those individuals who are, in this context, potentially frustrated in their education, and who are likely to experience concomitant loss of confidence and motivation. When designing screening instruments, a view has to be taken as to which type of error, false negatives or false positives, it is more important to minimise. It has been argued that a large number of false positives may have adverse consequences for these children (Fletcher and Satz, 1984). However, what is generally regarded as more serious is a large number of false negatives, where children's real difficulties are overlooked at the time of screening, and may not be properly recognised and addressed until much later in their education.

Jansky (1977) argues cogently that false negative and false positive rates in excess of 25% ought not to be acceptable in any screening instrument.

It should be noted, however, that a distinction must be drawn between *incidence* of false negatives and false positives, and the real percentages of these measures, which must be calculated not as a percentage of the overall sample (which would be misleading) but of the appropriate sub-sample. In other words, of the children identified at risk, we must ask: what percentage subsequently fail?[1] And of the children who actually failed, we must ask: what percentage were shown to be at risk?[2] Kingslake (1982) argues that if either of these indices falls below 75% then we should reject the instrument. The real percentage of false positives can be derived by subtracting the first index from 100, and the real percentage of false negatives by subtracting the second index from 100. Very few screening devices are found to meet these fundamental requirements.

A hypothetical case illustrates this point. Suppose 100 children have been screened, with the following results:

Found to be at risk?

		Yes 31	No 69
Predicted to be at risk?	Yes 34	True positive 22	False positive 12
	No 66	False negative 9	True negative 57

Obviously, as the total sample comprises 100 children these incidence figures may be also regarded as percentages. Superficially, the outcome looks fairly satisfactory, with percentages of false positives and false negatives appearing reasonably low. The majority of the children predicted to be at risk turned out to be genuinely at risk (22 out of 34), while only a relatively small proportion of those not predicted to be at risk turned out to be at risk after all (9 out of 66). However, by applying the proper formulae we can see that our satisfaction is less justified than it first appeared. Of the children identified at risk (34), the percentage which subsequently fail is actually 65% ($22/34 \times 100$). Of the children who actually failed, the percentage which were shown to be at risk is actually 71% ($22/31 \times 100$). Both these indices fall below the critical 75% mark, so the proper conclusion should be that the instrument in question is not an adequate predictor. The *real* percentage of false positives in this case is 35% (not 12%), and the *real* percentage of false negatives is 29% (not 9%). (For further discussion of the use of discriminant function analysis in the computation of predictive accuracy, see Carran and Scott, 1992.)

The evaluation of screening instruments as predictors of reading

De Hirsch *et al.* (1966) conducted a pioneering study of predictive screening for reading failure in the USA, involving a sample of premature babies and infants who had experienced normal gestation. The children were given a total of thirty-seven tests while in kindergarten and the results were correlated with educational attainment at the end of the first grade. Not only were children in the premature group found to be much more likely to have reading difficulties, but also poor reading ability was associated with predictive measures of poor visual and auditory analysis, poor auditory memory, confusions of directionality, and poor motor control.

Feshbach *et al.* (1974) evaluated two American screening devices for the detection of literacy problems. The *Student Rating Scale*, comprising five factors (impulse control, verbal ability, perceptual discrimination, recall, and perceptual-motor skills), was administered by teachers in late kindergarten, with follow-up at the end of Grade 1. The *de Hirsch Predictive Index* (Jansky and de Hirsch, 1972) was also administered simultaneously. Accuracy rates of 77% for the *Student Rating Scale* and 73% for the *de Hirsch Predictive Index* were reported but these are misleading as the figures only indicate the true positives and true negatives. Satz and Fletcher (1979) re-examined the data and after adjusting for errors in calculations found that the accuracy rates were spuriously inflated by high numbers of true negatives, namely the correct identification of good readers (97% in the case of the *Student Rating Scale* and 93% in the case of the *de Hirsch Predictive Index*). It was found that both these devices had disquietingly high false negative rates of 70% or above (*Student Rating Scale* = 70% and *de Hirsch Predictive Index* = 74%).

Fletcher and Satz (1984) compared teacher-based and test-based screening for the prediction of later reading attainment in the USA. Children were followed from kindergarten to the end of Grade 2. There were 571 children in the sample and nearly all were male. The four predictor measures consisted of the *Peabody Picture Vocabulary Test*, the *Beery Test of Visual-Motor Integration*, a perceptual matching test, and an alphabet recitation task. Teacher judgements about the likelihood of the child developing a learning problem were obtained after nine months of teaching had taken place. A standardised reading test was used for the criteria measure and severely disabled readers were classified as those who were at least one standard deviation below the mean. Using discriminant function analysis the teachers had an overall accuracy rate of 74% and the test battery had an overall accuracy rate of 77%. What is interesting about the results is that on closer inspection the teachers make fewer false positives for the prediction of high or moderate risk than the test battery. However, the test was more accurate for the prediction of low risk since it made fewer false negatives. Teacher judgements of high risk had a false positive rate of 14% and a false negative rate of 87%. The false positive rate for the test's prediction of high risk was 54% and the false negative rate was 34%. In other words, teacher judgement tends to err on the side of caution in the sense that it is better to include a child who *may* be at risk rather than to exclude that child only to have him or her fail later.

The Bullock Report (1975) cited two pioneering screening studies in the UK. The first was a simple instrument for screening 6- to 7-year-old children which had been developed in Birmingham by Tansley (1976). This included items on auditory perception and discrimination, copying skills, fine motor co-ordination and handedness. Unfortunately, there does not appear to have been any scientific evaluation of this instrument, and Lindsay (1980) reported that he could find no evidence to support its use as a means of identifying children with learning difficulties. The second screening test had been developed in the London Borough of Croydon by Wolfendale and Bryans (1979). The *Croydon Check List* comprised nineteen items divided into areas covering speech and communication, perceptual motor skills, emotional and social behaviours and response to learning situations. Each item is scored with either a 'yes' or a 'no' by the teacher. Wolfendale and Bryans (1979) maintained that the *Croydon Check List* was a valid predictor of attainment in literacy, and in particular that reading attainment on the *Neale Analysis of Reading Ability* (Neale, 1966; now in a revised version, 1989) at age 7 had been shown to correlate significantly with the check-list administered at age 5 (r = 0.68). However, when Potton (1983) evaluated the *Croydon Check List* using a sample of 395 children he discovered that 60% of the children who had reading problems at age 8 (on *Young's Group Reading Test*; see Young, 1968) had not been picked up by the *Croydon Check List* at age 5. Apart from anything else, this illustrates the importance of evaluating screening instruments not only in terms of correlation, but also in terms of predictive accuracy. Potton's analyses revealed that of the nineteen items in the check-list, only six contributed significantly to the prediction of reading difficulties. The remaining thirteen, he says, can be dismissed straight away since they 'are neither good long-term predictors nor do they aid teacher vigilance by drawing attention to remediable positive antecedents of reading handicap' (p. 39). As a matter of interest, the six successful predictors were: (1) can pursue a learning task when given freedom of choice; (2) can reproduce a circle shape; (3) can reproduce a square shape with diagonals; (4) organises thought to narrate experiences; (5)listens to stories with interest, and (6) draws or paints recognisable objects. One must ask: is a test actually needed when all teachers should already be competent to monitor children's development in terms of these six, apparently 'key factors', or something very much like them?

Several screening tests were published in the US during the 1970s, perhaps the most well known being the *Boehm Test of Basic Concepts* (now a revised version; see Boehm, 1986) and the *Slingerland Screening Tests* (Slingerland, 1974). However, reviews by Lindsay (1988), Lindsay and Wedell (1982) and Wedell and Lindsay (1982) found that rarely, if ever, did these tests meet satisfactory criteria for accuracy. Hardly any of the original screening instruments devised by local education authorities in the UK have been properly evaluated. Two exceptions are the *Infant Rating Scale* (Lindsay, 1981) and the *Swansea Evaluation Profiles for School Entrants* (Evans *et al.*, 1978). The *Infant Rating Scale* consists of sixty-five items covering such categories as behaviour, social integration, expressive language, receptive language, attitude to learning, early learning, gross motor skills and general development. These were to be rated by the teacher on a scale of 1 to 5. The predictive validity of the scale was measured against *Young's Group Reading Test* on a sample of 480 children and an overall correlation coefficient of 0.45 reported (Lindsay, 1980). However, using the formulae given above the percentage of false positives is found to be 64%, and false negatives 69%. Similarly, Kingslake (1982) evaluated the predictive accuracy of the *Swansea Evaluation Profiles* against the *Burt* and *Holborn Reading Tests* and found 41% false positives and 49% false negatives. Hence, the predictive accuracy results suggest that neither of these screening instruments is entirely satisfactory.

Relatively few UK screening tests were published or achieved a usage outside their place of origin. Three which did get as far as publication and which are worthy of more detailed examination because they are still available are the *Bury Infant Check* (Pearson and Quinn, 1978; revised 1986), the *Humberside Infant Screening* (Randall, 1981) and the *Aston Index* (Newton and Thomson, 1976; revised 1982). The *Bury Infant Check* covers five areas: language skills, learning style, memory skills, number skills and perceptual motor skills. Only thirteen out of the total of sixty items are teacher-rated, the remainder being simple test items. Although a sample of 177 children were tested on *Young's Group Reading Test* at age 7, two years after being screened with the *Bury Infant Check*, correlation coefficients were not reported. However, figures quoted in the manual enable the predictive accuracy of the instrument to be calculated using the formulae given above. While the percentage of false negatives is acceptably low at 6.7%, the percentage of false positives is unacceptably high at 63%. In other words, few children with difficulties will be missed, but a relatively large number of children who do not have difficulties will be mis-classified, which could have serious implications for resourcing.

The *Humberside Infant Screening* system comprised two teacher-rated check-lists, the first (largely developmental) to be used on school entry, and the second (mainly on learning and behaviour in the classroom) to be used at age 6+. A scoring system enables the teacher to identify those children to be regarded as 'at risk'. Several further diagnostic tests and teaching programmes are explained. The test manual for the *Humberside*

Infant Screening system reports significant correlations of 0.27–0.80 between the various screening indices and reading ability, the latter being measured by the *Carver Word Recognition Test* (Carver, 1970), but no proper prospective validation study of the system appears to have been carried out. An overall 85% of cases is reported as being correctly classified by the screening system into 'normal' and 'at risk' groups, these groups being those to which the children had been independently assigned by their teachers, using their own judgement. This seems to demonstrate that such a screening system can produce results that are largely congruent with teachers' judgements, and presumably are therefore acceptable to the teacher. However, whether teachers are themselves accurate in their unstructured judgements is not addressed.

The *Aston Index*, which was primarily designed as an early screening measure for dyslexia, involves the assessment of general intellectual ability (on the basis of vocabulary knowledge, copying designs and a draw-a-man test) as well as analysis of performance in reading- and dyslexia-related skills (such as visual and auditory sequential memory, auditory discrimination and sound blending, and laterality). A predictive validation study in which children were screened at age 5 years 6 months and re-tested two years later revealed significant correlations with the *Schonell Reading Test*, auditory sequential memory and sound blending tests, indicating that these were the most predictive items (Newton *et al.*, 1979). Analysis of the predictive accuracy of the instrument, calculated using the formulae given above, indicates that although the percentage of false negatives is within satisfactory limits at 21%, the percentage of false positives is unacceptably high at 47%.

Another possible way of evaluating screening instruments is to ask: do they help the teacher to identify specific problems that otherwise might have gone unnoticed? Potton (1983) carried out a modest survey of forty-eight teachers who had been using the *Croydon Check List*. Only about one-third felt it had been helpful in assessing the child, and less than 30% said that it had pointed to specific problems. Less than 10% said it had told them something new about the child. After a three-year trial in one local education authority, however, forty headteachers gave their verdict on the system, and about 70% thought that it had been helpful in their schools. Potton concludes: 'screening is helpful in the assessment and discussion of children and their problems because of the enforced concentration it requires, although it seldom reveals anything new' (p. 50).

THE DECLINE IN SCREENING

During the 1980s there appears to have been a steady decline in the use of all types of screening tests among schools and local education authorities in the UK. In 1991 Pumfrey and Reason reported that only about 23% of local education authorities surveyed in England and Wales mentioned the use of screening instruments, although this figure could be an underestimate as the inquiry was primarily about specific learning diffi- culties. A survey of LEAs requested by the Secretary of State to address public concerns about reading standards generated by the publication of findings by Turner (1990) revealed that because attainment screening had fallen into disuse, only twenty-six out of a total of 116 were in a position to provide satisfactory data for the evaluation (Cato and Whetton, 1991). What caused this downturn in screening popularity? Three primary factors may be identified:

1 Practicality–accuracy dilemma

The evidence cited above should be sufficient to demonstrate that, to date, screening instruments have not achieved very impressive levels of accu- racy, nor have they given teachers information that they have greatly valued. One reason for this may be the inherent variability in learning growth patterns seen in many children, and which we have known about for many years (Clarke, 1978). Francis (1992) points out that concerns about reading development require attention to assessment over time, not to assessment at one particular point alone. In her study, Francis carried out assessments of fifty children at intervals of six months from the age of 5 years 9 months until they were 7 years 3 months. Using the Schonell Graded Word Reading Test she reported an overall correlation between first and last assessments of 0.68. Although the best readers in the sample showed a steady progress with linear gradient over two years, the remainder of the sample showed curvilinear patterns, many being char- acterised by slow progress over some months and steep bursts of achieve- ment over others. The poorest readers in the group, however, showed very slow progress and had not reached the point of 'take-off' in reading by the end of the study.

Gradually, educational psychologists have discovered that for screening tests to achieve acceptable levels of accuracy and yield information over and above that which the teacher knows already, they must of necessity be complex. Furthermore, they probably need to be administered at several points in a child's educational development. Consequently, since the pioneer screening devices such as the simple nineteen-item teacher- rated check-list devised by Wolfendale and Bryans (1979) there has been a steady elaboration and embellishment of screening procedures in the attempt to create instruments that will be of better accuracy and greater value to teachers. The *Bury Infant Check* (Pearson and Quinn, 1986) comprises sixty assessment items, only thirteen of which are teacher-rated.

We have also seen new screening systems being tied much more closely to teaching activities. One of the most recently published instruments for use in screening or baseline assessment on school entry is the *Early Years Easy Screen* (EYES), which was devised specifically with the National

Curriculum in mind (Clerehugh *et al.*, 1991). It is a complex instrument divided into six modules: pencil co-ordination skills, active body skills, number skills, oral language skills, visual reading skills, and auditory reading skills. Administration of EYES will take over two hours of observation alone, not to mention time in preparation and analysing results. Although the activities can be carried out in small groups, which allows some time-saving, this can introduce further complications into the assessment situation. For example, because many children in the 4- to 5-year age range are still rather egocentric, they often find it difficult to be patient while other children in the group take their turn to perform the set tasks, and may interfere with the activities in an undesirable way. Some of the tasks involve group games in which competitive urges displayed by some children can dominate the proceedings and make it difficult for the teacher to determine whether the child is able to perform the cognitive task correctly (e.g. when 'cheating' occurs). Each module comprises several (sometimes quite elaborate) assessment procedures, with extensive lists of follow-up teaching activities. The visual reading skills module includes observations of visual memory, visual discrimination, word and letter matching. The auditory reading skills involve identification and localisation of sounds and auditory memory. EYES was developed from an action research project involving teachers in Buckinghamshire and neither the theoretical rationale for the choice of items nor their validity is given. The approach is fundamentally qualitative rather than psychometric – i.e. 'can do/can't do' – with the aim being to identify specific strengths and weaknesses and to provide particular activities designed to remediate weaknesses rather than to give any overall prediction of later difficulty.

We have thus progressed to the point at which many educational 'screening tests' are no longer rough-and-ready instruments that can provide a quick, but nonetheless, psychometrically acceptable classification of children who are at risk of learning difficulties. Instead, educational screening tests are now increasingly presented as fairly time-consuming structured procedures for the qualitative assessment of young children's strengths and weaknesses, the validity and reliability of which is difficult to ascertain. Unfortunately, such complex assessment procedures are not widely regarded as a practical proposition for today's busy and hard-pressed teachers. In principle, this more complex approach to screening could be encompassed within psychometric principles, so that the items which comprise EYES, say, might be standardised with national norms. In practice, the requirements for objectivity and precision of measurement would increase the complexity of the testing procedure beyond the point of acceptability. The outcome would be a test that was more characteristic of those used by psychologists, such as *WISC-III* or the *British Ability Scales*. It should not be forgotten that educational screening instruments are primarily intended for use by teachers rather than by psychologists. A system of universal screening by educational psychologists – even supposing that the profession was willing to undertake such a task (which is unlikely) – would be totally impractical. There are insufficient psychologists available in the education sector to accomplish this.

2 Economic factors

Screening invariably turns up pupils who require special provision of some sort, and resources often fall short of the requirements for such provision. The most popular type of screening has always been classificatory attainment screening to identify children who are failing. In the economic recession experienced in the 1980s, and in the financial squeeze on schools which has prevailed since then, the discovery not only of numbers of children who were demonstrably failing (according to attainment tests) but also of children who might subsequently fail would not have been good news for education officers and headteachers holding the educational purse strings. Under these economic circumstances, therefore, many schools and local education authorities in the UK have been forced to eschew screening not for educational reasons but for economic ones. If schools do not have the resources to address properly the needs of children who are failing in reading, there is little point in regular screening, which will only identify more children with needs that cannot fully be met.

In tandem with the waning of screening, however, local education authorities have in recent years witnessed a dramatic rise in the requests for formal assessment of children's special educational needs under the 1981 Education Act. Whether rightly or otherwise, many parents have come to regard the Statement of Special Educational Needs as the *only* method by which they can secure for their children the additional educational resources which they believe are required. Schools, desperate for additional resources, may overtly or covertly condone such claims. The *Code of Practice for the Identification and Assessment of Special Educational Needs* (DfE, 1994) not only gives statutory force to the ethic of early identification of learning difficulties but also places primary responsibility for this on schools rather than on LEAs, offering dissatisfied parents the prospects of legal redress. Whether the objectives of the Code to promote earlier recognition and better provision for children with special needs will ultimately be realised remains to be seen.

3 Educational and political ethos

Arguably, the prevailing attitude that the 1981 Education Act fostered towards special needs was one of acceptance of the principle that before special educational provision can be made children first had to fail. This philosophy was in sharp contrast to that of the Bullock Report six years earlier, which recommended the identification of special needs *before* children experience failure. Children, under the 1981 Act, having failed

and hence demonstrated their needs, could then have their learning difficulties addressed by provision of additional resources though the medium
of a Statement of Special Educational Needs. Clearly, such a mechanism
does not encourage the use of screening techniques for predicting failure
– only when failure has actually been shown can children get substantive
help. Through the 1980s this doctrine steadily began to make its mark and
eroded the position of screening on the educational agenda.

With the arrival of the National Curriculum in England and Wales as
a provision of the Education Reform Act 1988, it is now a legal requirement for children to be tested at the four Key Stages. The SATs (Standard
Assessment Tasks) for 7 year olds (Key Stage 1) cover English (or Welsh),
mathematics and science and are intended to provide a yardstick regarding
what children of this age 'ought' to be able to do. (Notwithstanding
commentators who have pointed out that the distinction between 'ought'
and 'is' in the SATs has already become blurred so that they can be used
in national comparisons of what schools have accomplished.) *The National
Curriculum and its Assessment Final Report* (Dearing, 1993) quoted the
Office for Standards in Education: 'The assessment requirements of
the National Curriculum have a vital role in raising the expectations of
teachers, pupils and parents. In particular, assessment should ensure that
individual learning is more clearly targeted and that shortcomings are
quickly identified and remedied' (p. 25). However, if SATs are intended
to provide a sound basis for remedying deficiencies in learning, their
validity and reliability stands in great need of improvement. Pumfrey *et
al.* (1992) examined the results of the Key Stage 1 SATs for reading for
a sample of 199 children and discovered that the SATs were highly unreliable. For example, on the *British Ability Scales Word Reading Test*,
reading ages of the children who attained Level 2 on the SATs ranged
from 5.7 years to over 12 years! The validity and reliability of the SATs
has recently been challenged by a number of authorities, including Davies
et al., (1995); James and Conner (1993), and Pumfrey and Elliott (1991).
Furthermore, the substance of the SATs has been condemned as trivial,
telling teachers nothing that they do not already know (Whitehead, 1992).
However, since teachers are now *compelled* to carry out statutory assessment of all children at age 7+, predictive or attainment screening during
the infant or early primary stage represents an additional burden which,
with debatable justification, may be abandoned. If screening, instead of
declining during the 1980s, had become a universal approach in British
infant education, there would possibly have been no need for SATs at
age 7. On the other hand, this attitude could have been fostered by an
absence of appropriate screening instruments at the time.

Perhaps largely in reaction to the political ethos which engendered the
National Curriculum and the SATs during the 1980s there has been a
growing educational ethos that has attributed to screening and assessment
an undesirable and negative connotation, emphasising what children

cannot do, rather than what they *can* do, and coming into play only when things go wrong. Norm-referenced assessment is regarded as competitive and therefore elitist, and ipsative assessment (comparing an individual not with norms or external criteria, but against his or her own previous accomplishments across a range of skill areas) is advocated as more educationally beneficial. Ipsative assessment, especially if relying on teacher judgement rather than objective tests, favours a holistic approach in which the relative strengths and limitations of the individual can be profiled (Kelly, 1992). Not surprisingly, adherents to this educational philosophy do not subscribe to the use of standardised screening instruments to identify children who are failing (or who are likely to fail) in reading, any more than they support the SATs.

By contrast, current government thinking, as embodied in the *Code of Practice for the Identification and Assessment of Special Educational Needs* (DfE, 1994) strongly espouses the screening approach in facilitating early identification. Indeed, the Code echoes the philosophy of the Bullock Report (1975) in its belief that 'The earlier action is taken, the more responsive a child is likely to be, and the more readily can intervention be made' (Section 2:16). The Code places on schools the responsibility for identifying children with special educational needs as early as possible, adopting a staged response to their needs. It also urges schools to make use of appropriate screening or assessment tools (Section 2:17), and in the case of specific learning difficulty (e.g. dyslexia) it expects that schools will be able to provide clear, recorded evidence of clumsiness; significant difficulties of sequencing or visual perception; deficiencies in working memory, or significant delays in language functioning (Section 3:61). In other words, there is an expectation that schools should obtain quite detailed information about underlying cognitive limitations of pupils who are believed to have special educational needs. Furthermore, the Code stresses that lack of competence in English (e.g. in children from minority ethnic groups) should not be equated with learning difficulties, and insists that assessment tools should be 'culturally neutral' (Section 2:18).

THE PROSPECTS FOR SCREENING

Baseline assessment

With the advent of the National Curriculum and its statutory assessment requirements, headteachers have become increasingly concerned that national 'league tables' of schools based on performance of pupils in the SATs will be published, which could damage the reputation of their schools. Although this is a concern throughout the school system, it affects primary schools in particular, because assessment at age 7, when children have only had the benefits of schooling for two years or so, will be exceptionally vulnerable to the effects of social background. Inevitably, primary schools in disadvantaged areas or with large proportions of children from various ethnic backgrounds for whom English is not their first language, will tend to have SATs results somewhat lower than other schools. Hence there is strong support within education for a system that assesses not absolute levels of attainment but, rather, the progress which children have made while in school, generally known as 'value added assessment'. In order to give a measure of value added, schools must first have a measure of children's abilities and level of development when they first enter school. This is called 'baseline assessment' (Lindsay, 1993; Wolfendale, 1993). Baseline assessment, according to Blatchford and Cline (1992) has the following four main purposes:

1   Testing on entry as a basis for measuring future progress.
2   Getting a picture of the new intake.
3   Getting a profile of the new entrant.
4   Identifying children who may have difficulties at school.

It can be seen that the first and second functions are largely administrative and can subserve any value added evaluation carried out at a later date. The last two functions are essentially those of early screening that should identify each child's strengths and weaknesses and so enable teaching to be more appropriately adapted to individual learning needs. Hence screening appears to be on the way back, albeit under a new name.

Towards the end of 1996, the British government announced its intention to make baseline assessment compulsory in all state schools from September 1998. The School Curriculum and Assessment Authority has published draft proposals on how this might be achieved. One of the key principles of these proposals is that 'The National Framework will require baseline assessment schemes to be sufficiently detailed to identify individual children's learning needs, including special educational needs, in order to support effective and appropriate planning for teaching and learning' (SCAA, 1996, p. 12). If the National Framework subsequently endorses only baseline schemes of the traditional observation and check-list type it is difficult to see how this principle could be adhered to. Identification of individual learning needs (especially if they are exceptional in any way) requires some form of diagnostic assessment, and traditional baseline approaches have proved incapable of meeting this requirement to any acceptable degree of validity and reliability. Hence a rethink of what baseline assessment should comprise would seem to be called for.[3]

Lindsay (1993) reports preliminary findings of a baseline assessment project in Sheffield, using a simple check-list that is linked directly to the National Curriculum. Sixteen attainment areas were identified (e.g. language skills, number skills, social development) and for each area, three levels of performance were drawn up. A sample comprising 25% of the children entering Sheffield schools in January 1993 was administered this check-list, with follow-up at the end of Key Stage 1 planned. Lindsay portrays the merits of this approach as providing both a baseline assessment for evaluating the progress of all children through Key Stage 1, as well as a general screening of all children at age 5 to identify those who have developmental difficulties, with follow-up using more detailed assessment where required. Whether this is a viable solution will to a large extent depend on the predictive validity of the screening instrument, which has yet to be established. However, the check-list has now been published under the title of the *Infant Index* (Desforges and Lindsay, 1995). It comprises fifteen items, grouped into four sub-scales: literacy skills, mathematical skills, social behaviour and independent learning. It is intended for use in screening and/or baseline assessment during the first half-term of school entry. For each sub-scale there are from three to five items, each of which can be scored 0, 1, 2 or 3, according to the child's ability or behaviour. For example, in the reading item (one of three in the literacy sub-scale), the choice for the teacher giving the test is between: 'Shows an enjoyment of books and knows how books work' (Score 1), 'Can recognise individual words or letters in familiar context' (Score 2), 'Can read from a simple story book' (Score 3) or 'None of the above' (Score 0). In the listening item (one of five in the social behaviour sub-scale) the choice is between: 'Participates as a listener in a 1:1 conversation' (Score 1), 'Participates as a listener in group activities' (Score 2), 'Listens attentively to stories' (Score 3), or 'None of the above' (Score 0).

In essence, the *Infant Index* is a measure of social disadvantage. The items show a distinct bias to accomplishments that are correlated with socioeconomic class, and consequently it would be expected that the *Infant Index* should predict educational progress with some degree of accuracy. However, whether the instrument really tells the teacher much more than would be apparent from knowing the child's socioeconomic background (other than in cases of significant developmental delay) is doubtful. The test also contains some astonishing anomalies. For example, in the independence/self-help item of the independent learning sub-scale a score of 1 is given for being 'Dependent on adults for dressing/undressing'. A score of 2 or 3 is awarded if the child displays somewhat greater independence in these skills. Although it would appear that a score of 0 could never be given for this item, nevertheless the item includes the option 'None of the above' (Score 0)!

As far as early literacy is concerned, the *Infant Index* does not appear to be particularly discriminating (although, of course, there are as yet no measures of predictive validity for the instrument). On the literacy skills sub-scale, the score range is 0 to 9 (three items – reading, writing and spelling – each with a maximum score of 3). The manual suggests that the bottom 2% of children should be regarded as 'high risk' and a further 15–18% as 'moderate risk'. On this basis, a score of 1 on the literacy scale would be regarded as 'moderate risk', and a score of 0 would be 'high risk'. However, the median score given in the manual is 3, which means that there will be large numbers of children who will obtain scores lower than this. The result is that this sub-scale shows a pronounced positive skew or 'floor effect', and has little capacity to discriminate within the lower range. The majority of children know very little about reading, writing and spelling when they first enter school, and what these children do know is not very helpful in discriminating those who are going to have problems from those who are not. Hence the authors' claim that the *Infant Index* 'can help the teacher identify the level of a pupil's development in a number of specific areas, highlighting strengths and weaknesses, and giving pointers to suitable areas for particular interventions by the teacher' (Desforges and Lindsay, 1995, p. 4) appears to be a gross overstatement, at least as far as literacy development is concerned. The *Infant Index* is not going to help teachers differentiate the literacy learning of most children. It is not altogether surprising that the manual for the *Infant Index* refers to 'highlighting strengths and weaknesses', because that is exactly the terminology of the Code of Practice, and publishers of educational tests are naturally keen to establish a role for their products within the framework of the Code. However, despite its claims, the *Infant Index* can hardly qualify as a screening instrument for the purposes of the Code, since it is not culturally neutral, nor can it discriminate between the underlying cognitive difficulties which the Code specifies.

Reading recovery

The desire for more effective early intervention in cases of children who are failing in reading is not entirely driven by governmental behest, nor by schools' anxiety about possible litigation. There is a genuine educational movement towards early intervention which in recent years has been spearheaded by the technique known as 'reading recovery'. This is an early intervention programme which focuses on children who have failed to make satisfactory progress in reading after one year in school (Clay, 1979). It has been adopted widely in New Zealand (where it originated), Australia and in several states in the USA, and has been trialled in the UK with claims of considerable success (e.g. Wright, 1992). The programme involves the provision of individual teaching for thirty minutes each day to the lowest attainers in the target group for up to twenty weeks. Clay designed a battery to be used as a classificatory screening system to help to identify children who, at age 6, are in need of reading recovery. Known as the *Diagnostic Survey,* this instrument comprises a record of the child's reading behaviour with books using miscue analysis, a letter identification test, a 'concepts about print' test (e.g. concepts of 'word' and 'letter'), word tests (reading high-frequency words out of context), writing vocabulary and writing to dictation. A similar early reading assessment system was devised in the UK by Reason and Boote (1986), involving measures of visual word recognition, phonic skills and concepts and approaches to reading. Perhaps not surprisingly, a proper evaluation of the predictive accuracy of the *Diagnostic Survey* employing a sample for whom no intervention has been given does not appear to have been carried out. However, Stuart (1995) reported on an small-scale study with thirty children, in which the *Diagnostic Survey* was compared with a battery of tests of phonological awareness and basic phonic knowledge (grapheme-phoneme correspondence), both instruments being administered on school entry. Although no figures for predictive accuracy are given, the two different screening instruments were found to correlate significantly ($r = 0.78$), and both correlated significantly with reading age on the *British Ability Scales Word Reading Test* one year later: $r = 0.80$ for the *Diagnostic Survey* and $r = 0.73$ for the phonological/phonics battery. A comparison was also made between screening on school entry and screening at the end of the first year. Screening on school entry was found to be as effective as the latter, but more useful, since it permits an earlier intervention.

Other studies have furnished further support for the use of measures of children's concepts about written language as predictive indicators of reading growth. Many of these have employed the LARR Test (*Linguistic Awareness in Reading Readiness*; see Ayres and Downing, 1982; Ayres *et al.*, 1977; Mason, 1990). Although the *Diagnostic Survey* is obviously not intended as a predictive instrument since its purpose is to select children for intervention, in reflecting on its scientific validity it is nevertheless pertinent to ask what percentage of children found to be at risk by this method and who do *not* receive intervention will actually go on to have longer-term reading difficulties. In the light of this, it is particularly interesting that the principal study of reading recovery in the UK reported by Wright (1992) reveals that the children *not* in the reading recovery group actually showed gains in reading ability from pre-test to post-test which, despite the small sample, were nevertheless statistically significant. Three measures (book level, Burt Graded Word Reading Test and writing vocabulary) were all significantly higher on post-test with the non-intervention group than they had been on the pre-test one school term earlier. The reading recovery group made significant gains only in book level, letter identification and writing to dictation. This suggests that although reading recovery appears to bring about significant benefits (which in view of the substantial input of individual teacher time is, arguably, only to be expected), the ability of the *Diagnostic Survey* to provide an accurate early classification of children who without special help will continue to fail must remain in doubt.

Phonological and cognitive screening

Researchers in psychology and education are currently in a much more favourable position to devise accurate screening tests for reading development than they were fifteen or twenty years ago. This is because of the growing volume of empirical studies on the precursors and predictors of reading failure (Singleton, 1987, 1988; Whyte, 1993). The core cognitive processes in reading involve the decoding of a written representation of spoken language. According to current psychological theory, therefore, linguistic skills are believed to be critical prerequisites for successfully learning to read. Beginning with the pioneering studies in the UK by Bradley and Bryant (1978), in the USA by Mann *et al.* (1980), and in Sweden by Lundberg *et al.* (1980), numerous studies have demonstrated the importance of phonological awareness as a predictor of early reading development (for reviews see Goswami and Bryant, 1990; Rack, 1994; Snowling, 1995). An intensive longitudinal study of reading development with children in the UK revealed that only three out of a total of forty-four variables reliably differentiated children with specific reading difficulties from their better-reading peers (Ellis and Large, 1987). The variables in question were short-term memory, phonological segmentation and reading vocabulary. Comparable results were reported in a large-scale study in Australia (Jorm *et al.*, 1986), and these findings have been supported by many independent studies (e.g. Gathercole and Baddeley, 1993; Torgesen, 1987). Most findings on memory relate to auditory working memory, but Awaida and Beech (1995) found visual memory ability at age 4 correlated with reading skills one year later. Moreover, if children with specific reading difficulties are compared with children who have more general reading problems it is in visual processing that differences most typically emerge (Ellis and Large, 1987; Willows, 1990). Early letter-name knowledge and speed of naming pictures are also both good predictors of later literacy development (Rack, 1994; Snowling, 1995; Wolf and Obregón, 1992). Grogan (1995) conducted a longitudinal study of tasks taken from the revised version of the *Aston Index* (Newton and Thomson, 1976; revised 1982) using all the pupils entering one primary school in the UK, being a total of fifty-one subjects. The children were re-tested two years and nine months later using the *Primary Reading Test*, level 1 (France, 1979). When intelligence was partialled out, reading ability was found to be significantly correlated with only visual memory and auditory sequential memory. Letter naming was found to be related to reading indirectly, only though intelligence, although it must be pointed out that in the *Aston Index* intelligence is assessed by means of a draw-a-man test, which is an extremely crude measure.

Badian (1994) added three additional sub-tests to the Holbrook Screening Battery, the additional tasks being rapid automatised naming of objects, syllable tapping and visual–orthographic matching. The Holbrook Battery comprises a diverse range of items divided into verbal IQ, language, pre-academic (letter, shape, colour naming, etc.), visual motor and pre-school reading ability (parental questionnaire). The 118 subjects were first tested six months before kindergarten entry (mean age 60.2 months) and were followed up nineteen months and twenty-four months later. The additional tests, together with pre-school reading ability and letter naming, were responsible for 62% of the variance in early first grade reading and spelling. Variables that contributed significantly to the prediction of later first grade reading comprehension were letter naming, sentence memory, object naming speed, orthographic matching and socioeconomic status. The overall accuracy rate of this augmented and extensive battery was 91%.

However, although certain 'core' cognitive factors are powerful predictors we should not assume that they can account for all the variance in later reading development. Catts (1991) used discriminant function analysis to assess the ability of some phonological and other measures to predict a combined reading measure for a group of speech-language impaired children. The best predictive accuracy achieved was 75.6%, which is good but by no means outstanding. Much will depend on the reliability of the cognitive tests. Some tests (e.g. the original Bradley and Bryant 'oddity task' for assessing phonological awareness) can be quite difficult to administer to very young children. Nevertheless, new tests of phonological skills and awareness modelled on this approach are currently being researched – how children will take to them remains to be seen. Some recent research (e.g. Francis, 1994; Gathercole, 1995) has focused on establishing the reliability of instruments for early screening. Furthermore, assessing complex cognitive functions such as working memory in an objective and reliable manner is extremely troublesome, even for experienced educational psychologists. If screening tests are to encompass such measures (which they probably must do if they are to have acceptable levels of predictive accuracy) then a further dilemma presents itself – how can teachers, in a busy classroom, give children complex tests which even psychologists would find difficult to administer? As if that were not bad enough, the final straw is that young children are notoriously difficult to assess anyway, since they soon get bored with conventional testing materials. Many educational psychologists, who know this full well, quite understandably avoid testing children under age 7 if they can.

Screening for dyslexia

Dyslexia is a neurological condition, usually of genetic origin, that affects the development of literacy skills in about 4–10% of children. Phonological and memory deficits are the most common underlying cognitive features of the syndrome. The 'phonological deficit model of dyslexia' hypothesises that the status of children's phonological representations determines the ease with which they learn to read, and that the poorly developed phonological representations of children with dyslexia are the fundamental cause of their literacy difficulties (Hulme and Snowling, 1992; Snowling, 1995). However, children with dyslexia often 'slip through the net' for a variety of reasons (Singleton, 1988). First, there is a lack of awareness of the condition among ordinary teachers. The phonological and memory weaknesses of dyslexia are not appreciated by the teacher, and children with dyslexia typically have to suffer many years of failure and frustration before a proper diagnosis is forthcoming. Second, there has been a tradition among some educational psychologists of scepticism about the existence of dyslexia and this has often been reflected in the anachronistic policies of LEAs which have refused to recognise the condition (although financial factors have probably also played a part here). Third, the subsumption of the concept of dyslexia under that of specific learning difficulty (SpLD), together with the procedures instituted by the 1981 Education Act (see above) have perpetuated a 'wait for failure' approach. Diagnosis of SpLD has always been based on the cardinal principle of establishing a significant discrepancy between intelligence and literacy attainment (in general, psychologists look for evidence that literacy development is lagging at least two years behind expected levels with no obvious social, emotional, or medical cause). Inevitably, this has precluded the identification of dyslexia (or SpLD) in children under the age of about 7 or 8, since before that age children will not have had sufficient time to fall significantly behind expected levels. Fourth, while children with dyslexia often have deficits in the cognitive skills that subserve the acquisition of phonics, they may have intact abilities which can subserve visual strategies in reading. The success that an early reliance on such visual strategies may bring can result in them becoming ingrained. Although visual strategies can be quite effective for some time, in the absence of phonic analysis skills they will eventually prove to be inadequate for the child's needs. This typically occurs towards the later years in primary school, when the child is encountering new or unfamiliar words in print on an almost daily basis. When this happens, not only will the child begin to fall steadily behind other children in literacy development, but it is also likely to retard their progress right across the curriculum. Remediation at this stage is much more complicated and costly than it would have been to take appropriate steps to ensure that the child did acquire phonic skills in the first few years of schooling.

Hence screening systems for identifying children with dyslexia at an early stage of their schooling are regarded as highly desirable by many psychologists and teachers. More appropriate educational provision could then be made before the cumulative effects of long-term failure have taken their toll. However, creating dyslexia screening tests which are both valid and reliable presents considerable challenges. We have seen from discussion earlier in this chapter that the *Aston Index*, an early British attempt at such a system, as well as being quite complex to administer, suffers from very high levels of false negatives and false positives (Kingslake, 1982). Furthermore, there is the tricky issue of premature labelling of children. Labels for different special educational needs (especially the label 'dyslexia') have been unpopular for the best part of a generation.

However, labels are not always undesirable, and there are signs of a change of opinion among educationalists. Although all children with special educational needs are individuals, nevertheless there are broad categories which are useful in teaching. The 1981 Education Act, which encouraged a non-labelling approach to special educational needs, has now been superseded by the 1996 Education Act and the *Code of Practice for the Identification and Assessment of Special Educational Needs* (DfE, 1994). It is interesting that the latter embodies a fairly broad labelling of special educational needs categories, including the category 'Specific Learning Difficulties (e.g. dyslexia)' (Code of Practice, 1994, Section 3:60). This development is an acknowledgement of the fact that SEN labels are often necessary to ensure that the child receives the right sort of support in learning. On the other hand, there is still a need for differentiation of teaching and learning activities within a single category. This is particularly true of the category 'dyslexia' (or Specific Learning Difficulty), in which some children may be affected more in the auditory/verbal domain, others in the visual/perceptual domain, and a few in both domains or who may have motor difficulties. Hence, children with dyslexia may exhibit a variety of difficulties and dyslexia has been described as a variable syndrome (Singleton, 1987). Nevertheless, dyslexia is a condition that can usually be helped tremendously by the right type of teaching, even though children with dyslexia cannot all be taught in exactly the same way (Augur, 1990; Pollock and Waller, 1994; Thomson, 1989; Thomson and Watkins, 1990).

On the other hand, many teachers are justifiably worried that labelling a child – especially at an early age – carries with it some dangers, and could create a self-fulfilling prophecy. Whether most teachers will find that the label 'dyslexic' at age 4 or 5 is of itself a significant help to teaching strategies is doubtful, and some may regard the prospect with alarm. Many schools and local education authorities, while now accepting the concept of dyslexia in principle, may in practice be wary of what they regard as premature labelling, especially as the label in question ('dyslexia') often creates anxieties about vociferous demands on the part of parents for statements of Special Educational Need. Rather, what teachers and schools are seeking is a screening system that will identify strengths and weaknesses in core cognitive abilities which are known to underpin the processes of literacy development, so that this information can be used to shape a learning programme that is appropriate for the individual child – in other words, to *differentiate* learning, in the true sense of that frequently misused and misunderstood term. Hence, if a child is discovered to have poor phonological awareness, then rhyming and other phonological activities can be provided to help remedy the deficiency. Likewise, if the child's auditory working memory is found to be rather weak, then the teacher will realise that learning phonics is likely to be problematic for that child, and consequently phonics instruction will have to be given with particular care involving ample over-learning. An effective screening system should carry with it implications for teaching, and it is essential that a *multi-dimensional* technique is used, i.e. that a variety of cognitive abilities is assessed. Although one dimension can in theory yield a prediction of risk, a uni-dimensional technique is undesirable because it is liable to degenerate into a simplistic labelling approach (albeit, perhaps, one in which children are categorised not as 'dyslexic' but as 'phonologically deficient'). Moreover, the teacher cannot rely on a single dimension (not even phonological awareness) to provide all the information that will be required in order to differentiate a learning programme effectively. Of course, even a complex cognitive screening system will still not tell the teacher everything; other important factors – such as home background and the child's motivation, concentration and attention – will obviously need to be taken into account when differentiating learning activities. However, it hardly needs a screening test to measure things that the teacher, using his or her own awareness and knowledge, can evaluate a great deal more efficiently. Assessing underlying cognitive abilities, however, is quite another matter; for these a psychometric approach is essential in order to obtain information that is both valid and reliable.

Griffin *et al.* (1988) developed a quick screening procedure for dyslexia based on two earlier American tests, the *Boder Test of Reading–Spelling Patterns* (Boder and Jarrico, 1982) and the *Dyslexia Determination Test* (Griffin and Walton, 1987). The new test, called the *Dyslexia Screener* is intended to identify three types of dyslexic coding patterns: *dyseidesia* (deficit in the ability to perceive whole words as visual gestalts and to match these with auditory gestalts); *dysphonesia* (deficit in phonetic word analysis synthesis skills), and *dysphoneidesia* (deficits in both eidetic and phonetic coding skills). The *Dyslexia Screener* is designed for use with students in Grades 2 to 9 and takes about five minutes to administer. It involves oral reading and spelling of regular and irregular words graded in difficulty. Guerin *et al.* (1993) carried out a study on the efficiency of the *Dyslexia Screener* using a sample of 100 children age 10, comparing it with reading tests taken from the *Woodcock–Johnson Psycho-Educational Battery* (Woodcock and Johnson, 1977), and reported an overall hit rate of 87%.

However, the *Dyslexia Screener* could not be claimed to address the problem of *early* identification, since its applicability only starts at second grade and it is based on analysis of deficits in reading and spelling skills. Furthermore, its predictive validity with children under age 10 is not known. The *Dyslexia Early Screening Test* (DEST) (Nicolson and Fawcett, 1994, 1995, 1996) represents a new British attempt to create a simple screening device for children in the age range 4:6 to 6:6. These authors also have a similar test for older children (age range 6:6 to 16:6) under development (*Dyslexia Screening Test* (DST)). The rationale for the items is based not only on the cognitive measures outlined above, but also on the authors' own research on the involvement of cerebellar processes in the development of automaticity in learning (Nicolson and Fawcett, 1990, 1994, 1995). Hence, in addition to expected items with good face validity such as rapid naming, rhyme detection (phonological awareness), digit span (auditory sequential memory) and letter naming, a test of cerebellar function (postural stability) is included. The full test takes about thirty minutes and is intended for administration by teachers. (It should be noted that an earlier research version of this test incorporated computer-delivered items, which now appear to have been abandoned; see Fawcett *et al.*, 1993, and Chapter 13, this volume.) The manual says that children with four or more scores less than the tenth centile (or seven or more scores below the twenty-fifth centile) for individual tests are to be considered 'at risk'. Alternatively, an at risk quotient may be calculated by use of a formula; in a standardisation sample of over 1000 children aged 4:6 to 6:11, 11% were classified as 'at risk' by this method. Although the DEST is a promising addition to the screening repertoire, it must remain for the time being an unknown quantity, and a fuller evaluation must await its use and follow-up in schools. No concurrent validity measures are currently available, and investigation of its predictive validity has yet to be carried out.

A psychometric screening system for dyslexia and other special educational needs, known as CoPS 1 (*Cognitive Profiling System*), has been devised by Singleton *et al.* (1996). Since this is a fully computerised system its development is described in more detail in Chapter 13 of this volume. CoPS 1 is intended for use as a screening and/or assessment device with children age 4 to 8, and comprises nine sub-tests of various cognitive skills, including auditory and visual working memory, phonological awareness and auditory discrimination. However, instead of attempting to categorise children as 'dyslexic' or 'not dyslexic' in the manner of the DEST test (Nicolson and Fawcett, 1996), CoPS 1 allows both a normative and an ipsative[3] profile to be derived. The CoPS 1 graphical profile, in addition to flagging up a child's cognitive limitations in normative terms, also indicates the child's cognitive strengths. Hence it provides an ipsative framework from which the teacher can derive insights into the child's learning styles and which can be used as a basis for curriculum development, for differentiation within the classroom, and for more appropriate teaching techniques. Hence it is not necessary to use labels such as 'dyslexic' when describing a child assessed with CoPS 1, although it is apparent that certain profiles are statistically associated with dyslexia (Singleton *et al.*, 1996). On the other hand, if CoPS 1 is used to assess children who already show a significant discrepancy between ability and literacy attainment, and particular cognitive limitations are thereby uncovered, then arguably the term 'dyslexia' is more defensible. Nevertheless, the principal purpose behind CoPS 1 is that children who are at risk and who might otherwise have slipped through the net can be identified at an early age. The intention is that by using CoPS 1 for early screening, such children may be taught in a more appropriate way from the start and hence any discrepancies will be prevented from developing (Singleton, 1991). In this manner, any cognitive weaknesses will be much less likely to be translated into de-motivating and debilitating literacy failure, provided of course that the teachers possess the skills and materials required for a proper differentiation of the learning experience for the individual pupil. This, in turn, has significant implications for initial and in-service teacher training.

The overall prediction rate for CoPS 1 administered at age 5 (the predicted variable being the *British Ability Scales Word Reading Test* at age 8) was 96%, with a false negative rate of 16.7% and a false positive rate of 2.3% (Singleton, 1995). Being computer-delivered, the test is easy for teachers to administer and enjoyable for young children, and its complex cognitive content not only allows for a more accurate prediction but also provides a fairly detailed picture of children's strengths and weaknesses which is valuable in devising learning programmes for the individual. Hence it may be argued with some conviction that the combination of a computer-based method of test administration together with a complex cognitive test content offers the most promising prospect for resolution of the practicality/complexity dilemma which has beset this field for so long.

CONCLUSION

Despite the apparent decline in popularity of screening tests in the UK over the past decade or so, screening remains firmly on the educational agenda, although in the future it may increasingly appear in the guise of 'baseline assessment'. The check-list approach was largely discredited for the purposes of predicting literacy development over a decade ago; nevertheless, its obvious attractions for baseline assessment (principally the ease of administration) remain. Indeed, the very fact that check-lists and other 'at risk' measures still attract vociferous criticism (e.g. Crossland, 1994; Pellegrini, 1991) is testimony to a perceived dogma about screening which some educationists feel the need to discredit. Pellegrini (1991) rejects 'at risk' concepts altogether on the grounds that they typically locate problems within the child, the family or the school (or some combination of the three) and imply that at least one of these factors (and probably all three) will require rectification. His somewhat enigmatic solution to the problem of literacy failure is that we should look more closely at how the rules which operate at home and at school differ, and seek to eliminate any discrepancies. Crossland (1994) points out that the fundamental weaknesses of screening lie in the inherent instability of development, and in the problem of where the line is to be drawn between 'at risk' and 'not at risk', which he says is like 'chasing shadows'. He also comments that much screening has little to offer in the way of advice that fits easily into normal classroom teaching, and cites by way of illustration the fact that the EYES test (Clerehugh *et al.*, 1991) gives sixty follow-up activities for 'visual and auditory reading skills', none of which involves any reading.

On the other hand, if check-lists are going to be used *solely* as a speedy method of estimating levels of social disadvantage on school entry and as a subsequent basis for allocation of resources and for calculating value added, then their lack of predictive validity will not be a major drawback (provided, of course, that they have significant correlation with accepted indices of social disadvantage). However, if such instruments are going to be used for screening in the belief that they are capable of discriminating children at risk of literacy difficulties or other learning problems then that gives cause for grave concern. There is a serious danger that children who *are* at risk because of underlying cognitive weaknesses will be missed by such crude instruments, especially if these children come from middle-class homes. Any problems that such children do experience may be disregarded by the teacher because the screening test has pronounced the child to be 'not at risk'. This false sense of security could easily result in the child's problems not being properly diagnosed until much later in schooling, with all the deleterious effects such late diagnosis brings. The legal implications of this are worth considering. What would be the outcome if parents sued their child's school because of alleged failure to recognise their child's learning problem sufficiently early and if, in its defence, the school maintained that a screening test had been used (as recommended by the Code) and that the test had shown the child not to be at risk, but the publishers of the test had actually made exaggerated claims with regard to their product? It may be argued that the test publishers should be liable, but on the other hand it might be contended that teachers have the ultimate responsibility for evaluating the methods which are used to assess children and ensuring that those chosen are reliable and appropriate. Undiscriminating faith in a screening test (especially one as crude as a check-list) might itself be regarded as professionally negligent. It therefore behoves teachers to study very carefully the validity and reliability of the test instruments that they adopt and to exercise caution when making decisions about educational provision being made for children who are perceived to be (or not to be) at risk.

The provisions of the 1996 Education Act and of the *Code of Practice for the Identification and Assessment of Special Educational Needs* (DfE, 1994) undoubtedly represent significant steps towards the goal of earlier identification of special educational needs and the prevention of literacy failure. Indeed, these statutory developments reinstate many of the worthy objectives expressed in the Bullock Report almost twenty years earlier. Not only do the 1996 Act and the Code both stress the importance of early identification of special education needs, the Code also goes on specifically to mention screening as one of the tools which schools should consider using in order to accomplish early identification. Furthermore, if schools fail to address the issue of early identification they become vulnerable to litigation by disaffected parents who believe that their children's special educational needs have not been recognised and addressed as early as they should have been. Hence, we are likely to witness increased development of screening systems for these purposes, and test publishers will offer schools a selection of techniques that are purported to fulfil their legal obligations under the Code. However, which type of screening tests schools should adopt is a problem that is still far from being resolved. The crux of the matter still rests in the practicality–accuracy dilemma and the enduring requirement for screening tests which are reliable but easy for teachers to use with young children. The most favourable outlook for resolution of this dilemma currently lies not with any purported improvements to the check-list approach, nor with increasingly elaborate teacher-administered tests, but in the ability of the computer to administer, precisely and objectively, testing materials that are sufficiently complex to yield acceptable degrees of accuracy, but in a manner that is efficient for teachers.

Of course, identification of a risk of literacy failure or of some other special educational need is only part of the story – *addressing* that risk or need effectively is paramount. The Code locates this responsibility, in the first instance, in the school. However, if the school has inadequate resources or lacks teachers who have the appropriate skills to meet this need, then the outcome could well be the opposite of what was intended by the Code. We are already seeing that, in some cases, the system which the Code has instigated will permit a delay of several years before the LEA is prepared to accept that a child's difficulties are sufficiently serious for it to assume responsibility for support. Hence, the prospects of the Code bringing about a significant reduction in the incidence of literacy failure by encouraging earlier identification are predicated on improved teaching skills and better provision of educational resources in ordinary schools. Such educational developments should proceed in unison with the psychological quest for practicable screening instruments which will reliably predict those children who are likely to experience difficulties in reading. Only when schools are fully able to take on board their responsibilities for providing education which, from the outset, is adapted to *individual* learning needs, will such screening systems be of significant benefit to children who are at risk of literacy failure.

NOTES

1 This may be calculated by the formula $TP/(TP + FP) \times 100$.
2 This may be calculated by the formula $TP/(TP + FN) \times 100$.
   (where TP = incidence of true positives, FP = incidence of false positives and FN = incidence of false negatives.)
3 In 1997 SCAA published revised criteria which specified that in addition to assessment of literacy and mathematics, baseline assessment must cover aspects

of language, personal and social development. The revisions also stipulate that baseline assessment should be accomplished in no more than about 20 minutes per child, which, given the nature and range to be covered, makes it very difficult to use a scheme other than a simple check-list. SCAA also acknowledged that such a scheme would not, as originally intended, be capable of identifying pupils with special educational needs. Although the time restrictions are perhaps understandable in the light of pressures on teacher time, it must be regretted that a significant national opportunity for earlier identification of special educational needs and of pupils at risk of literacy difficulties has thereby been missed.

4 i.e. a comparison of the individual not with norms or external criteria, but against his or her own previous accomplishments across a range of skill areas.

REFERENCES

Augur, J. (1990). Dyslexia – have we got the teaching right? In P. Pinsent (ed.) *Children with Literacy Difficulties*. London: David Fulton.

Awaida, M. and Beech, J.R. (1995). Children's lexical and sublexical development while learning to read. *Journal of Experimental Education*, 63, 97–113.

Ayres, D. and Downing, J. (1982). Testing children's concepts of reading. *Educational Research*, 24, 277–83.

Ayres, D., Downing, J. and Schaefer, B. (1977; revised 1982). *The Linguistic Awareness in Reading Readiness (LARR)*. Windsor, Berks: NFER-Nelson.

Badian, N.A. (1994). Preschool prediction: orthographic and phonological skills, and reading. *Annals of Dyslexia*, 44, 3–25.

Blatchford, P. and Cline, T. (1992). Baseline assessment for school entrants. *Research Papers in Education*, 7, 247–70.

Boder, E. and Jarrico, S. (1982). *The Boder Test of Reading–Spelling Patterns*. New York: Grune & Stratton.

Boehm, A.K. (1986). *Boehm Test of Basic Concepts (Revised Version)*. New York: The Psychological Corporation.

Bradley, L. and Bryant, P.E. (1978). Difficulties in auditory organisation as a possible cause of reading backwardness. *Nature*, 17, 746–7.

Bullock, A. (Chair) (1975). *A Language for Life*. London: HMSO.

Carran, D.T. and Scott, K.G. (1992). Risk assessment in preschool children: research implications for the early detection of educational handicaps. *Topics in Early Childhood Special Education*, 12, 196–211.

Carver, C. (1970). *Word Recognition Test/Manual* and *Record Form*. London: Hodder & Stoughton.

Cato, V. and Whetton, C. (1991). *An Enquiry into LEA Evidence on Standards of Reading of Seven Year Old Children*. Slough: NFER.

Catts, H. W. (1991). Early identification of dyslexia – evidence from a follow-up study of speech-language impaired children. *Annals of Dyslexia*, 41, 163–77.

Clarke, A.D.B. (1978). Predicting human development: problems, evidence and implications. *Bulletin of British Psychological Society*, 31, 249–58.

Clarke, A.M. and Clarke, A.D.B. (1976). *Early Experience. Myth and Evidence*. London: Open Books.

Clay, M.M., (1979). *The Early Detection of Reading Difficulties*. London: Heinemann Education.

Clerehugh, J., Hart, K., Pither, R., Rider, K. and Turner, K. (1991). *Early Years Easy Screen (EYES)*. Windsor, Berks: NFER-Nelson.

Cornwall, K. and Spicer, J. (1982). DECP enquiry: the role of the educational psychologist in the discovery and assessment of children requiring special education. *Occasional Papers of the Division of Educational and Child Psychology*, 6, 3–30.

Crossland, H. (1994). Screening early literacy: ideology, illusion, and intervention. *Educational Review*, 46, 47–62.

Davie, R., Butler, N. and Goldstein, H. (1972). *From Birth to Seven. A Report of the National Child Development Study*. London: Longman.

Davies, J., Brember, I. and Pumfrey, P.D. (1995). The first and second reading Standard Assessment Tasks at Key Stage 1: a comparison based on a five-school study. *Journal of Research in Reading*, 18, 1–9.

Dearing, R. (1993). *The National Curriculum and its Assessment. Final Report*. London: School Curriculum and Assessment Authority.

De Hirsch, K., Jansky, J.J. and Langford, W.S. (1966). *Predicting Reading Failure. A Preliminary Study*. New York: Harper & Row.

Desforges, M. and Lindsay, G. (1995). *Infant Index*. London: Hodder & Stoughton.

Department for Education (DfE) (1994). *Code of Practice on the Identification and Assessment of Special Educational Needs*. London: HMSO.

Ellis, N.C. and Large, B. (1987). The development of reading. *British Journal of Psychology*, 78, 1–28.

Evans, R., Davies, P., Ferguson, N., and Williams, P. (1978). *Swansea Evaluation Profiles for School Entrants*. Windsor, Berks: NFER-Nelson.

Fawcett, A.J., Pickering, S. and Nicolson, R.I. (1993). Development of the DEST test for the early screening for dyslexia. In S.F. Wright and R. Groner (eds), *Facets of Dyslexia and its Remediation*. Amsterdam: Elsevier Science.

Feshbach, S., Adelman, H., and Fuller, W. W. (1974). Early identification of children with high risk of reading failure. *Journal of Learning Disabilities*, 7, 639–44.

Fletcher, J M. and Satz, P. (1984). Test-based versus teacher-based predictions of academic achievement: a three-year longitudinal follow-up. *Journal of Pediatric Psychology*, 9, 193–203.

France, N. (1979). *The Primary Reading Test (Levels 1 and 2)..* Windsor, Berks: NFER-Nelson.

Francis, H. (1992). Patterns of reading development in the first school. *British Journal of Educational Psychology*, 62, 225–32.

Francis, H. (1994). Literacy development in the first school – what advice? *British Journal of Educational Psychology*, 64, 29–44.

Gathercole, S.E. (1995). The assessment of phonological memory skills in preschool children. *British Journal of Educational Psychology*, 65, 155–64.

Gathercole, S.E. and Baddeley, A. (1993). *Working Memory and Language*. Hove: Erlbaum.

Gipps, C., Steadman, S., Blackstone, T. and Stierer, B. (1983). *Testing Children: Standardised Testing in LEAs and Schools*. London: Heinemann.

Goswami, U. and Bryant, P. (1990). *Phonological Skills and Learning to Read*. Hove: Erlbaum.

Griffin, J.R. and Walton, H.N. (1987). *Dyslexia Determination Test*. Los Angeles: Instructional Materials and Equipment Distributors.

Griffin, J.R., Walton, H.N. and Christenson, G.N. (1988). *The Dyslexia Screener (TDS)*. Culver City, CA: Reading and Perception Therapy Center.

Grogan, S.C. (1995). Which cognitive abilities at age four are the best predictors of reading ability at age seven? *Journal of Research in Reading*, 18, 24–31.

Guerin, D.W., Griffin, J.R., Gottfried, A.W. and Christenson, G.N. (1993). Concurrent validity and screening efficiency of The Dyslexia Screener. *Psychological Assessment*, 5, 369–73.

Hulme, C. and Snowling, M. (1992). Deficits in output phonology: an explanation of reading failure? *Cognitive Neuropsychology*, 9, 47–72.

James, M. and Conner, C. (1993). Are reliability and validity achievable in National Curriculum assessment? Some observations on moderation at Key Stage 1 in 1992. *The Curriculum Journal*, 4, 5–19.

Jansky, J.J. (1977). A critical review of 'Some developments and predictive precursors of reading disabilities'. In A. L. Benton and D. Pearl (eds), *Dyslexia*. New York: Oxford University Press.

Jansky, J.J. and de Hirsch, K. (1972). *Preventing Reading Failure*. New York: Harper & Row.

Jorm, A.F., Share, D.L., MacLean, R. and Matthews, R. (1986). Cognitive factors at school entry predictive of specific reading retardation and general reading backwardness: a research note. *Journal of Child Psychology and Psychiatry*, 27, 45–54.

Kelly, V. (1992). Concepts of assessment: an overview. In G.M. Blenkin and A.V. Kelly (eds). *Assessment in Early Childhood Education*. London: Paul Chapman.

Kingslake, B. (1982). The predictive (in) accuracy of on-entry-to-school screening procedures when used to anticipate learning difficulties. *Special Education*, 10, 23–6.

Laming, D. (1995). Screening cervical smears. *British Journal of Psychology*, 86, 507–16.

Lichenstein, R. (1981). Comparative validity of two preschool screening tests: correlational and comparative approaches. *Journal of Learning Disabilities*, 13, 102–8.

Lindsay, G.A. (1980). The infant rating scale. *British Journal of Educational Psychology*, 50, 97–104.

Lindsay, G.A. (1981). *The Infant Rating Scale*. Sevenoaks: Hodder & Stoughton.

Lindsay, G.A. (1984). *Screening for Children with Special Needs. Multidisciplinary Approaches*. London: Croom Helm.

Lindsay, G.A. (1988). Early identification of learning difficulties: screening and beyond. *School Psychology International*, 9, 61–8.

Lindsay, G.A. (1993). Baseline assessments and special educational needs. In S. Wolfendale (ed.) *Assessing Special Educational Needs*. London: Cassell.

Lindsay, G.A. and Wedell, K. (1982). The early identification of educationally 'at risk' children: revisited. *Journal of Learning Disabilities*, 15, 212–17.

Lundberg, I., Olofsson, A. and Wall, S. (1980). Reading and spelling skills in the first school years predicted from phonemic awareness skills in kindergarten. *Scandinavian Journal of Psychology*, 21, 159–72.

Mann, V.A., Liberman, I.Y. and Shankweiler, D. (1980). Children's memory for sentences and word strings in relation to reading ability. *Memory and Cognition*, 8, 329–35.

Mason, J. (1990). The development of concepts about written language in the first three years of school. *British Journal of Educational Psychology*, 60, 266–83.

Neale, M.D. (1966; revised 1989). *Neale Analysis of Reading Ability*. Windsor, Berks: NFER-Nelson.

Newton, M.J. and Thomson, M.E. (1976; revised 1982). *The Aston Index*. Wisbech: LDA.

Newton, M.J., Thomson, M.E. and Richards, I.L. (1979). *Readings in Dyslexia*. Wisbech: LDA.

Nicolson, R.I. and Fawcett, A.J. (1990). Automaticity: a new framework for dyslexia research. *Cognition*, 30, 159–82.

Nicolson, R.I. and Fawcett, A.J. (1994). Comparison of deficits in cognitive and motor skills in children with dyslexia. *Annals of Dyslexia*, 44, 147–64.

Nicolson, R.I. and Fawcett, A.J. (1995). Dyslexia is more than a phonological disability. *Dyslexia*, 19–36.

Nicolson, R.I. and Fawcett, A.J. (1996). *The Dyslexia Early Screening Test (DEST)*. Sidcup, Kent: The Psychological Corporation.

Pearson, L. and Lindsay, G.A. (1986). *Special Needs in the Primary School*. Windsor: NFER-Nelson.

Pearson, L. and Quinn, J. (1978; revised 1986). *Bury Infant Check. Teacher's Manual.* Windsor, NFER-Nelson.

Pellegrini, A.D. (1991). A critique of the concept of At Risk as applied to emergent literacy. *Language Arts,* 68, 380–5.

Pollock, J. and Waller, E. (1994). *Day-to-day Dyslexia in the Classroom.* London: Routledge.

Potton, A. (1983). *Screening.* London: Macmillan.

Pumfrey, P.D. and Elliott, C.D. (1991). National reading standards and Standard Assessment Tasks: an educational house of cards. *Educational Psychology in Practice,* 7, 74–80.

Pumfrey, P.D. and Reason, R. (1991). *Specific Learning Difficulties (Dyslexia). Challenges and Responses.* Windsor, Berks: NFER-Nelson.

Pumfrey, P.D., Elliott, C.P. and Tyler, S. (1992). Objective testing: insights or illusions? In P. Pumfrey (ed.) *Reading Standards: Issues and Evidence.* Leicester: British Psychological Society, Division of Educational and Child Psychology.

Rack, J.P. (1994). Dyslexia: the phonological deficit hypothesis. In A. Fawcett and R. Nicolson (eds) *Dyslexia in Children: Multidisciplinary Perspectives.* London: Harvester Wheatsheaf.

Randall, P.E. (1981). *The Humberside Infant Screening Test.* Windsor, Berks: NFER-Nelson.

Reason, R. and Boote, R. (1986). *Learning Difficulties in Reading and Writing: A Teacher's Manual.* Windsor, Berks: NFER-Nelson.

Satz, P. and Fletcher, J.M. (1979). Early screening tests: some uses and abuses. *Journal of Learning Disabilities,* 12, 43–50.

Satz, P. and Fletcher, J.M. (1988). Early identification of learning disabled children: an old problem revisited. *Journal of Consulting and Clinical Psychology,* 56, 813–19.

School Curriculum and Assessment Authority (SCAA) (1996). *Baseline Assessment: Draft Proposals.* London: School Curriculum and Assessment Authority.

Sharp, F. (Chair) (1987). *Report of the Intercollegiate Working Party on Cervical Cytology Screening.* The Royal College of Obstetricians and Gynaecologists.

Singleton, C.H. (1987). Dyslexia and cognitive models of reading. *Support for Learning,* 2, 47–56.

Singleton, C.H. (1988). The early diagnosis of developmental dyslexia. *Support for Learning,* 3, 108–21.

Singleton, C.H. (1991). Computer applications in the diagnosis and assessment of cognitive deficits in dyslexia. In C.H. Singleton (ed.) *Computers and Literacy Skills.* Hull: Dyslexia Computer Resource Centre, University of Hull.

Singleton, C.H. (1995). *Computerised Screening for Dyslexia.* Paper delivered at the Conference of the British Psychological Society, London, December 1995.

Singleton, C.H., Thomas, K.V. and Leedale, R.C. (1996). *CoPS 1 Cognitive Profiling System.* Nottingham: Chameleon Educational Systems Ltd.

Slingerland, B. (1974). *A Multi-sensory Approach to Language Arts for Specific Language Disability Children.* Cambridge, MA: Educators Publishing Service.

Snowling, M. J. (1995). Phonological processing and developmental dyslexia. *Journal of Research in Reading,* 18, 132–8.

Stuart, M. (1995). Prediction and qualitative assessment of five- and six-year-old children's reading: a longitudinal study. *British Journal of Educational Psychology,* 65, 287–96.

Tansley, A.E. (1976). Special educational screening in infant schools. In K. Wedell and E.C. Raybould (eds) *The Early Identification of Educationally 'At-risk' Children. Educational Review,* Occasional Publication No. 6, University of Birmingham.

Thomson, M. (1989). *Developmental Dyslexia.* (3rd edn). London: Whurr.

Thomson, M. and Watkins, B. (1990). *Dyslexia: A Teaching Handbook.* London: Whurr.

Tizard, J. (Chair) (1972). *Children with Specific Reading Difficulties. Report of the Advisory Committee on Handicapped Children* (Department of Education and Science). London: HMSO.

Torgesen, J.K. (1987). Academic difficulties of learning disabled children who perform poorly on memory span tasks. In H.L. Swanson (ed.) *Memory and Learning Disabilities.* Greenwich, Conn: JAI Press.

Turner, M. (1990). *Sponsored Reading Failure.* Warlingham: Independent Primary and Secondary Education Trust.

Wald, N., Frost, C. and Cuckle, H. (1991). Breast cancer screening: the current position. *British Medical Journal,* 302, 845–6.

Wedell, K. and Lindsay, G.A. (1982). Early identification procedures: what have we learned? *Remedial Education,* 15, 130–5.

Whitehead, M. (1992). Assessment at Key Stage 1: core subjects and the developmental curriculum. In G.M. Blenkin and A.V. Kelly (eds). *Assessment in Early Childhood Education.* London: Paul Chapman Publishing.

Whyte, J. (1993). Patterns of development in good and poor readers age 6–11. In S.F. Wright and R. Groner (eds) *Facets of Dyslexia and its Remediation.* Amsterdam: Elsevier Science Publishers B.V.

Willows, D.M. (1990). Visual processes in learning disabilities. In B. Wong (ed.) *Learning about Learning Disabilities.* New York: Academic Press.

Wolf, M. and Obregón, M. (1992). Early naming deficits, developmental dyslexia, and a specific deficit hypothesis. *Brain and Language,* 42, 219–47.

Wolfendale, S. (1993). *Baseline Assessment for Children Starting School: Issues and Challenges.* Stoke-on-Trent: Trentham Books.

Wolfendale, S. and Bryans, T. (1979). *Identification of Learning Difficulties. A Model for Intervention.* Stafford: National Association for Remedial Education.

Woodcock, R.W. and Johnson, M.B. (1977). *Woodcock–Johnson Psycho-Educational Battery.* Hingham, MA: Teaching Resources Corporation.

Wright, A. (1992). Evaluation of the first British reading recovery programme. *British Educational Research Journal,* 18(4)., 351–68.

Young, D. (1968). *Group Reading Test.* London: University of London Press.

5 Assessment of visual problems in reading

Bruce J. W. Evans

INTRODUCTION

It is the visual nature of reading that distinguishes it from speech, yet the role of visual problems in reading has long been the source of debate. Some authorities have argued that visual deficits are not associated with reading problems, while others have argued that visual anomalies are the major cause of reading difficulties. Controversy seems to have been fuelled by two main issues: the vagueness of the term 'vision' and a failure to appreciate that visual correlates of reading disability are not necessarily the sole or main cause of poor reading.

Vision begins with light being focused by the lenses of the eyes on to the retinae at the back of the eyes. Sensory aspects of visual function then occur in the retinae, visual pathway and visual areas of the brain. In addition to these sensory processes, there are also important motor aspects of visual function. These include the precise co-ordinated alignment of the two eyes. The distinction between sensory and motor visual function is not always clear. For example, depth perception (stereopsis) requires (but does not always accompany) co-ordination in the alignment of the two eyes (a motor function) and good visual acuities (a sensory factor).

Further confusion arises from cognitive tests or profiles which identify a 'visual' or 'visuo-spatial' anomaly. Here, the term visual refers to deeper conceptual processing of complex visual information. These types of visual deficits are distinct from the ocular motor and afferent visual pathway anomalies discussed below.

This chapter will concentrate on the visual problems that have been identified as correlates of reading difficulty, often of dyslexia. A concentration on this area is unavoidable since most of the research on vision and reading has concentrated on the emotive issue of dyslexia. It is appreciated that the term 'dyslexia' is itself controversial, but it is used here because it has been employed in many of the original papers that are under review. The meaning of the term in most of these studies can be summarised by the generic definition of a marked specific difficulty in learning to read (and usually to spell) in individuals who suffered no manifest barrier to the acquisition of these skills.

THE ASSOCIATION BETWEEN VISUAL ANOMALIES AND READING SKILLS

Ocular health

Ocular diseases are rare in childhood. Poor ocular health will not necessarily cause symptoms and some pathologies cause a loss only of peripheral vision so that a child may be able to read a letter chart normally. Interestingly, people with ocular pathology that does interfere with vision often seem to automatically adjust their reading rate so that they would be unlikely to make as many errors as a person with good ocular health and a specific reading disability. Similarly, individuals with the severe eye movement anomaly of nystagmus (in which the eyes constantly oscillate) do not usually have severe reading difficulties. This fact may support the argument that subtle eye-movement anomalies are unlikely to hold the key to dyslexia. However, nystagmus sometimes occurs as a consequence of grossly impaired vision following some other type of pathology (e.g. cataracts), and such individuals will need large-size type.

Pathology causing visual field defects may, depending on the field loss, interfere with reading. Hemianopias (loss of half the visual field) affecting the right visual field will present greater difficulties for reading English than hemianopias of the left field. It should be noted that cortical damage which causes a hemianopia might also affect non-visual cortical areas which are involved in the higher functions of reading. There has been little research on the effect of a loss of central visual field in children, although adults seem to adapt rapidly to using the remaining area of maximum visual acuity in the place of the fovea (in a healthy eye, the fovea is the central area of the retina which has maximum resolving ability).

Severe cataracts are usually removed by surgery but may leave a residual visual loss. People with milder cataracts, which may not require surgery, can sometimes be helped by controlling the level of illumination. Some individuals are helped by increasing the illumination and others by reducing it. It is always important to investigate the effect of varying the strength and type of illumination in any case of visual impairment.

People with severe visual impairment can be helped by low vision aids (e.g. spectacle-mounted telescopic systems), but these are often difficult to learn to use and individuals should be prepared to persevere and to experiment with different types of aid. Low vision aids are usually obtained free of charge through the Hospital Eye Service. Reading by Braille for people who have a very severe visual impairment is beyond the scope of this chapter.

Visual acuity and refractive error

Visual acuity refers to the angular subtense of the smallest size of detail that the eye can resolve. It is usually expressed as a fraction in which the numerator refers to the testing distance in metres (feet in the USA). Six metres is the reference distance (20 feet in the USA) and the denominator changes proportionally in either direction according to the proportional change in size of the lettering, while reading from the same reference distance. Average visual acuity is 6/6 (in feet, 20/20), where the height of letters sub-tends an angle of five minutes of arc (one minute of arc is one-sixtieth of a degree). The bottom line of many letter charts is 6/3 (half the size of 6/6 letters), and the top line of most letter charts is 6/60 (ten times the size of 6/6 letters). Most of the near print that 6- or 7-year-old children would be expected to read is equivalent to about 6/24, and typical text for a 9 year old is equivalent to about 6/18. The smallest print that any children are expected to read (e.g. dictionaries) is equivalent to about 6/12. Although this is approximately twice the threshold acuity, this margin may be necessary for comfortable vision.

Short-sightedness (myopia) blurs distance vision and the prescribing of spectacles for myopia by eye care practitioners is usually a fairly straightforward decision. Most children can read 6/5 easily and an optometrist might consider prescribing a refractive correction if the myopia reduced the binocular acuity to 6/9 and would almost certainly prescribe if it was reduced to 6/12. Low to moderate myopia will not impair near vision and some studies have even found a correlation between myopia and supranormal reading performance (Evans and Drasdo, 1990).

Young people have an ability to compensate for low to moderate degrees of hypermetropia (or hyperopia: long-sightedness), although this ability decreases with age. The eyes compensate by accommodating, which is the process whereby the shape of the lens inside the eye is changed to increase its power. Because accommodation naturally occurs during near vision, there is a neural cross-link between accommodation and convergence (a turning in of the eyes which is necessary for single vision during close work). Hence, when accommodation is used to compensate for hypermetropia it induces a turning inwards of the eyes and uncorrected hypermetropia is a common cause of convergent strabismus (squint). A constant accommodative effort to overcome hypermetropia may also cause eye-strain, headaches and blurred vision. Hypermetropia in children would not usually be detected by a distance letter chart test, and frequently does not even affect performance at brief near vision tests. Unilateral hypermetropia will not be detected by measuring binocular visual acuity and, although unlikely to affect reading, can result in a permanent visual loss if not detected in the first five or six years of life. Some studies have found a weak correlation between hypermetropia and reading difficulties; others have suggested that this may result from a weak negative correlation between hypermetropia and IQ (Evans and Drasdo, 1990).

Astigmatism is the refractive error that results when an eye has a different refractive power in different meridians (e.g. in the horizontal and vertical meridian). Low astigmatism is ubiquitous and harmless, higher astigmatism will lead to blurred distance and near vision and may cause eyestrain.

Refractive errors can be determined objectively and subjectively. The principal objective technique uses a hand-held instrument, the retinoscope, to shine light through the pupil and to neutralise (with lenses) the rays that are reflected back from the retina. Eye care practitioners rely more on objective techniques when examining younger and less reliable children; patient co-operation is not essential for such an eye examination. Sometimes, cycloplegic eye drops are used to relax the accommodative mechanism and thus reveal the full refractive error. Modern drugs only sting a little on insertion and the duration of blurred vision is only a few hours (the pupils remain dilated for longer so that sunglasses may still be needed on the day after the drops are inserted).

Accommodation

Accommodation describes the ability of the eyes to maintain a clear focus on objects at a wide range of distances. The amplitude of accommodation is recorded in diopters as the inverse of the smallest distance from the eye that clear vision can be maintained. Young children can usually focus clearly very close to; they have a high amplitude of accommodation. The amplitude of accommodation reduces with age, but should be more than adequate for all near visual tasks during school years. An apparent low amplitude of accommodation can result from uncorrected long-sightedness, as described above, and this possibility must be excluded before poor accommodation can be diagnosed. To read comfortably for sustained periods the amplitude of accommodation needs to be substantially greater than that predicted for clear vision at the viewing distance.

Research has shown that the mean amplitude of accommodation of a group of children with dyslexic difficulties is significantly reduced compared with control good readers (Evans *et al.*, 1994). However, despite this *average* difference, the majority of children with reading difficulties have an amplitude of accommodation that exceeds the level necessary for clear and comfortable reading.

The amplitude of accommodation is measured by bringing a target of fine print towards subjects until they report blurring. It can also be measured objectively by using reflected light (retinoscopy). Some optometrists include other tests of accommodative function in their assessment of children with reading difficulties. The two most common of these are tests of accommodative lag and facility. During near vision, the eyes are not usually precisely focused on the object of regard, but the accommodation lags a small amount behind the target. If the accommodative lag is small then the blur it causes is insignificant; if it is large then it can result in blurred reading. Accommodative lag is measured objectively with a retinoscope. Accommodative facility is a measurement of ability to rapidly change focusing.

It is rare for a patient to have very poor accommodation, although accommodative paralysis is occasionally encountered and is usually corrected with glasses. A milder degree of accommodative dysfunction is more common and requires treatment if it is associated with symptoms (e.g. blurring, eye-strain, headaches). Some children may become so used to their symptoms that they fail to report them, so accommodative dysfunction may occasionally be treated in the absence of symptoms, if it is of a degree that would be expected to interfere with academic performance. Treatment often consists of eye exercises (vision therapy) or, if exercises are unsuccessful, spectacles (possibly bifocals).

Binocular vision (orthoptics)

Binocular vision refers to the ability of the two eyes to work together in a co-ordinated way. Perfect binocular vision requires that the two eyes are precisely aligned (to within about 0.03°) in their fixation of the object of regard. Strabismus (synonyms: squint, cast, turning eye) describes the condition where the eyes manifestly fail to maintain alignment and affects about 2.5% of the population. In young children, the image in the eye that turns will be at least partially suppressed to prevent double vision. This almost invariably results in a permanent visual loss (amblyopia, or 'lazy eye') in that eye. This visual loss can, to some extent, be prevented or treated in young children (up to about 7 years) by patching the non-strabismic (normal) eye. The strabismus may be of a small angle and is often undetected by parents, and sometimes is not discovered by school screening tests.

Most types of strabismus are not usually thought to be associated with reading difficulties and some authorities have suggested that a stable unilateral strabismus might actually be associated with better-than-average reading because the ocular dominance is well established. For this reason, it has been suggested, controversially, that excessive patching to treat amblyopia in early life could cause problems with unstable ocular dominance in the school years (Fowler and Stein, 1983). Although most cases of strabismus are unilateral, a few patients alternate freely from using one eye to the other. If this alternation occurs during reading then this could cause a confused perception of text.

Eye care practitioners assess strabismus with a variety of tests, but the most important is the cover test (Evans, 1997). In this test, each eye is covered in turn while the patient fixates a target and the movement of the uncovered eye is observed. If, for example, when the right eye is covered the left is seen to move in to take up fixation then it can be deduced that there is a left divergent strabismus. This test requires very little co-operation and no verbal response from the subject. Not all cases of strabismus require treatment, but those that do are variously treated with spectacles, eye exercises or surgery, in addition to the patching described above.

Most people do not have a strabismus but instead manifest a heterophoria. A heterophoria occurs when the eyes are normally aligned, but their resting position is out of alignment. This is best demonstrated by an example with the cover test described above. With a heterophoria the eye behind the cover moves and, because the eyes are aligned during normal viewing, when the cover is removed the previously covered eye is seen to move to take up fixation once more (Evans, 1997). During everyday visual tasks, a slight constant effort has to be maintained through vergence eye movements (convergence or divergence) to overcome the heterophoria, but usually this effort is insignificant and causes no symptoms. The amount of convergence or divergence that is 'held in reserve' to overcome a heterophoria is called the 'fusional reserve'. Sometimes, the heterophoria is unusually large and/or the fusional reserves unusually low and the heterophoria becomes 'decompensated'.

Typical symptoms of decompensated heterophoria include eye-strain, headaches, blurred vision, double vision and perceptual distortions. Some people with these symptoms develop the habit of covering one eye (possibly by holding their head in an unusual position) when reading. Optometrists diagnose decompensated heterophoria using symptoms, the objective cover test and subjective tests (including fixation disparity and stereo-acuity tests). Occasionally, a person can have a decompensated heterophoria without any symptoms by suppressing a small central area of vision in one eye. It is possible that these, and other cases of decompensated heterophoria, may break down to a strabismus if left untreated.

Low fusional reserves are a correlate of dyslexia and there may, therefore, be a greater prevalence of decompensated heterophoria in those with reading difficulties. One research study found specific reading difficulties to be associated with low fusional reserves and an unstable heterophoria (Evans *et al.*, 1995). Together, these two visual anomalies are termed 'binocular instability' (Evans, 1997). Although binocular instability and/or a decompensated heterophoria are unlikely to be the sole or main cause of a severe reading difficulty, they may be a contributory factor. It should be noted that some people with these binocular vision anomalies read very well, so there is unlikely to be a simple causal relationship. Decompensated heterophoria usually responds very well to treatment, either by exercises or spectacles.

One other very common binocular vision anomaly in children is convergence insufficiency. If a child observes an object that is approaching their nose then their eyes will usually continue to turn inwards (converge) until the object is less than about 5 cm away from their eyes. A convergence insufficiency is when a person is unable to converge closer than a certain distance, usually 10 cm. A marked convergence insufficiency is often associated with a decompensated heterophoria at a normal reading distance and may require treatment. Most convergence insufficiencies respond well to simple exercises.

Ocular dominance

A great deal has been written about the role of ocular dominance in reading and many theories have risen and fallen in popularity. One cause of confusion is that there are at least three different types of ocular dominance: sighting, motor and sensory dominance. For example, sighting dominance can be determined by the usual pointing tests, motor dominance by the eye, which first loses fixation when the near point of convergence is reached, and sensory dominance by the eye with better acuity. There are several methods of assessing dominance within each of these categories.

There is little homogeneity in the results of different tests of ocular dominance (Moseley, 1988). In a given individual, the right eye might be the dominant eye for a sighting task and the left for a motor task; and it may even be the case that the right eye is the dominant eye for one motor task and the left for another motor task. It is not known which, if any, of these types of ocular dominance is most relevant for reading.

Sighting tests of ocular dominance were once used to determine whether an individual was 'crossed dominant' (sighting dominant eye contralateral to dominant hand); crossed dominance was thought to be related to reading difficulties. However, some studies have failed to support this hypothesis and the general consensus now seems to be that sighting dominance is irrelevant to the assessment and treatment of reading and spelling problems (Moseley, 1988).

More recently, it has been claimed that an unstable result on a test of motor ocular dominance, the Dunlop Test, can diagnose 'visual dyslexia', which is treated by occluding one eye (Stein and Fowler, 1985). The use of the term 'visual dyslexia' has caused some confusion since it is probably not intended to be equivalent to the visual-spatial sub-type of dyslexia identified by Boder and other classifications (see below on higher visual processing). It was later asserted that an unstable result on the Dunlop Test indicated 'poor visuomotor control' or 'binocular instability'. The Dunlop Test has been criticised on many grounds and, although preliminary research supported the use of this test, most subsequent studies have failed to replicate the original findings (Bishop, 1989; Evans, 1993). There is fairly wide agreement that the Dunlop Test is unreliable, although there is growing evidence that many dyslexic children have some form of binocular instability (the classic meaning of this term is described above). It is unlikely that any single test, let alone one as unreliable as the Dunlop Test, possesses the sensitivity and specificity to diagnose binocular instability. The best approach would seem to be for eye care practitioners to apply a battery of tests to assess binocular function.

Eye movements

During reading, the eyes constantly make saccadic eye movements. The eyes typically fixate on a group of letters for about 250 ms (a quarter of a second) while the information from these is assimilated and then make a saccadic eye movement to the next group of letters, and so on. At the end of the line the eyes make a large backwards saccade to the beginning of the next line. Occasional smaller backwards saccades, regressions, occur to aid comprehension. Both 'bottom-up' (occurring independently of cognition) and 'top-down' (influenced by cognition and comprehension) factors have been shown to influence the pattern of eye movements when reading.

It should be noted that the general pattern of fixations separated by saccadic eye movements is not specific to reading (Stark *et al.*, 1991). It is the visual system's basic method of acquiring information from any visual scene in which the observer and target are relatively stationary. The unusual factors in reading are the sequential and predominantly horizontal nature of successive targets, and the similarity, in gross spatial terms, of these targets.

Generally speaking, with more difficult reading material or with less expert readers the number of fixations is increased, the duration of fixations is increased so that the reading rate is slower, and the number of regressions increases. The reading eye movements of people with severe reading difficulties are therefore somewhat atypical. A key question is whether these atypical eye movements are, as has been implied above, the result of poor reading skills or whether they are underlying causes of poor reading. This question has been addressed in two ways (Evans and Drasdo, 1990). First, many researchers have studied the sequential horizontal saccadic eye movements of disabled readers in non-reading tasks. The second approach has been to compare the reading eye movements of people with a specific reading difficulty (SRD) with those of younger, good readers whose reading age was at the same level as the SRD group.

Although a large body of research has used these paradigms, the results have been contradictory and there is still a lack of agreement in this area (e.g. Stark *et al.*, 1991; cf. Pavlidis, 1981, and Biscaldi *et al.*, 1994). Although case studies have identified one or two individuals who have an irrepressible tendency to read from right to left, this appears to be abnormal, even in dyslexic individuals. It would seem to be prudent to conclude that, in view of the large amount of research, abnormal eye movements are unlikely to be the explanation for poor reading in the majority of cases.

It is interesting to note, in passing, some research findings on pursuit eye movements. These are the following eye movements that occur in pursuit of a moving target. If the target moves too quickly then the smooth pursuit eye movements break down into 'jerky' saccadic eye movements. Some researchers have noted that people with dyslexic difficulties often exhibit saccadation of their pursuit eye movements for target speeds where this does not usually occur. This observation has received relatively little attention because pursuit eye movements are not used during normal reading tasks. Some authorities have described pursuit eye movements as an extreme case of a fixation reflex (the reflex that occurs to keep the image of the object of regard on the fovea) and fixation instability has been described in a group of children with poor reading performance (Eden *et al.*, 1994).

The term 'tracking skills' is sometimes used to describe subjective estimates of ocular motor function in relation to reading performance. Unfortunately, the term is vague and is used variously to refer to saccadic eye movements (e.g. changing fixation between two pens), saccadation of pursuit (e.g. non-smooth movements when following a slowly moving pen), or a remote near point of convergence (e.g. eyes appear unable to converge on a pen approaching the nose). It is possible that all three types of observation may be related to lapses of concentration by the subject. The high co-morbidity between specific reading difficulty and attention deficit disorder (with or without hyperactivity) might account for much of the controversy surrounding the relationship between eye movement dysfunction and specific reading difficulty and is discussed below. It should also be noted that even when a subject can converge to their nose, when asked to make the effort, this does not necessarily mean that they have a full range of vergence eye movements, nor that their binocular vision is normal.

Behavioral optometry

Behavioral optometry (BO) is a sub-discipline of optometry which has some practitioners in the USA and has a few followers in the UK. The term is difficult to define since it covers a broad range of activities. The simplest interpretation of BO is that optometrists should take account of the whole person and his or her environment. This is unquestionably sound advice which is likely to be followed by all good eye care practitioners. Many behavioral optometrists, like other conventional optometrists, concentrate on a very thorough orthoptic investigation as outlined above, and the treatment of anomalies detected in this way is not controversial. However, most behavioral optometrists seem to investigate unconventional areas of visual function and often prescribe exercises and glasses to the vast majority of children they examine, even when these patients would not be thought to be abnormal following a thorough eye examination by a conventional optometrist or ophthalmologist. For example, many behavioral optometrists regularly treat saccadic or pursuit eye movements in those with reading disability, although the literature suggests that these types of eye movement dysfunction have not been clearly established as a strong correlate of reading difficulties, let alone a cause.

One of the areas that BO concentrates on is perceptuo-motor function and exercises, which are reminiscent of the 'patterning treatment' of Dolman and Delacato (Silver, 1986). Often BO involves the assessment of functions which might conventionally be thought to lie within the domain of psychology, such as analysing reading errors, sub-typing dyslexia, and investigating higher visual processing skills such as decoding and short-term memory skills. The research supporting BO is copious, but often of rather poor quality and not usually published in interdisciplinary peer-reviewed journals. The therapies usually involve giving the child considerable extra attention; yet there is a dearth of rigorous placebo-controlled trials. The case for behavioral optometry is, perhaps, best represented by Birnbaum (1993); the opposite view is given by Beauchamp (1986). It seems likely that at least some of the successes in improving reading that have been attributed to BO are simply manifestations of the placebo effect. These cases may have benefited more if the resources had been spent on conventional management, such as extra teaching tailored to the child's individual needs.

Meares-Irlen Syndrome

Critchley (1964) cited a case study by Jansky in 1958 of a dyslexic child who was unable to read words on white card, but could manage to read words printed on coloured card. Meares (1980) suggested that some children's perception of text and reading disabilities are influenced by print characteristics. She found that in some cases the white gaps between the words and lines masked the print and caused perceptual anomalies, such as words blurring, doubling and jumping. She noted that this was helped by reducing the size of the print, using coloured paper, reducing the contrast, or using white print on black paper.

Following these early reports Helen Irlen established a proprietary system, based on 'Irlen Institutes', in several countries including the USA, UK and Australia to detect and treat 'Scotopic Sensitivity Syndrome'. This term is probably etymologically inappropriate and 'Meares-Irlen Syndrome' may be a suitable alternative. The condition is characterised by symptoms of eye-strain and visual perceptual distortions when reading. The eye-strain predominantly is said to occur with reading and is typified by sore, tired eyes, visual discomfort and headache. The distortions include blurring, doubling, fading, shimmering, movement of words or letters and seeing patterns and shapes on the page. Treatment of Meares-Irlen

Syndrome is with coloured filters, either coloured sheets (overlays) placed on the page or with coloured glasses. It is claimed that the required colour differs from person to person and is very specific: if a person is given coloured glasses of a colour that is similar but slightly different to their required colour then they will receive much less benefit than with the appropriate colour (Irlen, 1991).

Proponents of the Irlen system claim that up to 60% of people with a reading problem and 10% of good readers suffer from this disorder and cite case studies or open trials in which the use of coloured filters appears to be associated with a vast improvement in symptoms. However, until recently Meares-Irlen Syndrome has lacked both an adequate scientific explanation and placebo-controlled research and this has led many eye care professionals to dismiss it as a placebo or attributional effect.

Wilkins developed an instrument, the Intuitive Colorimeter, which facilitated a double-blind placebo-controlled trial of the purported beneficial effect of coloured filters. In this trial we tested children who had the symptoms described above with the Intuitive Colorimeter to determine the precise colour of filter that most improved their perception of text (Wilkins *et al.*, 1994). One pair of tinted glasses was made up to this 'optimal tint', while a second pair was made up with a tint that was similar, but slightly different to their optimal one (the 'control tint'). The optimal and control tints were each worn for a period of four weeks, in random order. Thirty-six children, who completed daily diaries reporting symptoms of eye-strain and headaches throughout the study, reported significantly fewer symptoms with their optimal than with their control tints ($p < 0.003$). During testing with the Intuitive Colorimeter, people adapt to the colours they view so that they are unable to precisely name or remember their optimal colour. It is this feature that facilitated a double-blind protocol, which was confirmed by the inability of the subjects in our study to reliably recall which pair of glasses was most similar to their optimal colorimeter setting (Wilkins *et al.*, 1994).

This study did not investigate whether Irlen's claims about the high prevalence of Meares-Irlen Syndrome are accurate, although one recent study suggests that about half of a sample of typical schoolchildren report a benefit from coloured overlays and, if given their preferred overlay, about one-fifth of these would still be using it after ten months (Jeanes *et al.*, submitted).

Several potential mechanisms have also been proposed. Some are based on a hypothetical link between the benefit from colour and other visual correlates of reading disability. However, these hypotheses do not seem to be able to account for the high degree of specificity of the required colour which has been stressed by Irlen and substantiated by the placebo-controlled trial (Evans *et al.*, 1995). An alternative mechanism, initially proposed by Wilkins, is based on 'pattern glare' (Wilkins *et al.*, 1984). Striped patterns (Figure 5.1) can be unpleasant to look at and some people

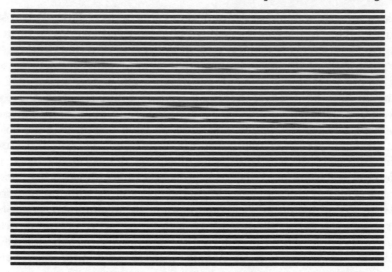

Figure 5.1 A pattern which may cause pattern glare
Warning: DO NOT STARE AT THE PATTERN IF YOU SUFFER FROM EPILEPSY
OR MIGRAINE.

experience eye-strain and visual perceptual distortions when viewing these.
In fact, these symptoms are remarkably similar to those reported by
patients with Meares-Irlen Syndrome. Some people with photosensitive
epilepsy are particularly prone to these symptoms, as are others with
migraine, and the mechanism for these symptoms is likely to be a hyperexcitability of the visual cortex. Lines of print on a page form a striped
pattern which can have the spatial properties of a pattern that may cause
pattern glare and it seems likely that this mechanism is responsible for
at least some patients' symptoms of 'visual stress' with reading. Some of
the cortical neurones are sensitive to specific colours and this could
account for the benefit from specific coloured filters (Wilkins, 1995).
Recent research suggests that pattern glare is a correlate of Meares-Irlen
Syndrome (Evans *et al.*, 1995).

The Intuitive Colorimeter was developed by Wilkins at the Medical
Research Council (MRC) Applied Psychology Unit and is manufactured
under licence (to the MRC) by Cerium Visual Technologies.[1] Wilkins also
developed a system of Precision Tinted Lenses to facilitate the accurate
reproduction of colours chosen in the Intuitive Colorimeter and a system
of coloured plastic sheets that can be placed on the page to inexpensively,
yet systematically, screen children for a benefit from colour (Intuitive
Overlays[2]). A clinical system is in operation where teachers, optometrists
and psychologists screen children with the coloured overlays. Children
who show a sustained benefit from an overlay are then referred to an
optometrist or hospital department with an Intuitive Colorimeter.

Three caveats should be stressed about this system. First, about one-third of children who are issued with a coloured overlay return for Intuitive Colorimetry. This suggests that the system of trying overlays first is a good method of differentiating the 'genuine' cases from those who may simply want to try colour for a novelty; but it does mean that the failure to use this type of screening process could result in the over-prescription of coloured glasses. Second, there are good optical reasons to predict, and clinical evidence to support, Irlen's claim that the colour of a person's preferred overlay is different from the colour of their preferred lens. Spectacle lenses should not be tinted on the basis of a preferred overlay colour. Finally, several studies have shown a high prevalence of ocular motor anomalies in patients presenting with the symptoms of Meares-Irlen Syndrome. In some cases these symptoms are resolved after eye exercises, although other cases still need coloured filters. Therefore, people should be referred to an eye care practitioner who is skilled in the assessment of people with reading difficulties before providing coloured overlays.

Deficit of the transient visual sub-system

The foregoing sections on accommodation, binocular vision and eye movements predominantly relate to motor visual functions. The role of sensory visual factors in reading will be discussed initially in terms of the processing of the afferent visual pathway which carries information from the retina to the primary visual cortex. The integration and interpretation of this visual information using higher association cortical regions will then be considered.

It is generally accepted that visual processing under daytime (photopic) light levels takes place in parallel through the transient (magnocellular) and sustained (parvocellular) sub-systems (Lennie *et al.*, 1990). These two pathways are compared and contrasted in Table 5.1. It should be stressed that the functional segregation is not as distinct as Table 5.1 suggests and these two sub-systems can demonstrate considerable overlap and complementarity.

Lovegrove *et al.* (1986) reviewed four lines of evidence suggesting that about 75% of people with specific reading difficulties have a deficit of the transient visual system. First, people with specific reading difficulties have been shown to have abnormal visual persistence, although this measure is subject to criterion errors. The second line of evidence comes from experiments assessing subjects' ability to detect low contrast striped patterns of various spatial frequencies (low spatial frequency patterns have coarse, widely spaced stripes and high spatial frequency patterns have fine, closely spaced stripes). Children with specific reading difficulties show a reduced ability to detect low contrast coarse patterns, but a normal ability to detect low contrast fine patterns. The transient system is likely to play

Table 5.1 Characteristics of sustained and transient channels

Sustained	Characteristic	Transient
P-cells	Ganglion cells	M-cells
Parvocellular	Layer of LGN	Magnocellular
Temporal lobe	Ultimate cortical destination	Parietal lobe
Long (low pass)	Response property	Short (band pass, 20 Hz)
Static targets/ low frequency flicker	Temporal conditions for maximum response	Moving targets/ high frequency flicker
High spatial frequencies	Spatial conditions for maximum response	Low spatial frequencies
Small	Receptor field size	Large
More central	Retinal location	More peripheral
Yes	Sensitive to blur	No
Throughout stimulus	Persistence of response	At onset/offset of stimulus

Note: LGN = lateral geniculate nucleus

a greater role in the analysis of these low spatial frequencies than in the analysis of higher spatial frequencies (Table 5.1). A better measure of transient visual system function is perhaps the ability to detect flicker and this has been shown to be reduced in subjects with dyslexia. Lovegrove *et al.* (1986) also reviewed a fourth series of experiments investigating sustained system function, and showing this to be normal in specifically disabled readers. This latter finding may explain why many researchers have concluded that there are no visual correlates of reading disability since vision tests tapping the sustained sub-system have been used most frequently. In addition to these psychophysical measures of visual function there are also electrophysiological data which may, controversially, support the transient deficit hypothesis.

Predictably, several theories have been proposed to transform this visual *correlate* of reading difficulty into a *cause* of reading problems. One of these theories is based on a model of visual perception during reading which proposes that text is perceived through the sustained system during fixations. The transient system is thought to prevent visual persistence of the 'sustained image' by inhibiting this during saccades (saccadic suppression). Hence, a transient deficit might cause a superimposition of subsequent sustained images and thus some visual confusion when reading. Other theories rely on hypothetical perceptual consequences of a transient deficit. For example, it has been argued that the sustained and transient systems are predominantly involved in figure and ground perception respectively (Weisstein *et al.*, 1992). One weakness of these 'perceptual consequence' hypotheses is the lack of research carrying out the simple tests of low-level visual function that identify a transient deficit in the reading of disabled subjects who are said to manifest the perceptual consequences of such a deficit.

Higher visual processing

There have been many attempts to classify dyslexia, although it should be noted that one large study using cluster analysis failed to support the concept of clearly defined subgroups (Naidoo, 1972). Nevertheless, many authors have classified dyslexia into three subgroups and a good example is the classification of Boder (1971). Her system is based upon three reading–spelling patterns. Dysphonetic dyslexia is characterised by people who read words globally, as instantaneous visual wholes from the limited sight vocabulary, rather than analytically; and as a result could not cope with new or unusual words. The opposite is dyseidectic dyslexia, exemplified by the analytic reader who cannot perceive letters or words as visual wholes and who consequently read laboriously and cannot deal with words that are irregularly spelled or pronounced. The final group, mixed dysphonetic-dyseidectic dyslexia-alexia, exhibit the combined deficits of both groups and are usually the most severely handicapped educationally.

The type of high-level cognitive visual deficit that, for example, Boder's dyseidectic subgroup manifest is very different from the visual deficits that have been described earlier in this chapter. The relationship between these two types of visual deficit has been studied very little and is far from clear. Lovegrove *et al.* (1986) argued that the visual disabilities shown by the dyseidectic (visuo-spatial) subgroup do not reflect visual processes of the type characterised by their research on a transient system deficit. More recently, it has even been hypothesised that a transient deficit precedes and causes phonological language deficiency (Williams and Lovegrove, 1992).

A similar distinction needs to be drawn between the 'visual IQ' assessed by tests such as the British Ability Scales and the type of visual deficits described in this chapter. One author (Koslowe, 1991) did hypothesise that poor performance at a coding task was caused by ocular motor anomalies, but this was not supported by a recent study (Evans *et al.*, 1996).

LINKING THE VISUAL CORRELATES OF READING DIFFICULTY

The visual correlates of specific reading difficulty can be summarised as motor deficits in accommodation and vergence, the sensory transient visual system deficit, and a benefit from coloured filters (possibly owing to cortical hyperexcitability resulting in pattern glare). An obvious hypothesis is that some of these correlates may be linked to one another.

It is well known that there is a strong cross-link between the accommodative and vergence systems, although the role of this link in the visual correlates of dyslexia remains to be established. There is fairly compelling

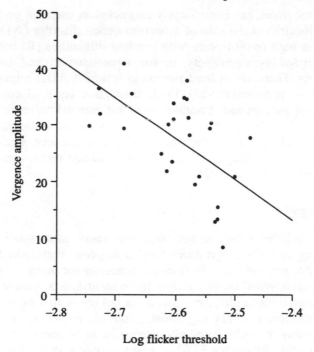

Figure 5.2 Regression of vergence amplitude, in prism diopters, on log temporal contrast threshold for a dyslexic group. No points are hidden by overlap

evidence that the transient visual system may be paramount in the control of vergence eye movements, although it would be simplistic to suggest that the sustained system did not have some role. The hypothesis that the transient deficit in dyslexia may be linked to poor vergence control was investigated by Evans *et al.* (1996). They compared thirty-nine dyslexic children with forty-three control good readers; the groups were matched for chronological age, gender and performance IQ. The dyslexic group manifested a reduced sensitivity to faint flicker (previously taken to be a sign of a transient deficit) and significantly reduced vergence amplitudes. These sensory and motor visual correlates were very significantly associated in the dyslexic group (Figure 5.2; $r = -0.627$), but not in the control group ($r = -0.116$).

It has been hypothesised by many authors that the transient visual system deficit may explain the benefit that some individuals experience from coloured filters, although a recent study did not support this hypothesis (Evans *et al.*, 1995). This study did demonstrate an association between the motor visual correlates of dyslexia described above and a reported benefit from colour, although the data suggested that it is unlikely that motor visual factors were the underlying cause of the benefit from colour. The search for a common cause of these visual factors will no doubt continue.

One factor which has been largely neglected in research on vision and reading difficulties is the role of attention deficit disorder (ADD). ADD, which has a high co-morbidity with reading difficulties (Richards, 1994), is characterised by impulsivity, motor impersistence, and (sometimes) hyperactivity. There are at least two ways in which ADD might influence the results of optometric tests. First, through a lapse of concentration during a test and second, because of motor impersistence (e.g. fixation instability). The role of ADD in the aetiology of the visual correlates of reading difficulty should be the subject of future research. Unfortunately, ADD is not easy to diagnose; simple questionnaire techniques are probably inadequate (Taylor, 1994).

CAUSALITY

While it is relatively easy to establish that visual factors are correlated with reading difficulties, it is much harder to prove that these factors are causes. Unfortunately, there has been a tendency for many researchers to conclude that a visual correlate they have identified is a cause. Vision is clearly essential for reading, but this does not mean that all visual anomalies will interfere with reading. Most, if not all, of the optometric correlates of reading difficulty listed above also occur in some people who do not have reading difficulties. Further, many people with reading difficulties do not have any visual problems. So the relationship between visual problems and reading performance cannot be a simple causal one.

Ocular motor factors and Meares-Irlen Syndrome might, in severe cases, have a direct effect on reading through perceptual distortions and could have an indirect effect if eye-strain and headaches were making a person reluctant to read. There is some evidence that ocular motor anomalies might cause a greater prevalence of certain types of reading errors (Cornelissen *et al.*, 1992), although one study suggested that visual problems are unlikely to be a major cause of dyslexia (Evans et al, 1996). The evidence for visual factors causing reading difficulties is probably less compelling than the argument that phonological factors are major causes of reading problems. The finding that the transient deficit is often present in children with poor phonological coding suggests that the discovery of low-level visual anomalies or of phonological weaknesses in a poor reader should not preclude the investigation of both areas of function. Optometric and psychometric assessments of people with reading difficulties are complementary, not mutually exclusive.

DETECTION

Many authors have criticised the adequacy of the visual screening procedures in the UK for pre-school and school-aged children. In particular, the use of a distance letter chart test for school screening would be very unlikely to detect any of the visual correlates of reading disability described in this chapter. Some schools use screening instruments which include binocular vision tests, but these tests are generally coarse and create conditions very different from normal reading. This is in direct contrast with optometric binocular vision tests which have, in recent years, evolved so as to more closely resemble normal viewing conditions (Evans, 1997).

Not all the children who require optometric intervention have symptoms. As far as the author is aware, no simple screening tests have been validated which could reliably detect those children who should be referred to an optometrist. Until such a tool has been developed, it seems most appropriate for all children with suspected learning difficulties to receive a specialist eye examination.

The largest eye care profession in the UK is optometry. There are approximately 7000 optometrists who are trained to detect pathology, detect and treat refractive and orthoptic (binocular vision) anomalies and to dispense spectacles and contact lenses. There are about 1500 ophthalmologists who are medical specialists trained in eye examination, and medical and surgical treatment of ocular pathology. There are about 1000 orthoptists, most of whom work with ophthalmologists. Orthoptists are principally concerned with detecting and treating binocular vision anomalies. About 3500 registered dispensing opticians supply and fit spectacles and sometimes, with additional qualifications, contact lenses.

The vast majority of optometrists work in primary care, usually in city centre locations, and patients do not need a referral from a GP to see an optometrist. Few ophthalmologists work in primary care and most of the patients seeing ophthalmologists have been referred by GPs or optometrists. Most orthoptists work in hospital practice and receive the majority of their patients via an ophthalmologist. The government privatised primary eye care in the UK in 1989, with the exception of certain exempt groups, mainly children and those on very low incomes. Optometrists and ophthalmologists working in primary care can therefore still receive a fixed fee for a child's eye examination. This fee has reduced in real terms since its introduction and, although most practitioners will see patients under the NHS, only the basic eye examination is usually covered by the NHS fee. Because of the various optometric anomalies that need to be looked for in a person with reading difficulties, an eye examination of such a person usually takes about twice as long as a normal eye examination. Therefore, practitioners who have specialised in investigating children with reading difficulties almost always charge a private fee for these additional tests.

Unfortunately, there are no specific qualifications that eye care practitioners can take to indicate specialist expertise in the assessment of people with specific learning difficulties. Interest in this area seems to be high among optometrists since courses in this subject and which the Institute of Optometry has run since 1992 have been over-subscribed. In 1991 the College of Optometrists commissioned a continuing education module on dyslexia, and specific learning difficulties have been a priority for optometric continuing education and training. It is the hope of this author that the College of Optometrists will eventually create a specialist diploma to indicate expertise in this area (with proof of continuing education as a prerequisite for continued certification). In the meantime, the best method of finding eye care practitioners who have specialised in this area is by personal recommendation.

Under the 1993 Education Act parents of children with reading difficulties can request to undergo a staged process of investigation which, in the initial stages, is carried out by the school and, in later stages, by the local education authority. The culmination of this process is, in severe cases, a statement of the child's special education needs. Certain advice must be appended to this statement, including 'medical advice', and frequently this includes the description of vision as being 'normal'. It seems that commonly the basis for this assumption of normality is distance visual acuity, which is virtually irrelevant to reading performance. It is to be hoped that it will become more commonplace for the opinion of appropriately specialised eye care practitioners to be sought. Ideally, this should happen long before the stage of drawing up a statement of special educational needs.

CONCLUSION

Ocular pathology is rare in childhood and is not a major cause of reading difficulties. Poor visual acuities and refractive errors are only rarely severe enough to interfere with reading, although long-sightedness is often missed by school vision screening and can cause visual discomfort and blurred vision with much reading. People with specific reading difficulties tend, on average, to have a slightly reduced amplitude of accommodation compared with control good readers. In a few severe cases this may cause eye-strain and blur when reading. Similar problems can result from binocular inco-ordination, which also has a high prevalence in specific reading difficulties. Both these types of visual problems may need treatment with eye exercises or spectacles.

Ocular dominance is not currently thought to be one of the key issues in reading, and the Dunlop Test is widely recognised as being too unreliable for diagnostic use. The type of binocular inco-ordination that this test is thought to detect may be identified by more conventional optometric techniques. There is still considerable controversy about the role of abnormal eye movements in reading disability, although the consensus seems to be that eye movements are unlikely to hold the key to dyslexia. The claims that some people with reading difficulties have symptoms of eye-strain and perceptual distortions which are helped by coloured filters have been supported by one double-blind placebo-controlled trial. This suggests that the tints do need to be individually prescribed and a new instrument for this, the Intuitive Colorimeter, is in fairly widespread use within optometry in the UK. Many people who consult practitioners for this treatment are found to have conventional optometric (orthoptic) anomalies and these should be treated in the first instance.

There is considerable evidence for the existence of a certain type of visual sensory deficit in specific reading disability: a deficit of the transient visual system. There are no reliable clinical tests or therapies for this and it is unclear whether detection or treatment would be of any benefit. All these visual correlates of reading disability are not necessarily related to the higher-level visual perceptual skills which may be assessed in a typical psychometric evaluation.

Although there has been some success in linking several of the visual correlates of reading disability (in particular, the transient deficit and binocular inco-ordination), more work needs to be done in this area and this should also take account of the effect of attention deficit disorder. Some evidence suggests that optometric anomalies may, in some cases, contribute to a reading difficulty, but most authorities accept that phonological factors may be more important in the aetiology of reading disability. Nevertheless, it would seem prudent for children with suspected reading difficulties to be referred to an eye care practitioner who has specialised in this subject. This applies not only to children with symptoms, but also to those without. The best way of finding such a practitioner is by personal recommendation, or asking the family optometrist for referral to a practitioner who has specialised in this way. It is a cause of some concern that many children are statemented without having had a specialist detailed eye examination.

ACKNOWLEDGEMENTS

I am grateful to Anne Busby for providing typical samples of text that might be read by different age groups, so that equivalent visual acuities could be calculated. I am also grateful to the following for their comments on an earlier version of this manuscript: Arnold Wilkins, Anne Busby, and Judith Morris.

NOTES

1 Cerium Visual Technologies, Cerium Technology Park, Appledore Road, Tenterden, Kent, TN30 7DE.
2 Intuitive Overlays available from I.O.O. Marketing Ltd, 56-62 Newington Causeway, London, SE1 6DS.

122 Bruce J.W. Evans

REFERENCES

Beauchamp, G.R. (1986). Optometric vision training. *Pediatrics*, 77, 121–4.
Birnbaum, M.H. (1993). *Optometric Management of Nearpoint Disorders*. Boston: Butterworth-Heinemann.
Biscaldi, M., Fischer, B. and Aiple, F. (1994). Saccadic eye movements of dyslexic and normal reading children. *Perception*, 23, 45–64.
Bishop, D.V.M. (1989). Unfixed reference, monocular occlusion, and developmental dyslexia – a critique. *British Journal of Ophthalmology*, 73, 209–15.
Boder, E. (1971). Developmental dyslexia: prevailing diagnostic concepts and a new diagnostic approach. In H.R. Myklebust (ed.) *Progress in Learning Disabilities*. New York: Grune and Stratton, pp. 293–321.
Cornelissen, P., Bradley, L., Fowler, S. and Stein, J. (1992). Covering one eye affects how some children read. *Developmental Medicine and Child Neurology*, 34, 296–304.
Critchley, M. (1964). *Developmental dyslexia*. London: Whitefriars.
Eden, G.F., Stein, J.F., Wood, H.M. and Wood, F.B. (1994). Differences in eye movements and reading problems in dyslexic and normal children. *Vision Research*, 34, 1345–58.
Evans, B.J.W. (1993). Dyslexia: the Dunlop Test and tinted lenses. *Optometry Today*, 33, 26–30.
Evans, B.J.W. (1997). *Pickwell's Binocular Vision Anomalies*, (3rd edn). London: Butterworth.
Evans, B.J.W. and Drasdo, N. (1990). Review of ophthalmic factors in dyslexia. *Ophthalmic and Physiological Optics*, 10, 123–32.
Evans, B.J.W., Drasdo, N. and Richards I.L. (1994). Investigation of accommodative and binocular function in dyslexia. *Ophthalmic and Physiological Optics*, 14, 5–19.
Evans, B.J.W., Drasdo, N. and Richards, I.L. (1996). Dyslexia: the link with visual deficits. *Ophthalmic and Physiological Optics*, 16, 3–10.
Evans, B.J.W., Busby, A., Jeanes, R. and Wilkins, A.J. (1995). Optometric correlates of Meares-Irlen Syndrome: a matched group study. *Ophthalmic and Physiological Optics*, 15, 481–7.
Fowler, M.S. and Stein, J.F. (1983). Consideration of ocular motor dominance as an aetiological factor in some orthoptic problems. *British Orthoptic Journal*, 40, 43–5.
Irlen, H. (1991). *Reading by the Colours*. New York: Avery.
Jeanes, R., Busby, A., Martin, J. and Wilkins, A. Prolonged use of coloured overlays for classroom reading. Submitted.
Koslowe, K.C. (1991). Binocular vision, Coding tests, and classroom achievement. *Journal of Behavioral Optometry*, 2, 16–19.
Lennie, P., Trevarthen, C., Van Essen, D. and Wassle, H. (1990). Parallel processing of visual information. In L. Spillmann and J.S. Werner (eds) *Visual Perception: The Neurophysiological Foundations*. San Diego: Academic Press, pp. 163–203.
Lovegrove, W., Martin, F. and Slaghuis, W. (1986). A theoretical and experimental case for a visual deficit in specific reading disability. *Cognitive Neuropsychology*, 3, 225–67.
Meares, O. (1980). Figure/ground, brightness contrast, and reading disabilities. *Visible Language*, 14, 13–29.
Moseley, D. (1988). Dominance, reading and spelling. *Bulletin of the Audiophonology University Franche-Comté*, 4, 443–64.
Naidoo, S. (1972). *Specific Dyslexia: The Research Report of the ICAA Word Blind Centre for Dyslexic Children*. London: Pitman.
Pavlidis, G.Th. (1981). Sequencing eye movements and the early objective diagnosis of dyslexia. In G.Th. Pavlidis and T.R. Miles (eds) *Dyslexia research and its Application to Education*. Chichester: John Wiley & Sons, pp. 98–165.

Richards, I. (1994). ADHD, ADD and dyslexia. *Therapeutic Care and Education*, 3, 145–58.

Silver, L.B. (1986). Review: controversial approaches to treating learning disabilities and attention deficit disorder. *American Journal of Diseases of Childhood*, 140, 1045–52.

Stark, L.W., Giveen, S.C. and Terdiman, J.F. (1991). Specific dyslexia and eye movements. In J. Cronly-Dillon (ed.) *Vision and Visual Dysfunction*. London: Macmillan, Vol. 13, pp. 203–32.

Stein, J. and Fowler, S. (1985). The effect of monocular occlusion on visuomotor perception and reading in dyslexic children. *Lancet*, 13 July, 69–73.

Taylor, E. (1994). Hyperactivity as a special educational need. *Therapeutic Care and Education*, 3, 131–44.

Weisstein, N., Maguire, W. and Brannan, J.R. (1992). M and P pathways and the perception of figure and ground. In J. Brannan (ed.) *Applications of Parallel Processing in Vision*. Amsterdam: Elsevier Science.

Wilkins, A.J. (1995). *Visual Stress*. Oxford: Oxford University Press.

Wilkins, A.J., Evans, B.J.W., Brown, J., Busby, A., Wingfield, A.E., Jeanes, R. and Bald, J. (1994). Double-blind placebo-controlled trial of precision spectral filters in children who use coloured overlays. *Ophthalmic and Physiological Optics*, 14, 365–70.

Wilkins, A.J., Nimmo-Smith, I., Tait, A., McManus, C., Della Sala, S., Tilley, A., Arnold, K., Barrie, M. and Scott, S. (1984). A neurological basis for visual discomfort. *Brain*, 107, 989–1017.

Williams, M.C. and Lovegrove, W. (1992). Sensory and perceptual processing in reading disability. In J. Brannan (ed.) *Parallel Processing in Vision*. Amsterdam: Elsevier Science.

6 Assessment of phonological skills and their role in the development of reading and spelling skills

John P. Rack

INTRODUCTION

There is now a tremendous body of research evidence which highlights the central importance of phonological skills in learning to read and spell. Much of this evidence has been reviewed elsewhere (see e.g. Bryant and Bradley, 1985; Goswami and Bryant, 1990; Hatcher *et al.* 1994; Lundberg, 1994; Rack *et al.* 1993, and Wagner and Torgesen, 1987). This chapter will therefore be more narrow in its focus. It is divided into four main sections. In the first I will review selected studies which have investigated the relationships between phonological skills and success in reading and spelling using longitudinal designs. In doing this I will attempt to illustrate the range of tasks which have been used to assess phonological skills. The second section considers how knowledge about the importance of phonological skills might be used predictively to allow those at risk of specific reading and spelling difficulties to be identified. The third section considers, briefly, some of the studies which have looked at phonological skills training. Finally, we consider some of the remaining problems of interpretation and theoretical issues still facing us.

The focus in this chapter is on 'normal' reading and spelling development and we will touch only briefly on studies of dyslexia. However, it is worth noting at the outset that studies of developmental dyslexia converge well with longitudinal studies in highlighting the central role of phonological skills. Indeed, the Orton Dyslexia Society (Research Committee) has published a definition of dyslexia which is explicit in attributing reading failure to inefficient phonological skills.

This definition has not been accepted universally partly because it places dyslexia *within* a class of specific learning difficulties, rather than *equating* dyslexia with specific learning difficulties. Relatedly, there is a concern that some children with specific difficulties in reading and spelling may not have phonological processing difficulties; is it advisable therefore to reserve the term dyslexic for those who do? These issues will not be resolved quickly, but they need not detract us from the central finding that the *majority* of people with dyslexia experience difficulties with phonological processing and that this is very probably why they find

---

Box 6.1 Orton Dyslexia Society definition of dyslexia

Dyslexia is one of several distinct learning disabilities. It is a specific language-based disorder of constitutional origin characterised by difficulties in single-word decoding usually reflecting insufficient phonological processing abilities.

These difficulties in single-word decoding are often unexpected in relation to age and other cognitive and academic abilities; they are not the result of generalised developmental delay or sensory impairment.

Dyslexia is manifest by variable difficulties with different forms of language often including, in addition to problems in reading, a conspicuous problem with acquiring proficiency in writing and spelling.

Source: Shaywitz *et al.* (1995)

---

learning to spell and read difficult. The problems of short-term memory, naming (labelling) and word finding which are characteristic of dyslexia can also be accommodated within a phonological deficit hypothesis (e.g., Rack, 1994).

Defining dyslexia more positively in terms of a phonological processing deficit represents significant progress from the exclusionary definitions which view dyslexia as something 'unexpected' or 'inexplicable'. We do now have strong hypotheses about why dyslexic children have difficulties and this has important consequences for screening and early remediation. There are many complex issues regarding screening which will not be dealt with in this chapter, but they are considered elsewhere in this book. However, central to these more applied questions is the issue of how phonological skills are assessed and how these influence reading and spelling development. These are the very questions which have been addressed in a number of longitudinal studies and it is to these that we will turn in a moment. Before doing so it is necessary to review briefly what is meant by phonological skills.

Phonological skills may be thought of simply as word–sound processing skills: the ability to process words in terms of their sound characteristics as distinct from their meanings or their typical usage. In the context of reading and spelling development the term phonological awareness is often used. The intention here is to distinguish between implicit knowledge of the sound system – which is acquired through the processes of spoken language acquisition – and explicit awareness of the structure of the sound system – which seems necessary for reading and spelling. The term 'awareness' is unfortunate since, in common usage, it refers to a fairly clear state of knowing when, in fact, such knowledge of sound structure may be partial or only partially accessible. It is for these reasons that the term 'phonological skill' is preferred. We simply define this operationally as the ability to do tasks which involve phonological processing; it is then an empirical matter to determine whether there are important differences between tasks which may reflect, say, different levels of word–sound analysis or different levels of awareness.

LONGITUDINAL STUDIES OF THE RELATIONSHIP BETWEEN PHONOLOGICAL SKILLS AND READING DEVELOPMENT

In their landmark study, Bradley and Bryant (1983) tested a sample of 403 4 to 5 year olds who were then followed until they were aged 8 or 9 (by this time 363 children remained in the sample). Of principal interest was whether scores on the Bradley (1980; Bradley and Bryant, 1978) sound-categorization task predicted reading ability several years later. Subjects who had begun to learn to read at the start of the project were excluded. In this way, Bradley and Bryant could be sure that the sound-categorization scores were not confounded with reading ability. In the sound categorization task, subjects were given a sequence of three or four words and asked to pick the odd one out. Three types of condition were given. In the rhyming condition, all except one of the words rhymed (hit pin sit). In the alliteration condition, all except one of the words began with the same sound (sun sock see rag) and in the final sound condition all except one of the words shared the same final sound (cot hut man fit).

The question of interest concerned the relationship between children's pre-school skill in sound categorization and their later success in reading and spelling. Some of the variation among children was related to 'global' factors such as IQ and age at initial testing. After allowing for this, sound categorization accounted for between 4 and 10% of the variance in reading and between 6 and 10% of the variance in spelling. A control outcome measure was also taken (mathematics) to assess the specificity of the effects of sound categorisation. After removing the effects of extraneous factors, sound categorization accounted for between 1 and 4% of the variance in mathematics also.

An earlier longitudinal study of the role of phonological skills in reading acquisition was conducted by Helfgott (1976). Helfgott chose to test segmentation ability using a modification of the Elkonin procedure. In her modification the children were given a visual model of a three-phoneme (consonant-vowel-consonant) word comprising either three squares (for C-V-C segmentation) or a rectangle and a square (for CV-C segmentation) or a square and a rectangle (for C-VC segmentation). In the segmentation task a spoken word was presented to the subjects along with a picture cue. The subjects had to move counters into the model as they spoke the individual segments of the word. In the blending task, the experimenter moved counters, speaking the segments at the same time. Each subject's task was to blend the segments into the whole word and a picture was then shown for confirmation. Helfgott's initial sample comprised 103 kindergarten children (mean age 6).

It was found that C-V-C segmentation and blending were by far the hardest tasks with segmentation in general being harder than blending in general. Interestingly, subjects found C-VC segmentation easier than CV-C segmentation but the reverse was true for blending. However, the main question that concerns us here is the relationship between segmentation skills and later reading achievement. Helfgott (1976) only reports data for the thirty-one children who had been tested with C-V-C segmentation where a correlation of 0.72 was found between kindergarten segmentation and later reading ability. Blending correlated to a lesser degree (r = 0.49) as did mental age (r = 0.41).

Stanovich *et al.* (1984) administered ten different tests of phonological awareness to a sample of forty-nine children aged 5 to 6 years. The tasks were broken down into two main groups. Two tasks required rhyming responses: (1) Supply a rhyme to a given word; (2) choose a rhyming word for a given word (from three choices). A third task, phoneme substitution, also appeared to involve rhyming skills. In this task, children are asked to substitute the initial phoneme of a word for a specified phoneme; for example, 'what is "hat" if the first sound is changed to a "c"?' A good strategy is to think of rhymes for 'hat' until coming up with one beginning with 'c'. These phoneme substitution and rhyming tasks were the easiest; the distributions of scores were negatively skewed indicating ceiling effects. The other two groups were made up from the seven non-rhyming tasks. One of these, the phoneme deletion task, was the hardest and scores were positively skewed (approximately half the subjects scored 0). Five of the non-rhyming tasks were very similar. In these tasks the subjects are asked to identify: (1) the word (from a choice of three) that had the same initial sound as a given word; (2) the word (from a choice of three) that had the same final sound as a given word; (3) the word (from a choice of four) which had a different beginning sound to the others; (4) the word (from a choice of four) that had a different end sound to the others, and finally, (5) the word (from a choice of three) that did not begin with the same sound as the target. The remaining task was somewhat like the deletion task. The subjects were instructed to say, for example, 'cat', and then to say 'at' (that is, the word without its initial consonant); their task was to specify the missing sound.

Reading ability was assessed one year later for thirty-one of the initial sample of forty-nine. All the non-rhyming measures correlated with year end reading achievement. The best predictors of reading ability were the two tasks involving detection of the word with a different initial consonant; together, these accounted for 66% of the variance. Stanovich *et al.* (1984) concluded that the seven non-rhyming tasks were measuring the same underlying ability, an ability which turns out to be causally related to later reading success. The fact that the rhyming measures did not correlate significantly with year end reading achievement is probably due to ceiling effects – the tasks were too easy and therefore did not discriminate well.

These studies provide strong evidence for the importance of phonological skills as *predictors* of success in reading. Interpretation beyond this simple predictive level is, however, more complex. One difficulty relates to the possible confounding effects of some more general 'third' factor. For example, it may be the case that the phonologically skilled children in kindergarten are also the more intelligent children (or simply the older children in the class) and then when tested later those children are also found to be the better readers. It can be difficult to tell whether their superior reading is caused by their superior intelligence or by their superior phonological skills. More worrying is the possibility that the correlation between (early) phonological skills and (later) reading and spelling attainment is mediated by some unknown 'third' variable. This is why it is important to conduct intervention studies, as we discuss below. However, in practice, it is still useful to know about early indicators of later difficulties, and, especially where testing resources and facilities are limited, it is helpful to know which are the best early indicators.

Stanovich *et al.* (1984) found that their measure of IQ correlated 0.25 with year end reading performance. All seven of the phoneme awareness tasks correlated at higher levels (range 0.39 to 0.60) with year end reading. IQ and a standardised reading readiness test together accounted for 59% of the variance in year-end reading; two of the phonological awareness tasks together accounted for 66% of the variance, the median amount of explained variance for any two of the phonological awareness measures being 57%. Although it would have been desirable to see the increases in variance explained as variables entered on a stepwise basis, there is certainly evidence in these results for a unique contribution of phonological awareness measures to year-end reading. The correlation of 0.25 between IQ and reading tells us that 6.25% of the variance in year-end reading can be explained by variation in IQ. This figure is clearly less than the amount explained by the phonological awareness measures in combination. Thus the small effects of IQ on year-end reading achievement cannot remove all the effects of the phonological awareness measures.

A theory of reading development needs to account for relationships between variables observed in large samples of the population. But it also should have something to say about the development of skills in individuals. Indeed, it may be necessary to look at individuals or small groups in order to get the level of detail required to test specific mechanistic hypotheses. One study of this nature was done by Stuart and M. Coltheart (1988). Thirty-six children were first tested at the age of 4 years 5 months and twenty-three children remained by the time the sample had reached 8 years 5 months. Subjects were given a battery of tests of phonological skill before entering school and after one year in school; measures of reading skill, letter-sound and letter-name knowledge were given repeatedly during the first two years of the project; standardised reading tests were given at the end of each school year.

The measures of phonological skill were: rhyme production; rhyme detection; generation of the final phoneme or final syllable of an incomplete word; initial phoneme identification, and initial phoneme segmentation. These measures were all found to corrclate significantly and were combined into a composite phonological score for further analysis.

Stuart and Coltheart regressed reading age, at different points in time, on IQ scores and pre-school phonological scores simultaneously. IQ, but not phonological skill, was found to contribute to reading ability at the end of year 1; both predictor variables contributed to reading at the end of year 2 and the end of year 3; phonological score, but not IQ contributed towards reading at the end of year 4. Simply put, the results revealed a decreasing contribution of IQ and an increasing contribution of phonological skills to reading ability over the four years of the project. As pointed out by Goswami and Bryant (1990), it would have been nice to know what percentage of the variance in reading ability was uniquely related to pre-school phonological skill after controlling for differences in IQ. None the less, the reported results do demonstrate that phonological skills make a significant independent contribution to reading ability at the end of years 2 through 4. This pattern of results is interesting for, as Stuart and Coltheart (1988) point out, it suggests that general intellectual abilities influence children's initial success in reading, but progress will be limited in the longer term unless the child is phonologically skilled.

The regression analyses reported by Stuart and Coltheart are informative, but the strength of their data and argument is really to be found in the detailed qualitative analyses of reading errors. Reading errors were classified into six categories. The incidence of errors in one category showed a clear positive correlation with reading age. This type of error preserved both the beginning and end letters of the intended word; for example, *bird* read as *bad*; *Robert* as *rabbit*; *boots* as *boats*. The tendency to make errors in three other categories showed a clear negative correlation with reading age. These three error types reflected use of partial or irrelevant information (*rat-tat* as *ice-cream*; *play* as *sister*); use of letters or letter segments (*school* as *home*; *play* as *help*), and use of final letters (*hat* as *cat*; *birthday* as *Sunday*). The most frequently occurring error type reflected use of beginning letters (*cat* as *car*; *postcard* as *postman*) but the tendency to make this type of error was unrelated to reading ability. Stuart and Coltheart wish to argue that the errors associated with higher levels of reading ability should also be associated with higher levels of phonological skill. Likewise, errors associated with low levels of reading ability should be associated with low levels of phonological skill. In support of this, they found that subjects with good letter-sound knowledge tended to make more errors reflecting use of both beginning and end letters or just use of beginning letters. In general, the other three categories of errors were made more frequently by subjects with poor (or less good) letter-sound knowledge.

To chart these effects developmentally, Stuart and Coltheart classified subjects into groups on the basis of the time at which they showed some success in all of the tests of phonological skill. (They were required to know at least half of the letter sounds and be above chance or off the floor on the phonological tests.) One group never achieved these criteria for success and they were found to make a higher proportion of the 'non-phonological errors' associated with low levels of reading ability throughout the period of intensive data collecting. The other three groups all made more of the 'non-phonological errors' initially, but the proportion of 'phonological errors' gradually increased and was found to exceed the proportion of 'non-phonological errors' at almost exactly the point in time that children achieved the criterion of phonological skill. Summarising these findings, Stuart and Coltheart state:

> errors incorporating the first letter or letters of their targets, and errors incorporating the first and last letters or letter groups of their targets, began to predominate just at the point at which children were able to perform phonemic segmentation tasks and knew at least half the letters of the alphabet. If a preponderance of these kinds of errors indeed indicates phonological processing, our ideas about the role of phonological processing in beginning reading need to be radically rethought.
> (1988, p. 170)

It is interesting to note that there were large individual differences in Stuart and Coltheart's sample in the age at which subjects reached the criterion of 'phonologically able'. One group of five subjects showed this pattern at roughly age 5.25 years, some four months after they entered school. At the other extreme, one group (eleven subjects) had not achieved a degree of phonological skill and were still making a larger proportion of 'non-phonological' errors some two or three months into their second school year.

PREDICTING READING DIFFICULTIES

Mann (1984) looked at groups of good (N = 10), average (N = 22) and poor (N = 12) readers defined by their first grade abilities in reading. These groups did not differ on measures of verbal IQ nor in age when in kindergarten but they did differ on measures of letter-naming speed and verbal short-term memory taken in kindergarten. The subjects had also been given two more direct tests of phonological skill in kindergarten in which they were required to reverse the order of (1) syllables and (2) phonemes in auditorily presented nonwords. The phoneme task stimuli contained two phonemes, the syllable task stimuli contained two or three syllables.

The groups were not differentiated by the syllable reversal task. This appears to be because all three groups had average scores in excess of 14 out of 16 – close to the test ceiling. The phoneme task did differentiate between good and poor readers very reliably. The mean score was 0 out of 16 for the poor readers compared to 5.2 for the good readers. Kindergarten scores on the phoneme reversal test correlated at 0.75 with first grade reading ability, a coefficient that is particularly high considering that the measures were taken a year apart and given customary levels of unreliability. Corresponding correlations for letter-naming speed, letter-naming errors and verbal memory were reported as –0.42, –0.52 and 0.56 respectively. Syllable reversal did not correlate significantly with first grade reading, probably because of the ceiling effect already noted.

Ellis and Large (1987) identified three groups, each of five children, on the basis of their reading abilities at age 8: group A had high IQ and low reading ability; group B had high IQ and high reading ability, and, group C had low IQ and low reading ability. We should note that the terms low and high were relative; the low reading children were actually around age appropriate levels. The children had been given a battery of forty-four tests at ages 4, 5 and 6 and a complex analysis of variance was conducted in order to see what factors discriminated between the groups. The test profiles were different for the three groups as indicated by a group-by-test interaction. The overall scores of the group B ('normal') children tended to increase over the three measurement points whereas the overall scores of the two poor reader groups went down. (Note: the scores were relative and not absolute.) The test profiles were similar for the three groups over the three years in the majority of cases, as indicated by nonsignificant group-by-test interactions. However, for some of the tests there was a significant group-by-year interaction resulting from the fact that the poor readers declined (relatively) whereas the 'normal' readers tended to increase over the years. The tests that showed this pattern of divergent development were all the reading tests, vocabulary, spelling, auditory word span, letter search, WISC coding and block design, and phoneme segmentation. In the case of the reading tests this is not too surprising since the groups must all, at some stage, have been matched at a level of *no reading ability* although they are defined in terms of differences in their current abilities. As Ellis and Large note, the other tasks that show this divergent development must be especially related to reading ability. We cannot, however, tell the nature and direction of this relationship from these data. It is interesting to note the association of these skills with reading across development, but we cannot say which skills influence reading and which are influenced by reading.

Ellis and Large (1987) compared the three groups to determine what factors distinguish normal from specifically disabled readers, what factors distinguish normal from generally backward readers, and finally, what factors distinguish between the two poor reader groups. Where this study is unusual is that the discriminators were obtained one, two and three years before the criterion variable was obtained. In answer to the first of these questions, it was found that specifically disabled readers were worse than the 'normals' on measures of: rhyme generation and detecting the odd one out on the basis of rhyme; two measures of vocabulary, and, auditory digit span. The generally backward group differed from the normals 'in almost every way' (ibid. p. 14). Forty of the forty-four tests were significant discriminators. This, Ellis and Large argue, demonstrates the need for IQ control in studies of reading ability. Without this control, any ability that one may choose will discriminate between the groups. The final comparison between the two poor reader groups revealed advantages for the specifically disabled group on measures of visual processing. These tests included a letter-search test and a visual closure test as well as the performance scales from the WISC (although the results on Wechsler scales would seem to reflect group definition). These results are important as these contrasts have rarely been made. However, as we noted before, the same problem applies. Although the results indicate a causal role for the rhyme, vocabulary and memory measures, we cannot tell the direction of causation. Ellis and Large note that one vocabulary measure actually involves reading so here we would expect reading ability differences to emerge.

Scarborough (1989) reported data from a longitudinal study that was primarily concerned with the prediction of reading disability. This study is interesting because Scarborough's sample consisted of thirty-eight children who came from families with a history of reading problems and twenty-eight children from families with no reported history of reading problems. Parents were also given a battery of tests which enabled Scarborough to look at familial factors as well as individual difference factors as predictors of reading disability.

The sample of sixty-six children was tested at age 5 (by which time eighteen had begun kindergarten) and again at age 8. Pre-school tests included measures of general cognitive ability, measures of language (syntax, naming), visual discrimination, story comprehension, word reading, and sounds and letters from the Stanford Early School Achievement Test. The sounds and letters test comprised letter identification (eight items), letter-sound correspondence (sixteen items) and phonological awareness (twenty items), the latter involving matching of spoken words on the basis of rhymes or initial phonemes. The children were given a full assessment of cognitive and reading skills at age 8.

Regression analyses were conducted on the sample of children with no family history of reading problems in order to determine the expected reading cluster score from full-scale IQ and socioeconomic status. Subjects were then classified as specifically reading disabled if their expected reading was two Standard errors below expectations (sixteen subjects) or low achievers if their reading was a year or more behind age expectations (seven children). In this sample, all the specifically reading disabled children were also low achievers. The remaining forty-three children were classified as normal. The important question then became: what factors distinguished these groups three years earlier before they had begun to read? The normal group was superior to both poor reader groups on the Boston Naming Test and superior to the specifically reading disabled group on the sounds and letters test. No other differences were found on the pre-school measures. These results therefore show that pre-school differences on a composite measure of letter-knowledge, letter-sound correspondence and phonological skill are causally related to specific reading difficulties. This was supported by an analysis of the whole sample in which the Boston Naming Test ($r = 0.32$) and the Sounds and Letters test ($r = 0.31$) were the only pre-school measures to correlate with 2nd grade reading after partialing out the effects of IQ.

Scarborough's data also revealed that familial factors were highly predictive of later reading disability. Parents were classified in a similar way to the children as specifically reading disabled, low ability or normal. Using these classifications, fifty out of sixty-two children (80.6%) were correctly predicted to be good or poor readers. It was also interesting that grade 2 reading was predicted very strongly by family history when another family member had a measured specific disability (36% of the variance). Self-report family history was a weaker, but still substantial predictor of grade 2 reading (17% of variance). Further discussion of familial risk factors can be found in Olson *et al.*, (1990) and Pennington (1990).

TRAINING STUDIES

As already noted, intervention studies are important in helping to address questions about causality. Only when subjects are randomly assigned to experimental and control groups and given different 'treatments' can we be confident about claiming a causal influence (see Bryant and Bradley, 1985 for more discussion). There is, of course, still the potential for disagreement over what aspect of the intervention has produced the experimental effect and usually, therefore, there need to be several different 'experimental' interventions. Such designs then come close to studies contrasting the effectiveness of different approaches and these have obvious practical implications. Further discussion of intervention studies can be found in chapters by Hatcher (1994); Lundberg (1994), and Tunmer (1994). We review two of the earliest and most influential studies and a more recent extension from these.

Lundberg *et al.* (1988) conducted a longitudinal intervention study to assess the impact of phonological awareness training on later reading and spelling development. Two hundred-and-thirty-five Danish kindergarten children were given the phonological awareness training, and 155 children served as controls. The two groups were geographically separated but matched in terms of socioeconomic background. The separation was intentional in order to avoid aspects of the intervention programme being taken up by control schools. The school system in Denmark is said to be fairly homogeneous and therefore the geographical separation was thought not to be a problem in terms of the generality of the findings.

All the subjects were given a battery of linguistic and metalinguistic tests at the beginning and end of their kindergarten year (September to May). In the intervening period, the experimental group received daily 15–20-minute training sessions designed to promote phonological awareness. The control group was given no special attention but followed the normal pre-school activity programme. Neither group was given any direct training in reading. Using this design, it was possible to assess the effects of 'pure' phonological awareness training. In most other cases, phonological awareness training occurs alongside reading development and the outcome may well be a function of the interaction of these activities.

Lundberg *et al.* needed first to establish that they could alter children's phonological abilities without the support of written materials. The training programme consisted of a carefully constructed series of games and exercises. This began with simple listening games and rhyming games; moving through segmentation of sentences into words, words into syllables; and on to segmentation of initial phonemes and finally phonemes within words. The experimental group did indeed outscore the control group on the post-test measures of phonological abilities despite the fact that the control group had slightly (but significantly) higher scores on the pre-test. In contrast, general language comprehension and letter knowledge increased equally for both groups over the training period. The effects of phonological skills training were thus highly specific to the phonological domain. This is important since the experimental group might have shown greater improvements across the range of tests simply because they received special attention and the control group did not. Phonological skill was also assessed three months into the first year in school using a different set of tasks. Differences favouring the experimental group remained, indicating that the effects of training were persistent.

The effect of training was observed on a composite measure of seven phonological tests. Confirmatory factor analysis showed that a two-factor structure provided a good fit to the data. One factor consisted of the three tasks requiring a phonemic segmentation and another consisted of the three measures requiring word and syllable segmentation. The two factors were moderately correlated at 0.40. Rhyming ability was not entered into this analysis since only one measure was available. Looking at the changes in these three abilities (rhyme, phoneme segmentation and syllable/word segmentation) revealed that the most dramatic changes occurred on the phoneme-segmentation tasks. The trained group did improve significantly more than the control group on the other two measures but the differences were modest in comparison to the effects of training on phoneme-segmentation skills. The lack of a strong effect for rhyming may be due to the fact that both groups were already fairly good at rhyming before the intervention.

At the beginning of the training period, only one person in the experimental group and two in the control group had any reading ability as assessed by a crude screening test. By the end of training this number had not changed for the control group, but fifteen of the trained group now showed some reading ability. Lundberg *et al.* (1988) speculate that this might be one of the effects of the training programme. The more permanent effects of the phonemic awareness training were investigated by measuring reading and spelling some seven months into the children's first year in school and again in the middle of their second year. The experimental group outscored the control group on reading and spelling in grades 1 and 2. The difference in reading in grade 1 was not significant on a simple test; differences in grade 2 were significantly larger. In contrast, the control group outscored the experimental group on a test of mathematics given in the first year. This important control test indicates that the training had not had a global effect on all school subjects but it had specifically affected the targeted skills of reading and spelling.

A second part of Bradley and Bryant's (1983) longitudinal prediction study involved an intervention programme on a group of sixty-five children from the original sample who had poor sound categorisation skills (Bradley and Bryant, 1985). The children were divided into four groups on the basis of the training that they were given: (1) sound categorisation training; (2) sound categorisation training supported by concrete materials (plastic letters); (3) semantic categorisation training; (4) no treatment control. The subjects were initially matched on the basis of age, sex, sound categorisation ability and IQ. The training sessions were given weekly over a period of two years. The children were trained individually and progressed through the programme at their own rates.

After two years, the effects of training were evaluated by standardised tests of reading and spelling. Sound categorisation training seemed to have a beneficial effect on later reading and spelling, but it was only significantly better than the semantic categorisation control when plastic letters were also used as part of the training. The group which received sound categorisation supplemented by concrete materials (group 2) were nine months ahead of the control group (group 3) in reading and seventeen months ahead in spelling. The group which had sound categorisation without the plastic letters (group 1) were four months ahead of the control group in both reading and spelling which were not significant differences. Groups 1, 2 and 3 did not differ in the progress made in mathematics, indicating a specific role for the sound categorisation training.

Hatcher *et al.* (1994) considered directly the possibility that phonological training which is linked to reading experience might be more effective than phonological skills training alone or reading instruction alone. This hypothesis – which they termed the phonological linkage hypothesis – is based on Bradley and Bryant's finding that the significant gains in reading come from training in sound categorisation with the use of plastic letters. Hatcher *et al.* conducted a county-wide screening programme to identify 7–year-old children who were experiencing difficulties learning to read, but who were not being given any additional teaching programmes. The subjects were assigned to four matched groups and received either no training, 'reading alone', 'phonological skills training alone' or 'reading with phonology'. The 'phonology alone' group had the greatest exposure to phonological activities and did make the most progress on phonological tasks. However, the 'reading alone' group, which received the greatest exposure to printed materials, were outperformed in reading and spelling by the 'reading-with-phonology' group. Thus the linked training of reading with phonology produced the greatest gains in reading and spelling.

Hatcher *et al.*'s (1994) study is consistent with a number of other studies which have looked at the effectiveness of teaching programmes. For example, Iversen and Tunmer (1993) compared the reading recovery programme (Clay, 1985) with a modified version which included explicit training in phonological recoding (using procedures similar to those used by Bradley and Bryant, 1985). The dependent variable in this study was the number of lessons required to reach a set of criteria. Both groups reached the standards set, but the group which had been given the phonological training did so significantly sooner; the standard reading recovery was found to be 37% less efficient.

THEORETICAL AND PRACTICAL ISSUES

Direction of causality

Hatcher *et al.*'s (1994) linkage hypothesis has brought us some way from the simple notion of skills at one time predicting success in reading and in spelling at another. Indeed, it has long been claimed that there is a bi-directional relationship in development such that phonological skills influence the acquisition of reading skills, but reading ability also influences phonological skills. Support for this view comes from studies of non-literate adults who find segmenting words by phonemes very difficult (see Morais, (1991) for a review). Thus it seems that reading ability and phonological skills are interdependent (or reciprocal) during development – each being influenced by the other skill.

In direct tests of their 'reciprocal causation hypothesis', Perfetti *et al.* (1987) gave first grade children tests of nonword reading, phoneme deletion and phoneme synthesis on four separate occasions during the school term (at intervals of seven, eleven and thirteen weeks). One group of children was taught letter–sound relationships as part of their reading instruction (the 'direct code group'), a second group was given little or no phonics-based instruction (the basal groups). The repeated testing of phonological skills and nonword reading allowed the use of time-lagged correlations to investigate how the two skills were causally related.

Performance on the synthesis task predicted later nonword reading performance for both groups, although the timing was different. The basal group showed the strongest relationship between synthesis ability after eight weeks and nonword reading ability after nineteen weeks. For the direct code group, the strongest association was between synthesis at nineteen weeks and non-word reading at thirty-two weeks. For phoneme deletion, the predictive relationships were at the same times for both groups. However, in this case, it was nonword reading that predicted later success in the deletion task. In the basal groups, deletion skill went on to become a predictor of final nonword reading, but this was not true for the direct code group.

These results demonstrate how measures of phonological skill and reading skill are interdependent; not only does phonological skill influence reading skill, but reading skill also influences phonological skill. Perfetti *et al.* (1987) refer to this as a reciprocal relationship. The finding that the strength of relationships between the variables is different at different testing times indicates that changes over time are not linear. It is therefore important to test repeatedly over a time period if the critical relationships are to be discovered.

Different levels of phonological skill?

A variant of the reciprocal causation argument was put forward by Goswami and Bryant (1990). They argued that awareness of the onset-rime division (see Treiman, 1985) is the crucial factor in learning to read; awareness of smaller speech segments (phonemes) arises at least partly as a consequence of learning to read. One task that taps young children's sensitivity to rimes is rhyme detection; for example, asking children to pick the odd (non-rhyming) word out from a group of four spoken words (Bradley and Bryant, 1978). As we have seen, this task can be performed quite adequately by many 4 and 5 year olds before they have learned to read, and is highly predictive of their later success in reading and spelling.

Bryant *et al.* (1990) conducted a study to determine whether phoneme awareness was a result of reading ability, whether it was a co-predictor of reading ability or whether it was a necessary intermediary between rhyming and reading ability. To address these questions Bryant *et al.* studied a group of sixty-four children when they were approximately 4.5, 5.5, 6 and 6.5 years of age. The children were given tests of rhyme and alliteration at the first two testing times. At 4.5 years a modification of the Bradley (1980) oddity task was used. In the new version, three pictures were used and the child's task was to choose the one that did not rhyme with the other two or, in the alliteration task, the one that began with a different sound to the other two. At 5.5 years the children were given a more difficult rhyme and alliteration task. In this task they were shown three pictures such as *coat*, *coach* and *boat*; they were then asked to say which one began with the same sound as *code* and ended with the same sound as *rote* (answer: *coat*). At 5.5 years the children were given a test requiring them to delete the initial phoneme from either the beginning or the end of a word. At 6 years the children were given a phoneme tapping task in which they had to tap out the number of phonemes in 1-, 2- and 3-phoneme words. When the children were approximately 6.5 years old they were given measures of reading, spelling and arithmetic.

Multiple regression analyses were used to assess the causal relations between the various measures. First, Bryant *et al.* (1990) wanted to see what factors predicted phoneme segmentation ability, once extraneous factors (such as IQ and age at testing) had been taken into account. The rhyme and alliteration task at 5.5 years accounted for variance in phoneme segmentation even after these additional controls. Eleven percent of the variance in phoneme tapping, and 8% and 5% of the variance in first- and end-sound deletion, respectively, was explained by the rhyme/alliteration measure. The rhyme and alliteration oddity tasks given at the first testing time accounted for variance in first-sound deletion (13% and 9% respectively). Alliteration also accounted for additional variance in end-sound deletion.

The second question that Bryant *et al.* asked concerned the contributions of the various predictor measures to reading, spelling and arithmetic. Once again, extraneous variables were controlled for by entering them in the regression equation before entering the segmentation measures. The rhyme/alliteration test given at 5.5 years accounted for an additional 7% of the variance in Schonell spelling and 9% in Schonell reading. The rhyme oddity task at 4.5 accounted for 5% and 9% additional variance in spelling and reading. Alliteration at 4.5 accounted for even more variance in spelling and reading (11% and 17%). However, this measure also accounted for significant variance in mathematics (5%). Phoneme tapping suffered from a similar problem, accounting for more variance in maths (8%) than in spelling (5%) and reading (4%). Deletion of an initial phoneme accounted for significant variance in spelling (5%) and reading (8%) but not mathematics. Deletion of a final phoneme accounted for variance only in reading (3%).

Overall, the phoneme segmentation measures predicted reading and spelling to a lesser extent (median 4% unique variance) than did the rhyme and alliteration measures (median 9%). It was therefore not too surprising that rhyme and alliteration were found to make independent contributions to reading and spelling scores even after the phoneme segmentation measures were entered into the equation. After entering initial phoneme deletion or final phoneme deletion or phoneme tapping the median variance still explained by the rhyme and alliteration measures was 4%, 8% and 7% respectively. The only exception to this pattern was for the rhyme oddity measure given at 4.5 years. When initial phoneme deletion was entered as the penultimate step, rhyme oddity did not make a significant contribution to spelling ability. Rhyme oddity did contribute significantly to spelling when the other two phoneme segmentation measures were entered in penultimate steps.

What these analyses suggest is that rhyme exerts a double influence on reading ability. It has one influence that is mediated by phoneme awareness and a second direct influence. In addition, they suggest that phoneme awareness is not simply a product of reading ability; some of the variance in phoneme awareness comes from rhyme.

A couple of reservations need to be noted about the interpretation of this study. First, no data about the children's reading are available at the earlier points in time when segmentation ability was measured. Thus we do not know how much the children's measures of phoneme segmentation at 5.5 and 6 years were confounded with reading ability. For example, the children who were good at phoneme segmentation at these points in time might also be the children who have progressed most in reading. Their phoneme segmentation skills might be products of their reading skills which could explain why they turn out to be predictive of later reading. It is also just possible that rhyme ability at 4.5 and 5.5 years were influenced by children's reading levels. While we know that individual differences in rhyme exist before reading, we do not know that rhyming ability is uninfluenced by reading ability. A second reservation concerns the amalgamation of rhyme and alliteration. One might just as well argue that alliteration and initial phoneme deletion should be grouped together. Bryant *et al.* have not established that their distinction between types of phonological segmentation skill is valid. Finally, it is unfortunate that the children were never given tests of rhyme and of phoneme-segmentation at the same time. So we do not know, for example, whether phoneme deletion at 5.5 years might have been more predictive of later reading than was rhyme at 5.5 years.

Issues in assessment

We have seen that it is difficult to assess phonological skills in isolation. One reason for this is that phonological skills are influenced by reading and spelling ability (and vice versa). Second, phonological skills have to be assessed within some 'carrier task' or vehicle. The challenge is to find a task which is accessible (which participants can understand), which discriminates between participants (which is not too easy or too hard) and does not introduce extraneous demands. Bradley and Bryant's (1978) sound categorisation task is one which some have suggested introduced additional short-term memory demands (see Wagner and Torgesen, 1987 and Rack *et al.* 1993 for further discussion). It could be argued that a task

140 *John P. Rack*

such as phoneme deletion places demands on a working memory system over and above its demands on segmentation or sound-analysis skills. Clearly, a basic minimum level of 'conceptual ability' is needed to understand the often complex instructions in many tasks.

Researchers attempt to control for these additional factors by entering all other predictor variables into the regression equation before entering the measures of phonological skill. So, for example, a score on a test of phonological skill may partly reflect general conceptual abilities. If a measure of conceptual ability (IQ) is entered into the equation first, then any additional variation which is explained by the measure of phonological skills is picking up on something which is unrelated to IQ. This procedure is fine in research when the unit of analysis is the sample, but it is another matter to interpret an *individual's* result on a test of phonological skills. This certainly cannot be done in isolation and so an assessment of phonological skills needs to be conducted alongside a broader cognitive assessment. In the absence of fully standardised tests which would support a statistical analysis of discrepancies, interpretation depends on knowledge of and experience in the use of tests with different age and ability groups. This situation is likely to change in the next few years in the UK as tests of phonological skills become developed commercially, but as yet the practitioner must rely on experience and be guided by the sorts of research findings presented in this chapter.

CONCLUSION

In this chapter, I have reviewed a number of studies in some detail which I believed was necessary in order to illustrate the complexity of the issues involved. Yet a number of quite simple, practically relevant findings have emerged. First, it is possible to measure, at age 4.5 to 5 years, abilities which are important for the successful development of reading and spelling skills. Second, measures of phonological skill predict reading and spelling outcomes more strongly than do measures of general intellectual ability. Third, groups of children who are later found to be poor readers can be distinguished (statistically) from those who read without difficulty: measures of phonological skill are the most consistent discriminators. Fourth, intervention that links training of phonological skills with reading experience is more effective than an approach based mainly on exposure to reading materials. Fifth and finally, children whose phonological skills predispose them to difficulties do respond (differentially) to training that links phonological skills with print.

ACKNOWLEDGEMENT

Preparation of this paper was supported by Grant SPG 8920217 from the Tri-Council Initiative in Cognitive Science to C. Hulme and M.J. Snowling.

REFERENCES

Bradley, L.L. (1980). *Assessing Reading Difficulties*. London: Macmillan Educational.

Bradley, L.L. and Bryant, P. (1978). Difficulties in auditory organization as a possible cause of reading backwardness. *Nature*, 271, 746–7.

Bradley, L.L. and Bryant, P.E. (1983). Categorizing sounds and learning to read: a causal connexion. *Nature*, 301, 419.

Bradley, L.L. and Bryant, P.E. (1985). *Rhyme and Reason in Reading and Spelling*. Ann Arbor: University of Michigan Press.

Bryant, P.E., and Bradley, L.L. (1985). *Children's Reading Problems*. Oxford: Blackwell.

Bryant, P.E., MacLean, M., Bradley, L.L. and Crossland, J. (1990). Rhyme and alliteration, phoneme detection, and learning to read. *Developmental Psychology*, 26, 429–38.

Clay, M. (1985). *The Early Detection of Reading Difficulties*. Auckland: Heinemann.

Ellis, N.C. and Large, B. (1987). The development of reading ability: as you seek so shall you find. *British Journal of Psychology*, 78, 1–28.

Goswami, U. and Bryant, P.E. (1990). *Phonological Skills and Learning to Read*. London: LEA.

Hatcher, P. (1994). An integrated approach to encouraging the development of phonological awareness, reading and writing. In C. Hulme and M.J. Snowling (eds) *Reading Development and Dyslexia*. London: Whurr.

Hatcher, P., Hulme, C. and Ellis, A.W. (1994). Ameliorating early reading failure by integrating the teaching of reading and phonological skills: the phonological linkage hypothesis. *Child Development*, 65, 41–57.

Helfgott, J.A. (1976). Phonemic segmentation and blending skills of kindergarten children: implications for beginning reading acquisition. *Contemporary Educational Psychology*, 1, 157–69.

Iversen, S. and Tunmer, W.E. (1993). Phonological processing skills and the reading recovery program. *Journal of Educational Psychology*, 85, 112–26.

Liberman, I.Y., Shankweiler, D., Fischer, W.F. and Carter, B. (1974). Reading and the awareness of linguistic segments. *Journal of Experimental Child Psychology*, 18, 201–12.

Lundberg, I. (1994). Reading difficulties can be predicted and prevented: a Scandinavian perspective on phonological awareness and reading. In C. Hulme and M.J. Snowling (eds), *Reading Development and Dyslexia*. London: Whurr.

Lundberg, I. Frost, J., and Peterson, O. (1988). Effects of an extensive program for stimulating phonological awareness in preschool children. *Reading Research Quarterly*, 23, 263–84.

Lundberg, I. Olofson, A. and Wall, S. (1980). Reading and spelling skills in the first school years predicted from phonemic awareness skills in kindergarten. *Scandinavian Journal of Psychology*, 21, 159–73.

Mann, V.A. (1984). Reading skill and language skill. *Developmental Review*, 4, 1–15.

Morais, J. (1991). Metaphonological abilities and literacy. In M.J. Snowling and M. Thompson (eds) *Dyslexia: Integrating Theory and Practice*. London: Whurr.

Olson, R.K., Wise, B., Conners, F.A., and Rack, J.P. (1990). Organization, heritability, and remediation of component word recognition and language skills in disabled readers. In T.H. Carr and B.A. Levy (eds) *Reading and its Development: Component Skills Approaches*. New York: Academic Press.

Pennington, B.F. (1990). *Diagnosing Learning Disabilities*. New York: Guilford Press.

Perfetti, C.A., Beck, I., Bell, L.C. and Hughes, C. (1987). Phonemic knowledge and learning to read are reciprocal: a longitudinal study of first grade children. *Merrill Palmer Quarterly*, 33, 283–319.

Rack, J.P. (1994). Dyslexia: the phonological deficit hypothesis. In A. Fawcett and R. Nicolson (eds) *Dyslexia in Children: Multi-disciplinary Perspectives*. Harvester Wheatsheaf.

Rack, J.P, Hulme, C. and Snowling, M.J. (1993). Learning to read: a theoretical synthesis. In H. Reese (ed.) *Advances in Child Development and Behaviour* (Vol. 24). New York: Academic Press.

Scarborough, H.S. (1989). Prediction of reading disability from familial and individual differences. *Journal of Educational Psychology*, 81, 101–8.

Shaywitz, B.A., Fletcher, J.M. and Shaywitz, S.E. (1995). Defining and classifying learning disabilities and attention-deficit/hyperactivity disorder. *Journal of Child Neurology*, 10(1), 550–7.

Stanovich, K.E. (1988). Explaining the differences between the dyslexic and the garden-variety poor reader: the phonological-core variable-difference model. *Journal of Learning Disabilities*, 21, 590–612.

Stanovich, K.E., Cunningham, A E., and Cramer, B.B. (1984). Assessing phonological skills in kindergarten children: issues of task comparability. *Journal of Experimental Child Psychology*, 38, 175–90.

Stuart, M. and Coltheart, M. (1988). Does reading develop in a sequence of stages? *Cognition*, 30, 139–81.

Treiman, R. (1985). Onsets and rimes as units of spoken syllables: evidence from children. *Journal of Experimental Child Psychology*, 39, 161–81.

Tunmer, W.E. (1994). Phonological processing skills and reading remediation. In C. Hulme and M.J. Snowling (eds) *Reading Development and Dyslexia*. London: Whurr.

Wagner, R.K. and Torgesen, J.K. (1987). The nature of phonological processing and its causal role in the acquisition of reading skills. *Psychological Bulletin*, 101(2), 192–212.

7 Assessment of memory and reading

by John R. Beech

INTRODUCTION

Difficulties in learning to read arise when trying to extract the meaning of text from print. Difficulties in spelling occur when writing or typing text to express what the writer is trying to communicate. A first guess from the armchair would be that such difficulties are due to a problem with memory somewhere along the line, or as a second guess, a problem with operations performed on that stored information.

This chapter will begin with a discussion of some basic concepts that are relevant to making an assessment of the role of memory in reading problems. There is a well-established connection between problems in being able to retain sequences of verbal information and being able to read (see e.g. reviews by Baddeley, 1986; Brady, 1986; Jorm, 1983; Wagner and Torgesen, 1987). An examination of this association needs to assess if problems in memory are causally related to those in reading. The main areas of interest are (1) in the use and retention of phonological representations while using phonics; (2) in the retention of visual or orthographic codes for the development of reading vocabulary, and (3) in working memory as part of the process of reading comprehension. However, this last aspect is left principally to Chapter 9 on assessing reading comprehension. I will concentrate mainly on the role of memory in the use of phonics. Later I will examine the issue of the causal relationships between memory and reading and the actual importance of memory in relation to other factors affecting reading performance. I will also examine comparisons between verbal and visual memory. In the last section I will look at the ways in which memory can be measured as part of an overall reading assessment. First, I will examine and define the important concepts. Assessment invariably comes with a bundle of theoretical assumptions that are used as a basis for assessing data, and assessing memory as part of the reading process is no exception.

SOME BASIC CONCEPTS

It is as well to bear in mind that there are disagreements between theorists on many of the following conceptual issues. Perhaps there is none more controversial than the role of intelligence in assessment, which is discussed in more detail in Chapter 1. Many assessments of reading of individual children refer to the child's reading in relation to his or her potential reading given his or her underlying intelligence. The most widely used test is the Wechsler Intelligence Scale for Children (WISC). At present, most testers should have moved over from using the revised form (WISC-R) to the third form (WISC-III).

There are three tests within the WISC that are overtly testing short-term memory: digit span, mental arithmetic and coding. Digit span, which will be examined in more detail later, is testing the number of digits that can be retained in memory and repeated forwards or backwards without error; the second, mental arithmetic, requires the retention of information within a question while answering it. For instance, 'If you buy two dozen pencils at 45 pence a dozen, how much change should you get back from £1?' Coding, the third memory task, is about referring to a key of numbers and retaining a representation of an abstract symbol (such as an upside down T), copying it down as quickly as possible and then going on to the next one in sequence within a set period. These all require the retention of information; two of these need to retain verbal information (digit span and arithmetic) and the other needs visual information (coding), but of course, they require other related skills as well.

Some practitioners prefer to exclude these three sub-tests when making overall estimates of intelligence. As there is a known association between below-potential reading and performance on such memory tests, the intelligence of poor readers could be underestimated, they would reason. However, the WORD test provides expected scores, based on the full-scale intelligence score on WISC-III, for basic reading (reading words in isolation), reading comprehension and spelling and levels of significant difference between obtained and expected performance. Therefore, it is probably unnecessary to exclude tests sensitive to short-term memory (digit span and mental arithmetic) as part of the estimate of intelligence, because the norms have included children of all abilities. For any measured level of full-score intelligence the tester can look up the margin of difference between actual reading or spelling performance and see if it is significantly greater than would be expected at the 1% or 5% level. In practice this will mean that some children will be found to be significantly worse in reading than would be expected, even though they have a poor memory performance on the intelligence test. Their intelligence in the rest of the subcomponents will be sufficiently high to indicate that their reading is significantly worse than would be expected. Other children who this time do not have problems in memory will also be found to have significant problems in reading.

The term 'short-term memory' has a long and respectable history and is generally considered to be about being able to retain information for a brief period of time. This concept used to be couched in terms of information being retained in a 'buffer' (a term borrowed from computing concepts) or a holding store. At present, it might be more likely to be conceptualised in terms of latency of neural firing. This process can involve retention of phonemes or units of orthography during listening or reading. The typical paradigm in early work would be to present a list of items (such as random words) and the list would usually stop unexpectedly with the requirement for as many items to be recalled as possible in any order. Information is considered to decay over a fairly short period of time under these conditions, but the time course varies according to the type of modality (e.g. visual, auditory, tactual, etc.), the depth of initial processing, the extent of interference during retention, and so on. The information in short-term memory can resist decay if it is restructured by rehearsal or some other strategy, such as associating items with something already stored in memory.

The short-term memory span task is slightly different. Verbal information (e.g. digits or pronounceable nonwords) is presented and when presentation finishes recall is immediate and is only scored correct if it is in the correct sequence. Sometimes it is called a 'serial recall' task as the intactness of the sequence is important. This is usually the sort of task that is used to assess memory impairment and its relationship with reading.

Another type of memory that also operates in the short term is called 'working memory', which involves retaining a short sequence of information while having to perform some kind of conceptual task. The memory load typically impairs performance on the conceptual task. The term 'working memory' now has a broader meaning to encompass the idea that information is being processed while being held. This definition is unclear on the point whether this stored information needs to be the same or entirely different from the information being processed.

Baddeley and Hitch's working memory model (Baddeley and Hitch, 1974) proposed a central executive and two slave systems. The first slave system is an articulatory loop which circulates phonemic information. Information decays and has to be reactivated by being articulated; if it is not then the traces soon die away. The ability to retain such information will rely on the time for information to fade and the rate at which it can be articulated. For instance, longer words take longer to articulate and span for these will therefore be shorter (e.g Baddeley *et al.*, 1975). The second slave component is the visuospatial sketch pad, which by analogy is equipped to retain visual information in the short term.

Sublexical processes in reading (meaning phonic processes and/or analysis of groups of graphemes) involve working memory because phonological information has to be retained (or articulated, perhaps). At the same time conceptual resources are required to amalgamate or process this information and to decide which word from vocabulary is appropriate. Reading by searching for analogous words within words would require similar demands on working memory. There is evidence from Swanson (1994) of a clear distinction between short-term memory and working memory for both the normally achieving and the learning disabled (defined as below the twenty-fifth percentile in reading, but with intelligence in the normal range). Both working memory and short-term memory for the problem readers were important predictors of reading comprehension, but working memory made the most important contribution to reading recognition. For those without reading problems, working memory was more important than short-term memory for reading recognition and comprehension. The two types of memory make distinctive contributions. Although working memory was the better predictor of reading recognition, it only accounted for 13% and 5% of the variance, for the normal and the learning disabled respectively. Swanson suggests that the important source of the difference between the two types of memory is that short-term memory is a passive storage system, whereas working memory involves an interaction between verbal processes and storage demands.

What do we call the sort of verbal short-term memory that would be involved in the processes of learning to read? Terms such as 'short-term memory' and 'working memory' would be quite useful descriptions of what is happening in the sublexical process. However, in practice many investigators use the term 'phonological coding' or 'phonological memory' as umbrella terms for both the phonological analysis of information and for the retention of such information. There are times when it would be better to refer to the component skills of phonology (e.g. blending, synthesis, retention, articulation).

SHORT-TERM MEMORY AND PHONICS: A THEORETICAL PERSPECTIVE

The dual-route view of reading development proposes on the one hand lexical development, involving the build up of sight vocabulary, and on the other a sublexical (or phonics) route, including among other things letter–sound translation. From this view, a short-term verbal memory problem would be considered mainly to be connected with the sublexical route rather than the lexical. In other words, sublexical processes are involved in decoding unfamiliar, or vaguely familiar, words; they include translating letters to sounds, *retaining these sounds*, performing a blending operation, and then deciding if the resulting phonological code is appropriate in the preceding context.

There is a problem here, as another research finding is that there is a linear relationship between memory span and articulation rate. If articulation rate is the crucial link between memory span and phonology, it is difficult to see how articulation rate can have a role to play in sub-lexical processes. Perhaps it is not all that important; and this is why when comparing the two (memory and phonology) memory is considerably less effective as a causal factor in subsequent reading development. There will be more discussion of this later.

Thus one important question for the assessor of reading is this: does having a problem with short-term retention of the sequence of verbal information form a crucially important part in reading development? Could it be the case that such a problem is not really to do with retention at all, but concerns other phonological processes? If this second alternative were the case, it would not really be necessary to make an assessment of memory as part of the evaluation of reading. On the other hand, if problems in phonemic memory are of causal significance, we ought to give memory problems due emphasis and furthermore determine what would be the most appropriate tests to measure this crucial process.

There are several aspects of the phonology versus memory division that require attention. The first is that a weak memory span is going to affect phonology. If an attempt is made to perform operations on a string of phonemes which are beyond span, clearly the task becomes impossible. The second is that if there is a problem with perceiving and representing phonology, this would take away resources that may be required in order to store sounds in words. Third, the rate of articulation probably has a relationship with memory decay. Repeating back items rapidly usually improves memory span. If any articulation is involved in sublexical processes, faster articulation would improve performance. Fourth, there might be several different types of retention required in sublexical processes: there is the level of the phoneme generated from each grapheme, perhaps the retention of the increasing phonemic blend as the word is constructed and then there is the retention of other information if the word is not presented in isolation. If analogy is used, then known printed words will be retrieved and their sounds compared. Again, the retention of sounds will be required. Finally, poor or erratic short-term retention may be more a function of poor concentration than an actual poor short-term memory. If these distinctions are important, assessment tests would ideally be able to pinpoint where the weakness lies. That is, if these distinctions are important to future reading performance and as indicators of possible areas of remediation. A consideration of the experimental evidence helps to clarify this discussion.

MEMORY AND READING: CAUSE, DIRECTION AND EFFECT SIZE

Wagner *et al.* (1994) tested 244 children from kindergarten for three years using a battery of phonological tests and tests of memory in a longitudinal study. They found that memory made only a small contribution to decoding in first and second grade, whereas phonemic skills were much more important. They also demonstrated a bi-directional influence in which reading progress also affected phonological processing. It may be noted that the memory measures of memory span here were not for span of phonemic units but for more meaningful units containing words or digits.

Awaida and Beech (1995) in a longitudinal cross-sectional design examined 236 beginning readers in the UK aged 4 to 6 years using a battery of phonological, memory and visual tasks. Reading quotients were not predicted by phonological memory, as measured by a nonword mimicry span task; however, phonological memory at age 5 predicted nonword reading at age 6 years. This suggests that phonemic memory span influences sublexical processes (measured by nonword reading), as discussed above, rather than directly affecting the development of reading vocabulary. In this same group, reading quotient at age 5 was the most important determinant accounting for 32% of the variance, with nonword repetition contributing a further 10%. From this and other evidence it seems that assessing phonological memory will probably not help to further clarify a child's likely outcome in reading, but it may be useful in assessing the development of the sublexical route.

Nicolson et al. (1995) assessed children with dyslexia on tests involving motor skills, phonological skills, working memory, speed of information processing and balance. They computed an effect size based on the difference in performance on each measure with controls using z-scores. The greatest effect was on balance, followed by a rapid decline in the effect of eighteen other skills. For our purposes it is instructive to see that memory span came some way down the list at seventeenth out of nineteenth in the ranking. However, this was a memory span of meaningful units rather than of phonemic memory span. Nonword repetition, which tests phonemic memory span, was a slightly more important component in twelfth position. Furthermore, it might be argued that there could be something special about dyslexic children compared to poor readers in general, especially when dyslexic children appear to have mild difficulties with processes connected with the cerebellum, according to their theory.

MEMORY SPAN: SOME RELATED FACTORS

Several studies have shown a relationship between memory span and articulation rate. For instance, Das and Mishra (1991) examined normal fifth and sixth graders and found linear relationships between memory span and speech rate and between naming time and speech rate. Memory span involved repeating a series of words in the same order. Naming rate was the time to read a series of simple words; speech rate was the time to repeat words a set number of times. The children were split into three groups according to level of reading performance. Eleven (22%) of the forty-nine poor readers had a span of four words or fewer, whereas five (10%) had a span of six or above. On the other side, among the forty-nine good readers, five (10%) had a span of four words or fewer. Thus some children are poor readers despite a good short-term memory span, whereas others are good readers despite a poor short-term memory. Perhaps studying in depth good readers with poor memories in order to examine their natural coping strategies might be an instructive way to find out what could help other children with memory problems.

Torgesen and Houck (1980) made such a detailed comparison with children with dyslexia, using digit span as their memory measure. They found that the differences in memory were not due to lack of effort, nor in differences in strategies to memorise materials; but they found that the type of material used for memorisation was critical with the greatest distinction found when familiar digits were used and no distinction when nonsense syllables were employed, suggesting a problem in the retention of familiar items for the memory-deficient children.

Henry and Millar (1991) analysed memory span in more detail to tease out the relative effects of identification time and rate of articulation. The important aspect of the identification time hypothesis is that performance could be affected by the rate at which items are identified as they are received. Identification time was manipulated by comparing familiar with unfamiliar words. Slowness with processing any item would be disruptive for retention. A fast articulation rate enables a fast rate of rehearsing the items while retaining them. Neither hypothesis on its own could account for age differences in span. They also discussed the role of rehearsal as opposed to passive decay and concluded that few children under the age of 7 use rehearsal. In the context of children with reading problems, if they had poor phonological skills, there could be identification problems if the materials were unfamiliar sequences of phonemes. On the other hand, if the task involves the retention of digits, unfamiliarity is unlikely to be a factor.

Investigators interested in the relation between speech rate, memory span and reading difficulty have proposed that the real connection is not between memory span and reading as such, but between speech rate and reading and between speech rate and memory span. Avons and Hanna (1995) examined memory span and articulation in three groups of children according to specific learning difficulty, chronological age (CA) controls and younger readers at the same level of reading age (RA controls) as the discrepant readers. Articulation rate between the RA and the discrepant readers was similar, but different from the RA controls. These rates accounted for the differences between the two groups in memory span. McDougall and Hulme (1994) divided children aged between 7 and 9 years into three bands according to single-word reading on the British Ability Scales. They showed that controlling for speech rate differences between the three bands eliminated differences in memory span. They also found, using multiple regression, that speech rate made an independent contribution to reading performance, controlling for short-term memory, phonological awareness and IQ. On the other hand, memory span had no residual effect on reading, once speech rate had been incorporated into the regression model. Thus, the effect of memory span on reading may just boil down to differences in rate of articulation.

McDougall and Hulme wonder why this should be so and suggest that articulation rate is an index of efficiency of activation of phonological representations in memory. During the act of reading the child who activates these representations quickly will learn to read more easily. More importantly it seems to me, it needs to be established that there is a causal relationship between naming rate and subsequent reading, and this can only be done in a longitudinal design. The Awaida and Beech longitudinal study described above included tests of fluency which examined speed of naming digits, pictures (of different animals) or rate of counting to ten. While not exactly like the tasks measuring articulation rate in the two studies described above (Avons and Hanna, 1995; McDougall and Hulme, 1994), test performance on these did not have a significant influence on reading one year later for children aged 4, 5 and 6 years on initial testing. Remember though that our test of nonword mimicry, which had children repeating back nonwords which increased in length until phonemic span was determined, had an influence on subsequent nonword reading. This indicates that phonic development could be influenced by the ability to retain phonemes. By contrast, the articulation rate effect may simply be an effect of learning to read. Those who learn to read faster develop better phonology which in turn increases their memory span.

Gathercole and Baddeley (1993) have proposed that there is a connection between phonological working memory, reading and vocabulary development. Vocabulary development should be related to the development of reading. As noted in Chapter 1, a typical reading test of isolated words starts with short, familiar and therefore frequently encountered words. As it progresses the words become more abstract, longer and less frequent in usage. The child who has not read many words soon starts to stumble as the words become unfamiliar. The more fluent reader, who has much better skills in phonics, encounters words which look familiar but which they do not understand even when they use phonics. This is where a good receptive vocabulary becomes important because the generated phonological code is then more likely to be matched with a lexical entry. Gathercole and Baddeley argue that this is turn could be affected by the ability to retain phonemic information in memory. In a longitudinal study of children who started at 4 years and who were monitored until they were 8 years of age, vocabulary and nonword repetition of words such as *blonterstaping* were monitored. Using cross-lagged correlations they found that for children aged between 4 and 5 years vocabulary acquisition is influenced by the nonword task, but for those aged between 5 and 6 years the causal influence switches to vocabulary influencing phonological memory. This pattern persists, but not significantly, for children aged between 6 and 8 years of age. One reason for the switch could be that their vocabulary from the age of 5 onwards could be used in the phonology task. Interestingly they also found that reading ability at age 6 helped vocabulary scores at age 8 ($r = 0.68$), indicating that reading was helping to develop vocabulary knowledge. They also looked at the effect of phonological memory on reading and, to an extent, the result is disappointing. A partial correlation analysis partialled out age and nonverbal intelligence (*not* including vocabulary), and found no effect on three out of four reading measures. There was a small significant correlation of 0.09 with the primary reading test, which appeared to be more amenable to a phonic strategy than the other tests. Again, keeping the Awaida and Beech (1995) findings in mind, it would seem that phonological memory in the early years is more important for phonic than lexical reading development.

VISUAL AND VERBAL SHORT-TERM MEMORY COMPARED

Many investigators maintain that the problems with short-term memory are entirely verbal rather than visual. However, there is a small number of studies that suggest otherwise. For example, Fein *et al.* (1988) examined verbal and nonverbal short-term memory in children with or without dyslexia. The children with dyslexia were carefully selected to exclude, for instance, any with clinical neurological problems. Several hundred participants were excluded to arrive at a sample of sixty-nine 10 to 12 year olds. Their study produced a scatterplot of the relationship between performance on composite scores of verbal memory versus nonverbal memory for those with dyslexia. Verbal performance was based on a composite of memory span for words presented orally and pictures of common objects presented visually (1 sec./object) and recalled orally. Visual memory was based on a composite of two tests which both involved reproducing difficult-to-name designs with paper and pencil.

The distributions are normal with no clustering, and showed clearly that those with dyslexia have deficits in verbal as well as visual memory. Furthermore, visual and verbal memory are separable, but not clustered; for the thirty-four participants with dyslexia, only half were below normal performance on both visual and verbal memory performance. For the rest, twenty-three (41%) were below in only one type of memory, five (9%) had normal visual and verbal memory scores, nine (16%) had normal verbal memory scores. Fein *et al.* conclude that neither verbal memory nor verbal memory deficits are a necessary condition for dyslexia. Where there have been findings that visual memory can be important for dyslexia, they have usually been dismissed as using tasks which are contaminated by the possible use of verbal processing. Given the disparity in the performance of individuals between the two types of memory task, clearly there is not much verbal commonality in this study. Other analyses also indicated a clear distinction between the two types of test.

We have so far seen that some children with dyslexia and also some poor readers do not demonstrate memory deficits. The Fein *et al.* (1988) result also suggests a separate problem in being able to retain a visual representation in the short term for many, but not all those with dyslexia. Taking first the lack of memory deficits in some children with reading problems, one hypothesis could be that this is because these particular children have simply not been explicitly taught to use phonics when learning to read, even though they might find it relatively easy to do so, and are attempting to learn each word they encounter as an abstract visual pattern. However, those with poorly developed phonology, by contrast, may find it very difficult to learn phonics (see Beech, 1994).

A more visual approach to learning to read may also lie behind the problem for those with difficulties in visual memory; but some of these children also have a problem with both visual and verbal short-term memory.

Fein *et al.* (1988, 193) put forward yet another possibility: 'Our results suggest that memory deficits and reading disability are separate and mostly unrelated sequelae of an underlying lesion or that they are related in a very complex manner that may change over time.' Interestingly, the weak cerebellum hypothesis mentioned earlier may be relevant as there is recent neuro-imaging evidence of a connection between this structure and linguistic processing, mental imagery, word processing and working memory (Nicolson *et al.*, 1995).

PRACTICAL CONSIDERATIONS

What value can be derived from assessing memory as part of reading assessment? Memory assessment has to be seen in the context of the component skills that are required in the development of the reading process (Beech, 1989). Verbal short-term memory appears to play a minor role in reading development, relative to that of the role of developing phonology. It may have an important part to play, in particular, in the development of phonic skills that in part require the ability to retain phonemic information while it is being manipulated. The best test of such a skill is one that directly measures the retention of unfamiliar sequences of phonemes, such as the nonword mimicry task, available from the author. A similar test is the nonword repetition test for use with children aged between 4 and 8 years employed by Gathercole and associates. It has a test-retest reliability of 0.77 (Gathercole, 1995). There is also a simpler version for those aged under 3 years (Gathercole *et al.* 1994). Wells (1995) provides some criticisms of the test and discusses areas in which there should be caution in administration, scoring and interpretation.

Nonword reading is often used in assessments and might be considered to be another test of phonological memory. Typically the test materials have increasingly longer words, which makes it quite a good working test of sublexical (or phonic) processes. Each word has never been seen before. The letters, or combinations of letters, have to be translated to sounds. The sounds are stored in memory while an attempt is made to blend them together. In this sense, the retention of phonemes is involved and so it is indirectly testing verbal working memory in the appropriate setting.

If the child has a poor phonological memory then this test should reveal it, but of course poor performance could be put down to other processes as well. This is not just a test of phonic skills. I have come across older poor readers (aged about 18 years) who can do this task reasonably well but report that they use a mixture of phonics and analogy. This strategy would break down if the nonword test used material that was very difficult to read using analogy.

Beech and Awaida (1992) gave 108 nonwords to poor readers and younger reading-age matched controls, with both groups ranging between 7 to 8 years in reading age. The children were also matched in phonemic processing by means of a nonword mimicry task. Liberal scoring meant positive marking for both correct grapheme–phoneme translation and reading by analogy. We found that the poor readers read significantly fewer nonwords correctly. Second, the proportional difference in each of the words correct between the two groups served as the dependent variable in a multiple regression. Among the independent variables were measures called N and NSUM. The variable N was based on finding the number of real words generated by changing each letter of each nonword, using a computerised search of a corpus of about 18,000 real words. The NSUM measure made an adjustment for frequency of occurrence. However, neither of these measures was significant in the regression. The third finding to note was that poor readers had a slightly (but significantly) poorer memory span for concrete simple words, suggesting a slight verbal memory deficit. Beech and Awaida concluded that the nonword difference between the two groups was more likely to be due to poorer grapheme–phoneme conversion by the poor readers than by differences in the use of analogy.

No one has tried so far to separate these two alternative strategies within the framework of a standardised nonword reading test, but it could be a useful diagnostic measure. A frequently used test for nonword reading comes from the Woodcock Reading Mastery Test (Woodcock, 1987). A new test, the Dyslexia Screening Test (Fawcett and Nicolson, in press), has a test of nonsense passage reading, for instance, ' "Good lub," said the dix. "My name is Norgin" ', which is for children aged 6 years 6 months to over 16 years.

But what is the investigator to make of children who are poor readers but who have no problems with verbal short-term memory? This highlights that assessment of memory is only one part of the assessment procedure. It may also indicate that the child is behind in reading because he or she has not been taught to use phonics. However, we are on speculative ground here as no work has been done on this problem.

In practical assessment work (as opposed to experimental work) a great deal of emphasis can be placed on such tasks in the WISC as digit span, mental arithmetic and phonemic tasks. The digit span task is usually considered to be the best indication of short-term memory by many practitioners, and indeed, many children with dyslexia have problems in digit span and the connected task of mental arithmetic. The digit span task is a component of most intelligence tests but it suffers from (1) variability between testers in rate and quality of articulation (although rate is specified at 1 digit/sec.); (2) differences in speed of repeating back across children; (3) uncertainty about when the sequence has finished (Wagner *et al.* (1994), got around this by presenting their sequences in random order but ending each with a click); (4) the inclusion of backward span in the calculation, which may be tapping a slightly different process; (5) possible distortions if the children use strategies (e.g. visual imagery) to recode the material in other ways than those intended; (6) in the context of its being useful for reading, it is different in many important respects to what is hypothesised to happen during sublexical processing. To give just one instance, when letters are translated into sounds, the sounds are internally generated, rather than listened to passively, as in the case of digit span. Therefore it might be considered as too crude for the purposes of getting a more careful diagnosis. On the other hand, the digit span task is quick and easy to apply and it has an average test-retest (one-month interval) reliability of 0.78 in the WISC-R, which is about the middle of the range compared with the other subtests.

If assessing a poor reader who has a poor digit memory span, we might want to consider the work of Wagner *et al.* (1994), described above, who found that memory span for digits made a small contribution to decoding in the initial stages of reading. One consideration may be to look at the age equivalence on digit span. Suppose the reader has a poor memory span; this would only be in relation to his or her peers, and further suppose that the child in question is aged 10 years 9 months. On the WISC-R a score of 6 on digit span would be quite poor in relation to an average scaled score of 10 for other age peers, but among 6 year olds this score would represent average performance. It should represent a memory span that would be good enough for the early stages of reading, if this is the reading level of the poor reader.

It is generally the case in experiments that do reading age matches (comparing one group of poor readers with another where readers are rather younger but who have the same reading age as their chronological age) that memory span is equivalent, on average, to the reading level of both groups (e.g. Beech and Harding, 1984; Avons and Hanna, 1995). We have seen that there is a connection between phonological development and reading and between memory span and phonological development. Thus from present evidence a memory span age equivalent to reading age is more likely to be epiphenomenal, or due to developmental lag in reading, than an indication of a causal connection. First, the underlying phonology (perhaps rate of articulation, in particular) is an important determinant of both (lexical) reading age and memory span. Second, reading development itself can improve memory span for words, probably because being more able to visualise how the word looks will help the better reader retain words (Ellis, 1991). There is an important rider that nevertheless, a short-term memory problem does suggest a poor prognosis for the development of phonic skills, as opposed to the development of sight-reading vocabulary. If memory span age is substantially below reading age, I would propose that this indicates a more important connection between short-term verbal memory and reading development and serious problems for subsequent phonic development. For example, JM, who had developmental phonological dyslexia, was studied longitudinally by Snowling and Hulme (1989). They found phonological processing problems including a poor memory span. His biggest problem was reading nonwords, indicating great difficulty in developing phonics.

At a more informal level, when testing a child, the child might frequently ask for questions to be repeated. This might be particularly the case when a child is asked more conceptually difficult questions, for instance, while doing mental arithmetic. This could imply a problem in working memory when processing more complex linguistic information.

Another area where short-term memory is important is in the retention of sequences of letters and their connected semantic representation. This might sound obvious, but strangely this is an area that is largely neglected by investigators. We have seen the demonstration by Fein *et al.* (1988) that such retention is difficult for a subset of those with dyslexia. Furthermore, Awaida and Beech (1995), reported above, also found that ability in the retention of letter-like forms at the age of 4 years contributed 15% of the variance to reading quotient one year later. If the investigator would like to investigate short-term memory in this domain there is the British Ability Scales Matching Letter-Like Forms test which has norms available. In this test one target letter-like character has to be found within a string of similar characters. It is designed to test the ability of the child to discriminate and retain these characters while performing the task and is for children aged between 4 years old and 8 years 11 months. Maximum performance at the top age range would only be equivalent to the forty-second percentile; therefore an age limit of 8 years 5 months would be preferable.

Assessment is the precursor to training a person in order to rectify problems. Suppose a problem in memory and in reading has been identified, what kind of training would be worthwhile? There has been quite a lot of effort in training children in their letter-to-sound knowledge. For instance, Cunningham (1990) made a comparison between training these skills by drill with training the children and showing the context in which those skills can be applied. She found that she was more successful using the contextual method. Snowling (1996) provides a recent review of other training studies of reading, particularly those involving phonological training. There have also been experiments on letter-sound training using multisensory methods, but with mixed results (e.g. Beech *et al.*, 1992). There have been experiments on training adults to improve their memory spans (e.g. Chase and Ericsson, 1981). But it would be questionable whether such an approach would produce a transferable skill in the case of poor readers with memory span problems. Improving memory for strings of digits would be far removed from the task of retaining a string of phonemes in order to blend them together. Nevertheless it would make an interesting experiment to see if, for example, training children to increase their articulation rates would in turn help their efficiency in learning phonics. Alternatively, training in the use of more appropriate chunking of information might prove more effective. As we have seen, ability in nonword mimicry has an influence one year later in phonic development, in the early stage of reading. Similarly, normal teaching of phonics involves generating single phonemes from graphemes (e.g. *t*, *ch*) and then blending them. Children with memory problems could be encouraged to blend phonemes into larger units than single sounds, in order that there should be less of a memory problem in retaining the information while the process of blending is taking place. For the expansion of sight vocabulary and spelling the use of mnemonics, such as little poems, and visual imagery can be useful. For instance, the spelling of the word *locomotive* can be visualised with the letter *O* representing the wheels of a train (not that that word is used very often). We have also seen how phonology affects oral vocabulary; improving oral vocabulary should feed back into the development of reading vocabulary as well.

A memory problem in a poor reader does not mean that the problem is insurmountable. However, there may be special cases of children with severe problems in phonics and in short-term verbal memory. I have argued (Beech, 1994) that if efforts in training phonics are getting nowhere, certain cases could be encouraged to use other means of development. One important aspect would be that whenever children cannot identify a word, they have the means, by computer, teacher, parent, friend or dictionary, to find out the identity of difficult words quickly. Thus their reading of text may continue without too much disruption.

Concluding that the poor reader has a memory problem in an ideal world should mean that one can relate precisely how their particular memory problem could be affecting reading. Unfortunately, there seem to be many ways in which a poor short-term memory could be potentially detrimental.

In the case of poor short-term verbal memory we have examined problems in retention of blending and retention within the phonics task and problems in the development of receptive vocabulary which could be affecting sight-reading vocabulary. There could also be problems in learning rules of orthography. For instance, the teacher might be trying to teach the final *e* rule (e.g. *late*, *vote*) to help both reading and spelling. This is a rule which can be learned naturally by most readers by encountering many examples. The teacher who teaches explicitly the abstract generalisation may find that the child with working memory problems has great difficulty with such rule-learning without many concrete examples. Problems for those who have difficulty in remembering visual sequences may mean that later they have problems in remembering spellings. For the more developed reader a working memory difficulty could mean problems in understanding text. To make diagnosis even more difficult, it could also be the case that the level of difficulty in memory is not really a retarding influence for reading development, which is why age equivalence in memory should be a useful consideration, as suggested above. From the experimental work done so far, although memory can be a factor, it does not seem to be a major factor in learning to read when the acquisition of sight vocabulary is considered, but could be an important aspect in the development of phonics. There are most probably other areas in which the role of memory in reading development will be found to be important in the future. To end on the old cliché: further research is needed.

REFERENCES

Avons, S.E. and Hanna, C. (1995). The memory-span deficit in children with specific reading disability: is speech rate responsible? *British Journal of Developmental Psychology*, 13, 303–11.

Awaida, M. and Beech, J.R. (1995). Children's lexical and sublexical development while learning to read. *Journal of Experimental Education*, 63, 97–113.

Baddeley, A.D. (1986). Working memory, reading and dyslexia. In E. Hjelmquist and L. Nilsson (eds), *Communication and Handicap: Aspects of Psychological Compensation and Technical Aids*. Amsterdam: Elsevier Science.

Baddeley, A.D. and Hitch, G. (1974). Working memory. In G.H. Bower (ed.), *The Psychology of Learning and Motivation* (Vol 8). New York: Academic Press.

Baddeley, A.D., Thomson, N. and Buchanan, M. (1975). Word length and the structure of short-term memory. *Journal of Verbal Learning and Verbal Behavior*, 14, 575–89.

Beech, J.R. (1989). The componential approach to learning reading skills. In A.M. Colley and J.R. Beech (eds), *Acquisition and Performance of Cognitive Skills*. Chichester: Wiley.

Beech, J.R. (1994). Reading skills, strategies and their degree of tractability in dyslexia. In A. Fawcett and R. Nicolson (eds), *Dyslexia in Children: Multi-disciplinary Perspectives*. London: Harvester Wheatsheaf.

Beech, J.R. and Awaida, M. (1992). Lexical and nonlexical routes: A comparison between normally achieving and poor readers. *Journal of Learning Disabilities*, 25, 196–206.

Beech, J.R. and Harding, L.M. (1984). Phonemic processing and the backward reader from a development lag viewpoint. *Reading Research Quarterly*, 19, 357–66.

Beech, J.R., Pedley, H. and Barlow, R. (1992). Training letter-to-sound connections: the efficacy of tracing. *Current Psychology: Research & Reviews*, 13, 153–64.

Brady, S. (1986). Short-term memory, phonological processing and reading ability. *Annals of Dyslexia*, 36, 138–53.

Chase, W.G. and Ericsson, K.A. (1981). Skilled memory. In J. R. Anderson (ed.) *Cognitive Skills and their Acquisition*. Hillsdale, NJ: Erlbaum.

Cunningham, A.E. (1990). Explicit versus implicit instruction in phonemic awareness. *Journal of Experimental Child Psychology*, 50, 429–44.

Das, J.P. and Mishra, R.K. (1991). Relation between memory span, naming time, speech rate, and reading competence. *Journal of Experimental Education*, 59, 129–39.

Ellis, N.C. (1991). Spelling and sound in learning to read. In M.J. Snowling and M. Thompson (eds), *Dyslexia: Integrating Theory and Practice*. London: Whurr.

Fawcett, A.J. and Nicolson, R. (in press). *The Dyslexia Screening Test*. London: Psychological Corporation.

Fein, G., Davenport, L., Yingling, C.D. and Galin, D. (1988). Verbal and nonverbal memory deficits in pure dyslexia. *Developmental Neuropsychology*, 4, 181–97.

Gathercole, S.E. (1995). Nonword repetition: more than just a phonological output task. *Cognitive Neuropsychology*, 12, 857–61.

Gathercole, S.E. and Baddeley, A.D. (1993). Phonological working memory: a critical building block for reading development and vocabulary acquisition? *European Journal of Psychology of Education*, 8, 259–72.

Gathercole, S.E., Willis, C.S., Baddeley, A.D. and Emslie, H. (1994). The Children's Test of Nonword Repetition: a test of phonological working memory. *Memory*, 2, 103–28.

Henry, L.A. and Millar, S. (1991). Memory span increase with age: A test of two hypotheses. *Journal of Experimental Child Psychology*, 51, 459–84.

Jorm, A.F. (1983). Specific reading retardation and working memory: a review. *British Journal of Psychology*, 74, 311–42.

McDougall, S. and Hulme, C. (1994). Short-term memory, speech rate and phonological awareness as predictors of learning to read. In C. Hulme and M. Snowling (eds), *Reading Development and Dyslexia*. London: Whurr.

Nicolson, R.I., Fawcett, A.J. and Dean, P. (1995). Time estimation deficits in developmental dyslexia: evidence of cerebellar involvement. *Proceedings of the Royal Society, London. B*, 259, 43–7.

Snowling, M.J. (1996). Annotation: contemporary approaches to the teaching of reading. *Journal of Child Psychology and Psychiatry*, 37, 139–48.

Snowling, M.J. and Hulme, C (1989). A longitudinal case study of developmental dyslexia. *Cognitive Neuropsychology*, 6, 379–401.

Swanson, H.L. (1994). Short-term memory and working memory: do both contribute to our understanding of academic achievement in children and adults with learning disabilities? *Journal of Learning Disabilities*, 27, 34–50.

Torgesen, J.K. and Houck, D.J. (1980). Processing deficiencies of learning-disabled children who perform poorly on the digit span test. *Journal of Educational Psychology*, 72, 141–60.

Wagner, R.K. and Torgesen, J.K. (1987). The nature of phonological processing and its causal role in the acquisition of reading skills. *Psychological Bulletin*, 101, 192–212.

Wagner, R.K., Torgesen, J.K. and Rashott, C. (1994). Development or reading-related phonological processing abilities: New evidence of bidirectional causality from a latent variable longitudinal study. *Developmental Psychology*, 30, 73–87.

Wells, B. (1995). Phonological considerations in repetition tests. *Cognitive Neuropsychology*, 12, 847–55.
Woodcock, R.W. (1987). *Woodcock Reading Mastery Test – Revised*. Circle Pines, MN: American Guidance Service.

8 Assessment of affective and motivational aspects of reading

Peter D. Pumfrey

INTRODUCTION

The aims of this chapter are: (1) to identify some challenges concerning affective aspects of reading; (2) to describe some promising approaches to the conceptualisation of attitudinal and motivational aspects of reading; (3) to outline the importance of assessment in the related areas of attitudes and motivation to read, and (4) to provide sources of information for readers wishing to pursue particular lines of enquiry.

CHALLENGES

Helping all pupils to value and enjoy reading and to accept, in part and increasingly with the passage of time, their own reciprocal responsibilities in learning to read and reading to learn, are important educational objectives. Reading enriches the individual and society, intellectually, emotionally and materially. Not to be able to read in a democracy is to be impoverished and marginalised. Not to enjoy reading is to be culturally deprived. To accept a degree of personal responsibility for making the efforts necessary to learn to read and to benefit from opportunities that the ability to read presents are attributes of an autonomous learner.

Or are these suspect assertions? Consider the words of one of the most esteemed social scientists in the UK, Sir Claude Moser, Master of Wadham College, Cambridge University: 'The illiterate person is tragically handicapped. Without well-developed literacy skills, you are an outsider in our culture.'

Now consider the position represented by Dominic Diamond, the highly educated and erudite presenter of an English television computer games programme entitled *Games Master*: 'traditionalists obsessed with the teaching of reading and writing are failing to understand that this generation needs visual literacy and a sophisticated imagination to be forerunners in the year 2000' (Neustatter, 1993).

Sir Claude Moser is now 76 years of age; Dominic Diamond is 29.

Does the difference in their views reflect a conceptual rather than merely a generational gap? Can they both be right? The average of twenty-three hours per week spent by children in this country watching television is already greater than the time pupils spend in school. The rapidly growing access to, and popularity of, a wide range of increasingly sophisticated computer games has to be acknowledged. The challenge to education is to capitalise on the potential of *all* forms and modes of communication available through Information Technology (IT). The advent of a high technology multi-media-based pedagogy represents a recognition of the educational potential of IT. Does this indicate a reduction in the importance of reading as a means of communication?

In the 1960s, McLuhan predicted that the printed word would be made obsolete. People would stop reading. They would communicate through the electronic media. In his book *Understanding Media – The Extensions of Man*, he was mainly concerned with radio, telephone and television (McLuhan, 1964). In the electronic communications world of the late 1990s, is he being proved correct? We are in the midst of a communications revolution. Advances in microelectronics and information technology facilitate both the expression and reception of ideas expressed in many genres. The spoken word can be immediately transformed into text on a television screen. The blind can 'read' typed text. Information is power. Irrespective of its genre, it still has to be accessed, understood and its import evaluated.

Reading text is, above all, a thinking process. Reading requires the development and deployment of critical acumen. Thinking is characterised by reflection and decision making. The selection and self-pacing that is possible in reading printed text, coupled with the opportunities of reconsidering earlier sequences, contrasts with a somewhat differing control of sequence and pace with which materials are addressed when text is presented on a video screen. Both modes of text presentation have their respective strengths and limitations. The modes complement each other. The personal computer screen may well replace the printed page for many individuals and groups, but not for some time. Irrespective of whether text is presented or displayed in printed or electronic form, the ability to read (decode and comprehend) remains essential in appreciating the significance of the symbols and evaluating the practical and aesthetic costs and benefits contained within the message. The challenges of maintaining and improving both reading attainments and attitudes towards reading are currently important and likely to remain so for some time in our text-dominated culture.

The Reading Teacher is a publication of the International Reading Association and is of particular importance to the classroom teacher. An analysis of the content of the articles published therein over the period from 1948–1991 reached the conclusion that the topics of attitudes to reading, reading habits and interests in reading maintained a consistent appeal to practitioners (Dillon *et al.*, 1992). That interest has not been as marked among research workers whose studies have tended to be more into cognitive aspects of reading (Mathewson, 1994). Far more effort has been put into the measurement of cognitive aspects of reading than has been spent on the measurement of affective and motivational aspects of reading. In part, this may be because the affective aspects are less amenable to assessment and did not as readily lead to the prediction of specific behaviours (Ajzen, 1989).

Cognitive, affective and connative (innate) facets of human development, of communication and of reading are all related. Typically, positive attitudes towards reading and a willingness to engage in reading are linked to high attainments in reading. The converse also applies. Despite these generalisations, there are examples where pupils' attitudes to reading and their reading attainments are not positively correlated (Pumfrey, 1991, 1993). More adequate theoretical models of reading acquisition, maintenance and development are needed for generating predictions and guiding practice. There are some promising signs (McKenna, 1994; Mathewson, 1994; Ruddell and Unrau, 1994; McKenna *et al.*, 1995).

> Prior belief and knowledge consist of pre-existing factors, both *affective* and *cognitive*, that influence the reader's comprehension and construction of meaning. . . . Beliefs influence and shape affective conditions critical to the reader's meaning construction process. These conditions consist of *motivation to read, attitude toward reading and content* and *socio-cultural values and beliefs*.
> (Ruddell and Unrau, 1994, p. 1001; emphasis in original).

This chapter focuses on the conceptualisation and measurement of selected affective and motivational aspects of reading. Pupils' attitudes towards reading and the responsibility that they take for their learning to read are important to both pupils and teachers. Typically, teachers sample such aspects of children's reading-related behaviours informally and incidentally during their work with pupils. There are more systematic approaches that merit consideration.

DEFINITION OF TERMS

Reading is the ability to comprehend the thoughts and feelings of another mind via the medium of text. Grapho-phonic, semantic, syntactic and pragmatic awarenesses are involved in reading (Adams, 1990). The skills of the child learning to read are not as integrated, automatic or elaborated as those of the competent reader. At all stages, learning to read and reading to learn are complementary processes. For the competent reader, grapho-phonic and syntactic skills are typically so automated that the majority of the reader's attention is focused on reconstructing the meaning of the text. For the child learning to read, accuracy in decoding can, at times, detract from sufficient attention being available to deal adequately with the meaning of the text. The contexts in which a child experiences successes or failures in learning to read have powerful affective concomitents. Attitudes towards reading and attributions for successes and failures are largely determined by the proportion of successful and enjoyable encounters with texts to those involving failure and frustration.

Attitude has been defined generally as 'a learned predisposition to respond in a consistently favourable or unfavourable manner with respect to a given object' (Fishbein and Ajzen, 1975, p. 6). In relation to reading, overall attitude can be construed as a continuum ranging from positive, through neutral, to negative feelings that result in the pupil being, respectively, attracted, indifferent to or avoiding engagement with texts. Attitude to reading is not unitary and static but multidimensional and dynamic. For example, attitude towards reading varies with the appeal (interest) and accessibility (availability and difficulty level) of the text content and form. In solitary confinement, the opportunity to read almost anything could be a highly prized activity. At a holiday resort, the activity of reading might not be as positively perceived. To most individuals, everyday life as a pupil, parent or professional is not as polarised: options involving reading versus other activities are less extreme, but still differ, depending on context. In all circumstances, the cost/benefits ratio of reading is a function of the alternatives available. The power of Premack's pre-potent response hypothesis cannot be ignored.

The importance of social learning theory is apparent. The following dimensions are central to current theorising concerning attitudinal influences affecting reading and learning to read.

- The beliefs of the individual in relation to the activity.
- Behavioural intentions towards the activity.
- The feeling aroused in the individual during the activity.
- The differential motivational consequences of success and failure in reading.

Belief has been defined as an aspect of attitude involving 'the recognition or acceptance of something as real' (Drever, 1962). Some theorists consider attitudes to be primarily affective in nature and construe behavioural intentions and belief systems as *contributory* factors (Ajzen, 1989). Others consider the first three of the above list to be *components* of attitude. For example, Mathewson's model is concerned with the function of attitude during the acquisition of reading (Mathewson, 1994). McKenna acknowledges his own indebtedness to Mathewson. By synthesising the work of Mathewson and others, McKenna has developed a model that he considers 'more conducive to considering the long-term development of reading attitudes'. He has constructed a model that draws on earlier work by Fishbein and Ajzen (1975) and subsequently developed by Liska in a critical analysis of the causal structure of the Fishbein and Ajzen attitude–behaviour model (Liska, 1984). Attitudes to reading can be construed to include the individual's feelings, beliefs and values in relation to a wide range of reading-related experiences. McKenna's position is that 'attitude is largely affective in nature and that beliefs are causally related to it'. McKenna's model considers the following three factors as central in influencing changes in attitudes.

- beliefs about the outcomes of reading in the light of the judged desirability of those outcomes;
- beliefs about the expectations of others in the light of personal motivations to conform to those expectations;
- the outcomes of specific incidents of reading.

(McKenna *et al.*, 1995)

Motivation derives from the Latin word *movere*, meaning 'to move'. Psychologically, it is an exceedingly complex concept. The subject index of any psychology textbook will demonstrate both its complexities and its ubiquity in attempts to understand human involvement in, or avoidance of, particular activities in given contexts. Our interest is in the motivation-related aspects of attribution theory. When a child fails or succeeds in a task, for example, a reading-related activity, causal attributions are often made concerning where the responsibility for either the failure or the success lies. Previous experiences systematically affect the attributions made. Research in this area is problematic, but important (Weiner, 1983).

Measurement is *one* important component of assessment and can be defined as assigning numbers to objects or events, according to rules. There are different levels of measurement: categorical, ordinal, interval and ratio. Each level provides distinctive information concerning the inter and intra-individual characteristics of the individual and the group. Measurement is one important means of enabling teachers to be explicit concerning pupils' behaviour and beliefs, changes in these over time and the effects of interventions. Teachers and psychologists have a professional responsibility to conceptualise, operationalise, predict and intervene in the learner's reading acquisition processes when such actions are likely to benefit the pupil. Measurement can assist in this when used to evaluate the efficacy of educational practices that both derive from, and contribute to, the development of theory.

PROMISING PRACTICES

In this chapter, affective aspects have deliberately been narrowed to the assessment of attitudes towards reading; the motivational ones to the assessment of pupils' locus of control beliefs concerning their successes and/or failures in reading. Attitudes towards reading and motivation to engage with texts are complementary processes. The Affective Domain Special Interest Group (ADSIG) of the International Reading Association publishes a twice-yearly ADSIG Journal. It accepts articles related to affective aspects of reading. Theoretical, experimental, descriptive and review papers are included, and descriptions of innovative practices are also welcome. The existence of ADSIG is indicative of interest in this aspect of reading by members of the largest and most prestigious professional and scientific international organisation concerned with reading.

Instruments and techniques used to measure attitudes towards reading and locus of control belief in relation to learning to read are sometimes criticised. They can be seen as measuring only static products of the language curriculum in general and of the reading curriculum in particular, rather than the dynamics of the reading process and its acquisition. This criticism can be partially rebutted. Attitudes towards reading and locus of control beliefs are inferred from behaviours of various kinds. The closer, more detailed and reliable the observation of products, the more likely are the inferences about the processes to be valid in advancing understanding of the complexities of the attitudinal and motivational aspects of reading and the promotion of its development.

Attitudes to reading

If one wishes to assess some aspects of children's attitudes to reading, there are some interdependent questions to be asked and answered. They include the following:

- What is the purpose for which the information is required?
- What aspect of affect is of interest, and why?
- Will educational decision making be improved by assessing/measuring it?
- What is the population to be assessed?
- What assessment techniques and/or materials are available?
- How adequate is the evidence concerning the *validity* and *utility* of the scale or technique adopted to elicit the information?
- What will the cost/benefits (utility) of the assessment/measurement be to the various parties involved?

To answer such questions requires some knowledge of testing and assessment. A *Code of Fair Testing Practices in Education* has been prepared by the Joint Committee on Testing Practices (JCTP). The Joint Committee included the American Educational Research Association, the American Psychological Association, the American Association for Counselling and Development/Association for Measurement and Evaluation in Counselling and Development, and the American Speech–Language–Hearing Association (JCTP, 1988). In parallel, the Code considers testing from the viewpoints of both test developers and test users.

Its four sections cover:

1 Developing/Selecting Appropriate Tests.
2 Interpreting Scores.

3   Striving for Fairness.
4   Informing Test Takers.

In England, teachers are given little training in the theory and practice of assessment in education. In order to address this problem, the British Psychological Society Steering Committee on Test Standards published a brief eighteen page guide to psychological testing (British Psychological Society, 1992). Currently, the Steering Committee is consulting concerning the preparation of certification procedures that will enable test-using non-psychologists to obtain a qualification in psychological aspects of testing. The aim is to ensure that those who use published tests do so to an acceptable level of competence (British Psychological Society, 1995).

A wide range of techniques exist whereby attitudes in general, and attitudes towards reading in particular, can be conceptualised, observed, described and assessed (See Table 8.1). All have their conceptual and technical strengths and limitations (Edwards, 1957; Pumfrey and Dixon, 1970; Epstein, 1981; Ewing and Johnston, 1981; Athey, 1985; Ajzen, 1989; McKenna, 1994; Mathewson, 1994). Information on tests of all types can be found in the Buros Mental Measurement Handbooks (Krumer and Conoly, 1992). The Educational Testing Service at Princeton, New Jersey, probably has the most comprehensive collection and listing of tests in the English-speaking world. Their services include the provision of lists of various tests in print in given fields.

Generalised attitude scales have been developed that can be used to assess attitudes to *any* practice, *any* occupation and *any* school subject (Remmers: cited in Pumfrey, 1985). Measures are also available to assess teachers' attitudes towards the teaching of reading in the

Table 8.1 Techniques used to describe and assess attitudes to reading

A Observational approaches

  1 Direct observation by an adult of pupil behaviours in relation to reading materials whether in educational settings or elsewhere.
  2 Check-lists of reading-related behaviours from which the pupil's attitudes towards reading can be inferred.

B Self-report techniques

  1 Method of paired comparisons.
  2 Method of equal appearing intervals.
  3 Method of successive intervals.
  4 Method of summated ratings.
  5 Scalogram analysis.
  6 Adapted Rasch scaling.
  7 Factorial scales.
  8 Projective techniques.
  9 Semantic differential techniques.
  10 Repertory grid techniques.

Box 8.1 Examples of multidimensional batteries

(1) Individual development; (2) Utilitarian; (3) Enjoyment (Teale and Lewis: cited in Pumfrey, 1985, 1986).

(1) Affective (How much do I like this kind of reading?); (2) Instrumental (How useful is this reading to me?), and (3) Evaluative (How important is this for me at school?) (Ewing and Johnstone: cited in Pumfrey, ibid.).

(1) Pleasure in independent, extended reading; (2) Preference for reading as a leisure activity; (3) Preference for factual reading; (4) Reluctance towards extended reading; (5) Preference for reading aloud rather than to self; (6) Dislike of reading aloud; (7) Reading for self-improvement (primary education).

(1) Pleasure in independent, extended reading; (2) Reluctance towards extended reading; (3) Reading for self-improvement; (4) Preference for factual reading; (5) Attitude towards reading aloud; (6) Attitudes to school activities associated with reading (secondary education) (Gorman *et al.*: cited in Pumfrey ibid.).

(1) Attitude towards school-related reading; (2) Attitude towards recreational reading (McKenna and Kear, 1990).

subject specialisms. There are many scales that provide assessment of attitude towards reading using only a single dimension (ibid.).

Other researchers have identified a variety of factors characterising attitudes towards reading. Some examples are given above. The scales they have developed are presented in summary form. For each instrument, component attitude scales are listed by number, named, and their authors given. Examples of such multidimensional batteries are shown in Box 8.1.

One approach to the measurement of attitudes in young pupils is to provide a set of statements to which the pupils are required to indicate their degree of agreement using a modified five-point Likert scale. With young children, the scale is not presented in the usual format of 'strongly agree', 'agree', 'strongly disagree'. Instead, a set of three (or five) 'faces' is presented with each item. The expressions on the faces change from 'very happy' to 'very unhappy'. Agreement by the pupil with the former indicates identification/agreement with an item indicating a positive attitude. One such measure was used in a large-scale study of work in junior schools that included pupils' attitudes towards various aspects of school (Mortimore *et al.*, 1986, 1988). Technical comment concerning the instrument appeared later (Davies and Brember, 1994; West and Sammons, 1991).

Davies and Brember (1995) subsequently looked at the development of children's reading attitudes and habits through Key Stages 1 and 2 (5 to 11 years old) of the National Curriculum for England and Wales using a shortened version of the scale. A random sample of six primary schools was selected. The sample of pupils comprised 218 NC Year 2 (7 years old), 189 NC Year 4 (9 years old) and 209 NC Year 6 (11 years old) pupils. Pupils' attitudes towards 'reading to teacher at school', 'reading to self at school', 'reading to your parent at home' and 'reading to self at home' were studied. The distributions of scores showed that overall the pupils became *less positive* about reading as they became older. During the same period, their reading attainments had increased significantly. Similar overall results concerning the relationships between chronological age and attitudes to reading have been identified in the USA.

It has been demonstrated that attitudes towards recreational reading and towards school-related academic reading can be differentiated (McKenna and Kear, 1990). A national survey of attitudes towards reading for recreational and academic purposes, based on a stratified sample of 18,185 pupils in grades 1 to 6, has recently been reported (McKenna *et al.*, 1995). The instrument used was the Elementary Reading Attitude Survey (ERAS) (McKenna and Kear, 1990). This is a twenty-item pictorial Likert-type summated rating scale. Ten items cover attitudes towards recreational and ten towards academic (school-related) reading. Each item is scored on a four-point scale with 1 indicating the least favourable and 4 the most favourable attitude. Thus the scores on each of the sub-scales range from 10 to 40. Scores were analysed in relation to gender, grade level, ethnicity, reading ability and the use of basal readers. On average, attitudes towards recreational and academic reading became more *negative* over the six grades. An initial positive orientation declined to indifference. The decline in relation to recreational reading was most marked for pupils with the lower attainments in reading. In relation to attitudes towards academic reading, the negative trend was the same irrespective of pupils' reading attainments. Girls, on average, had more positive attitudes than boys at all grade levels and on both recreational and academic reading. Neither ethnicity nor the use of basal readers played a significant role in the trends identified (McKenna *et al.*, 1995).

Attribution theory: locus of control belief and motivation to succeed in reading

Attributions indicate motivationally important aspects of a child's beliefs concerning the child's control over the consequences of attempting a challenging task. Seeking the child's views concerning why *they* think they have difficulties and/or successes in reading opens up often overlooked motivational perspectives. Seeking pupils' attributions of the locus of control of both their successes and failures is one promising approach with important pedagogical implications. The characteristics of major attributions for achievement-related behaviour have been classified by Weiner as ability, effort, luck, others and task difficulty. Each is considered under three bi-polar dimensions: stability (stable vs. unstable); locus of causality (internal vs. external); and controllability (controllable vs. uncontrollable) (Weiner, 1980).

Learned helplessness means a dependence on others. Consider two boys. Both are unable to read. Both are in the same school. They are asked the same two questions (albeit less directly than indicated here). The first is 'Why are you having difficulties in reading?' Both children give the same reply, as follows:

It's a rotten school.
It's falling to pieces.
My teachers are no good.
There aren't enough books.
The books they've got are boring.

The second question is 'What can be done?'

One pupil answers, 'It's not my fault. The teachers and the school are to blame. *They* should do something about my reading.'

This pupil has an external locus of control belief. The responsibility for what has taken place is attributed entirely to *others*. From this it follows that the individual needs to do nothing. It is someone else's responsibility to rectify his illiteracy. It represents a form of learned helplessness (Dweck and Repucci, 1973).

The second pupil adopts a different viewpoint concerning what can be done to rectify the reading difficulty, and by whom. Irrespective of the material shortcomings that may have contributed to his reading difficulties, the pupil believes that he has some control over what happens.

The second pupil adopts an internal locus of control belief. His reply '*I* can do something about my reading' indicates that, irrespective of what others do or don't do, if he so chose, he could himself do something to learn to read. He accepts a degree of responsibility for his own learning.

Research evidence strongly indicates that individuals with an external locus of control belief have lower attainments than those with internal locus of control belief. Because responsibility for failure is attributed to others, personal involvement, commitment and responsibility are minimal. In contrast, the child with the internal locus of control belief accepts that personal efforts can, to an important extent, determine whether he learns to read (Lewis, 1992).

Typically, pupils develop a more internal locus of control belief as they grow older. Locus of control beliefs can be modified, but not necessarily simply (Bell-Gredler, 1986; Weiner, 1983, 1995a, 1995b). For example, if both the boys described earlier are asked to read a simple text well within their capabilities and both do so *successfully*, their reactions to this successful experience can differ significantly. It is *not* always the case that success breeds success. The child with the external locus of control will tend to attribute his success to 'luck', or some other aspect of the situation that is unpredictable and seen as out of his or her control. Thus the child's expectations of success, when next he or she encounters a book, are unlikely to have changed. It will once again be a matter of 'luck' whether or not he or she can read the text.

In contrast, the child with an internal locus of control will attribute his or her success to his or her *own* efforts. The next time he or she encounters a book, he or she will increasingly accept that, *provided the effort is made*, he or she can be successful.

In the first case, we have a motivationally downward spiral. It is likely to lead to alienation from reading-related activities and contexts (e.g. school) and an increasing likelihood of low attainments and lack of progress in reading. In the second case, we have the opposite. In practice, the polarisation outlined above is rarely as marked as in these extreme examples. Success in learning to read, in knowing that one is making progress, tends to encourage positive attitudes to reading and to an increasing acceptance of one's own control of that success.

The Intellectual Achievement Responsibility Scale (IARS) was originally developed by Crandall on the basis of social learning theory (Crandall, 1978). The IARS provides three indices of the extent to which the individual is willing to accept responsibility for learning-related events: internality for positive events (I+) (e.g. successes); internality for negative events (I–) (e.g. failures), and total internality (I+ plus I–) = (TI). The first two indicate the extent to which the pupil accepts personal responsibility for success and failure respectively. Internality for positive events (I+) is more readily acknowledged and expressed than for negative events (I–). The IARS also assesses attribution to effort (Ie) and attributions that are undifferentiated (Iu). As with the vast majority of such scales, it has its limitations (Lewis, 1992). In general, the internal locus of control belief of the individual increases with age.

A small-scale pilot study of the integration of statemented pupils with formally recognised Special Educational Needs (SEN) attending a primary school in England looked at pupils' popularity, self-esteem and IARS scores. The study involved a total of forty-five Learning Disabled (LD) and Non-Learning Disabled (NLD) pupils attending a primary school. The non-statemented pupils in each class were categorised by their teachers as either 'not having SEN' (NOSEN) or, when the teacher was uncertain whether a pupil had, or did not have, SENs, as 'undecided' (UND). The school was in a local education authority committed to integration. Members of staff were similarly committed. The staffing ratio was extremely favourable. With reference to their IARS scores, although the mean score of the LD pupils was lower than that of the other two groups (i.e. indicative of a more external locus of control belief), no statistically significant mean differences were found between the three groups. This was an encouraging finding, but it must be treated with extreme caution because of the many acknowledged threats to both internal and external validity inherent in the study (Pumfrey and Rath, 1995). Statistical non-significance can be psychologically and educationally highly significant.

A larger scale cross-cultural study compared reading comprehension attainments, attitudes to reading and locus of control belief across 1236 pupils in Kingston and St Andrew (Jamaica) and Manchester (UK) (Lewis, 1992). The samples were stratified by age (9-, 11- and 13-year-old age groups) and sex. The three-dimensional 'attitude to reading' model of Teale and Lewis distinguishes 'Individual Development' (ID), 'Utilitarian' (U), and 'Enjoyment' (E) aspects. Means for ID in the Jamaican sample showed similar levels across age groups. In the UK sample, the means declined with the increase in age. For both cultural groups, females showed more favourable attitudes to reading on this dimension. On the utilitarian dimension, the Kingston and St Andrews means increased between ages 9 and 11, but there was no significant increase between 11 and 13 years of age. A different pattern was found in the Manchester sample where a slight decline took place after the age of 11, following a significant increase over the first period. Attitude to reading for enjoyment decreases with age in both groups, albeit occurring earlier in the Manchester sample. In both groups, females show more positive attitudes to reading for enjoyment.

With reference to the Intellectual Achievement Responsibility Scale (IARS), in the Kingston sample, the 11-year-old pupils showed greater internality than the other two age groups. This is interpreted as one consequence of secondary school organisation. In the Manchester sample, internality increased with age.

Intercorrelations between reading attainments, attitudes to reading and locus of control belief vary between age groups and samples. Assuming that the patterns identified are not a consequence of weak instrumentation, or other threats to validity, their existence supports the importance of both cognitive and affective factors in understanding, describing and enhancing learning to read. There are important, but complex, messages for parents and professionals. A central one is that a reliance on any two of the above three variables is likely to be unjustified as a basis for understanding, predicting and modifying affective and cognitive aspects of pupils' reading development.

A recent study of spelling skills and causal attributions involved 128 children. In the context of their motivations when learning, the aim of the study was to explore the attributions children made after attempting a challenging spelling task (Dodds, 1994). The pupils comprised two groups; sixty-four from secondary school special needs department (poor spellers) and sixty-four younger children of equivalent spelling age (competent spellers). All were deemed to be of about average general ability. The pupils attempted two spelling and two non-spelling (puzzle) tests. Success or failure on each of these was controlled by the researcher. One half of each of the groups 'failed' the tests; the other half 'succeeded'. Order of presentation of the spelling and the puzzle task was also controlled. The subjects were randomly assigned to one of eight groups. Four sets of attribution cards were prepared for failure and success in each of the two tasks. These covered task level (difficult/easy), ability (not very clever/quite clever), luck (unlucky/lucky) and effort (didn't try hard enough/tried very hard).

The hypothesis that the older poor spellers would differ from the comparison group under the *failure* condition was confirmed. The poor spellers used an internal and stable attribution (lack of ability) more frequently than the others who tended to attribute their failure to a relatively unstable and unpredictable cause: bad luck. Both groups were equally unwilling to attribute failure to lack of effort. Both groups attributed their failure more frequently to task level, rather than to either ability or luck. In respect of *success* on the spelling test, there were no differences between the groups in their attributions. This was also true for both the *failure* and *success* conditions of the puzzle tasks. The author then considers the implications of the findings for the learning and teaching of spelling. Learning and performance goals in spelling, the functions of failure in learning how to spell and children's motivation in spelling are interestingly and constructively addressed.

Attribution theory has helped to identify important motivational issues in our schools and society. The competitive nature of education can become Darwinian. The consequences that such an ethos can have on pupils is not necessarily constructive. 'Competitiveness, by its very nature, relegates someone to last place, often in a race that has limited long-term value' (Bell-Gredler, 1986). Can competition, cooperation and compassion be combined in school and in society so that alienation from reading by pupils is reduced? Can we more effectively help pupils develop an increasingly internal locus of control belief in relation to their progress in reading? 'Learning to read' would then truly become 'reading to learn' (Cramer and Castle, 1994).

CONCLUSION

One paradox presented to professionals is represented by the call that 'The uniqueness of every individual pupil must be acknowledged and accepted: every child is special'. Currently, this is often paralleled by a call that 'Children should learn to read at about the same age'. The distinction between values, social policy and social science must be recognised.

When reading attainments, attitudes to reading and locus of control beliefs are considered, inter- and intra-individual differences cannot be ignored. Social science enables these differences to be observed and assessed. Even if every 5 year old could decode, comprehend and enjoy reading *War and Peace* or complex text in any other genre, some would do so more rapidly, more accurately and with greater comprehension than others. Would those who took longer, made more errors, understood less well and avoided reading when given the choice still be identified as 'underperforming'? The answer is almost certainly 'Yes' in a text-saturated culture.

The nature and functions of attitude and motivation in developing, establishing and maintaining reading are important for the following reasons. Because of their reciprocal effects on the individual's engagement with text, both attitudes to reading and locus of control belief affect the individual's levels of reading attainment and the perceived benefits of such encounters with text. As with other accomplishments, 'If you don't use it, you lose it'. This point is now known to be more than unsubstantiated folk wisdom. When faced with competing options, poor attitudes and an external locus of control to read materials that may present difficulties increase the likelihood that reading will be not selected (McKenna *et al.*, 1995). 'Pictures are easy; print is difficult.'

Values matter. Provided we can discount the anachronistic sexism, the words of William Godwin merit consideration by teachers and psychologists: 'He that loves reading has everything within his reach. He has but to desire and he may possess himself of every species of wisdom to judge and power to perform.'

The challenge to society in general, and education in particular, is to help all children acquire the skills, attitudes and belief in their ability to learn to read that concurrently encourages reading to learn (Cramer and Castle, 1994).

REFERENCES

Adams, M.J. (1990). *Beginning to Read: Thinking and Learning about Print*. Cambridge: MIT Press.

Ajzen, I. (1989). Attitude structure and behaviour. In A.R. Pratkanis, S.J. Becker and A.G. Grenwald (eds), *Attitude Structure and Function*. Hillsdale, NJ: Erlbaum, pp. 241–74.

Athey, I. (1985). Reading research in the affective domain. In H. Singer and B. Ruddell (eds), *Theoretical Models and Processes of Reading*. Newark, DE: International Reading Association (3rd edn), pp. 527–57.

Bell-Gredler, M.E. (1986). *Learning and Instruction: Theory into Practice*. New York: Macmillan.

British Psychological Society (1992). *Steering Committee on Test Standards. Psychological Testing: A Guide*. Leicester: BPsS.

British Psychological Society (1995). *Steering Committee on Test Standards. Competencies in Educational Testing: Use of Published Tests. A Consultation Document*. Leicester: BPsS.

Cramer, E.H. and Castle, M. (eds) (1994). *Fostering the Love of Reading: The Affective Domain in Reading Education*. Newark, DE: International Reading Association.

Crandall, V. (1978). New developments with the Intellectual Achievement Responsibility Scale. Paper presented in a symposium on Goal-specific Locus of Control Scales at the 86th Annual Convention of the American Psychological Association, Toronto.

Davies, J. and Brember, I. (1994). The reliability and validity of the 'Smiley' Scale. *British Educational Research Journal*, 20(4), 447–54.

Davies, J. and Brember, I. (1995). Stories in the kitchen: reading attitudes and habits of Year 2, 4 and 6 children. *Educational Research*, 37(3), 305–13.

Dillon, D.R., O'Brien, D.G., Hopkins, C.J., Baumann, J.F., Humphrey, J.W., Pickle, J.M., Ridgeway, V.R., Wyatt, M., Wilkinson, C., Murray, B. and Pauler, S.M. (1992). Article content and authorship trends in *The Reading Teacher* 1948–1991. *The Reading Teacher*, 54(5), 362–5.

Dodds, J. (1994). Spelling skills and causal attributions in children. *Educational Psychology in Practice*, 10(2), 111–19.

Drever, J. (1962). *A Dictionary of Psychology*. Harmondsworth: Penguin.

Dweck, C.S. and Repucci, N.D. (1973). Learned helplessness and reinforcement responsibility in children. *Journal of Personality and Social Psychology*, 25(1), 109–16.

Edwards, A.L. (1957). *Techniques of Attitudes Scale Construction*. New York: Appleton-Century-Crofts.

Epstein, I. (1981). *Measuring Attitudes Towards Reading*. Princeton, NJ: Educational Testing Service.

Ewing, I. and Johnstone, M. (1981). *Attitudes to Reading Measurement and Classification Within a Curricular Structure*. Dundee: Dundee College of Education.

Fishbein, M. and Ajzen, I. (1975). *Belief, Attitude, Intention, and Behaviour: An Introduction to Theory and Research*. Reading, MA: Addison-Wesley.

Joint Committee on Testing Practices (JCTP) (1988). *Code of Fair Testing Practices in Education*. Washington, DC: JCTP.

Krumer, J.J. and Conoly, J.C. (eds) (1992). *Eleventh Mental Measurement Yearbook*. Lincoln, NA: University of Nebraska Press.

Lewis, J. (1992). Reading comprehension, attitudes to reading and locus of control belief: a cross-cultural study. Unpublished Ph.D., University of Manchester School of Education.

Liska, A.E. (1984). A critical examination of the causal structure of the Fishbein/Ajzen attitude–behaviour model. *Social Psychology Quarterly*, 47, 61–74.

McKenna, M.C. (1994). Towards a model of reading attitude acquisition. In E.H. Cramer and M. Castle (eds) *Fostering the Love of Reading: The Affective Domain in Reading Education*, Newark, DE: International Reading Association, pp. 18–40.

McKenna, M.C. and Kear, D.J. (1990). Measuring attitudes toward reading: a new tool for teachers. *The Reading Teacher*, 43, 626–39.

McKenna, M.C., Kear, D.J. and Ellsworth, R.A. (1995). Children's attitudes towards reading: a national survey. *Reading Research Quarterly*, 30(4), 934–56.

McLuhan, M. (1964). *Understanding Media: The Extensions of Man*. London: McGraw-Hill.

Mathewson, G.C. (1994). Model of attitude influence upon reading and learning to read. In R.B. Ruddell, M.R. Ruddell and H. Singer (eds) *Theoretical Models and Processes of Reading*. Newark, DE: International Reading Association (4th edn), pp. 1131–61.

Mortimore, P., Sammons, P., Stoll, L., Lewis, D. and Ecob, R. (1986). *The Junior School Project Report Part D Technical Appendices*. London: Inner London Education Authority Research and Statistics Branch.

Mortimore, P., Sammons, P., Stoll, L., Lewis, D. and Ecob, R. (1988). *School Matters: The Junior Years*. Wells: Open Books.

Neustatter, A. (1993). Literacy in Britain. In *Wordpower, Part 1: Literacy*. London: *Sunday Times* in association with W.H. Smith.

Pumfrey, P.D. (1985). *Reading: Tests and Assessment Techniques*. London: Hodder & Stoughton (2nd edn).

Pumfrey, P.D. (1986). Measuring attitudes towards reading. In D. Vincent, A.K. Pugh and G. Brooks (eds). *Assessing Reading: Proceedings of the UKRA Colloquium on the Testing and Assessment of Reading*. London: Macmillan Education, pp. 115–35.

Pumfrey, P.D. (1991). *Improving Reading in the Junior School: Challenges and Responses*. London: Cassell (2nd imp. 1994).

Pumfrey, P.D. (1993). Encouraging literacy in a multicultural society: motivational issues. Evidence, and lessons to be learned. In: E. Olshtain (ed.), *Proceedings of the Sixth International Jerusalem Symposium on Encouraging Reading*. Jerusalem: Jerusalem International Book Fair.

Pumfrey, P.D. and Dixon, E. (1970). Junior children's attitudes to reading: comments on three measuring instruments. *Reading*, 4(2), 19–26.

Pumfrey, P.D. and Rath, K. (1995). 'The integration of pupils with and without Special Educational Needs in a mainstream junior school: a pilot study. *Education Section Review*, 19(1), 26–34.

Ruddell, R.B. and Unrau, N.J. (1994). Reading as a Meaning-Construction process: the reader, the text and the teacher. In R.B. Ruddell, M.R. Ruddell and H. Singer (eds), *Theoretical Models and processes of Reading*. Newark, DE: International Reading Association (4th edn), pp. 996–1056.

Weiner, B. (1980). *Human Motivation*. New York: Holt, Rinehart & Winston.

Weiner, B. (1983). Some methodological pitfalls in attributional research. *Journal of Experimental Psychology*, 75(4), 530–43.

Weiner, B. (1995a). Spontaneous causal thinking. *Psychological Bulletin*, 97(1), 74–84.

Weiner, B. (1995b). A cognitive–cmotion–action sequence: anticipated emotional consequences of causal attributions and reported communication strategy. *Developmental Psychology*, 21(1), 102–7.

West, A. and Sammons, P. (1991). *The Measurement of Children's Attitudes Towards School: The Use of the 'Smiley' Scale*. London: Centre for Educational Research, London School of Economics and Political Science.

9 Assessment of comprehension in reading

Jane V. Oakhill and Kate Cain

INTRODUCTION

This chapter will begin with a brief overview of how children's comprehension ability is typically measured by standardised tests, and the importance of distinguishing between specific comprehension difficulties and more general reading problems. In the remainder of the chapter, we will outline the ways in which good and poor comprehenders have been found to differ, and will go on to consider which of the poor comprehenders' difficulties might be predictive of later comprehension problems. This is a difficult area, since there is little or no work to indicate which, if any, of the poor comprehenders' specific difficulties are causally related to their problems in text understanding. However, with this caveat in mind, we suggest some measures which, if collected from pre-school or beginning readers, are likely to predict later reading comprehension ability. The measures we explore are: listening comprehension, vocabulary, syntactic abilities, inference skills, text structure understanding, and working memory. The research showing a link to comprehension skill in each of these areas is discussed, and the likelihood that these measures might predict later comprehension skill is considered.

In the final section, we consider some ways in which comprehension might be assessed, which are both more flexible and which might be more useful diagnostically than standardised tests.

(STANDARDISED) TESTS OF COMPREHENSION ABILITY

Probably the most widely used test of reading comprehension in the UK is the Neale Analysis of Reading Ability (Neale, 1989). This test is useful for diagnosing specific comprehension problems because comprehension can be assessed independently of the child's level of single-word reading ability. In the test, the children read a series of passages out loud, and a reading accuracy score is derived from their performance. However, if a child misreads a word, or hesitates for longer than a prescribed amount of time, the correct word is supplied for them by the tester, and they continue reading. Thus, at the end of a passage, the child has either read, or has had read for them, all the words. They are then asked a series of questions about each passage, and their comprehension score is derived from their performance on these questions. The Neale Analysis is very similar to the Macmillan Individual Reading Analysis (MIRA: Vincent and de la Mare, 1989). However, we have not found the latter test so useful for diagnostic purposes because the test administrator is not permitted to correct or supply words that arc read incorrectly or that are not attempted. The WORD Reading Comprehension sub-test works in a similar manner, and it is also the case that the tester is not allowed to help the children with words they cannot read, so single-word reading ability and comprehension skill cannot be de-confounded as they can in the Neale Analysis. One could argue that comprehension performance as measured by the Neale Analysis does not really constitute reading comprehension, since the children listen to, rather than read some of the words! Our view is that it depends on what one is trying to assess. If you want a measure of a child's overall ability to read independently, then the Neale is not an ideal tool. However, it does provide more detailed information about the child's relative abilities. Two children with poor decoding might have very different levels of comprehension ability, but such differences might not be fully revealed unless they are helped with words they are unable to decode. These differences can be highly relevant in assessing a child's problems: the better comprehender, for example, may well be more likely to be motivated to improve his or her reading, because reading is perceived to be an enjoyable and purposeful activity.

In fact, the Neale Analyis never turns into a listening comprehension test, because testing ceases once the child makes a certain number of errors in a passage. Since the passages are graded in difficulty, it is assumed that the child will find the next passage in the series not only very difficult to decode, but will also have a negligible level of comprehension for that passage. This assumption is based on the fact that, in the population in general, word reading and comprehension are very highly correlated. However, it is a limitation of the test, in that some children (for example, dyslexics) can have excellent comprehension but poor single-word reading. We will discuss the relationship between reading and listening comprehension in more detail later in this chapter. At the end of the chapter, we consider some other, less formal, ways in which comprehension might be assessed.

CHARACTERISTICS OF POOR COMPREHENDERS

In this section, we will be discussing the characteristics of children whose comprehension has been assessed using the Neale Analysis, since this is the most frequently used test in research in this area, and the test that we have always used in our own research. Children who show discrepancies between their word decoding ability and their comprehension skill on the Neale might have a specific comprehension deficit for a number of reasons. In this section, we consider some of the obvious reasons why children might be able to read (pronounce) the words in a text, but fail to answer questions about it. These reasons include deficiencies in vocabulary, inference making and working memory.

One obvious reason why a child may be able to read a text aloud, but not be able to understand that text is that, although they can decode the words, they do not know the words' meanings. In our own research, we attempt to rule out this reason by testing the children's silent word recognition in a group-administered picture–word matching task. In this task, the children are required to choose one (of four) words to go with each picture. Thus they have to know the meanings of the words in order to make the correct choice. Since the groups of good and poor comprehenders whose performance we contrast in our studies are matched on this test (Gates–MacGinitie vocabulary), we can be fairly sure that the poor comprehenders do not have a severe vocabulary deficit. Similarly, Stothard and Hulme (1992) matched the good and poor comprehenders they used in their studies for BPVS vocabulary (a test of receptive vocabulary). Later in this chapter, we discuss the empirical evidence for a link between vocabulary knowledge and comprehension skill.

SPECIFIC DIFFICULTIES OF POOR COMPREHENDERS: EXPERIMENTAL FINDINGS

In this section, we briefly outline research that has explored the differences between good and poor comprehenders, and suggest a number of areas in which poor comprehenders do (and do not) have difficulties. Perfetti, a prominent researcher in this area, has in particular (e.g. 1985) suggested that comprehension difficulties arise mainly because certain processes that can potentially become relatively automatic (e.g. lexical processes) fail to become so. Our own work, by contrast, has focused on text-level processes in comprehension. This does not mean we believe that poor comprehenders do not have problems in other areas, but only that comprehension difficulties can still be found in the absence of problems in lower level processes such as word recognition speed and automaticity (for a review see Oakhill, 1994). In our own studies, we have found no differences between groups of good and poor comprehenders in decoding speed, accuracy or automaticity.

Syntactic skills

Once the written word has been read and word meanings established, sentence and phrase structure must be worked out. (These stages will overlap within a discourse of any length.) Knowledge about syntactic constraints can help the reader to establish sentence meaning and, in some instances, it will be necessary to establish the correct interpretation of a sentence, for example, knowing who did the kissing in 'John was kissed by Mary'. Although basic syntactic principles are learned by about the age of 5, knowledge about more complex syntactic constructions is still developing until age 10 or 11 (Chomsky, 1969). Some poor comprehenders may have an incomplete understanding of sentence structure and therefore be unable to use this knowledge to guide their comprehension. Such difficulties may present more of a problem for reading comprehension than for listening comprehension since written text tends to employ more formal structures than spoken language, and punctuation provides fewer cues to the phrasing and grouping of words than prosody. Furthermore, syntactic difficulties might not emerge until reading has become fairly fluent, since books written for beginner readers typically use short and simple sentences, whereas those designed for independent reading are written in more complex language. Tunmer and Bowey have proposed two additional ways in which grammatical knowledge may influence reading comprehension skills: awareness of grammatical structures might facilitate the grouping of words into meaningful units (Tunmer and Bowey, 1984) and it might assist children in the detection and correction of reading errors and, therefore, enhance their comprehension monitoring (Bowey, 1986a; Tunmer and Bowey, 1984). Thus, there are many reasons to predict a strong relationship between comprehension performance and syntactic skill.

There is now a well-established relationship between syntactic skill, age and reading skill: older and more competent readers are better at correcting grammatically deviant sentences such as 'Yesterday, Steve eat a whole pineapple' (e.g. Bowey, 1986b) and at completing sentences with missing words such as 'It __ very cold outside yesterday.' (e.g. Siegel and Ryan, 1988). However, the relationship between syntactic ability and *comprehension* skill is far from clear.

Several studies report moderate to good correlations between syntactic awareness and reading comprehension ability (e.g. Bowey, 1986a; Siegel and Ryan, 1988), but correlational data alone cannot be used to argue for a causal relationship between two skills. In our own studies, we have not found differences between good and poor comprehenders on standardised tests of syntax (TROG, Bishop, 1983), though Stothard and Hulme (1992) report differences on this test with groups selected in a similar manner, so the role of syntactic abilities in text comprehension needs to be explored further.

Inferential skills and integration

We will now consider some of the higher level processes that are needed for efficient text comprehension. First, inferential skills will be needed to go beyond what is stated explicitly in a text: authors need to leave some information implicit, and readers need to be able to assess which of the myriad possible inferences need to be made.

Several studies have shown that good and poor comprehenders differ in their ability to make inferences (for a review see Yuill and Oakhill, 1991). Less-skilled comprehenders have problems with inferences of various types: they have difficulties inferring information that is only implied in a text (Oakhill, 1984), and they have problems inferring specific meanings of words, depending on the context (Oakhill, 1982). We briefly outline the first of these experiments, because the possible interpretations of the results are discussed later in this chapter. An early concern of our research was to assess whether the poor comprehenders' difficulties in answering questions about text were simply a memory problem. To explore this issue, Oakhill (1984) asked children questions about short stories in two conditions: in the first, the children had to answer a series of questions from memory; in the second, they could reread and look back over the texts to find, or check, their responses to the questions. The questions were either 'literal' in that they simply asked about information that was explictly stated in the text, or 'inferential' in that they required the children to go beyond what was explicitly stated, to make plausible, very simple, inferences from it. For instance, an inference question for one of the texts asked how a boy travelled to school. Although it was not stated explicitly that he travelled by bicycle, there were several clues in the text: that he 'pedalled' and that he ran over some broken glass and had to walk the rest of the way (presumably because the tyres on his bicycle were punctured). Although the good and poor comprehenders were equally able to answer the literal questions when the text was available for them to refer to, it was particularly interesting that, in this condition, the poor comprehenders still performed significantly worse on the questions requiring an inference. These findings indicate that the poor comprehenders' difficulties cannot simply be attributed to poor memory: even when a text is available for them to look over, they are still unable to answer a high proportion of the questions that require them to infer information that is not explicit in the text. There are several possible reasons for this pattern of results, some of which will be taken up later. First, poor comprehenders may lack the general *knowledge* to make the inferences. Such an explanation seems unlikely (we would expect a 7 year old to know that a creature which flaps its wings is likely to be a bird) and, indeed, has been ruled out in a later study in which similar differences were shown, even though the poor comprehenders had the relevant knowledge available to them (Cain and Oakhill, 1997). A second possibility may be that poor comprehenders do not realise that inferences are necessary or even permissible – perhaps they focus too much on getting the literal meaning from the text. Third, poor comprehenders may realise that inferences are legitimate, but may have difficulty accessing relevant knowledge, and integrating it with what is in the text, because of processing limitations. We will argue below that there is some evidence that both the second and the third of these possible explanations may be correct.

Good and poor comprehenders also have problems in making inferences to integrate information from different parts of a text, even when all of the necessary information is stated explicitly (Oakhill, 1982; Yuill *et al.*, 1989). Here, we will describe one of these experiments briefly, since it related to the hypothesis we discuss in more detail later – that poor comprehenders have a working memory deficit. In this experiment, the children were read short stories which described an adult's apparently strange response to a child's action (for example, a mother *praises* her child for refusing to share his sweets with his little brother). However, in some stories, this response (which conflicts with behaviour norms: it is good to share sweets) was explained by a further statement (in this case, that the little brother was, in fact, on a diet, and was not supposed to eat sweets). Children were asked various questions about the story, including one question which could only be answered correctly if they integrated two pieces of information in each story to 'explain' the adult's initially odd response or reaction. A further manipulation was the memory load intrinsic to successful integration. In some cases, the two sentences that needed to be integrated were adjacent in the text; in other cases, they were divided by a few other sentences. The finding of particular interest was that the poor comprehenders were perfectly able to integrate the two sentences when they were adjacent (in fact, they performed non-significantly better than the good comprehenders). However, their performance dropped off very markedly when integration over several sentences was required to answer the question correctly. Thus, good and poor comprehenders only differed on this task when the memory load was demanding, a point we will return to later.

In the next section, we turn to the issue of the precise nature of the link between comprehension skill and inference ability.

Understanding text structure

Readers need to have an understanding of the structure of the text. In the case of stories, for example, they need to identify the main characters and their motives, follow the plot and identify the causal structure of the story, and derive a coherent representation of the whole. It has been suggested that knowledge about how texts (and in particular narratives) are organised may facilitate memory for and understanding of them (e.g. Mandler and Johnson, 1977; Stein and Glenn, 1979). For instance, children recall chronologically ordered stories much better than those in which the sentences have been scrambled (Buss *et al.*, 1983). There is now a considerable body of evidence to demonstrate that children's knowledge about narrative structure becomes increasingly enriched and refined between the ages of 4 and 11 (e.g. Fitzgerald, 1984; Fitzgerald *et al.*, 1985; Haslett, 1986; Spinillo and Pinto, 1994, Stein and Glenn, 1982). In addition, some work has examined the relationship between reading skill and story knowledge. This work has shown that the two skills are related, for instance, better readers write stories with better structures (Juel, 1988). However, the relation between reading comprehension skill and story structure is less clear. If, as suggested, knowledge about how stories are structured aids memory and understanding of them, we would expect comprehension skill and story structure knowledge to be related. There is some evidence to support this view: better comprehenders are more likely to recall important story units, whereas poorer comprehenders' recall is less affected by the importance of the different story parts (Smiley *et al.*, 1977).

Our own studies of good and poor comprehenders' understanding of story structure illustrate the generality of the problem by showing that, in some circumstances, poor comprehenders have difficulties understanding even picture story sequences.

We have carried out some experiments in which children were asked to retell stories, prompted by picture sequences (see Yuill and Oakhill, 1991). One finding from such studies was that the less-skilled comprehenders did not seem to have an integrated idea of the stories as a whole – they tended to give picture-by-picture accounts. We do not mean to imply that poor comprehenders may have a deficit in story production *per se.* Rather, we view their difficulty in this area as an aspect of a more general problem in understanding the idea of cohesion in text, which underlies both comprehension and production.

One problem with this earlier work was that, in order to produce a story from a picture sequence, the child has first to *understand* the picture sequence! So, it was not clear with which component of the task the child was having problems. In a later study (Cain and Oakhill, 1996), picture and topic prompts were compared. This study is discussed in more detail in the next section, because it also addresses the issue of whether the skills that contribute to story production are causally linked to comprehension skill.

Comprehension monitoring

A further aspect of skilled comprehension is the meta-level skill of assessing whether or not one's comprehension is adequate. A skilled reader is able to assess whether they are having comprehension difficulties and, if so, will have some strategies to hand to try to remedy those difficulties. Children, in particular, may not realise that they are not understanding adequately, or may not know what to do about it, even if they do realise.

In an initial attempt to assess whether good and poor comprehenders differ in their ability to keep track of their own comprehension, we used a traditional inconsistency detection paradigm, of the sort favoured by Markman (e.g. 1977). In this experiment (Oakhill *et al.*, 1996), we used slightly older children than usual (9 and 10 year olds) partly because children find these tasks notoriously difficult, but also because we thought that older children would be better able to pinpoint and explain their problems with the texts. In this experiment, the children were asked to read a few short descriptive texts: some with inconsistent statements, and some without. The inconsistencies were blatant contradictions (e.g. 'Moles have good eyesight'; 'Moles cannot see very well'). They were either in adjacent sentences, or were separated by several sentences. The children read each passage, and underlined any problems they noticed. After reading each passage, the children were asked to identify anything they thought did not 'make sense', and to explain any problems they had found. The finding of interest was that, as in the study of integration outlined above, the poor comprehenders were affected by the distance manipulation far more than were the good comprehenders. Again, this finding suggests that poor comprehenders' performance is limited by their memory capabilities.

So, although we have some evidence that good and poor comprehenders differ in metacognitive monitoring, thus far there is no evidence for the direction of causality of this link. Indeed, Baker (1994) suggests that metacognitive knowledge may be acquired as a result of practice in performing the cognitive ability in question (in this case, reading). She further points out that, although empirical evidence is limited, the most likely relation between metacognition and cognition is that the two interact in development.

In fact, it is not clear whether comprehension monitoring is really an add-on skill, or whether poor comprehenders are bad at monitoring because they understand so little anyway. As Perfetti *et al.* (1996) state: 'If the text representation is impoverished, there is little for the monitoring skills to operate on. Comprehension cannot be monitored or evaluated if no comprehension has taken place' (p. 144). Until the precise relation between comprehension monitoring and comprehension ability has been more clearly established, it does not seem profitable either to explore or to speculate on possible causal links.

Working memory

Working memory has been defined as the ability to store and process information simultaneously, i.e. to hold the information from one sentence in mind while reading the next one. If poor comprehenders are less efficient at storing and processing information simultaneously in the working memory system they may have difficulty making links between different sentences and ideas to form a coherent, integrated model of the text.

Daneman and Carpenter (1980, 1983) developed the reading-span test which has both processing and storage components, in order to test working memory capacity. In this test, subjects are required to read and understand a series of sentences (the processing component) while concurrently remembering the final word in each of the sentences (the storage component). Subjects begin with pairs of sentences and the memory load is increased by incrementing the number of sentences in each trial. Performance on this task is significantly correlated to college students' comprehension skill.

Yuill *et al.* (1989) investigated whether working memory capacity was related to comprehension ability in young children. They tested groups of 7 to 8-year-old skilled and less-skilled comprehenders on a non-linguistic version of the reading-span test. In this test, subjects were presented with groups of three digits to read aloud (processing requirement) and had to remember the final digit from each group (storage requirement). The memory load was varied by increasing the number of sets of digits (and, therefore, the number of final digits to be recalled): 2, 3 or 4. So, for example, in a two-digit case, the child might read the sets 7–4–2 and 1–3–9 and then have to recall 2 and 9. The task becomes more difficult as the number of groups in the trials increases from two to four. Less-skilled comprehenders were poorer than skilled comprehenders on the more taxing levels of the task. Yuill *et al.* propose that this difference in the ability to store and process information concurrently may account for the less-skilled comprehenders' difficulties in resolving anomalies in text and answering inference-based questions about a text.

PREDICTORS OF COMPREHENSION SKILL

As discussed above, children who have problems with text comprehension experience difficulties with a range of reading-related skills, such as inference-making ability and metacognitive skills. In this section we consider which of these many problems may be causally related to comprehension skill. Unfortunately, there has been little work done to specifically investigate this issue, although we have recently begun to address it in our own work. So, bearing in mind these limitations, we will address the likelihood that early performance on some of these comprehension skills might predict later reading comprehension ability. The measures to be discussed are: listening comprehension, vocabulary, syntactic abilities, inference skill, knowledge about text structure and working memory. First, however, we briefly describe the three different types of design that are commonly used to investigate causal relations because these are used in the studies that follow. They are skill-level match designs, training studies and longitudinal research.

Skill-level design

Skill-level designs have been widely used in research investigating phonological awareness and the development of reading skill (e.g. Bradley and Bryant, 1983, 1985). In this work, researchers have typically compared poor readers' performance on a particular task to that of two groups: same-age good readers and younger children with equivalent reading skills to the poor readers. We have recently begun to use a similar design in our own work, comparing the performance of poor comprehenders to both same-age good comprehenders and a comprehension-age match (CAM) group. This latter group comprises younger children whose reading is developing normally for their chronological age and who have equivalent reading comprehension ability to the poor comprehenders. If the poor comprehenders are worse on a particular task than the comprehension-age match group, we can rule out the possibility that the difference is due to differential reading experience, since it is highly unlikely that this younger group will have more experience of reading and understanding text. Instead, such a result indicates that lack of inference-making skill is a candidate cause of poor reading comprehension.

Training studies

Another way to test the hypothesis that a certain skill is causally related to comprehension ability is by training good and poor comprehenders in this skill. If the less-skilled comprehenders' reading comprehension improves after training, we can infer that their comprehension deficit was probably caused by a deficit in the trained skill. Furthermore, if the skilled comprehenders' abilities were not affected by the training programme it would suggest that they were already using these skills, and thus strengthen our claim.

Longitudinal studies

Longitudinal research is perhaps the most obvious way to assess the relationship between two (or more) skills, but also the most time-consuming and expensive. It is therefore useful to identify candidate causes first (using the methods described above) before embarking on this type of study. By mapping the development of two skills over the course of time, it is possible to see precisely how they are related: the development of one skill might lead to greater proficiency in the other, either directly or indirectly or, alternatively, the two skills might be reciprocally related.

There are obvious limitations with the explanatory power of all the above designs. One problem, noted particularly in the literature using reading-level match designs, is the possibility that a third unmeasured factor influenced the results (see Bryant and Goswami, 1986, for a discussion of such problems). However, converging evidence from two or more of these designs would provide strong evidence that the skill being investigated is *causally* related to comprehension ability.

Listening comprehension skills

Although reading accuracy and reading comprehension are highly correlated skills, they are dissociable (e.g. Gough and Walsh, 1991). This relationship is encapsulated in the simple view of reading which holds that decoding skill and listening comprehension account for nearly all of the variance in reading comprehension (e.g. Gough and Walsh 1991; Hoover and Gough, 1990; Juel, 1988, 1994). According to this theory the nature of the input of each component will change over time: in the early stages of reading poor decoding skills will limit comprehension, but once these basic skills are mastered, reading and listening comprehension skills should be more comparable. Experimental work supports these predictions. Performance on decoding tasks is the strongest predictor of reading comprehension in young children, whereas the predictive power of listening comprehension increases with age (e.g. Hoover and Gough, 1990; Stanovich *et al.*, 1984) and is the best predictor of reading comprehension ability in older children (Curtis, 1980; Juel, 1988; Vellutino *et al.* reported in Vellutino and Scanlon, 1991). Furthermore, when decoding differences are negligible, as in a population of college students, very high correlations between reading and listening comprehension are obtained (Gernsbacher *et al.*, 1990; Palmer *et al.*, 1985).

If we assessed young children's listening and reading comprehension with two comparable texts, they might be expected to obtain higher scores on the listening task. This is because their reading comprehension is restricted by their word decoding ability, as noted above (see also sections on vocabulary and syntax below). However, that is not to say that an assessment of listening comprehension is not a useful way to predict reading comprehension. For instance, we have found that less-skilled comprehenders are poor at making inferences from spoken as well as written texts (e.g. Oakhill, 1982, 1984; Oakhill *et al.*, 1986). In work specifically designed to address the relationship between listening and reading comprehension it has been found that both types of assessment yield similar comprehension profiles in young children and that the two skills are highly correlated (Cain, 1994; Smiley *et al.*, 1977; Stothard and Hulme, 1992; Townsend *et al.*, 1987). In addition, Tunmer (1989) found that grade 2 children's listening comprehension and decoding ability were the only skills to make significant independent contributions to reading comprehension ability.

Thus, although there has been little work specifically designed to address this issue it appears that, once word decoding skill has been controlled for, listening comprehension is a good predictor of later reading comprehension skill.

Vocabulary

Word knowledge is strongly related to reading comprehension ability in both children and adults (e.g. Carroll, 1993). Although children may be competent communicators and comprehenders within spoken discourse, they may experience difficulties when they encounter the same words when reading, since receptive (or hearing) vocabulary is considerably larger than sight vocabulary until the later junior school years (Sticht and James, 1984).

Uncommon words may disrupt the flow of reading in several ways. For instance, lexical access may be slower for rare words or, in extreme cases, sentence context must be used in order to work out the meaning of the word. This additional processing can result in inadequate comprehension of text because part of the passage may have been forgotten and/or because there is insufficient cognitive capacity left to complete comprehension processing.

However, the extent to which vocabulary difficulties affect comprehension is disputed. For instance, although some studies have found that replacing common words with less common synonyms can disrupt young children's comprehension of stories (e.g. Wittrock *et al.*, 1975) other researchers report that difficult or rare vocabulary has to occur at a very high frequency (of one in three content words), or in prominent story propositions, before children's comprehension is adversely affected (e.g. Freebody and Anderson, 1983). Furthermore, if limited word knowledge is a significant factor in reading comprehension, then training in difficult vocabulary should result in better comprehension for the trained group relative to children with negligible prior exposure to such words. However, such studies have not always been successful. Some report gains in reading comprehension scores after vocabulary instruction (e.g. Beck *et al.*, 1982), whereas others find that such training does not improve reading comprehension (e.g. Pany *et al.*, 1982). It has been suggested that studies such as Beck *et al.*'s owe their success to improvements in general reading strategy brought about by their training regime (Mezynski, 1983). Thus, the work in this area demonstrates that, although comprehension skill and word knowledge are related, vocabulary knowledge *per se* is not sufficient for adequate comprehension.

Other work has shown that comprehension difficulties can still arise when vocabulary is familiar (Perfetti, 1985) and when decoding skill and word knowledge are controlled for (Ehrlich, 1996; Stothard and Hulme, 1992; Yuill and Oakhill, 1991). The less-skilled comprehenders whom we have studied experience comprehension difficulties which do not appear to be due to a vocabulary deficit: they are matched to good comprehenders on a test of sight vocabulary, the Gates–MacGinitie (1978). A different test, the British Picture Vocabulary Scales (Dunn *et al.*, 1982) has also been used successfully to select and match good and poor comprehenders (Stothard and Hulme, 1992). This latter test assesses receptive (or hearing) vocabulary: an individual's comprehension of the spoken word. However, we cannot equivocally state that such poor comprehenders do not experience some vocabulary deficits. We have found that skilled and less-skilled comprehenders with comparable sight vocabularies do differ when hearing vocabulary is assessed (Cain, 1994) and similarly, Stothard and Hulme (1996) report that their groups, selected to have equivalent hearing vocabulary skills (BPVS), differ on a measure of expressive vocabulary. However, there was no evidence that poor vocabulary was a likely cause of comprehension difficulties in either study: the vocabulary differences might have been the result of greater reading experience of the skilled group.

Indeed, work by Stanovich and colleagues supports such an interpretation. These researchers have shown that the amount of reading one does can predict vocabulary and verbal ability *independently* of reading comprehension skill (for a review see Stanovich, 1993). For instance, it is possible to find adult poor comprehenders who obtain high scores on measures designed to assess their reading experience who have larger receptive vocabularies than good comprehenders with limited exposure to print. In addition, it appears that the amount of reading that a child does can account for significant variance in vocabulary knowledge once other factors such as age and IQ have been controlled for (Allen *et al.*, 1992; Cunningham and Stanovich, 1991). These studies of children suggest that vocabulary differences might emerge as a result of differences in reading experience, independently of reading comprehension level.

In summary then, although vocabulary knowledge is a good indicator of reading comprehension skill in the general population and, as such, can be used as a fairly accurate predictor of reading comprehension ability, vocabulary deficits will not automatically lead to comprehension difficulties, nor vice versa. We should bear in mind, as Stanovich *et al.* (1984) note, that the relationship between reading comprehension and vocabulary might be one of mutual facilitation: good vocabulary knowledge aids comprehension skill, and comprehension development facilitates vocabulary growth.

Syntactic knowledge

As we discussed above, a number of studies have reported correlations between measures of syntactic awareness and comprehension skill, but most such studies have been purely correlational, and as such, have nothing to say about the direction of causality between the two skills. There have been few studies investigating the causal nature of this relationship. One, conducted by Tunmer (1989), provides some evidence for the hypothesis that knowledge about grammar and syntax influences reading comprehension ability. Tunmer used a word-order correction task as a measure of syntactic awareness and took measures of reading and listening comprehension (among other things) at grades 1 and 2. Path analysis revealed that syntactic awareness in grade 1 directly influenced grade 1 listening comprehension, but that listening comprehension did not significantly affect reading comprehension: the only variable to make a significant independent contribution to reading comprehension at grade 1 was a measure of word decoding. However, when looking at achievement on the comprehension measures when the children were in grade 2, Tunmer found that grade 1 syntactic awareness directly predicted grade 2 listening comprehension which, in turn, predicted reading comprehension skill. More recently, Leather (1994, expt 5) reports that awareness of grammar at 5 years was significantly related to reading comprehension at age 6.

Unfortunately, these studies do not provide any evidence for a *unique* relationship between comprehension ability and syntactic skill because they did not take decoding skill into account. Thus it is quite plausible that the influence of syntactic knowledge on comprehension skills has arisen indirectly through the relationship between decoding and comprehension. Indeed, some work has shown that different measures of syntactic awareness are more strongly related to decoding skill than to comprehension ability (Bowey, 1986a; Tunmer, 1989) and there is now ample evidence that early syntactic skills aid decoding skill (e.g. Rego and Bryant, 1993; Tunmer, 1989; Tunmer and Hoover, 1993). Thus, these longitudinal studies provide no concrete support for an independent relationship between syntactic skill and comprehension ability.

An additional problem with some of the work reporting a strong relationship between syntactic knowledge and reading comprehension ability is that verbal working memory was not assessed. Shankweiler and colleagues propose that sentence comprehension problems (as well as word decoding difficulties) stem from a general deficiency in the use of a phonological representation of verbal information, which makes it difficult to retain and process this information in verbal working memory (e.g. Mann *et al.*, 1980; Shankweiler *et al.*, 1979). For instance, although poor readers are not very good at acting out such syntactically complex spoken sentences as 'The dog that chased the sheep stood on the turtle' (Mann *et al.*, 1984), their difficulties arise because of their restricted memory rather than the syntactic demands of the task (Smith *et al.*, 1989). Furthermore, Leather (1994) found little evidence that syntax accounted for additional unique variance in the reading comprehension scores once memory span differences were controlled for.

In our own work investigating children with a specific comprehension deficit, we have found little evidence for syntactic difficulties. However, there is some work that has, like our own, controlled for decoding skill and has found a link between comprehension and syntax. In a study of native speakers of Hebrew, Bentin *et al.* (1990) compared the syntactic abilities of groups of children with equivalent reading accuracy skills who differed in comprehension ability. Relative to good comprehenders, the poor comprehenders were less able to use syntactic information to correct a range of syntactic violations in spoken sentences, and children with a more severe comprehension deficit were poor at even detecting such violations. An assessment of verbal memory indicated that this was not contributing to the poor comprehenders' difficulties. Thus, in Hebrew at least, there is some evidence that syntactic knowledge is related to reading comprehension skill once the obvious intermediary factors such as reading accuracy and memory are controlled for. There is also some recent evidence that syntactic differences might exist between British populations of good and poor comprehenders which cannot be accounted for by decoding differences (Stothard and Hulme, 1992). However, in a recent unpublished study of our own, we have been able to identify only small differences on fairly hard grammatical structures which have high processing requirements. Thus we have been unable to rule out a memory basis for such findings. More importantly, neither of these studies of good and poor comprehenders has found any evidence to indicate syntax as a likely cause of the poor comprehenders' difficulties.

The work reviewed in this section has shown that although there is a strong relationship between reading comprehension and syntactic knowledge, this is often mediated by decoding ability and memory capacity. Thus it is still far from clear how well early syntactic skills predict later reading comprehension.

Inference and integration skill

As already discussed, inference making is an important skill for text comprehension. Work by Oakhill and Yuill (for a review see Yuill and Oakhill, 1991) has revealed a strong link between this ability and reading comprehension skill. Recent work using training studies and the comprehension-age match design also points to a causal link between these two skills.

Several studies have found that encouraging children to make inferences can be effective in improving comprehension, though most of these studies have looked at the effects of training on poor readers generally, rather than on children who have a specific comprehension problem (for a review, see Oakhill and Yuill, 1991). The general aim of this experiment was to encourage the poor comprehenders to become more aware of, and more involved in, their own comprehension: in particular, to encourage inference making and comprehension monitoring. Training in question generation was combined with instruction in making inferences, to sensitise the children to the *types* of inferences they should make, as well as helping them in the *techniques* for drawing inferences. We also aimed to help the children to go beyond the information explicitly presented in the texts, by including a type of 'macrocloze' task, in which they read stories with sentences covered, and were encouraged to make hypotheses about what was missing. There were two control groups: children in one group were taught to decode the words in the same passages as quickly and as efficiently as possible, and a second who were given more traditional comprehension exercises, on the same passages, to complete (a full account of this study can be found in Yuill and Oakhill, 1988). After seven half-hour sessions of training, the children's comprehension ability was reassessed. The results showed that, for less-skilled comprehenders, inference training was both more beneficial than was decoding practice, and more helpful to them than it was to the skilled comprehenders. The effect of inference training was striking for the less-skilled group: their average increase in Neale comprehension age was seventeen months, over a training period of only two months. This result is particularly impressive given that most training studies reassess performance on the specific skills that are being trained, rather than on standardised tests. However, one puzzling aspect of the results was that the less-skilled comprehenders given inference training improved slightly, but not significantly, more than those given comprehension exercises. This unexpected finding may have arisen because the children in the exercise group often corrected one another, and discussed their answers. Thus they may have benefited from the discussion about the text in ways we had not anticipated. Furthermore, the passages we used were rather obscure, to encourage inferences, and they may have caused the children to engage in more inferential processing and reflection on their comprehension than would more traditional comprehension passages. Hence, the inference training may have been effective not because the children were taught particular strategies but, rather, because they developed a greater awareness of their own comprehension. So, inference training does appear to have pronounced effects, but it is not entirely clear that the improved perfomance we observed resulted from increases in the poor comprehenders' inference abilities, or from a more general improvement in awareness of comprehension.

In a more recent experiment (see Cain and Oakhill, 1997) we compared the less-skilled comprehenders' ability to make two different kinds of inferences with both less-skilled comprehenders and a comprehension-age match group. The first sort of inference, which we called inter-sentence inferences, were similar to the sort used by Oakhill (1982). These inferences, necessary to establish cohesion between sentences in a text, can be derived from information explicitly provided in the text. The other type of inference, a gap-filling inference, was like those used by Oakhill (1984), where general knowledge must be applied in order to make sense of information which is implicit in the text. Children read short stories and were then asked questions which required these inferences to be made. The less-skilled comprehenders made fewer of both types of inferences than both the skilled comprehenders and the comprehension-age match group. The less-skilled comprehenders' poor inference-making skill could not simply be attributed to poorer memory since their recall of verbatim detail from the story was comparable to that of the other two groups. Furthermore, in instances where children did not make the inference at first, further questioning revealed that they had the requisite knowledge to make these inferences. Instead, our findings indicated that knowing when and how to relate such general knowledge to the text, in order to fill in missing details, was a more likely source of the less-skilled group's problems.

These two lines of research indicate that inference-making skill may be causally related to reading comprehension ability.

Text structure

As we discussed earlier, good and poor comprehenders differ in their ability to produce coherent stories. In this section, we consider the direction of the link between this ability and comprehension skill.

Recent work of our own has indicated a causal link between comprehension skill and the ability to structure a story (Cain and Oakhill, 1996). We used a production task in which children were given two types of story prompt: topic titles, such as 'The Farm', which provided a theme for the children to base their stories around, and sequences of six pictures, which provided a more detailed and structured framework for their stories. When telling stories elicited by the topic prompts, poor comprehenders produced less coherent and integrated narratives than skilled comprehenders: they were more likely to tell a story where the outcome was not related to previous events in the story. In addition, the less-skilled comprehenders also produced poorer stories than did a comprehension-age match (CAM) group. However, the difference between the less-skilled comprehenders and the CAM group was not apparent when picture sequences were used to elicit the stories, suggesting that this type of prompt did provide some of the structural information about stories that the less-skilled comprehenders lacked. More importantly, the difference between the less-skilled comprehenders and the comprehension-age match group in the topic prompt condition indicates that inferior story knowledge is more plausibly a cause of poor comprehension than the result of it. A training study of relevance to this issue was conducted by Fitzgerald and Spiegel (1983). They devised a programme to teach children with poor knowledge of story structure about the different elements of a story. This programme improved the children's story-telling ability and also their reading comprehension. However, since Fitzgerald and Spiegel's study was designed to test their specific training procedure and did not include a group of children who already had a good sense of story structure, these findings do not shed any light on whether story knowledge and reading comprehension are causally related.

Thus, there is some evidence that knowledge about how stories are structured is a possible predictor of reading comprehension skill.

Working memory

The last candidate as a predictor of comprehension skill that we will consider in this section is working memory ability. Studies discussed earlier revealed a strong relationship between comprehension ability and working memory capacity, but this work did not indicate whether poor working memory is a likely cause of comprehension difficulties. Stothard and Hulme (1992) conducted a study which included a comprehension-age match group in order to explore the nature of this relationship. They used a test that is similar to the original Daneman and Carpenter listening span test. In contrast to Yuill *et al.*'s (1989) work using the digit-based task, Stothard and Hulme only found a small, and insignificant, difference in working memory span between skilled and less-skilled comprehenders. This result is somewhat surprising because their task comprised a sentence comprehension element and, if anything, one would expect a greater difference in working memory capacity between good and poor comprehenders with such a task. However, the children's performance on the task was very low, and therefore might not be sensitive enough to detect the group differences found by Yuill *et al.* Indeed, in recent unpublished work, Yuill and Oakhill have demonstrated a link between comprehension ability and verbal and numerical but not spatial tests of working memory. Of specific interest to this section was Stothard and Hulme's finding that the comprehension-age match group were slightly poorer on the task than the less-skilled comprehenders. We have found a similar difference in our own recent work (Cain, 1994). However, in a longitudinal study with slightly younger children, Leather (1994, expt 5) reports that a verbal measure of working memory taken at age 5 was a unique predictor of reading comprehension skill a year later.

With the exception of Stothard and Hulme's work, the literature reveals a strong relationship between working memory and comprehension ability. However, studies adopting the comprehension-age match design find that the younger CAM group have poorer working memory capacity than the less-skilled comprehenders. Thus, this work does not rule out the possibility that the relationship between working memory and comprehension skill has arisen through differential reading experience, rather than working memory being causally implicated in comprehension development. Indeed, this interpretation was proposed by Tunmer (1989): he suggested that practice at representing and manipulating linguistic information may facilitate working memory ability.

Summary

The skills we focused on in this section were listening comprehension, vocabulary and syntactic knowledge, inference making ability, knowledge about text structure, and working memory capacity. The experimental work discussed demonstrated that measures of all these skills taken in young children are likely to correlate with later reading comprehension skill. However, the emerging evidence suggests different patterns of relation between these various skills and comprehension performance. There is little evidence that deficits in vocabulary or syntactic awareness are primary *causes* of later poor reading comprehension skill: the relationship between comprehension and these skills may be an indirect one. For instance, as discussed earlier, it may be that syntactic awareness facilitates decoding ability which, in turn, affects reading comprehension skill. Thus, these two skills (vocabulary and syntactic knowledge) might be good predictors of early reading comprehension, which is highly constrained by decoding ability, but may not be very precise indicators once reading accuracy has been controlled for. In addition, although a strong case has been made for the role of working memory in comprehension deficits, there is not yet any evidence to indicate precisely how working memory limitations are linked to poor comprehension. There is much stronger support, however, for the contention that listening comprehension, inference-making skill and knowledge about text structure are all causally related to reading comprehension, independently of skills such as decoding ability. Since deficits in inference making and understanding story structure are apparent on tasks in both visual and oral modalities, it would appear that the most accurate predictor of reading comprehension ability would be listening comprehension. Furthermore, it would be interesting to assess and compare these two comprehension sub-skills (inference-making ability and story structure understanding) in both modalities. If, for example, poor inferencing skill is limiting comprehension of a text, as opposed to inefficient decoding reducing the cognitive capacity necessary to make such inferences, deficits of a similar magnitude should be found in both listening and reading tasks.

CONCLUSIONS

The 'simple view' of reading (e.g. Gough and Tunmer, 1986; Hoover and Gough, 1990; Tunmer and Hoover, 1992) proposes that individual differences in reading comprehension can be accounted for in terms of the product of decoding skill and listening comprehension. Intuitively, this conceptualisation makes a lot of sense: someone who cannot understand (in spoken form) the language he or she is decoding cannot be said to be 'reading' and, conversely, someone who has good listening comprehension, but who cannot decode any of the words in written form cannot be said to be reading either. A longitudinal study by Hoover and Gough (1990) provides strong support for this view of reading: they found that decoding and listening comprehension, and the interaction of these two measures, accounted for a very high proportion of variance in reading comprehension in grades 1 to 4 (between 73% and 90%, depending on grade level).

Another prediction of the model is that children should be able to read as well as they are able to listen, unless their decoding skills are holding them back. This prediction gives credence, from a theoretical perspective, to the view that listening comprehension will be a good predictor of potential reading comprehension ability in beginning readers. This idea is certainly not new. In 1977, Carroll argued for the use of a W-O (written-oral) scale to be used as a measure of reading competence. If there is little discrepancy between a child's comprehension whether measured in the written or oral mode, then the child could be said to be reading as well as he or she is able. However, if oral comprehension were higher than written comprehension, then the child's potential is not being realised.

We do not know of any standardised British test of listening comprehension (although at least one American test, the Woodcock–Johnson, is available). However, Royer and colleagues (see e.g. Royer *et al.* 1987) have developed a Sentence Verification Technique (SVT) test which can be readily produced from any text, following a few basic rules which are laid out in their paper, and which can be administered either as a listening or as a reading comprehension assessment. Royer distinguishes between a superficial representation of a text (which may be sufficient to answer a number of factual comprehension questions) and a more integrated and elaborated representation, which could be taken as an indication of a more profound understanding. Based on the idea that a good representation of a text may preserve the text's meaning, but not its form, he developed tests in which the child has to indicate which of a set of test sentences have the same meaning as sentences they have just read or listened to. Typically, four types of test item are included: original sentences, paraphrases of originals, meaning change items (which are original sentences, with a few words changed to alter their meaning) and distractors (which are sentences with a similar syntactic structure to a sentence in the passage, and related in meaning to the passage theme, but not related in meaning to any particular sentence). Good performance (understanding of the gist meaning of a passage) is typified by acceptance of the original and paraphrase sentences, and rejection of the others. A further aim of Royer's work was that such tests could be used as a diagnostic tool, to inform the teacher not simply that a particular child had good or poor comprehension, but to provide some more detailed information about the child's reading. Thus a child who paid too much attention to decoding the words, at the expense of deriving meaning, might be good at accepting originals and rejecting distractors (because they are completely different). However, they would also be expected to classify paraphrases wrongly (because the wording is different), and meaning changes wrongly (as having been in the passage, because the wording is similar). In contrast, a child who paid attention to overall meaning, rather than the details of the superficial form of the text, might be expected to be good on the originals, paraphrases and meaning changes, but relatively poor on the distractors because these are consistent with the meaning of the passage as a whole. A further advantage of SVT tests is that they can be used to assess understanding of a particular text, or type of text, or to assess comprehensibility of a text – situations in which standardised measures are not appropriate.

In the section on predictors of reading comprehension, we noted that listening comprehension performance can be a good indicator of reading comprehension ability under certain circumstances. Carlisle (1989) proposes that parallel measures of reading and listening comprehension should be taken to identify two separate groups of children with reading comprehension problems: those whose deficit is caused primarily by their decoding difficulties should show pronounced difficulties on a reading task relative to their performance on a listening task, whereas children who experience specific comprehension difficulties, of the kind that we have described, should obtain low scores on both measures (see also Aaron, 1991). Carlisle has developed a test battery, the Profiles in Listening and Reading (PILAR) (e.g. Carlisle, 1989), to enable identification of these sub-types. This battery comprises measures of both listening and reading comprehension, as well as a test to assess the automaticity of word recognition (but unfortunately does not have any norms). Poor performance on the latter test would support a diagnosis of a reading-specific deficit made on the basis of a discrepancy between reading and listening performance. The PILAR comprehension tests are based on Royer's Sentence Verification Technique (Royer *et al.*, 1987), because Carlisle proposes that this task assesses language comprehension without requiring the reader to employ reasoning skills and question-answering strategies (as do most other measures). Carlisle, however, adopts a different scoring procedure from that used by Royer. Whereas Royer calculates an overall score to control for biased responding, Carlisle looks instead at performance on each sentence type because of their individual diagnostic potential. For instance, one type of test sentence (distractor) presents information not in the original passage, that is, about a new, but related, topic. Carlisle argues that children who do not construct a representation of the meaning of the whole text will make a disproportionate number of errors on these items (see Carlisle and Felbinger, 1991 for further details). However, it should also be noted that Carlisle and Felbinger urge caution in extrapolating from one test to another, since they find some evidence that the comprehender may construct slightly different representations of the same text in the two modalities.

The tasks developed to assess comprehension and other reading skills by Paris and van Kraayenoord are similarly motivated. They have been concerned that many assessments of reading development are rather narrow and do not assess the strategies that children use in reading, their book-handling skills, their self-perceptions and their motivation. Much recent work has emphasised that children need to use appropriate strategies for efficient reading, and to have positive views of their own abilities. Comprehension problems might, in some cases, be related to inadequate strategies or low motivation. Paris and van Kraayenoord have devised a number of measures and assessments which can be used in the classroom, and suggest that these be used to supplement more traditional assessments. An account of some of these assessments can be found in van Kraayenoord and Paris (1996). Their tests are, however, still in the early stages of development, and their predictive power has not yet been properly assessed. Nevertheless, they point the way towards more flexible and informative measures of reading skill.

In conclusion, recent trends in assessing comprehension show a movement away from more traditional, standardised measures to a less formal approach, perhaps using assessments which can be integrated with the children's everyday activities and tasks. These assessments can be used to provide diagnostic information about a particular child's strengths and weaknesses. In particular, listening comprehension can provide a measure of later reading comprehension potential, and measures of reading and listening taken from the same child at different points in development can help the teacher to decide if a child is attaining his or her potential in reading.

REFERENCES

Aaron, P.G. (1991). Can reading disabilities be diagnosed without using intelligence tests? *Journal of Learning Disabilities*, 24(3), 178–86.

Allen, L., Cipielewski, J. and Stanovich, K.E. (1992). Multiple indicators of children's reading habits and attitudes: construct validity and cognitive correlates. *Journal of Educational Psychology*, 84(4), 489–503.

Baker, L. (1994). Fostering metacognitive development. In H. Reese (ed.) *Advances in Child Development and Behavior*, (Vol. 25). (pp. 201–39). New York: Academic Press.

Beck, I.L., Perfetti, C.A. and McKeown, M.G. (1982). Effects of long-term vocabulary instruction on lexical access and reading comprehension. *Journal of Educational Psychology*, 74, 506–21.

Bentin, S., Deutsch, A. and Liberman, I.Y. (1990). Syntactic competence and reading ability in children. *Journal of Experimental Child Psychology*, 48, 147–72.

Bishop, D. (1983). *Test for the Reception of Grammar*. Manchester: Chapel Press.

Bowey, J.A. (1986a). Syntactic awareness in relation to reading skill and ongoing comprehension monitoring. *Journal of Experimental Child Psychology*, 41, 282–99.

Bowey, J.A. (1986b). Syntactic awareness and verbal performance from preschool to fifth grade. *Journal of Psycholinguistic Research*, 15, 285–306.

Bradley, L. and Bryant, P.E. (1983). Categorising sounds and learning to read: a causal connection. *Nature*, 301, 419–21.

Bradley, L., and Bryant, P.E. (1985). *Rhyme and Reason in Reading and Spelling*. Ann Arbor: University of Michigan Press.

Bryant, P. and Goswami, U. (1986). Strengths and weaknesses of the reading level design: a comment on Backman, Mamen and Ferguson. *Psychological Bulletin*, 100 (1), 101–3.

Buss, R.R., Yussen, S.R., Matthews, S.R., Miller, G.E. and Rembold, K.L. (1983). Development of children's use of story schema to retrieve information. *Developmental Psychology*, 19(1), 22–8.

Cain, K. (1994). *An Investigation into Comprehension Difficulties in Young Children*. Unpublished D.Phil. thesis, University of Sussex.

Cain, K. and Oakhill, J. (1996). The nature of the relationship between comprehension skill and the ability to tell a story. *British Journal of Developmental Psychology*, 14, 187–201.

Cain, K. and Oakhill, J.V. (1997). Comprehension skill and inference making ability: issues of causality. In C. Hulme and R.M. Joshi (eds), *Reading and Spelling: Development and Disorder*. Mahwah, N.J.: Lawrence Erlbaum.

Carlisle, J.F. (1989). Diagnosing comprehension deficits through listening and reading. *Annals of Dyslexia*, 39, 159–76.

Carlisle, J.F. and Felbinger, L. (1991). Profiles of listening and reading comprehension. *Journal of Educational Research*, 84(6), 345–54.

Carroll, J.B. (1977). Developing parameters of reading comprehension. In J.T. Guthrie (ed.), *Cognition, Curriculum and Comprehension*. Newark, DE: IRA.

Carroll, J.B. (1993). *Human Cognitive Abilities: A Survey of Factor-Analytic Studies*. New York: Cambridge University Press.

Chomsky, C. (1969). *The Acquisition of Syntax in Children from Five to Ten*. Cambridge, MA: MIT Press.

Cipielewski, J. and Stanovich, K.E. (1992). Predicting growth in reading ability from children's exposure to print. *Journal of Experimental Child Psychology*, 54, 74–89.

Cunningham, A.E. and Stanovich, K.E. (1990). Assessing print exposure and orthographic processing skill in children: a quick measure of reading experience. *Journal of Educational Psychology*, 82(4), 733–40.

Cunningham, A.E. and Stanovich, K.E. (1991). Tracking the unique effects of print exposure in children: associations with vocabulary, general knowledge and spelling. *Journal of Educational Psychology*, 83(2), 264–74.

Curtis, M. (1980). Developmental components of reading skill. *Journal of Educational Psychology*, 72, 656–69.

Daneman, M. and Carpenter, P.A. (1980). Individual differences in working memory and reading. *Journal of Verbal Learning and Verbal Behavior*, 19, 450–66.

Daneman, M. and Carpenter, P.A. (1983). Individual differences in integrating information between and within sentences. *Memory and Cognition*, 9, 561–84.

Dunn, L.M., Dunn, L.M., Whetton, C. and Pintillie, D. (1982). *British Picture Vocabulary Scales*. Windsor, Berks: NFER-Nelson.

Ehrlich. M.F. (1996). Metacognitive monitoring in the processing of anaphoric devices in skilled and less-skilled comprehenders. In C. Cornoldi and J. V. Oakhill (eds), *Reading Comprehension Difficulties: Processes and Intervention*. Hillsdale, NJ: Lawrence Erlbaum.

Fitzgerald, J. (1984). The relationship between reading achievement and expectation for story structures. *Discourse Processes*, 7, 21–41.

Fitzgerald, J. and Spiegel, D. L. (1983). Enhancing children's reading comprehension through instruction in narrative structure. *Journal of Reading Behaviour*, 15(2), 1–17.

Fitzgerald, J., Spiegel, D.L., and Webb, T.B. (1985). Development of children's knowledge of story structure and content. *Journal of Educational Research*, 79(2), 101–8.

Freebody, P., and Anderson, R.C. (1983). Effects on text comprehension of differing proportions and locations of difficult vocabulary. *Journal of Reading Behaviour*, 15(3), 19–39.

Garnham, A. (1985). *Psycholinguistics: Central Topics*. London: Methuen.

Gates, A.I. and MacGinitie, W.H. (1978). *Gates–MacGinitie Reading Tests*. New York: Columbia University Teachers' College Press.

Gernsbacher, M.A., Varner, K.R. and Faust, M.E. (1990). Investigating differences in general comprehension skill. *Journal of Experimental Psychology: Learning, Memory and Cognition*, 16(3), 430–45.

Goswami, U. and Bryant, P. (1990). *Phonological Skills and Learning to Read*. Hove, UK: Lawrence Erlbaum.

Gough, P.B. and Tunmer, W.E. (1986). Decoding, reading and reading disability. *Remedial and Special Education*, 7, 6–10.

Gough, P.B. and Walsh, M.A. (1991). Chinese, phoenicians, and the orthographic cipher of English. In S.A. Brady and D.P. Shankweiler (eds), *Phonological Processes in Literacy: A Tribute to Isabelle Y. Liberman* (pp. 199–209). Hillsdale, NJ: Lawrence Erlbaum.

Haslett, B. (1986). A developmental analysis of children's narrative. In D.G. Ellis and W.A. Donohue (eds), *Contemporary Issues in Language and Discourse Processes*. Hillsdale, NJ: Lawrence Erlbaum.

Hickmann, M.E. (1985). The implications of discourse skills in Vygotsky's development theory. In J.V. Wertsch (ed.), *Culture, Communication and Cognition: Vygotskian Perspectives*. New York: CUP.

Hoover, W.A., and Gough, P.B. (1990). The simple view of reading. *Reading and Writing*, 2, 127–60.

Juel, C. (1988). Learning to read and write: a longitudinal study of fifty-four children from first through to fourth grade. *Journal of Educational Psychology*, 80, 437–47.

Juel, C. (1994). *Learning to Read and Write in one Elementary School*. New York: Springer Verlag.

Leather, C.V. (1994). *The Role of Memory, Phonological Awareness and Syntactic Awareness in Reading*. Unpublished D.Phil. thesis, University of Reading.

Leather, C.V. and Henry, L.A. (1994). Working memory span and phonological awareness tasks as predictors of early reading ability. *Journal of Experimental Child Psychology*, 58(1), 88–111.

Liberman, I.Y. and Shankweiler, D. (1991). Phonology and beginning reading: a tutorial. In L. Rieben and C.A. Perfetti (eds) *Learning to Read: Basic Research and its Implications* (pp. 3–17). Hillsdale, NJ: Lawrence Erlbaum.

Mandler, J.M. and Johnson, N.S. (1977). Remembrance of things parsed: story structure and recall. *Cognitive Psychology*, 9, 111–51.

Mann, V.A., Liberman, I.Y., Shankweiler, D. (1980). Children's memory for sentences and word strings in relation to reading ability. *Memory and Cognition*, 8, 329–35.

Mann, V.A. , Shankweiler, D. and Smith, S.T. (1984). The association between comprehension of spoken sentences and early reading ability: the role of phonetic representation. *Journal of Child Language*, 11(3), 627–43.

Mark, L.S., Shankweiler, D., Liberman, A.M. and Fowler, C.A. (1977). Phonetic recoding and reading difficulty in beginning readers. *Memory and Cognition*, 5, 623–9.

Markman, E. (1977). Realizing that you don't understand: a preliminary investigation. *Child Development*, 48, 986–92.

Mezynski, K. (1983). Issues concerning the acquisition of knowledge: effects of vocabulary training on reading comprehension. *Review of Educational Research*, 53(2), 253–79.

Neale, M. D. (1989). *The Neale Analysis of Reading Ability – Revised.* Windsor, Berks: NFER-Nelson.

Oakhill, J. V. (1982). Constructive processes in skilled and less-skilled comprehenders' memory for sentences. *British Journal of Psychology*, 73, 13–20.

Oakhill, J.V. (1983). Instantiation in skilled and less-skilled comprehenders. *Quarterly Journal of Experimental Psychology*, 35A, 441–50.

Oakhill, J.V. (1984). Inferential and memory skills in children's comprehension of stories. *British Journal of Educational Psychology*, 54, 31–9.

Oakhill, J.V. (1994). Individual differences in children's text comprehension. In M. A. Gernsbacher (ed.), *Handbook of Psycholinguistics*, (pp. 821–48). New York: Academic Press.

Oakhill, J.V. and Garnham. A. (1988). *Becoming a Skilled Reader*. Oxford: Basil Blackwell.

Oakhill, J.V., Hartt, J. and Samols, S. (1996). Comprehension monitoring and working memory in good and poor comprehenders. Paper presented at the XIVth Annual Meeting of the ISSBD, Quebec City, August.

Oakhill, J.V. and Yuill, N.M. (1991). The remediation of reading comprehension difficulties. In M. Snowling and M. Thomson (eds) *Dyslexia: Integrating Theory and Practice*. London: Whurr.

Oakhill, J.V., Yuill, N.M. and Parkin, A. (1986). On the nature of the difference between skilled and less-skilled comprehenders. *Journal of Research in Reading*, 9, 80–91.

Omanson, R.C., Warren, W.M. and Trabasso, T. (1978). Goals, inferential comprehension and recall of stories by children. *Discourse Processes*, 1, 337–54.

Palmer, J., MacLeod, C.M., Hunt, E. and Davidson, J.E. (1985). Information processing correlates of reading. *Journal of Memory and Language*, 24(1), 59–88.

Pany, D., Jenkins, J.R., and Schreck, J. (1982). Vocabulary instruction: effects of word knowledge and reading comprehension. *Learning Disability Quarterly*, 5, 202–15.

Paris, S.G. and Lindauer, B.K. (1976). The role of inference in children's comprehension and memory for sentences. *Cognitive Psychology*, 8, 217–27.

Paris, S.G., Lindauer, B.K. and Cox, G.L. (1977). The development of inferential comprehension. *Child Development*, 48, 1728–33.

Paris, S.G. and Upton, L.R. (1976). Children's memory for inferential relationships in prose. *Child Development*, 47, 660–8.

Perfetti, C.A. (1985). *Reading Ability*. Oxford: Oxford University Press.

Perfetti, C. A. (1991). Representations and awareness in the acquisition of reading competence. In L. Rieben and C.A. Perfetti (eds), *Learning to Read: Basic Research and its Implications* (pp. 33–44). Hillsdale, NJ: Lawrence Erlbaum.

Perfetti, C.A. (1994). Psycholinguistics and reading ability. In M.A. Gernsbacher (ed.), *Handbook of Psycholinguistics*, (pp. 849–94).

Perfetti, C.A. and Hogaboam, T. (1975). Relationship between single word decoding and comprehension skill. *Journal of Educational Psychology*, 67, 461–9.

Perfetti, C.A. and Lesgold, A.M. (1977). Coding and comprehension in skilled reading and implications for reading instruction. In L.B. Resnick and P. Weaver (eds), *Theory and Practice of Early Reading*, (Vol. 1). Hillsdale, NJ: Lawrence Erlbaum.

Perfetti, C.A., Marron, M.A. and Foltz, P.W. (1996). Sources of comprehension failure: theoretical perspectives and case studies. In C. Cornoldi and J.V. Oakhill (eds), *Reading Comprehension Difficulties: Processes and Intervention*. Hillsdale, NJ: Lawrence Erlbaum.

Perfetti, C.A., Beck, I., Bell L.C. and Hughes, C. (1987). Phonemic awareness and learning to read are reciprocal: a longitudinal study of first grade children. *Merrill-Palmer Quarterly,* 33(3), 283–319.

Rego, L.L.B. and Bryant. P.E. (1993). The connection between phonological, syntactic and semantic skills and children's reading and spelling. *European Journal of Psychology of Education,* VIII(3), 235–46.

Royer, J.M., Greene, B.A. and Sinatra, G.M. (1987). The sentence verification technique: a practical procedure for testing comprehension. *Journal of Reading,* February, 414–22.

Shankweiler, D. (1989). How problems of comprehension are related to difficulties in decoding. In D. Shankweiler and I.Y. Liberman (eds), *Phonology and Reading Disability: Solving the Reading Puzzle* (pp. 35–68). Ann Arbor: University of Michigan Press.

Shankweiler, D., Liberman, I.Y., Mark, L.M., Fowler, C.A. and Fischer, F.W. (1979). The speech code and learning to read. *Journal of Experimental Psychology: Human Learning and Memory,* 5, 521–45.

Siegel, L.S. and Ryan, E.B. (1988). Development of grammatical-sensitivity, phonological, and short-term memory skills in normally achieving and learning disabled children. *Developmental Psychology,* 24, 28–37.

Singer, M. (1994). Discourse inference processes. In M.A. Gernsbacher (ed.), *Handbook of Psycholinguistics* (pp. 479–515).

Smiley, S.S., Oakley, D.D., Worthen, D., Campione, J. and Brown, A.L. (1977). Recall of thematically relevant material by adolescent good and poor readers as a function of written versus oral presentation. *Journal of Educational Psychology,* 69, 381–7.

Smith, S T., Macaruso, P., Shankweiler, D. and Crain, S. (1989). Syntactic comprehension in young poor readers. *Applied Psycholinguistics,* 10, 429–54.

Spinillo, A.G. and Pinto, G. (1994). Children's narrative under different conditions: a comparative study. *British Journal of Developmental Psychology,* 12, 177–94.

Stanovich, K.E. (1993). Does reading make you smarter? Literacy and the development of verbal intelligence. In H. Reese (ed.), *Advances in Child Development and Behaviour,* (Vol. 24) (pp. 133–80). New York: Academic Press.

Stanovich, K.E., and West, R.F. (1989). Exposure to print and orthographic processing. *Reading Research Quarterly,* 24, 402–33.

Stanovich, K.E., Cunningham, A.E. and Feeman, D.J. (1984). Intelligence, cognitive skills and early reading progress. *Reading Research Quarterly,* 19(3), 278–303.

Stanovich, K.E., Nathan, R.G. and Vala-Rossi, M. (1986). Developmental changes in the cognitive correlates of reading ability and the developmental lag hypothesis. *Reading Research Quarterly,* 21, 267–83.

Stein, N.L. and Glenn, C.G. (1979). An analysis of story comprehension in elementary school children. In R.O. Freedle (ed.), *New Directions in Discourse Processing,* (Vol. 2) (pp. 53–120). In the series, Advances in Discourse Processes. Norwood, NJ: Ablex.

Stein, N.L. and Glenn, C.G. (1982). Children's concept of time: the development of a story schema. In W.J. Friedman (ed.), *The Developmental Psychology of Time* (pp. 255–82). New York: Academic Press.

Stein, N.L. and Policastro, M. (1984). The concept of a story: a comparison between children's and teachers' viewpoints. In H. Mandl, N.L. Stein and T. Trabasso (eds), *Learning and Comprehension of Text* (pp. 113–51). Hillsdale, NJ: Lawrence Erlbaum.

Stein, N.L. and Trabasso, T. (1981). What's in a story: an approach to comprehension and instruction. In R. Glaser (ed.), *Advances in the Psychology of Instruction,* (Vol. 2) (pp. 213–67). Hillsdale, NJ: Lawrence Erlbaum.

Stenning, K. and Michell, L. (1985). Learning how to tell a good story: the development of content and language in children's telling of one tale. *Discourse Processes*, 8, 261–79.

Sticht, T.G. (1979). Applications of the audread model to reading evaluation and instruction. In L.B. Resnick and P. Weaver (eds), *Theory and Practice in Early Reading*, (Vol. 1) (pp. 209–26). Hillsdale, NJ: Lawrence Erlbaum.

Sticht, T.G., and James, H.J. (1984). Listening and reading. In P.D. Pearson (ed.) *Handbook of Reading Research*, New York: Longman.

Stothard, S.E., and Hulme, C. (1992). Reading comprehension difficulties in children: the role of language comprehension and working memory skills. *Reading and Writing*, 4, 245–56.

Stothard, S.E. and Hulme, C. (1995). A comparison of phonological skills in children with reading comprehension difficulties and children with decoding difficulties. *Journal of Child Psychiatry and Psychology*, 36, 399–408.

Stothard, S.E. and Hulme, C. (1996). A comparison of reading comprehension and decoding difficulties in children. In C. Cornoldi and J.V. Oakhill (eds), *Reading Comprehension Difficulties: Processes and Intervention*. Mahwah, NJ: Lawrence Erlbaum.

Townsend, D.J., Carrithers, C. and Bever, T.G. (1987). Listening and reading processes in college and middle school-age readers. In R. Horowitz and S.J. Samuels (eds), *Comprehending Oral and Written Language* (pp. 217–42). San Diego, CA: Academic Press.

Tunmer, W.E. (1989). The role of language-related factors in reading disability. In D. Shankweiler and I.Y. Liberman (eds.), *Phonology and Reading Disability: Solving the Reading Puzzle* (pp. 91–132). Ann Arbor: University of Michigan Press.

Tunmer, W.E. and Bowey, J.A. (1984). Metalinguistic awareness and reading acquisition. In W.E. Tunmer, C. Pratt and M.L. Herriman (eds) *Metalinguistic Awareness in Children*. New York: Springer-Verlag.

Tunmer, W.E., and Hoover, W.A. (1992). Cognitive and linguistic factors in learning to read. In P. Gough, L. Ehri and R. Treiman (eds), *Reading Acquisition* (pp. 175–214). Hillsdale, NJ: Lawrence Erlbaum.

Tunmer, W.E., and Hoover, W.A. (1993). Language-related factors as sources of individual differences in the development of word recognition skills. In G.B. Thompson, W. E. Tunmer and T. Nicolson (eds) *Reading Acquisition Processes*. Clevedon: Multilingual Matters.

van den Broek, P. (1994). Comprehension and memory of narrative texts: inferences and coherence. In M.A. Gernsbacher (ed.), *Handbook of Psycholinguistics* (pp. 539–88).

van Kraayenoord, C.E. and Paris, S.G. (1996). Story construction from a picture book: an assessment activity for young learners. *Early Childhood Research Quarterly*, 11(1), 41–61.

Vellutino, F.R. and Scanlon, D.M. (1991). The preeminence of phonologically based skills in learning to read. In S.A. Brady and D.P Shankweiler (eds), *Phonological Processes in Literacy: A Tribute to Isabelle Y. Liberman*. Hillsdale, NJ: Lawrence Erlbaum.

Vincent, D. and de la Mare, M. (1989). *Macmillan Individual Reading Analysis*. London: Macmillan Education.

Wittrock, M.C., Marks, C. and Doctorow, M. (1975). Reading as a generative process. *Journal of Educational Psychology*, 67, 484–9.

Yuill, N. and Joscelyne, T. (1988). Effect of organisational cues and strategies on good and poor comprehenders' story understanding. *Journal of Educational Psychology*, 80 (2), 152–8.

Yuill, N.M. and Oakhill, J.V. (1988). Effects of inference awareness training on poor reading comprehension. *Applied Cognitive Psychology*, 2, 33–45.

Yuill, N. and Oakhill, J. (1991). *Children's Problems in Text Comprehension. An Experimental Investigation.* Cambridge: CUP.

Yuill, N.M., Oakhill, J.V. and Parkin, A.J. (1989). Working memory, comprehension skill and the resolution of text anomaly. *British Journal of Psychology*, 80, 351–61.

10 Assessment of spelling and related aspects of written expression

David V. Moseley

INTRODUCTION

It has long been recognised that poor spelling can interfere with the quality and quantity of written expression. This does not happen with all students and one hopes that teachers do what they can to minimise the effect, but the fact is that English spelling is difficult, mainly because English orthography is irregular. In Italian, where there is a virtually complete correspondence between pronunciation and spelling, children can write as many words as they can read (Thorstad, 1991), but in English the proportion is significantly lower. While Whiting and Jarrico (1980) found that average readers between the ages of 8 and 11 years could spell correctly between 80% and 91% of the words they could read from flash cards, according to Boder and Jarrico (1982) the figure is typically below 50% for children assessed as having dyslexia.

Writing is the act of constructing and organising meaning and involves a wide range of motor, perceptual and cognitive processes. The language used in writing has to be appropriate for the purpose, social context and audience. The teacher, in assessing written work, has to take many factors into account and there is a tendency among English teachers to regard spelling as a low-level set of 'secretarial' skills. The emphasis on meaning and genre in writing is such that if spelling did not feature strongly in National Curriculum documents, many would avoid teaching it. In a recent evaluation of English teaching, observers of classroom practice found little or no evidence of the systematic teaching of spelling at Key Stage 2 (SCAA, 1994). While some teachers see poor spelling as a 'special needs' problem, there is little structured teaching in which all pupils study spelling in a linguistic context. The regular class use of dictations in assessment and teaching is not very common, perhaps because low achievers experience too much failure with passages pitched at the middle range of ability. Teachers rarely carry out formal assessments of spelling and many are critical of spelling tests in much the same way as they are critical of word-recognition tests, saying that they test skills in isolation, not in context. Criterion-referenced National Curriculum assessment procedures reinforce the widely held belief that norm-referenced tests have little curricular relevance.

Psychologists often become involved in the assessment of writing and spelling when dyslexia is suspected. While both reading and spelling are often below expected levels in children with dyslexia, it has long been recognised that some students can read competently but have extreme difficulty with spelling (Naidoo, 1972). This slows them down in written work and means that they take inadequate notes and perform badly in examinations where extended written answers are required. It is important in all cases of specific learning difficulty that assessment is undertaken within a problem-solving framework which results in practical suggestions for intervention. Referrals need to be made at an early date, preferably before a new course of study is to begin.

It is less common for psychologists to be consulted when a school or college is formulating a writing policy or seeking to improve standards of written work. Yet a systems approach of this kind is likely to be more effective than one based on response to individual referrals since more pupils would benefit.

Both teachers and psychologists have contributions to make to the assessment, teaching and learning of spelling. However, the vast majority of publications on the subject are statements of opinion and belief which lack a sound basis in empirical studies. There is a need for wider dissemination of research such as that included in the *Handbook of Spelling* (Brown and Ellis, 1994) in terms that can be understood by teachers as well as by cognitive psychologists. The nature of the task facing the learner in learning to spell has to be understood and certain widespread misconceptions have to be dispelled. At the same time, the onus is on applied psychologists to set up effective interventions if the sceptics are to be convinced. The writer has reviewed a number of these (Moseley, 1994) and a further example is a single case study by Brooks (1995) in which a 'words in words' strategy proved effective.

In this chapter the interplay between qualitative and quantitative aspects of writing is discussed and age-related 'productivity' norms are presented for a simple writing task. Suggestions are made for assessing handwriting speed and accuracy and the current emphasis on the early teaching of cursive script is questioned. Spelling is identified as a core component of 'accuracy' in writing and the phonological and morphemic aspects of spelling are emphasised, since there is little evidence that spelling depends on holistic visual processing. The validity of different approaches to spelling assessment is discussed and the conclusion is reached that single-word measures are no less valid than others. Spelling error analysis is also considered and guidelines are provided to keep this as simple, reliable and informative as possible.

QUALITATIVE AND QUANTITATIVE ASPECTS OF WRITTEN EXPRESSION

National Curriculum English level descriptions and programmes of study (DfE, 1995) emphasise the communication of meaning through writing by the use of descriptors such as 'interesting', 'lively', 'imaginative', 'thoughtful', 'reasoned', 'clear', 'coherent' and 'organised'. Great value is placed throughout on learning how to write in different forms for different purposes and audiences, as well as on planning and reviewing. The need for collaborative input and feedback is also stressed. All these aspects are concerned with the process of writing and are largely qualitative in nature. They are best assessed by teachers who are fully aware of the classroom context. However, both teachers and psychologists may sometimes find it helpful to assess pupils' metacognitive knowledge about writing. Graham *et al.* (1993) devised an interview procedure with eight open-ended questions which could be scored in terms of whether pupils dwelled more on process ('substantive') or on mechanical ('production') aspects in their answers and in making suggestions for improving a test passage. It was found that pupils aged 9–13 with specific learning difficulties were more concerned with production than with process aspects, whereas age-matched controls gave equal weight to both. Similar findings have been reported by Englert *et al.* (1988) and by Wong *et al.* (1989).

Of the qualitative aspects of writing it is perhaps the imaginative, original and creative aspects that are the hardest to assess other than subjectively. They produce effects which the reader may not wish to analyse and which may depend on emotional associations. However, they are certainly important and are to some extent dependent on technical accuracy in writing. I found a moderate degree of correlation between ratings of 'originality' and 'accuracy' ($r = 0.48$) and between originality and percentage of correctly spelt words ($r = 0.44$) in twenty-five samples of writing produced by children at the end of year 5. The samples were those published as representative of the full range of originality in the large-scale study carried out by Hunter-Grundin and Grundin (1980).

Quantitative aspects of writing receive more attention than qualitative ones at National Curriculum Levels 1 and 2 and equal emphasis at Level 3 and above in the DFE document referred to above. One most important feature which has both quantitative and qualitative attributes is the use of vocabulary. The aspects of writing which are largely quantitative are: grammar, spelling, punctuation and handwriting. More implicit than explicit in the document is the idea that as children grow older they should be expected to write more often and to write more extended pieces.

The most substantial British study of children's language and literacy skills in primary schools was carried out for the Schools' Council by Hunter-Grundin and Grundin (1980). Up to 2800 children were assessed in each age group and one of the tasks was to write for ten minutes on the subject 'On the Way to School'. In terms of quantity, the results agreed quite closely with those of Myklebust (1973), who used a photograph as a stimulus for writing, and with the more recent British study by Alston (1995) in which children had to write for twenty minutes on 'My Favourite Person (or Personality)', 'Someone I Know Very Well' or 'Something in which I am Very Interested'. Alston offers norms based on 168 Cheshire pupils in years 3 to 6. Perhaps because the time given was longer and the topics more open-ended than in the Schools' Council study, the children wrote at a somewhat slower rate in Alston's study. For children in years 1 and 2 there is little published data to go on, but Robinson (1973) (cited in Clay, 1975) devised a writing vocabulary task in which children are encouraged (with suggestions) to write as many single words as they can in ten minutes.

If one combines the results of the above studies (seventeen data points in all over the age range 5 to 17 years), a linear relationship ($r = 0.94$) between age and mean writing speed in words per minute is found. The least-squares solution to fitting a straight line to these points yields the results shown in Table 10.1. It is reassuring to find that the mean writing speed of 15.5 words per minute for 15 year-olds is much the same as the figure given by Hedderly (1992). Also in Table 10.1, and based on the published standard deviations in the above studies, are cutting points at the tenth percentile, which may be taken to indicate a significant degree of slowness in writing. However, it should be noted that the writing speeds given are averages for boys and girls, and most studies have shown that girls write more fluently than boys at all ages, boys typically writing 15 to 20% less than the girls.

For most children, writing speed is much more a function of thinking time than of motor skill. Even for adults, thinking what to write takes up a large part of total writing time (Gould, 1980). While verbal ability in English must be an important general factor influencing writing speed, it is reasonable to believe that young writers with specific learning difficulties are slowed down considerably by having to work out how to structure a sentence, or how to express an idea using easy-to-spell words. Martlew (1992) showed that ten-year-old pupils with dyslexia are no slower than their peers in the physical process of handwriting, even with hard-to-spell words that are copied or written to dictation. So the slowness of children

Table 10.1 Norms for the number of words written in ten minutes by children aged 6 to 15 years

CA	6y 0m	7y 0m	8y 0m	9y 0m	10y 0m	11y 0m	12y 0m	13y 0m	14y 0m	15y 0m
50th percentile	20	35	50	65	80	95	110	125	140	155
10th percentile	4	9	15	23	31	41	52	66	79	95

with dyslexia and of others with reading, spelling and language problems (Myklebust, 1973) is more likely to be caused by problems in finding the right words and/or syntactical forms. This idea is supported by Myklebust's finding of a close relationship between number of words written by sixty-four children with dyslexia and their performance on a word-opposites task ($r = 0.82$) and by the fact that they made more syntax errors in their writing than age-matched controls at 9 and 11 years. In addition, there is undoubtedly a link between spelling competence and the amount written in classroom conditions. I have found a highly significant correlation ($r = 0.55$) between percentage of correctly spelt words and total number of words written in ten minutes, using twenty-five passages by year 5 children collected by Hunter-Grundin and Grundin. There is also substantial evidence (Moseley, 1989) that both poor spellers and pupils with dyslexia avoid the use of hard-to-spell words. When compared with good spellers, their written work included more regularly spelt words and fewer common hard-to-spell words such as 'friend', 'their' and 'until'.

If one wishes to compare speed when writing freely for ten minutes about a familiar topic with purely mechanical writing speed, a simple copying task like the one shown in Box 10.1 can be used to assess mechanical speed. The average length of the words in the sentence to be copied is 3.67 letters, which is close to average word length in the free writing of children aged 7 to 11 years. The suggested sentence makes minimal demands linguistically. Although a simple comparison can then be made between performance on the free-writing and copying tasks in terms of words written per minute, no norms are available to help with the evaluation of discrepancies.

Box 10.1 Sentence-copying task to measure mechanical writing speed

Sentence to be copied (written at top of sheet):
The snow was deep and cold.

Procedure
When I say 'Go', pick up your pen/pencil and copy the sentence in your usual handwriting. See how many times you can write the sentence before I say 'Stop'. Write each sentence on a new line. Give one minute and then say 'Stop'. Add up the number of words written.

Handwriting speed is undoubtedly one important determinant of writing fluency, with the greatest increase in speed taking place for most children between the ages of 7 and 9. However, the legibility of writing is generally viewed as a more important learning target than speed. Good writers generally manage not only to write more in terms of both quantity and quality, but also to write more legibly. In the year 5 samples referred to above, legibility ratings were significantly correlated with the word count totals (r = 0.46), as well as with accuracy ratings (r = 0.71), spelling accuracy (r = 0.41) and originality (r = 0.44).

So far as legibility is concerned, there are a number of published guidelines which add some detail to National Curriculum statements, such as those by Alston (1995), Hunter-Grundin and Grundin (1980) and Reason and Boote (1994). Alston attaches great importance to the early development of cursive script and appears to have influenced the National Curriculum expectation for joined writing at Level 3. However, the benefits of joined script may well be exaggerated and it certainly presents a more complex perceptual motor-learning task to young children. The argument is sometimes advanced that letter strings are established as the building blocks of spelling by writing them in cursive script, but there is little empirical support for this claim. In a study funded by the University of Reading Centre for the Teaching of Reading in 1984 which involved 395 Year 7 pupils in four Berkshire secondary schools, it was found that there was no significant difference in spelling ability between the 42% of pupils who had a good cursive hand and the 37% who wrote in a well-formed printed style. Furthermore, Vaughn *et al.* (1993) showed in a well-controlled study that there was no advantage either for 8 to 9-year-old learning-disabled pupils or for their age peers in actually writing the words they were learning to spell. Keyboarding, writing and tracing were equally effective in improving the accuracy of two-letter strings and whole-word spelling, which suggests that if letter strings are learned as units, this can be done purely by means of visual or linguistic 'chunking'. Consequently it is preferable for assessment purposes to focus less on the joining of letters than on pencil grip, position in relation to paper, the execution of basic movement patterns, and on aspects of letter formation such as shape, consistency of size, slope and the avoidance of shape reversals and unwanted capitals.

An adventurous psychologist may wish to experiment with biofeedback or relaxation techniques if it seems that difficulty with handwriting is associated with undue muscle tension especially in the hand and forearm. Biofeedback clearly has potential if one wishes to monitor the effects of a handwriting training programme. Pencil or pen pressure can also be monitored by low-tech means such as turning the paper over and looking at the extent of indentation on the other side, provided that the writing conditions have been constant.

Word usage, grammar, punctuation and spelling are all features of writing where computer analysis has been developed in packages such as 'Grammatik' and 'Perfect Copy'. Some packages offer built-in assessment and recording of progress. While there are limits to what can be achieved by computer assessment in these areas, it has the important advantage of providing immediate feedback. Even the application to writing samples of a readability formula which gives some weight to word frequency can provide useful evidence of growth in vocabulary and of the ability to handle longer sentences. However, it is unwise to base such evaluations on a single piece of writing, as some topics require simple language and reference to everyday experiences. It is probably for this reason that the writer found little evidence of an increase in vocabulary size, word and sentence length in the Hunter-Grundin and Grundin 'On the Way to School' passages between Years 3 and 6. There was, however, a year-by-year reduction in the repetition of words and phrases, suggesting that a measure of repetition such as type/token ratio might be a useful quantitative index of an increase in the ability to choose interesting and varied means of expression. One possible reason for the reduction in repetition with age is that as spelling ability improves the writer is not deterred from using common hard-to-spell words. There was clear evidence of this happening, with the proportion of words containing hard-to-spell features such as digraphs, silent letters, doubled consonants and neutral vowel spellings showing a substantial increase over the junior school years ($r = 0.80$).

Hunter-Grundin and Grundin provided guidelines for a composite 'accuracy' rating based on 'choice of words and phrases, sentence construction, spelling, capitalisation and the use of the full stop'. They found that at the end of Year 5 the norm was for children to make between ten and fifteen such errors per 100 words written, reducing to eight or ten at the end of Year 6. In the poorest 10% of Year 5 scripts typically 'well over a third of the words are either ill-chosen or misspelled or show some grammatical error', while at Year 6 this was true of 'well over a quarter of the words'. It is important to note that composite accuracy ratings of this kind reflect spelling more than any other variable, as is shown by the high correlation ($r = 0.80$) between 'accuracy' and the percentage of misspellings in twenty-five Year 5 passages. In the representative uncorrected writing samples provided by Hunter-Grundin and Grundin, the median percentage of spelling errors at the end of Year 3 was 14%, falling to 10% at the end of Year 4, and 5% at the end of Years 5 and 6. Spelling mistakes typically account for half of all 'accuracy' errors made by the average pupil, and for a still higher proportion among those who find spelling difficult. And it is to spelling that we now turn, since this provides for many pupils a major obstacle to gaining confidence as well as competence as writers.

SPELLING: THE MAJOR TASK COMPONENTS

It is well known that a core writing vocabulary of 100–200 words accounts for 50–70% of all writing samples (Sakiey and Fry, 1979). The spelling of these words can be separately assessed, using appropriate lists such as those produced by Graham *et al.* (1994) and by Moseley (1995). Both within and outside that vocabulary there are short words and longer words, words that are both regular and irregular in their spelling. Writers need to be able to spell words correctly, in their different morphological forms and in different contexts. To succeed in this they need both word-specific knowledge and knowledge of spelling patterns, especially those that are linguistically based. Whether or not spellchecks are used, writers also need proof-reading skills, notably the ability to tell whether words 'look right'.

According to Croft (1983), there are forty-five common words which collectively accounted for 25% of all errors made in writing samples by 1200 New Zealand children aged between 8 and 13 years. The sources of difficulty in these words can be classified under the following headings: unusual sound spellings, silent letters, neutral vowels, doublings, homonyms and splits (one word written as two, or two as one). It is clear that if these words are to be mastered, highly efficient strategies must be found to dispel the feelings of failure and confusion that are likely to be associated with them.

Using spelling error data in the reference books for the Hunter-Grundin Literacy Profiles as well as the research carried out by Graham *et al.* I have added fifteen more words to Croft's list to produce a list of sixty words that account for approximately 30% of all misspellings made by children in Years 3–6. These are listed in Box 10.2 by word length and constitute a useful assessment tool in their own right.

Researchers are agreed that a large proportion of spelling errors are more or less phonetically accurate renderings, using graphemes and letter sequences found elsewhere in English spelling. According to Sterling (1983), who studied the essays written by fifty-six 12 year olds, more than 50% of the total errors could be classified in this way, while according to Whiting and Jarrico (1980) (who used more liberal criteria), between 75% and 90% of spelling errors made by normal readers are 'good phonetic equivalents'. Gentry (1982) and Frith (1985) see phonetically plausible spelling as an important step towards complete orthographic mastery.

Phonetically plausible misspellings interfere little with intelligibility and demonstrate both auditory-vocal and linguistic awareness. If longer and unfamiliar words are tackled phonetically, most parts are likely to be correct and attention has to be given only to the 'tricky parts'. It is therefore sensible to encourage children to develop the skills of auditory analysis as a useful tool in learning to spell words of increasing complexity. If this is done then confusion is less likely to occur between acoustically similar consonants and vowels and fewer problems are likely to arise with consonant clusters. Bruck and Waters (1989) provided convincing evidence that spelling–sound correspondence is important in both spelling and reading for children with very different levels of reading and spelling attainment, with weaker spellers making a smaller proportion of phonetically plausible errors than good spellers. Similarly, Lennox and Siegel

Box 10.2 Core list of hard-to-spell words

These words (or some of them) can be given as a test. If used before and after teaching the results provide a measure of learning. If used for self-assessment they can provide an indication of self-awareness. Words for students to self-check whenever they have writing to do should be written on personal reference cards.

an   of

all   it's   (a)lot   off   saw   too   two   was

came   come   hour   into   kept   knew   know   said   then   they
want   went   were   when

again   could   heard   might   right   still   that's   their   there
tried   until   where

always   bought   caught   friend   houses   inside   myself
opened   people   played   police   school   turned

another   decided   outside   running   started   stopped   thought
through

because   suddenly

sometimes

(1994) compared good with poor spellers at all ages from 6–16, and found that good spellers 'more frequently use a phonological as opposed to a visual approach to spelling'. However, poor spellers who were also good readers were more likely than those who also had reading problems to make use of developing phonological skills in their spelling. Lennox and Siegel suggest that print exposure helps to develop phonological skills as well as an awareness of spelling patterns within words. They also claim that good spellers eventually come to rely on visual as much as phonological skills in their spelling, but usually not before the age of 11.

It is far from clear how people learn which particular letter combinations belong to individual words, but it is unlikely that this can happen purely on a word-specific visual recognition or rote-learning basis. The process seems to be based on a growing probabilistic awareness of linguistic features as well as of visual patterns. According to Sterling, a significant proportion of misspellings (29%) are morphemic in nature, most being concerned with plurals and tense endings. This suggests that in such cases it would be worthwhile to teach spelling in relation to the appropriate morphemic patterns. It is often held that spelling rules are too complex and have too many exceptions to be worth teaching, but this argument does not hold for basic grammatical word-endings. If these features can be taught to second language learners of English then why not to native speakers? As a minimum, the following word-endings should be taught and their use monitored:

- add 's' to form plurals
- add 's' to verb for third person singular present tense
- add 'es' instead of 's' to words ending in 'ss', 'ch' and 'sh'
- add 'ing' to verbs
- add 'ed' to regular verbs for past tense
- add 'er' and 'est' to adjectives.

When these have been mastered, more complex skills such as changing final 'y' to '-ies', the omission of final 'e' when adding a suffix and the rules governing consonant doubling should also be assessed and taught.

The ability to detect and self-correct errors is part of competence in spelling. This skill of recognising errors depends partly on the ability to recognise that a particular word does or does not 'look right'. Croft *et al.* (1981) devised the Proof-Reading Tests of Spelling (PRETOS) on the basis of a study carried out by the New Zealand Council for Educational Research in which it was found that a proof-reading format was more closely related to children's spelling in their written assignments than either a multiple-choice or a dictation format. However, conventional spelling tests in which children write down single words which they have heard used in a sentence also provide the opportunity to see if a spelling 'looks right'. Croft and others found that PRETOS scores were highly correlated (0.87 and 0.90) with scores on Vernon's Graded Word Spelling Test (Vernon, 1977) in which words are written in isolation. It may be that the 'looks right' component is relatively unimportant when compared with other phonological and linguistic skills. At college level, Tenney (1980) found that being able to write and visually compare correct and incorrect spellings (as opposed to listening to the spelt-out words) added relatively little to task accuracy (an increase from 71% to 74%). Weak spellers are typically very poor at detecting their own errors and it may be that the ability to tell whether a word looks right is well developed only in good spellers who are avid readers.

SPELLING TESTS

The form of a spelling test probably makes little difference to its validity, provided that the content is appropriate. Hunter-Grundin and Grundin (1980) developed a number of short spelling tests in which children had to write in missing words in a passage that was read to them. The validity of these tests was demonstrated by correlation coefficients in the range 0.81–0.84 with the number of words spelled correctly in a standard ten-minute free-writing activity. However, whether or not the test words are located in a passage is probably of little importance, as single-word spelling tests and dictation tests have been shown to yield very similar results. I (Moseley, 1980) compared two forms (single-word spelling and dictated passage) of a spelling test judged by teachers to include common sight words, commonly misspelt words and basic phonic patterns. The two forms were given to a sample of eighty-five 8-year-old pupils within a fortnight of each other and the scores on the sixty test words yielded a correlation coefficient of 0.94. A similar result was obtained by Clarke (1975), who obtained a validity coefficient of 0.90 between his own dictation spelling test and the long-established single-word spelling test by Schonell (1932). Single-word spelling and the recognition of a target word among four or five distractors have also been shown to yield highly correlated sets of scores (Carver and Moseley, 1994).

There are a number of published single-word spelling tests of good reliability, some of which are reviewed in this book. One of the most reliable is Vernon's (1977) *Graded Word Spelling Test*, which can be used with whole classes or individually and takes up to thirty minutes to administer. Young's *Parallel Spelling Tests* (Young, 1983) are of similar length and reliability, but have the advantage of an item bank from which an indefinite number of parallel forms can be generated. Taking less time (only ten minutes) to administer to a whole class, but covering only the junior school age range, the five spelling scales in the *Hunter-Grundin Literacy Profiles* (1980) are of good reliability (0.90–0.94) and have an attractive and meaningful format.

Standardised spelling tests, however reliable and valid, do have their limitations. It is argued below as well as in some of the test reviews, that it is rarely possible to glean diagnostic information of much value from standardised tests. A possible exception is the *Boder Test of Reading–Spelling Patterns* (Boder and Jarrico, 1982), which has norms based on rather small American samples but was designed primarily as a diagnostic instrument. However, most tests allow one to make an impressionistic judgement as to whether a phonetic approach has been used and whether regular or irregular words cause more difficulty. These judgements always need to be confirmed by analysing a larger sample of errors collected from the pupil's written work. However, spelling tests do have the advantage of pushing pupils to the limits of their ability and it is possible to gain from them not just a score, but an idea of the types of word an individual can and cannot spell. If successes and errors are examined in terms of word length, one can find out the length of word where there is a chance greater than one in three that an error will occur. This is useful information to have, since it means that in proof-reading, all words of that length or longer need careful checking. An example is given in Box 10.3, taken from Young's *Parallel Spelling Tests*. In this case, a spelling age of 6 years 11 months means that words of two and three letters are spelled correctly and that errors occur in more than a third of four-letter words.

Box 10.3 How to assess spelling accuracy in relation to word length

The example below is taken from a spelling test, but the same method can be used with any writing sample yielding enough errors. The aim is to find the point at which more than one-third of the words of the same length are misspelled.

WORDS ATTEMPTED		NO. CORRECT/ TOTAL
2-letter words	in be	2/2
3-letter words	men hat run leg cap	5/5
4-letter words	this thin (for then) make bist (for best) maeae (for melt) boat	3/5
5-letter words	cisp (for crisp) dive (for drive) papar (for paper)	0/3
6 letters or more		none correct

So far as content is concerned, spelling tests are usually based on studies of children's spoken and/or written language. They vary in the following ways:

- vocabulary gradient
- increase in average word length with age level
- the inclusion of commonly misspelt words and 'spelling demons'
- the proportion of regular to irregular spellings
- the built-in features which may support error analysis.

Vocabulary and word-length differences can be illustrated by comparing the *Boder Test of Reading-Spelling Patterns* and the *Proof-Reading Tests of Spelling* (Croft *et al.*, 1981). *The Boder Test* is designed to include words that are not immediately recognised on sight and all the words intended for 11 year olds lie outside a core vocabulary of 2000 words which I have compiled from a variety of published lists. On the other hand, the *Proof-Reading Test* passages were intended to be read and understood by the majority of New Zealand pupils in an age group, and the 69% of the spellings to be corrected by 11 year olds are to be found in the 2000-word core vocabulary list. *The Boder Test* words for this age group tend to be longer than those in the *Proof-Reading Test*, an average of 8.3 letters compared with 6.4. These differences reflect the different purposes of the two tests, since in *The Boder Test* a comparison is made between the spelling of 'known' and 'unknown' words and in the *Proof-Reading Test* the task of detecting misspellings adds to the overall difficulty. The *Proof-*

Reading Test has greater face validity, since it most closely resembles part of the writing process, that of detecting and correcting errors in passages of appropriate complexity. Unlike *The Boder Test*, it also includes in the proof-reading paragraphs a substantial proportion of high-frequency commonly misspelt words.

The majority of published spelling tests include more or less equal proportions of so-called regular and irregular words, although few define their characteristics in a rigorous manner. This is true of *The Boder Test*, where the proportion of regular and irregular known words spelled correctly is said to be a diagnostic indicator for 'dysphonetic' and 'dyseidetic' dyslexia. Dysphonetics spell correctly more irregular than regular words and fail to spell 'unknown' phonetic words of more than one syllable, producing under 50% of good phonetic equivalents for unknown words. On the other hand, dyseidetics, who find it hard to recall visual patterns, use a phonetic strategy, doing well with regular words and offering more than 50% of good phonetic equivalents for unknown words. Boder and Jarrico (1982) provide evidence for the criterion-related validity of these subtypes and for inter-rater agreement and test-retest stability regarding 'good phonetic equivalents' across the age range 6–15 years. However, with younger children (6–9 years) there was considerable variation over a period of up to two months in the number of known words spelled correctly ($r = 0.64$) and no data are presented concerning the stability of the ratio of phonetic to non-phonetic known words spelled correctly. Nevertheless, Boder's classification has some support in terms of underlying verbal and visuospatial cognitive processing and in its implications for teaching. Using receptive vocabulary and spatial visualisation measures to compare performance on verbal and visual tasks, I (Moseley, 1994) found that verbal strategies for learning spellings worked best in 9 to 10 year olds who were stronger verbally than spatially. Verbal strategies were also more effective than visual ones for pupils who were better at spelling regular than irregular words. On the other hand, visual strategies proved to be more effective for pupils who were better at spelling irregular words.

Nelson (1974) claimed that children whose problems lie in language development (e.g. slow speech development, slow word finding and lower verbal than non-verbal IQ) tend to have both reading and spelling problems and to make spelling errors that are phonetically inaccurate. These findings are similar to those of Ginn (1979). Nelson also described a second clinical group of children whose reading is adequate, but who have a specific problem with spelling. This group tend not to have a history of language problems and to make phonetically plausible errors, so resembling Boder's dyseidetics. If we follow the implications for teaching outlined above, the dyslexic pupil with phonological problems affecting both reading and spelling may respond best to spelling instruction with a visual emphasis, whereas those who read well enough but cannot spell may do best with verbal methods, such as using 'spelling pronunciation', simultaneous oral spelling, mnemonics and spelling rules.

SPELLING ERROR ANALYSIS

The categorisation of spelling errors is a complex and time-consuming process and spelling error analysis remains an academic exercise unless it is likely to result in an effective intervention. For most busy teachers who wish to keep records of individual progress, personalised spelling lists suffice, or the recorded results of regularly administered dictation passages. Published graded and diagnostic dictation passages in which different spelling patterns are repeated are readily available.

Some spelling tests claim to provide useful diagnostic information based on a system of error analysis. Here it is important to raise the question of reliability, since most tests generate only a small number of errors. There is also the related issue of overlapping error categories, which can lead to over-complex scoring procedures and lack of consistency between markers. I (Moseley, 1980) examined the test-retest reliability of a four-category non-overlapping diagnostic scoring system in a sample of eighty-five 8 year olds. It was found that shortening errors (using fewer letters than required) and vowel errors (incorrect representation of a vowel grapheme) were the most reliable, each with reliability coefficients of 0.79. Consonant errors came next, but the least common type of error (mistakes of letter order) was of low reliability ($r = 0.39$). The average number of order errors was 1, and this applied equally in all four quartiles of spelling ability, suggesting that order errors are usually chance occurrences of little diagnostic significance. On the basis of this study, as a result of applying the Spearman–Brown formula, it was inferred that for reliable error analysis, it is necessary to have a minimum of ten to twelve errors under each error category. This may well be feasible if we are basing the analysis on writing samples, since data collection can continue until that number has been recorded under all categories used, but it is unrealistic to expect most spelling tests to produce an appropriate range of errors. For example, the spelling test in the *Richmond Tests of Basic Skills* battery (Hieronymus *et al.*, 1988) identifies sixteen types of recognition error, but of these only the vowel substitution category occurs more than ten times at a particular level in the test.

There have been some studies of the incidence of spelling errors in tests, dictation passages and free writing (Livingstone, 1961; Williams, 1974) and these have established that shortening is one of the most common types of error. However, whereas in younger and less able children the omission of letters may suggest a memory weakness or a failure to move beyond a single-letter phonic strategy, in older and more able students it may reflect a willingness to attempt long and unfamiliar words. In similar ways, other error categories such as insertions and doubling may tell us more about the kinds of words the writer is attempting to spell than about an underlying cognitive profile. Nelson's (1980) failure to find any difference in error frequencies between children with dyslexia and younger controls of the same spelling age, using a three-category diagnostic system (phonologically inaccurate, orthographically illegal and order error), suggests that the search for distinctive cognitively driven patterns of 'dyslexic spelling' is probably mistaken. As Nelson put it, 'the quality of dyslexic children's spelling is essentially normal'.

Hepburn (1991) proposed a ten-category system for error analysis. Five of the categories can apply to almost any word:

- generalisation (an inappropriate use of a spelling pattern or rule), e.g. 'fisical' for 'physical';
- shortening, e.g. 'r' for 'are'; 'libry' for 'library';
- articulation (based on mispronunciation), e.g. 'somethink' for 'something';
- doubling a single consonant, e.g. 'boddy' for 'body';
- letter order reversals, e.g. 'muose' for 'mouse'.

We have already seen that both phonically plausible generalisation errors and shortening errors are very common and may have diagnostic significance. The other types of error listed above are less common, but may be worth considering in individual cases. In the early stages of word recognition and spelling it may also be worth making an assessment of relative strength and weakness in phonological awareness of consonant and vowel sounds. A group or individual test that provides an objective scoring system for doing this is the *Test of Word Recognition and Phonic Skills* (Carver and Moseley, 1994). This is the only group test which provides a reliable profile of strengths and weaknesses at different stages of development, with linked suggestions for teaching that can be built into individual education programmes.

Hepburn's other five categories relate to built-in features of the target words:

- morphological errors, e.g. 'keeped' for 'kept';
- homonym confusion, e.g. 'beech' for 'beach';
- single in place of double consonant, e.g. 'cal' for 'call';
- omission of silent letter, e.g. 'com' for 'comb';
- spacing error (omission or insertion between words), e.g. 'alot' for 'a lot'; 'in side' for 'inside'.

A case has been made above for the separate evaluation of morphological errors, since there can be clear implications for teaching when problems are found. Bentote *et al.* (1990) report the following empirically derived order of difficulty within the morphological category of suffixing: plurals, compound words, doubling rule, modified *e* words, *y* endings changing to *i* plus suffix. Hepburn's other four categories which apply to groups of words as well as those listed below may require separate assessment at certain ages and stages on an individual basis:

- letter rotations, e.g. 'bog' for 'dog';
- confusion of voiced and unvoiced and other similar sounding consonants, e.g. 'doe' for 'toe';
- inaccurate representation of consonant clusters, e.g. 'jaw' for 'draw';
- inaccurate representation of letter-string vowel spellings, e.g. 'vuw' for 'view';
- omission or insertion of the 'magic e', e.g. 'cam' for 'came';
- inaccurate representation of the neutral 'schwa' vowel sound, e.g. 'coler' for 'colour',
- inaccurate spelling of prefixes containing the letter 'e', e.g. 'rigret' for 'regret'.

It is clear that spelling error analysis can easily become over-elaborate and time-consuming. In order to simplify the process I suggest that diagnostic assessment should be based on a set of standard procedures (listed in Box 10.4). A small number of further options may then be selected that are appropriate to each individual case. These options and procedures can only be justified if they yield information that helps to shape effective educational intervention.

In order to ensure educational relevance and to increase reliability when evaluating types of error, it is suggested that both correctly and incorrectly spelled words be studied. One way of doing this is to make

---

Box 10.4 Recommended procedures for the diagnostic assessment of spelling

- evaluate spelling of high-frequency words, especially those that are frequently misspelt;
- when developmentally appropriate, evaluate proof-reading skills for spelling mistakes in a first draft;
- collect at least forty spelling mistakes from writing samples to evaluate in relation to choice of vocabulary;
- use a standardised test or a dictation passage to determine a spelling age or stage level;
- find out the word length at which more than one-third of all words are misspelled;
- evaluate the phonic plausibility of mispellings;
- compare the spelling of regular and irregular words;
- find examples of shortening errors and consider their significance;
- find examples of morphological errors and consider their significance.

two lists of longer words from writing samples and/or from test responses. It is not difficult to find the longest word correctly spelled by a particular student and then to find other long words (above a certain number of letters) that are correctly spelled – perhaps twenty or so in total. The next step is to compile a second list of misspelt words of similar or greater word length. The two lists are then examined to see which of the following features are causing problems: letter rotations, single consonant sounds, consonant clusters, doubled consonants, vowels, letter order reversals, morphological endings, homonyms, 'magic e', silent letters, neutral vowel sounds, and prefixes containing the letter 'e'. If, for example, it is thought that homonyms may be a significant problem, both lists are examined and both misspelled and correctly spelled homonyms are added up. The same procedure is followed for each error category where a number of misspellings are evident. It is important that both lists are examined in arriving at the totals. It can then be seen which types of error are most common and also where the chances of error are greatest. The implications for teaching will then be apparent.

ASSESSMENT AS A DYNAMIC PROCESS

There is little point in assessing spelling individually unless feedback is provided directly to the student and to those who will be working with that student. Individual assessment is best seen as a discussion or series of discussions in which problems are explored, views sought, feelings expressed, understanding developed and targets set. It should be a learning experience for the student in which hope is generated and strengths and achievements are confirmed.

A one-off assessment is unlikely to provide a good basis for predicting future progress, especially when there is a history of negative experiences and task avoidance. It is particularly risky to assess a student as 'having dyslexia' if the assessment does not include measures of learning style, process and outcome. For this reason, it is important that short-term learning targets be set and that learning be evaluated by the teacher or psychologist as an integral part of the assessment process. This approach is built into *The Code of Practice* (DfE, 1994) at stages 1–3 and should, in the writer's view, also be carried out routinely by psychologists.

At the simplest level, a dynamic approach to assessment means taking a baseline measure, providing some guidance or help, and checking to see whether learning has occurred. For example, the number of trials needed to learn spellings before and after modelling and teaching a new strategy can be measured. Similarly, accuracy in proof-reading for spelling errors can be measured and fed back to the student before agreeing on a suitable strategy for improving this skill. Precision teaching programmes can also be seen as a type of dynamic assessment.

'Precision spelling' was a five-week intervention with built-in dynamic assessment (Moseley, 1988). It succeeded in dramatically raising the achievement of four students with dyslexia in a short period, using a target-setting approach. More recently, a class-based intervention using the Vernon test for initial allocation to appropriate word lists raised the spelling ages of sixty-four pupils aged 8–11 years by an average of nineteen months in five months (Moseley, 1994). With an effect-size of 1.4, who needs a control group? With a reliable old car and a Haynes manual, who needs Galileo?

REFERENCES

Alston, J. (1995). *Assessing and Promoting Writing Skills*. Stafford: NASEN.

Bentote, P., Norgate, R. and Thornton, D. (1990). Special needs: spelling – some problems solved? *Educational Psychology in Practice*, 6(2), 76–81.

Boder, E. and Jarrico, S. (1982). *The Boder Test of Reading–Spelling Patterns*. New York: Grune & Stratton.

Brooks, P. (1995). A comparison of the effectiveness of different teaching strategies in teaching spelling to a student with severe specific learning difficulties/dyslexia. *Educational and Child Psychology*, 12(1), 80–8.

Brown, G.D.A. and Ellis, N.C. (eds) (1994). *Handbook of Spelling*. Chichester: Wiley.

Bruck, M. and Waters, G. (1989). An analysis of the component reading and spelling skills of good readers–good spellers, good readers–poor spellers, and poor readers–poor spellers. In T. Carr and B.A. Levy (eds), *Reading and its Development: Component Skills Approaches*. New York: Academic Press.

Carver, C. and Moseley, D. (1994). *Manual for a Group or Individual Diagnostic Test of Word Recognition and Phonic Skills*. London: Hodder & Stoughton.

Clarke, A. (1975). *A Dictation Spelling Test* (mimeo). London: Child Guidance Training Centre.

Clay, M.M. (1975). *What Did I Write? Beginning Writing Behaviour*. Auckland: Heinemann.

Croft, C. (1983). *Teachers Manual for Spell-Write: An Aid to Writing, Spelling and Word-study*. Wellington: New Zealand Council for Educational Research.

Croft, C., Gilmore, A., Reid, N. and Jackson, P. (1981). *Proof-Reading Tests of Spelling*. Wellington: New Zealand Council for Educational Research.

Department for Education (DfE) (1994). *The Code of Practice on the Identification and Assessment of Special Educational Needs*. London: DfE.

DfE (1995). *English in the National Curriculum*. London: HMSO.

Englert, C., Raphael, T., Fear, K. and Anderson, L. (1988). Students' metacognitive knowledge about how to write informational texts. *Learning Disability Quarterly*, 11, 18–46.

Frith, U. (1985). Beneath the surface of developmental dyslexia. In K.E. Patterson, J.C. Marshall and M. Coltheart (eds), *Surface Dyslexia: Neuropsychological and Cognitive Analyses of Phonological Reading*. London: LEA.

Gentry, R. (1982). *An analysis of developmental spelling in GNYS AT WRK*. The Reading Teacher, 36, 192–200.

Ginn, R. (1979). An analysis of various psychometric typologies of primary reading disability. Unpublished doctoral dissertation, University of Southern California.

Gould, J.D. (1980). Experiments on composing letters: some facts, some myths and some observations. In L.W. Gregg and E.R. Steinberg (eds), *Cognitive Processes in Writing*. Hillsdale, NJ: Lawrence Erlbaum.

Graham, S., Harris, K.R. and Loynachan, C. (1994). The spelling for writing list. *Journal of Learning Disabilities*, 27, 210–14.

Graham, S., Schwartz, S.S. and MacArthur, C.A. (1993). Knowledge of writing and the composing process, attitude toward writing, and self-efficacy for students with and without learning disabilities. *Journal of Learning Disabilities*, 26, 237–49.

Hedderly, R.G. (1992). Psychologists' assessment of specific learning disabilities (dyslexia) and examination boards: policies and practices. *Educational Psychology in Practice*, 8, 32–42.

Hepburn, J. (1991). Spelling categories and strategies. *Reading*, April, 33–7.

Hieronymus, A.N., Lindquist, E.F. and France, N. (1988). *Richmond Tests of Basic Skills* (2nd edn). Windsor: NFER-Nelson.

Hunter-Grundin, E. and Grundin, H.U. (1980). *Hunter-Grundin Literacy Profiles*. High Wycombe: The Test Agency.

Lennox, C. and Siegel, L.S. (1994). The role of phonological and orthographic processes in learning to spell. In G.D.A. Brown and N.C. Ellis (eds), *Handbook of Spelling*. Chichester: Wiley.

Livingstone, A. (1961). A study of spelling errors. In Scottish Council for Research in Education, *Studies in Spelling*. London: University of London Press.

Martlew, M. (1992). Handwriting and spelling: dyslexic children's abilities compared with children of the same chronological age and younger children of the same spelling level. *British Journal of Educational Psychology*, 62, 375–90.

Moseley, D.V. (1974). Some cognitive and perceptual correlates of spelling ability. In B. Wade and K. Wedell (eds), *Spelling: Task and Learner*. Birmingham: University of Birmingham Educational Review Occasional Publications, pp. 15–22.

Moseley, D.V. (1980). Patterns of spelling errors: some problems of test design. *Spelling Progress Bulletin*, 20(4), 17–18.

Moseley, D.V. (1988). New approaches to helping children with spelling difficulties. *Educational and Child Psychology*, 5(4), 54–8.

Moseley, D.V. (1989). How lack of confidence in spelling affects children's written expression. *Educational Psychology in Practice*, 5, 42–6.

Moseley, D.V. (1994). From theory to practice: errors and trials. In G.D.A. Brown and N.C. Ellis (eds), *Handbook of Spelling*. Chichester: Wiley.

Moseley, D.V. (1995). *ACE Spelling Dictionary* (7th edn). Wisbech: LDA.

Myklebust, H. (1973). *Development and Disorders of Written Language*, Vol 2. New York: Grune & Stratton.

Naidoo, S. (1972). *Specific Dyslexia*. London: Pitman.

Nelson, H. (1974). The aetiology of specific spelling disabilities. In B. Wade and K. Wedell (eds), *Spelling: Task and Learner*. Birmingham: University of Birmingham Educational Review Occasional Publications.

Nelson, H. (1980). Analysis of spelling errors in normal and dyslexic children. In U. Frith (ed.), *Cognitive Processes in Spelling*. London: Academic Press.

Reason, R. and Boote, R. (1994). *Helping with Reading and Spelling: a Special Needs Manual*. London: Routledge.

Robinson, S.M. (1973). *Predicting Early Reading Progress*. Unpublished M.A. thesis, University of Auckland.

Sakiey, E. and Fry, E. (1979). *3000 Instant Words*. Highland Park, NJ: Dreier.

SCAA (1994). *Evaluation of the Implementation of English in the National Curriculum at Key Stages 1, 2 and 3 (1991–1993)*. London: SCAA.

Schonell, F.J. (1932). *Essentials in Teaching and Testing Spelling*. London: Macmillan.

Sterling, C.M. (1983). Spelling errors in context. *British Journal of Psychology*, 74, 353–64.

Tenney, Y.J. (1980). Visual factors in spelling. In U. Frith (ed.), *Cognitive Processes in Spelling*. London: Academic Press.

Thorstad, G. (1991). The effect of orthography on the acquisition of literacy skills. *British Journal of Psychology*, 82, 527–37.

Vaughn, S., Schumm, J.S. and Gordon, J. (1993). Which motoric condition is most effective for teaching spelling to students with and without learning disabilities? *Journal of Learning Disabilities*, 26, 191–8.

Vernon, P. (1977). *Graded Word Spelling Test*. London: Hodder & Stoughton.

Whiting, S. and Jarrico, S. (1980). Spelling patterns of normal readers. *Journal of Learning Disabilities*, 13, 40–2.

Williams, A. (1974). A study of spelling errors. In B. Wade and K. Wedell (eds), *Spelling: Task and Learner*. Birmingham: University of Birmingham Educational Review Occasional Publications, pp. 45–50.

Wong, B., Wong, R. and Blenkinsop, J. (1989). Cognitive and metacognitive aspects of learning disabled adolescents' composing problems. *Learning Disability Quarterly*, 12, 21–30.

Young, D. (1983). *Parallel Spelling Tests*. London: Hodder & Stoughton.

11 Assessment of adult reading skills

David McLoughlin

INTRODUCTION

It is perhaps inevitable that the understanding and assessment of reading skills is always placed in an educational context. It has been said that while children learn to read, teenagers read to learn (Chall, 1983). Adults do read to learn but they also read to work. One might add that they read to play, as being able to read underlies many social activities. Although the assessment of reading skills of adults will resemble that of the assessment of reading skills of children, the aims and process can be quite different. In addition, the testing of adults will depend on context. This chapter concentrates on assessment mainly within the work situation. However, psychologists can also be called upon to assess students at universities and colleges to determine if they have dyslexia. This will mean a full psychometric appraisal including the application of an intelligence test. Recommendations will include whether an extra time allowance or some concessional arrangement needs to be made. There is now recognition that some kind of allowance should be made for literacy difficulties in formal examinations. There particular issues and related matters are dealt with in the Introduction to this book (Chapter 1). In this chapter the components of reading which should be included when assessing adults are outlined, and relevant measures of each component are described and discussed.

THE AIMS OF ASSESSMENT

There are essentially three aims in assessing an adult's reading skills, especially in the work setting:

1 Establishing whether the reader has sufficient competence in all aspects of reading as to enable them to deal with a particular occupation, or at least the programme of study leading to that occupation.
2 Diagnosing reading difficulties and establishing a starting point for remedial instruction.
3 Measuring progress on reading programmes.

THE PROCESS OF ASSESSMENT

It is assumed here that measures of cognitive and language functioning have already been taken. It is important, particularly when establishing remedial reading programmes, to separate the following:

1 *The unable* – those people whose overall level of cognitive and language functioning are such as to predispose them towards finding aspects of reading difficult. Limited expressive and receptive language skills can, for example, affect the process of reading comprehension.
2 *The disabled* – those people whose cognitive and language functioning is at an average or better than average level, but who have specific areas of weakness which undermine their acquisition of reading skills; for example, people with dyslexia.
3 *The unprepared* – those whose cognitive and language skills are adequate, but whose educational experience has been such that they leave school without having developed appropriate reading skills.

READING LEVELS

Where standardised tests have been used to assess the reading levels of children, scores have been expressed as reading ages, grade norms or percentile equivalents. The first two of these I would consider to be inappropriate for adults, particularly as many tests are limited to student populations. It may not be helpful for an adult to know they have a reading age of 10 years, for example, and it would be demoralising if handled insensitively. The same can be said of percentiles. Knowing that one has scored less well than 80% of the population could do on a particular reading task is not encouraging. In my view, it might not be relevant to the particular individual. We only need the reading skills we need; that is, the skills which enable us to deal with the demands placed upon us by our educational, work and social programme. The most enduring and important situation in which adults need reading skills is their work environment. Criteria for establishing levels of reading amongst adults are, therefore best derived from work tasks.

Adult reading skills can be rated as being at one of four levels. These are professional, technical, vocational and functional. For those who are more familiar with reading in an educational setting, these levels are set out below with their equivalent educational levels.

Professional GCE A level and above
Technical beginning of secondary school to GCSE level
Vocational primary school
Functional infant school

Professional reading skills are those required by GCE A level courses, as well as university studies and a professional occupation. Someone who has reached this level is capable of independent reading, has a wide reading vocabulary and the ability to understand sophisticated material.

Individuals who read at the *technical level* have sufficient competence in decoding and comprehension to enable them to complete GCSE courses and a programme of further education. They would be able to work in occupations such as sales, secretarial work and computing.

Those who are at *vocational level* in all aspects of reading would have difficulty completing secondary education but should be able to understand the fundamental needs of many jobs that require a moderate amount of reading. They should be capable of undertaking semi–skilled work that only requires a minimum amount of reading.

Adults who read at only the *functional level* will show considerable variation but it can be expected that they will find jobs which require even a moderate amount of reading difficult. Those at the upper end of the functional level may have sufficient reading survival skills to enable them to deal with jobs which place minimal demands upon reading skills but those at the lower end may not be able to deal with any type of job which requires some reading.

Within these four levels, individuals can be identified as being at an *independent, instructional* or *frustrational* stage. The first reflects a stage at which the reader demonstrates excellent proficiency and is able to deal with material without assistance. The instructional stage indicates that the reader requires minimal assistance. Performance at this stage suggests that the reader would benefit from tuition to bring on their skills within this level. It is the most useful piece of information. Once this stage has been established it is assumed that someone can be given materials which are written at the particular reading level. If, for example, someone reads between 91% and 93% of words correctly and answers between 75% and 90% of comprehension passage questions correctly, it is assumed they can profit most from materials and instruction at that level.

Individuals who score at the frustrational stage cannot deal with reading material at that particular level and should be provided with materials at a lower level.

THE COMPONENTS OF READING ASSESSMENT

Reading is a very complex skill. However, for the purpose of assessment, many researchers, such as Aaron and Baker (1991), have suggested that it can be regarded as having two major components:

1 *Decoding* – that is, the ability to pronounce the word, either overtly or covertly.
2 *Comprehension* – that is, the ability to understand the word and the text.

It is important to add to the first of these the ability to pronounce the word at an acceptable rate, as being able to read quickly is important in the adult years. To the second should be added 'when listening'. Listening comprehension underlies many adult activities including working, learning and socialising. The assessment of adult reading skills should therefore include measures of decoding, reading and listening comprehension, as well as reading rate. Each sub-skill should be evaluated separately, particularly when the aim of an assessment is to diagnose reading difficulties and plan remedial instruction. This is not as easy as it should be as there is a dearth of good tests designed for adults.

Decoding

Decoding skill has been measured typically by the use of single-word reading and prose reading tests. There are many examples of the first and they are much the same. They consist of lists of words graded in order of difficulty. The best known are those developed by Schonell (1950) and Vernon (1938) (but both are now considered to be out of date). Only the latter provides a score which is beyond the beginning of secondary school level. The *National Adult Reading Test* (Nelson and Willinson, 1991), although sometimes listed as a single-word reading test, was designed to estimate intelligence retrospectively, that is, prior to deterioration through physical or psychiatric illness. The *Wide Range Achievement Test – Revised* (WRAT-R) (Jastak and Wilkinson, 1984) has two forms for reading, Level 2 being for 12 year olds upwards. However, like other single-word reading tests its presentation of ninety words to be read may appear threatening to poor readers, although in practice it has been commonly used. Spreen and Strauss (1991) questioned its use outside of the USA because of a lack of correspondence with academic curricula in other English-speaking countries. They argued that due to a lack of availability of technical data regarding the properties of the test 'as well as shortcomings in the standardisation procedures the test should not be used as a diagnostic measure of academic difficulties' (p. 109). It has now been replaced by WRAT-3 (Wilkinson, 1993) which has overcome some of these criticisms. The number of words has been reduced to forty-two and more recent technical data have been provided. However, it still has an element of being culturally specific.

The *Spadafore Diagnostic Reading Test* (Spadafore, 1983) includes tests of single-word reading which are better presented than they are on most individual reading tests. That is, there are twenty words on a page for each grade level. This is far less threatening for the adult who has experienced problems with literacy than being presented with a large number of words all at once. It is criterion-referenced, indicating whether an individual has reached the independent, instructional or frustrational stage for each of the four levels of reading described above.

Although they do have a place in the assessment of decoding skill, single-word reading tests offer only one part of the overall picture. When assessing an adult's reading skills, one is really attempting to determine how well he or she can function in everyday life, as well as in academic and work settings. Most people have to deal with prose rather than individual words. Prose reading tests usually consist of a set of passages graded in order of difficulty, which the examinee has to read aloud. Examples of these are the *Neale Analysis of Reading Ability*, both the old form and new revised version (Neale, 1989), as well as the *Macmillan Reading Test*. Again, however, such tests were developed for use with children and the maximum score tends to be around the beginning of secondary school level. The *Spadafore Diagnostic Reading Test* does have a prose or oral reading component and consists of passages up to the professional level of reading.

Two other prose reading tasks have become quite widely used in the assessment of adult reading skills. These are Cloze procedure and Miscue Analysis. Cloze procedure is favoured by organisations such as the Adult Literacy and Basic Skills Unit (ALBSU, 1995). It involves presenting passages of particular readability from which words have been deleted. The person being assessed is expected to supply these missing words. Every fifth, seventh or tenth word is generally replaced by a blank space. Although it can be used as a measure of reading level, and in order to complete a Cloze task successfully decoding must be involved, the procedure is of limited diagnostic value because it does not separate individual sub-skills.

Miscue analysis (see e.g. Klein, 1993) measures how well a reader is able to use language clues, his or her own expectations and decoding skills to derive meaning. That is, when readers encounter the printed page they use a variety of language clues or cues, individual expectations about the message, and decoding cues to make rapid guesses about the words. Sometimes a reader makes wrong guesses and 'reads' words that are different from those on the page. These are not counted as errors but miscues. By careful examination of these miscues, the examiner is able to draw conclusions about strengths and weaknesses in the reading process. The examiner is looking for indications of how well a reader is interacting with the language. One of the main problems with miscue analysis is that it is an oral reading task, and the assumption is made that miscues in the silent reading process are reflected in oral reading. The precise relationship between the two is, in fact, unknown (Quandt, 1977). A further criticism is that, when asked to read material which is difficult and unfamiliar in content, even the best readers will make errors that do not fit the context.

Comprehension

Measures of reading comprehension take a number of forms. In general they involve answering questions about material which has been read aloud or silently. Tests such as the *Neale Analysis* and the *Macmillan*

Reading Test have a comprehension component. The passages are read aloud and then questions are asked about their content. It is arguable that reading comprehension can be measured accurately when someone has been asked to read aloud. The process of dealing with correct pronunciation and expression can interfere with comprehension. Measures of silent reading comprehension are much more important. It is silent reading comprehension which is fundamental to being able to pursue formal education and most occupations. If one were to choose a particular aspect of reading which would predict success in an occupation, it would be silent reading comprehension.

Tests of silent reading comprehension usually involve asking individuals to read a passage to themselves within a prescribed time and then to answer questions. The *Wechsler Objective Reading Dimensions Test* (Rust *et al.*, 1993) has a measure of silent reading comprehension, but the upper age limit is 17 years. There are no British tests of this skill designed for adults but the silent reading comprehension tests from the Spadafore and the *Scholastic Abilities Test for Adults* (Bryant *et al.*, 1991) have much to commend them. The first consists of passages graded up to the professional level. The reader is given a prescribed amount of time in which to read the passage; they are then asked questions about them and respond verbally. Further, it provides information about the level of reading skill required for specific occupations, so can be useful in career counselling. The latter also has a set of graded passages but questions are presented in written form and the response is in multiple-choice format.

When examining people who, on the basis of their educational background, are likely to be at a functional or vocational level, the *Basic Skills Tests* (Smith and Whetton, 1988) are quite useful. These were designed for use in occupational rather than educational settings. The reading section focuses on silent reading comprehension as the examinee is required to answer questions about articles and advertisements in a specially prepared mock local newspaper. It has good face validity as its relevance is obvious to examinees.

The greatest strength of both Cloze procedure and Miscue analysis lies in the fact that what they do best is measure reading comprehension. It has been suggested that Cloze only measures reading comprehension. Passages can be selected and analysed for readability, relevant to factors such as age and occupation. Miscue analysis suffers from the same problem as other oral reading tests. That is, the process of reading aloud can interfere with comprehension.

LISTENING COMPREHENSION

Listening comprehension is an important skill. This is the ability to analyse and understand what is presented aurally. A great amount of new knowledge is acquired through listening. Listening comprehension underlies performance in learning situations such as seminars, tutorials, work training programmes, as well as skills such as note taking. Adults with poor listening comprehension skills can have difficulty functioning in learning and work settings. At the professional level, reading is more efficient than listening, but below that people are heavily reliant on listening comprehension. Measures of listening comprehension consist mainly of the examiner reading passages to the person being tested and then asking them questions about what they have heard. The *Spadafore Diagnostic Reading Test* provides a measure of listening comprehension up to the professional level.

SPEED OF READING

There are adults who can decode words quite well but do so very slowly. Being able to decode words at the professional level does suggest that an adult might be able to tackle courses of advanced study or undertake a professional occupation, but if the process is very slow there will be limitations. Being able to read quickly is also important to comprehension. Biemiller (1977–8), for example, demonstrated that unless a person can read at least 150 wpm they cannot keep the content in memory long enough to comprehend it.

Reading speed is traditionally expressed in terms of words read per minute. However, single-word reading and prose reading tests often contain unfamiliar words. This introduces a complication because of the individual differences in the word knowledge of readers – some spend an unusually long time when they encounter an uncommon word that they cannot readily decode. Aaron and Baker (1991) have therefore suggested that a simple way of assessing reading speed is the use of lists of common words. Examples of the tests they use are shown in Box 11.1.

Reading aloud is not a particularly important skill for most adults. A more appropriate measure of reading speed or rate is based on silent reading. Reading rates tend to increase in predictable increments across the age span. Average reading rates for the four levels of reading are set out in Box 11.2.

Reading rate can be tested by asking the examinee to read a passage silently, without worrying about remembering the material. 'MARK' is called after one minute has elapsed, and the number of words read counted. The average for several passages at the same level of difficulty provides the most reliable measure (Manzo and Manzo, 1993).

METACOGNITION

An additional area which should be considered, particularly when working with readers operating at an advanced level is metacognitive skills; that is, people's own thinking about the way they learn and work. Brown (1980)

Box 11.1 Speed of reading test

Instructions: Here are some common words. Read them aloud as fast as you can taking care not to make mistakes.

List I	List II
let	every
has	never
ago	could
off	along
why	while
any	might
yet	often
nor	which
will	since
much	ahead
also	should
must	except
even	behind
such	though
once	during
soon	almost
ever	before
upon	without
else	perhaps
thus	although

Average rate at technical level

12 seconds   14 seconds

Box 11.2 Silent reading rate

Reading level	wpm
Functional	100
Vocational	150–175
Technical	200–250
Professional	+250

first applied the concept of metacognition to reading and underscored its crucial role in effective reading. Metacognitive skills related to reading can be described as reading for meaning (comprehension monitoring) and reading for remembering (studying or learning). A good reader possesses metacognitive skills in reading, is aware of the purpose of reading and differentiates between task demands. When reading text for a study assignment, for example, or reading a magazine for pleasure, the reader actively seeks to clarify the task demands through self-questioning prior to reading material. This awareness leads to the use of suitable reading strategies. A good reader varies his or her reading rate and comprehension level as a function of materials being read. The altering of reading rate according to the purpose of reading and the difficulty of the text is *flexibility*. This can be tested by calculating and comparing rates of reading for simple and difficult materials (Manzo and Manzo, 1993).

Awareness can also lead readers to monitor their reading comprehension. When a good reader encounters a comprehension difficulty he or she uses 'debugging' strategies. These attempts at problem solving reflect self-regulation. A good reader evaluates his or her own comprehension of material and this has important consequences. If readers are unaware of their failure to understand a particular part of given material, they will not employ suitable 'debugging' strategies such as backtracking or scanning ahead for possible cues to solve the difficulties. The fluent or mature reader is rarely conscious of his or her overall comprehension monitoring. When a comprehension failure arises, the fluent reader immediately slows down in reading and either reviews the difficult sections or reads on, seeking clues in subsequent text. Metacognition therefore does have two components: one is online monitoring of comprehension; the other is taking corrective action when encountering difficulty (Wray, 1994).

The assessment of metacognition in reading involves investigating two sub-skills:

1 Whether someone has a reasonably correct estimate of his or her own abilities.
2 Whether or not readers are comprehending what is read or heard.

Readers should be encouraged to ask questions such as:

1 When I read a book how often do I go back to a passage or sentence and reread it so as to clarify things?
2 How often do I ask a fellow student or tutor for clarification of ideas?
3 Do I find it difficult to grasp the main idea of a passage that I have read?
4 After an examination, how often do I feel I have done well but find the results are disappointing?

If the answer is 'rarely' to the first three and 'often' to the last, it might be that the reader is not good at comprehension monitoring (Wong, 1986), and instruction in metacognitive skills should be included in a remedial programme.

REPORTING

Proper reporting, whether verbally to the individual tested or in writing, is of course essential. When preparing written evaluations those testing the adult reader need to recognise that their reports can be read by a variety of people, some of whom are familiar with assessment techniques and scoring but others who are not. Misinterpretation by a training or personnel manager can have dire consequences for an employee.

Written reports of assessments must therefore be clear and meaningful. When test scores are included their significance should be explained. In my view the use of age levels should be avoided; it is preferable to relate them to the levels of reading described in this chapter. Two sample reports follow; the first (Box 11.3) concerns an individual working at an advanced level who wishes to develop his reading skills in order that he might cope better with the demands of his job. The second report (Box 11.4.) concerns someone who has severe problems with reading which have resulted in difficulties in employment and subsequent litigation.

OVERVIEW

1 The aims and process of the assessment of adult reading skills both resemble and differ from those involved when testing children. It is particularly important to use meaningful criteria, the best being based on the most significant activity in which an adult participates, that is, work. The reading skills of an adult can be regarded as being at one of four levels: functional, vocational, technical or professional.
2 Assessment should be relevant, comprehensive and include individual measures of decoding, reading as well as listening comprehension and reading speed.
3 When assessing adult readers working at an advanced level it is important to include a measure of metacognition related to reading.
4 Written reports of assessments need to be clear. In particular, the significance of scores should be explained as these can be easily misinterpreted by those who have no training in the interpretation of tests.

Box 11.3   Report of Reading Assessment A

Name: Paul

Age: 28 years

Reason for referral   Paul was referred by his employers. He is at present a junior manager and is in line for promotion. He approached his personnel manager, concerned that he was finding the amount of paperwork he had to deal with onerous. This was also affecting his performance on the part-time management certificate course he was undertaking.

Tests administered   Spadafore Diagnostic Reading Test.

Test scores
Single-word reading – technical level
Prose reading – professional level (instructional stage)
Silent reading comprehension – technical level
Listening comprehension – professional level
Rate of reading – 150 wpm

Interpretation   Paul was able to read lists of words accurately up to a technical level. His attempt at the first list from the professional level suggested that he was at the frustrational stage. He did much better when he could read words in the context of prose, scoring at the professional level (instructional stage).

Paul read passages to himself and was asked questions about them. He was able to do this independently up to the highest passage from the technical level. Paul read prose slowly, probably in an attempt to enhance comprehension. His rate of reading (150 wpm) is below an expected level. He did read more quickly when given a passage at a much lower level and this does suggest he is showing some flexibility in his rate of reading.

Skill development   Paul can improve his reading skills and would benefit from some tuition. The emphasis should be on the following:

1 Paul needs to expand his reading vocabulary. This is largely a matter of practice but he does need feedback on the correct pronunciation of words. Listening to tapes of printed material while following the text could be helpful.

2 It is particularly important that Paul develop improved reading comprehension strategies. Being able to extract information from text quickly is the most important reading skill. It would be better if he was to devote his attention to this rather than under-

take a speed reading course. Systematic approaches such as SQ3R (Survey, Question, Read, Recite, Revise) could be useful.

Special examination arrangements It would be appropriate to make special provision for Paul during a course of study. In particular, he should be allowed extra time to complete formal examinations as his slow reading rate and problem with reading comprehension will be a disadvantage.

Box 11.4   Report of Reading Assessment B

Name: George

Age: 48 years

Reason for referral George was referred by his solicitor. At the time of the assessment his employment had just been terminated. He had been working in an unskilled manual job, but sustained a physical injury. This led to five years on sick leave, during which time he had been offered clerical jobs by his employers. As he was well aware of the limits of his literacy skills, he had refused these positions. Cognitive testing had shown him to have dyslexia but his employers were refusing to accept this diagnosis. He was in the process of appealing against his dismissal.

Tests administered Spadafore Diagnostic Reading Test

Test scores
Single-word reading – functional level
Prose reading – functional level (instructional stage)
Silent reading comprehension – vocational level
Listening comprehension – technical level
Rate of reading – 90 wpm

Interpretation George was only able to read lists of words accurately at the functional level. The use of contextual cues when reading prose did not make a significant difference and his attempt at the lowest passage from the vocational level suggested that he was at the frustrational stage.

George read passages to himself and was asked questions about them. He was able to do this independently of the instructional stage on the highest passage from the vocational level. He took a long time to read the passages, his rate of reading (90 wpm) being very slow. George's best performance was when he was asked questions about material which had been read to him. He was successful at the technical level.

Conclusion   George has very limited reading skills. Although he can understand material at a level which would enable him to deal with semi-skilled work, his word-reading skills are at a very basic level and he reads very slowly. At present he does not have sufficient competence in reading to enable him to engage in clerical work.

This should be taken into account when considering his current employment situation. He will require a considerable amount of specialist teaching if he is to be successful in other than an unskilled occupation.

REFERENCES

Aaron, P.G. and Baker, C. (1991). *Reading Disabilities in College and High School* Penn, Bucks: York Press.

ALBSU (1995). *Assessing Reading and Maths*. London: The Adult Literacy and Basic Skills Unit.

Biemiller, A. (1977–8). Relationships between oral reading rates for letters, words, and simple text in the development of reading achievement. *Reading Research Quarterly*, 2, 223–53.

Brown, A.L. (1980). Metacognitive development and reading. In R.J. Spiro, B. Bruce and W.F. Brewer (eds) *Theoretical Issues in Reading Comprehension*. Hillsdale, NJ: Lawrence Erlbaum.

Bryant, B.R., Patton, J.R. and Dunn, C. (1991). *Scholastic Abilities Test for Adults (SATA)*. Austin, Texas: Pro-Ed.

Chall, J.S. (1983). *Stages of Reading Development*. New York: McGraw-Hill.

Jastak, S. and Wilkinson, G. (1984). *Wide Range Achievement Test – Revised*. Los Angeles, CA: Western Psychological Services.

Klein, C. (1993). *Diagnosing Dyslexia*. London: Avanti.

Manzo, A.N. and Manzo, U.C. (1993). *Literacy Disorders*. Orlando, Fda: Holt, Rinehart & Winston.

Neale, M.D. (1989). *Neale Analysis of Reading Ability* (Revised edn). Windsor, Berks: NFER-Nelson

Nelson, H. and Willinson, J. (1991). *National Adult Reading Test (NART)* . Windsor, Berks: NFER-Nelson

Quandt, I.J. (1977). *Teaching Reading: A Human Process*. Chicago: Rand McNally

Rust, R., Golombok, S. and Trickey, G. (1993). *Wechsler Objective Reading Dimensions Test*. London: Psychological Corporation.

Schonell, F.J. (1950). *Diagnostic and Attainments Testing*. London: Oliver & Boyd.

Smith, P. and Whetton, C. (1988). *Basic Skills Tests*. Windsor, Berks: NFER-Nelson.

Spadafore, G.J. (1983). *Spadafore Diagnostic Reading Test*. Novato, CA: Academic Therapy.

Spreen, O. and Strauss, E. (1991). *A Compendium of Neuropsychological Tests*. New York: OUP.

Vernon, P.E. (1938). *The Standardization of a Graded Word Reading Test.* London: London University Press.
Wilkinson, G. (1993). *Wide Range Achievement Test* (Revised 3rd edn) Delaware: Jastak Associates.
Wong, B.Y.L (1986). Metacognition and special education: a review of a view. *Journal of Special Education*, 20, 19–29.
Wray, D. (1994). Comprehension monitoring, metacognition and other mysterious processes. *Support for Learning*, 9, 3107–13.

12 Assessment of acquired disorders of reading

Janice Kay

This chapter is concerned with how to assess reading disorders that are acquired after neurological trauma of some kind, such as stroke, road traffic accident or tumour. It is written as a tutorial essay for clinicians who may be relatively inexperienced in assessment of the acquired dyslexias (though not necessarily in cognitive assessment in general), and I have also tried to make it accessible to people who are interested in reading and its impairments, but who perhaps have only a limited knowledge of clinical disorders. I have essentially tried to write a practical essay on how to assess acquired reading disorders. However, to do so requires that I also tell you not only about the kinds of disorder that can occur, but also why they may occur. In order to understand better why they occur, one needs an account of the processes that may operate when you and I, as competent readers, read. Note that by 'reading' here, I mean recognition, comprehension and pronunciation of written words, since the disorders I discuss below affect reading at the level of a single word.

In an article on the rehabilitation of acquired disorders of reading and writing, Patterson (1994) sets out a simplified flow diagram of the processes that may be involved in successful identification, comprehension and production of a written word. As she notes, although the scheme is simple, it is both speculative and controversial. For the purposes of instruction, however, it is a good place to start, and I will discuss any contentious issues as it becomes necessary.

Let us consider the bare bones of this scheme. The first stage in Figure 12.1 is one of visual letter identification. Of course, a lot more must go on before a written word even arrives at this stage. It must be analysed perceptually just as any visual stimulus is analysed, and this means that at a bare minimum, its location in space, and characteristics such as its length, and serial position of its letters, must be encoded in some way (Ellis *et al.*, 1987). As we can recognise words regardless of type font and most handwriting styles, a common assumption is that letters are transformed before a word is recognised into representations that are independent of letter case and style (i.e. print or handwriting) and these representations are referred to as abstract letter identities (Coltheart,

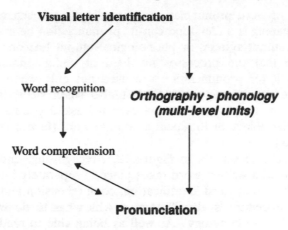

Pure alexia (letter-by-letter reading)
Surface dyslexia
Deep dyslexia
Phonological dyslexia

Figure 12.1 A simplified flow diagram of processes involved in recognising, understanding and pronouncing single written words, illustrating how four major types of acquired dyslexic disorder might arise from selective impairments to these processes
Source: adapted from Patterson, 1994

1981; McClelland, 1976). All this information about letter identities and their position in the word is transmitted in parallel to a system of visual word recognition (sometimes called the visual or orthographic input lexicon). The assumption that letter information is processed in parallel, rather than serially, one letter at a time, is supported by the finding that in competent adult readers, processing speed is relatively unaffected by word length. We shall see that, after brain damage, some patients are apparently no longer able to process letters in parallel.

The visual word recognition system itself consists of separate entries for all the written words known to the reader, and it is involved in identifying what the word is. Understanding what words actually mean takes place in a separate system for word comprehension, generally called the semantic system. Although considerable research effort is currently directed at trying to understand more about the complexities of how we represent meaning, it is reasonable to state that the semantic system is probably not organised like a dictionary, with meanings standing alongside individual words. It is more likely that our knowledge about the meanings of words is represented conceptually, and possibly even non-linguistically (Allport, 1985). The stage at which meaning is analysed is also separate from one of word pronunciation. According to this scheme, only after a word's meaning is understood can its pronunciation be made available in a speech output system, or phonological output lexicon. It is important to realise that the processes involved in understanding a word and retrieving it for pronunciation are used not only when we read aloud (which we do relatively rarely), but also when we speak in everyday conversation. They would also be used if I asked you to name a picture of a familiar object, or to repeat a familiar word (favourite clinical assessment tasks).

In the scheme set out in Figure 12.1, recognising, understanding and reading aloud a written word takes place in separately identifiable stages to do with written word identification, comprehension and pronunciation. Another procedure is also illustrated which has to do with 'multi-level orthography → phonology'. As well as being able to read aloud familiar words, we are also readily able to read aloud written words that we may never have seen before (in unfamiliar addresses, for example, such as *Shuttern Lane, Newton St Cyres*); indeed, to children learning to read, most words that they come across are at first unfamiliar. If our lexicons for reading and speaking consist of familiar words, then things that are not words will not be represented. As we have little difficulty in assembling pronunciations for them, we must have an alternative way of doing it. The procedure depicted in Figure 12.1 consists of spelling and sound segments that are smaller than words (and therefore called *sub*-lexical units). To pronounce the made-up word *shint*, for example, one might use information about the correspondence between individual letters and sounds. Note that 'grapheme' is more appropriate than 'letter' here: 's' and 'h' would be dealt with as a single graphemic unit 'sh', corresponding with the phonemic sound /sh/, rather than as two letters. One would expect the vowel 'i' to be given its short pronunciation /i/, when followed by a consonant ('n') or consonant group ('nt'). Alternatively, one might use information about larger-sized units, as well as graphemes, such as the end segment (technically called the 'rime'), '-int', and its more common pronunciation (/int/, in this case). The nature of these units, how they are derived, and how far they are separable from whole-word representations are issues of hot debate that do not concern us here (the interested reader is directed to Harley (1995) for an accessible introduction to this debate). The scheme we have followed assumes separable word and sub-word processes, with the latter consisting of multiple spelling–sound correspondences (from single letters and sounds (graphemes and phonemes) to larger spelling–sound units such as the rime). Following common practice, I will refer to the system that allows us to read aloud new words and nonwords as the *sub-lexical routine*, and the system for reading words as the *lexical routine*. Of course, neither of these systems knows the lexical status of a string of letters beforehand (whether it is a familiar word or something new), and so both will be involved in processing a written input, at least initially. Unfamiliar words, nonwords, will not be identified as words by the word recognition system and so will not undergo further processing. Many written words can be given a correct pronunciation both by the lexical route and by the sub-lexical route, but this will not apply in all cases. For a variety of historical reasons, written English is made up of many scores of words, often very common in the language, which have pronunciations that are not predicted by the regularities of spelling–sound correspondences. Some words, like *yacht* and *meringue*, have quite unusual spellings, as well as having unusual pronunciations. Others are exceptions to a more predictable spelling–sound pattern: *pint*, compared with *mint*, *tint*, *print*, etc., *have*, compared with *save*, *gave*, *cave*, etc. The pronunciation of such words, referred to as exception words, must be derived from word-based processes; sub-lexical procedures will produce incorrect, 'regularised' responses. In contrast, regular words (like mint and print), which conform to common sound–spelling patterns of English, can be provided with correct pronunciations by whichever route.

A basic model such as this can account for the performance of competent adult readers (of English) when they read, understand and pronounce both written words and novel letter strings successfully. Although under normal conditions different components of the model may not operate independently of each other, or indeed of the rest of the language system, its processes are separable in the sense that they can each be subject to impairment after brain damage. Detailed investigations of acquired disorders of reading that have taken place over the past thirty years have indeed revealed different and distinct patterns of deficit. Even if this model, or models like it, ultimately do not take us very far into understanding the mechanisms involved in written word recognition, comprehension and production, they provide us with a logic with which to begin to assess the symptomatology of acquired disorders (Kay *et al.*, 1996).

In-depth investigations of acquired reading impairments have distinguished four major patterns of disorder, each associated with a characteristic signature: pure alexia (letter-by-letter reading), surface dyslexia, deep dyslexia and phonological dyslexia. These are based on sensitivity to linguistic dimensions of words, such as their grammatical class, imageability (whether they are able to raise an image in the reader's mind), frequency/familiarity (how often a word occurs or is used in the language), regularity (whether they conform to common spelling–sound correspondences of written English) and lexical status (whether they are words, or just made-up strings) (Patterson, 1981), and on the types of reading errors that occur. Of course, this picture is not as clear-cut as I have made it appear. These are not the only patterns that can occur, and, within each type, variants of the main type are frequently observed. However, these major types crop up relatively frequently in the clinic, and, as Patterson (1994) notes, they are so far the only types of reading impairment in which systematic reading rehabilitation has been attempted in one or more cases.

I will therefore confine discussion of reading impairments and their assessment to these major patterns, with some discussion of the variations that can occur.

PURE ALEXIA OR LETTER-BY-LETTER READING

Pure alexia was described over a hundred years ago by Jules Dejerine (1892), and in a recent exposition of his work, Bub *et al.* (1993) provide evidence of a fascinating link between his views and current hypotheses of the nature of the disorder. The hallmark of pure alexia is that reading aloud single words is considerably slowed (to seconds rather than milliseconds). Thus, the longer the word, the longer it takes to be identified, and there is a monotonic relationship between word length (in letters) and reading speed. Sometimes, but not invariably, letters will be read aloud one letter at a time (hence the alternative label, letter-by-letter reading). Individual letters are sometimes misidentified, so that the patient makes errors such as the following: men → 'h, e, n, hen' (Patterson and Kay, 1982). At the same time, patients are often extremely good at identifying words spelled aloud to them.

This combination of symptoms has led some authors to conclude that the disorder stems from a problem in visual letter identification (e.g. Behrmann and Shallice, 1995), or in transmission of information from letter identification to word recognition (Kay and Hanley, 1991; Patterson and Kay, 1982). Warrington and Shallice (1980) suggest a more central problem, at the level of word recognition itself, but in order to explain the pattern of preserved word identification from oral spelling, they have to assume that patients carry out this task by using a lexicon for word spelling, rather than word reading. As Bub *et al.* (1993) note, there are almost as many accounts of pure alexia as case reports. Some authors have claimed that there is no unitary explanation of pure alexia since different problems both within and between stages of visual word processing can each produce the characteristic signature of an interaction between word length and reading speed (Kay and Hanley, 1991; Rapp and Caramazza, 1991). For example, while some letter-by-letter readers appear to read serially strictly left to right (e.g. Behrmann and Shallice, 1995; Behrmann *et al.*, 1990; Kay and Hanley, 1991), other letter-by-letter readers process word-strings 'ends-in', which is the normal case (Bouma, 1971). On the other hand, Behrmann and Shallice (1995) have claimed that a deficit in processing abstract letter identities is the core of the disorder (cf. Arguin and Bub, 1994).

Recently, a number of rehabilitation studies of letter-by-letter reading have been published. Behrmann and McLeod (1995) tried to reduce the word-length effect in a single pure alexic patient. Their therapy did not succeed, however, and the authors speculate whether compensatory procedures (e.g. Multiple Oral Rereading (MOR) technique – Moyer, 1979;

kinesthetic feedback – Nitzberg Lott *et al.*, 1994) may be more beneficial. On the other hand, Behrmann and McLeod's study was designed to directly address what was believed to be the functional problem in the subject SI's reading – strict left to right, serial, processing of written letter-strings (see also Arguin and Bub, 1994). The authors acknowledge that a more complete treatment programme might focus not only on first and last letters, but on all letters. Without more therapy studies for letter-by-letter reading, and ones which directly compare methods on the same patients, we do not yet know which treatments will be beneficial.

SURFACE DYSLEXIA

Surface dyslexia is characterised by poor reading of exception words. It is important to realise, however, that the difficulty is not absolute: some exception words can be read aloud correctly, and the pattern is one of poor exception word reading relative to regular word reading. The characteristic signature is therefore a regularity effect, while word variables such as imageability and grammatical class do not significantly affect reading success (although word frequency and word length may be significant determiners of reading success in some patients with surface dyslexia). Exception words are often given incorrect, 'regularised' pronunciations (*bear* → 'beer', *castle* → 'castul', *island* → 'izland'). This pattern suggests that word-specific pronunciations often cannot be retrieved, and that greater reliance than usual is placed on phonology constructed from the sub-lexical route (hence the alternative label of 'phonological reading'; Patterson *et al.*, 1986). If patients read using a sub-lexical phonological route, nonwords should be read aloud successfully, or at least to the same level as regular words. The degree of successful functioning of the phonological route appears to vary between patients in reported cases. Some patients are able to use the full range of sub-lexical units in reading aloud (Shallice *et al.*, 1983; Bub *et al.*, 1986), while others appear to rely on letter-sound correspondences, which may be intact, or impaired (Marshall and Newcombe, 1966; 1973; Temple and Newcombe, 1986). (Shallice and McCarthy (1985) refer to the former as Type I readers, and to the latter as Type II readers.)

Reliance on a sub-lexical or phonological routine happens because there is a difficulty in using lexical systems, and this can occur for a variety of reasons: impairment at any of the stages of word recognition, word comprehension and pronunciation illustrated in Figure 12.1 can hinder lexical reading. However, different types of lexical impairment will be accompanied by different patterns of comprehension. A common pattern is that phonological reading will go hand in hand with severely impaired comprehension, in which the understanding both of heard words and written words is substantially affected (e.g. Bub *et al.*, 1986; Schwartz *et al.*, 1980). In this case, written words will not be understood, even though they may be read aloud correctly, or given a regularised pronunciation. Phonological reading/surface dyslexia can therefore be a feature of progressive dementing disorders such as semantic dementia (Patterson and Hodges, 1992).

In a second pattern, words are sometimes misunderstood in terms of what the patient says, rather than by what is read: 'bear → I drink it, beer'; listen → 'that's the boxer, Liston' (Coltheart *et al.*, 1983; Marshall and Newcombe, 1973). Here, the difficulty appears to lie at a pre-semantic level, perhaps in visual word recognition itself, so that word meanings cannot be reliably addressed from the visual form. Instead, a regularised pronunciation will be produced, which can be used to access word meaning as if the word had been heard rather than seen (via a phonological pathway from speaking to hearing to meaning). In the case of regular words, the 'regularised' pronunciation will be correct and so comprehension will be correct. In the case of exception words, the regularised pronunciation will sometimes not correspond to an existing word (e.g. *castle* → 'castul'), making comprehension difficult, but in other cases it will correspond with a familiar, though incorrect, word (e.g. *bear* → 'beer'), resulting in a comprehension error ('I drink it').

In a third type of surface dyslexic reading, the word may be mispronounced, but understood in terms of what is read: *foot* → 'body, and it's my shoe ... /fut/' (Goldblum, 1986; Kay and Patterson, 1986). The picture is not usually so clear-cut as this, however: while the defining feature is the presence of phonological reading, some patients will show a mixture of correctly and incorrectly understood responses.

A small number of rehabilitation studies for surface dyslexia/phonological reading exist in the neuropsychological literature. For example, Byng and Coltheart (1986) and Coltheart and Byng (1989) constructed a successful remediation programme which was designed to improve access to word-specific pronunciations and to reduce the regularity effect in a patient with surface dyslexia. The patient appeared to have difficulty in accessing the system for visual word recognition, and appeared to understand by mentally listening to the sound of the written word. Even with only a small amount of therapy treatment, the patient's reading aloud of exception words improved, and flawless performance on at least one set was maintained one year later.

PHONOLOGICAL DYSLEXIA

If surface dyslexia represents one side of the coin of a two-route reading model, then phonological dyslexia represents the other. This disorder was first 'discovered' by Beauvois and Derouesne (1979), and by Shallice and Warrington (1980) and Patterson (1982). One might feel that it hardly qualifies as a reading disorder, since the primary characteristic is difficulty in constructing pronunciations for made-up words; word reading is relatively well preserved. Indeed, if 'nonwords' had not been used as a clinical tool, and if the 'two-reading-route' model had not predicted its existence, then one wonders whether the disorder would have been discovered and named. The patient finds it difficult to read aloud nonwords, often misreading them as visually similar words (e.g. *dusp* → 'dust'), but as the patient can repeat nonwords aloud correctly, the difficulty is not primarily one of articulation.

Arguably the purest case of phonological dyslexia so far reported is that of WB (Funnell, 1983). WB was unable to read any nonwords, although in other case reports nonword reading is not completely abolished. Like other cases, WB's ability to read words aloud was mildly affected; in particular, grammatical words (prepositions, conjunctions, determiners, etc.) were not read successfully, and neither were words that had grammatical endings, like tense and adjectival markers (e.g. *played, magical*) (Patterson, 1982). Word variables such as regularity, imageability and length are not determiners of word reading success. No specific rehabilitation reports of phonological dyslexia have been published, although a number of studies have concentrated on devising treatment routines to improve sub-lexical reading (Berndt and Mitchum, 1994; DePartz, 1986, Mitchum and Berndt 1991).

DEEP DYSLEXIA

Perhaps the most curious and most studied of the acquired dyslexias is deep dyslexia. The primary characteristic of this disorder is that semantic errors are produced in reading aloud (e.g. *present* → 'gift', *cannibals* → 'savages'). As well as semantic errors, patients also make visual errors (e.g. *spy* → 'shy') and morphological errors (e.g. *magical* → 'magic', *cutting* → 'cuts'). Some people have claimed that morphological errors are further cases of either semantic and/or visual errors (Funnell, 1987), particularly since patients with deep dyslexia also make combination reponses, such as semantic-then-visual errors (e.g. *sympathy* → 'orchestra') (presumably involving the mediating visual error, *symphony*). It is also perhaps worth mentioning at this point that visual errors (e.g. *shed* → 'shelf') occur in each of these four major patterns of acquired reading disorder and therefore do not have any power to distinguish between disorders.

Hand in hand with semantic errors in single-word reading, patients with deep dyslexia also show a strong imageability effect: words that are high in imageability (e.g. *school, summer*), are read aloud more successfully than words of low imageability (e.g. *truth, system*), even when high and low imageability words are matched for how often they occur in written English. It is also reported that deep dyslexic patients are better at reading aloud nouns than words of other parts of speech. It appears, however, that this may have more to do with imageability (nouns are generally higher in imageability than adjectives, verbs and particularly than grammatical words), than part of speech (Allport and Funnell, 1981). Other variables such as regularity and word length do not play a significant role in word reading success.

Nonword reading is usually completely abolished, and as in phonological dyslexia, visually similar word responses are produced instead. Deep dyslexia and phonological dyslexia both seem to involve reading disturbances which affect the operation of the sub-lexical reading routine. While in phonological dyslexia the word reading routine appears to be operating relatively well (although still sub-optimally: the patient WB described above could read aloud only approximately 85% of words), in deep dyslexia this procedure seems to be impaired, resulting in semantic reading errors. As in surface dyslexia, it is clear that impairment to the lexical routine is not consistent between patients with deep dyslexia. While some appear to have word comprehension difficulties regardless of whether the word is written or spoken (Marshall and Newcombe, 1973), other patients with deep dyslexia make semantic errors in the course of addressing a pronunciation, even though the word itself may be fully understood (Caramazza and Hillis, 1990). This observation led to the proposal by Morton and Patterson (1980) of a 'response blocking' effect in at least some cases of deep dyslexia.

Rehabilitation studies for deep dyslexia have focused on improving the patient's ability to use the sub-lexical route, by 're-educating' in segmenting written letters, assigning phonology and blending to form words (by focusing on the structure of words themselves through segmentation and blending, it was hoped that the number of semantic errors would also be reduced). The patient with deep dyslexia described by DePartz (1986) had little difficulty in performing segmentation and blending operations. On the other hand, the patient reported by Berndt and Mitchum (1994), although somewhat impaired in segmenting letters, was considerably more impaired in sounding out letters, and in fact no longer appeared to have any appreciation that words could be analysed into component sounds. However, practice in manipulating sound segments auditorily seemed to enhance letter sounding, and, using the DePartz technique, the patient learned to produce individual phonemes relatively quickly. Sadly, however, she was entirely unable to learn to blend the phonemes together. Nickels' (1992) patient with deep dyslexia was also discovered to be unable to blend. Nickels turned this to good advantage by training the patient to generate phonemic cues in response to seeing a picture, allowing him to name the picture by 'self-cueing'. In sum, recent studies that have attempted to rehabilitate sub-lexical reading in deep dyslexia have had some success, although it is clear that the sub-lexical reading routine can be impaired in a number of ways, and that particular remediation programmes can have more success with some kinds of difficulty than with others.

ASSESSING ACQUIRED DISORDERS OF READING

This, then, is a brief summary of the four major patterns of acquired reading disorder and the types of linguistic variables and reading errors that distinguish between them. How then do we identify them in a clinical setting? Unfortunately, widely available clinical batteries such as the Boston Diagnostic Aphasia Examination (BDAE) (Goodglass and Kaplan, 1983) and the Western Aphasia Battery (Kertesz, 1979) are not sufficiently sophisticated to distinguish between different types of acquired reading disorder. They are not designed for this purpose, and focus on acquired disorders of reading only to the extent that they accompany major aphasic syndromes such as Wernicke's and Broca's Aphasia. Similarly, individual sub-tests are not constructed to test for the effects of specific linguistic variables like frequency, imageability, regularity and word length that we know to be important in acquired language disorders. Certain batteries designed to evaluate developmental reading disorders can also sometimes provide useful measures of particular reading skills, such as the word attack sub-test of the Woodcock Reading Mastery Test – Revised (Woodcock and Johnson, 1987), which provides a normatively based estimate of nonword reading skills. There are a few specific reading tests such as the Nelson Adult Reading Test (NART – Nelson and O'Connell, 1978), although the NART is actually designed to assess pre-morbid intellectual functioning in the presence of current dementing disorder. As many of the individual words in the test are unusual exception words (e.g. *psalm*, *sidereal*, *drachm*), it does not serve its purpose for patients with surface dyslexia. What is needed is a number of tests that are directed at individual components of the reading system (e.g. visual word recognition, spelling–sound correspondences), and which take linguistic variables such as word frequency and regularity into account.

A COGNITIVE PERSPECTIVE

Recently, along with Ruth Lesser and Max Coltheart (of the universities of Newcastle upon Tyne, UK, and Macquarie, Australia, respectively), I have developed a battery of sixty tests designed to assess language processing in aphasia (*Psycholinguistic Assessments of Language Processing in Aphasia* (PALPA) – Kay *et al.*, 1992). Other psycholinguistically sophisticated language batteries are available: *The ADA Comprehension Battery* (Franklin *et al.*, 1992) and the *Psycholinguistic Assessment of Language* (Caplan, 1995). There are a number of tasks in the PALPA battery that are designed to test the functioning of components of the reading system (see Table 12.1). The tests themselves systematically assess the effects of linguistic variables both individually (e.g. frequency) and in interaction (e.g. frequency × imageability), while keeping other factors constant. Critically, they make use of the same items across different tests, both within modality

Table 12.1 Summary of reading assessments in the PALPA

Letter tasks
Letter discrimination: Mirror reversal
Letter discrimination: Upper → lower-case matching
Letter discrimination: Lower → upper-case matching
Letter discrimination: Matching across words and nonwords
Spoken letter → written letter matching
Letter naming
Letter sounding

Word tasks
Visual lexical decision: Legality
Visual lexical decision: Imageability × frequency
Visual lexical decision: Morphological endings
Visual lexical decision: Regularity
Homophone decision
Oral reading: Letter length
Oral reading: Syllable length
Oral reading: Imageability × frequency
Oral reading: Grammatical class
Oral reading: Grammatical class × imageability
Oral reading: Morphological endings
Oral reading: Regularity
Oral reading: Nonwords

Sentence tasks
Oral reading: Different syntactic structures

Source: Kay *et al.*, 1992

of input (e.g. visual lexical decision and reading aloud) and between modality (e.g. visual and auditory lexical decision). Information is therefore provided about the role of word variables in patients' ability to identify, comprehend and read aloud, and, at the same time, allow for qualitative analyses of error types that are produced. To give a more definite idea of how the tests can be used to assess acquired reading disorders, and how they can be related to the four major patterns of acquired dyslexia I have distinguished, I will go through each type of test in detail (although I will not describe every test that is available). The heart of the reading assessment battery is the series of oral reading tests, which allow the effects of different word variables on word reading to be systematically identified. As I have already discussed their roles in letter-by-letter reading, surface dyslexia and deep and phonological dyslexia, I will mention them only as they relate to the other reading tasks.

Letter-processing tasks

PALPA has a number of tasks which can be used to assess letter-processing abilities. For example, upper-case/lower-case matching (and vice versa) tests the ability to identify single letters across case (e.g. b/B vs b/P). A related task examines the ability to process letters across words and nonwords by using pairs which differ by just one letter (e.g. brown-BROWN vs. brown-CROWN). The place of difference in the word is also manipulated (beginning, middle, end). Finally, a letter-naming task is included (in which the patient is required to produce the name of a written letter: M as 'em'), and a letter-sounding task (M as 'muh'). I have claimed that, in order to recognise written words, we must be able to process them (and their constituent letters) into an abstract form which is independent of case or handwriting style. It is assumed that we have some way of transforming letters into an abstract letter identity (e.g. that allows us to know that B and b are variants of the same letter), and that letters are coded for position as well as for identity. It is further assumed that, prior to word recognition, letter processing is carried out in parallel and 'ends-in'.

As we have seen, pure alexic or letter-by-letter readers sometimes make errors in letter identification, although often these do not occur in single letter-processing tasks, but only with letters in words (or nonwords). It is therefore important to contrast performance on cross-case matching tasks using both single letters and letters in words (e.g. b/B vs. brown-BROWN). Some, but not all, letter-by-letter readers appear to process words in a strictly serial, left-to-right fashion (Behrmann and McLeod, 1995; Kay and Hanley, 1991). They can therefore be much slower (and make more errors) in detecting letter differences that occur at the ends of words than at the beginning, which is why the cross-case word-matching tasks build in differences at beginning, middle and end position (e.g. brown-CROWN, bench-BEACH, grasp-GRASS). Patients with attentional difficulties such as neglect dyslexia may also make more errors at the ends of words (e.g. Baxter and Warrington, 1983), although others may make more errors at the beginnings of words (e.g. Ellis *et al.*, 1987). This task is derived from one constructed by Friedrich *et al.* (1985) which compared reaction-time measures across patient and non-brain-damaged groups, and it is important to note that difficulties with letter identity and position may only appear under reaction-time conditions. Slow response times and position effects on letter detection tasks suggest that the patient may be reading in a letter-by-letter fashion. If assessment is begun with letter-processing tasks, it is therefore important to go on to test for letter-length effects in oral reading.

Patients with deep dyslexia have real difficulties in sounding letters, although they can often name them, or produce words which begin with the letter (e.g. M as 'mother'). It is sometimes assumed that the fact that they have apparently lost knowledge about letter sounds is linked with their difficulties in reading aloud nonwords, and with the production of semantic errors in reading (knowing about letter sounds might allow semantic errors to be 'edited out').

Visual lexical decision

In visual lexical decision, the patient is asked to indicate the familiar words in a list of words and word-like nonwords:

summer √   sammer
andience   audience √

In each of the tests, the words have been chosen to vary systematically on a particular linguistic variable, while keeping others constant (e.g. regular and exception words which are matched for frequency, image-ability and word length). Across the tests nonwords also vary in their 'word-like-ness'. In one test, for example, nonwords are not word-like and so the decision is an easy one. In another, nonwords are constructed by changing just one letter of the words, and the task becomes much more difficult. There are a number of ways in which performance can be impaired on visual lexical decision tasks, and it is important to realise that these do not necessarily relate to particular types of acquired disorder in obvious ways, but are perhaps more to do with confidence and motivation. For example, two patients with the same underlying disorder may respond differently to the demands of the task; both may have difficulties, but one may favour 'Yes, a word', the other, 'No, not a word'. The former will seem to have a well-preserved ability to identify all the words, but will also make a high number of false positives (marking nonwords as familiar words); the latter may seem to be good at picking out the nonwords, but will miss a substantial number of familiar words. Note that performance on visual lexical decision should always be compared with that on auditory lexical decision using the same words: if the patient shows a relative deficit on visual lexical decision the problem is likely to be specifically to do with reading, and not simply with the demands of the task.

Some researchers claim that the lexical decision task taps the 'lexical system' involved in visual word recognition, though it is certainly possible to decide whether a letter string is a word based on what it means (at the level of word comprehension), rather than on what it looks like. However, it has been clearly demonstrated that at least some patients such as those with deep dyslexias who are impaired in knowing what written words mean, particularly if they are low in imageability, are well within the normal range on written lexical decision tasks using such words.

What are the characteristics of the different types of acquired reading disorder on written lexical decision? One might expect letter-by-letter readers to be slow at making visual lexical decisions just as they are slow in reading aloud, and, if letter misidentifications occur, inaccurate as well. Equally, patients with surface dyslexia who have difficulties with visual word recognition are impaired in written lexical decision (Newcombe and Marshall, 1985). On the other hand, patients with surface dyslexia who have difficulties with comprehension or in addressing word pronunciations may be relatively less impaired, though they may still show effects of variables like word frequency and orthographic regularity (e.g. Margolin *et al.*, 1985). Thus, visual lexical decision tasks that include exception words and 'pseudohomophones' (nonwords like *brane* that sound like real words when pronounced) are particularly difficult for patients with surface dyslexia, regardless of the nature of their lexical impairment. In contrast, patients with deep dyslexias and phonological dyslexias tend to be relatively well preserved on tasks of visual lexical decision, generally failing to show effects of imageability and/or frequency, even when these are present in reading aloud.

Word comprehension

PALPA has a series of tasks designed to assess word comprehension abilities. One that we have found particularly useful in distinguishing even relatively mild semantic impairments is a word–picture matching task in which a written word is matched to a corresponding picture (e.g. *axe*). Although the word–picture matching task is a standard feature of existing aphasia assessment batteries, this one includes distractor pictures which allow patients to make errors that are closely (*hammer*), or more distantly (*scissors*), related to the target, as well as errors that are visually related (*flag*), or unrelated (*kite*). A preponderance of visual errors suggests difficulties in object recognition. Semantic errors suggest problems in comprehension.

Deep dyslexic patients can show problems in access (so that performance on written word–picture matching can be impaired relative to the spoken version of the test; see Shallice and Coughlan, 1980), or in semantic storage (so that written and spoken versions are both impaired and to the same level; see Hillis *et al.*, 1990). On the other hand, patients with deep dyslexia can be relatively unimpaired in this task, since the semantic errors they produce when reading aloud appear to arise post-semantically (Caramazza and Hillis, 1990).

Just as the performance of patients with deep dyslexia fractionates on this task, so does that of readers with surface dyslexia. Although many of the cases in the literature have not used written word–picture matching tasks, it is reasonable to infer that some surface dyslexic patients, who appear to rely on sub-lexical reading, and whose written lexical decision is severely impaired, will be impaired on this task (Newcombe and Marshall, 1985). In such cases, written comprehension appears to be mediated by a phonologically recoded stimulus. However, since the task does not include phonological distractors (e.g. axe / tracks), the semantic context may be sufficient to suggest the correct answer. Other cases of patients with surface dyslexia, who appear to read aloud sub-lexically but whose deficit seems to arise post-semantically, would be expected to perform well on this task (Margolin *et al.*, 1985). The performance of phonological dyslexic patients might also be expected to fractionate: compare the impaired semantic processing abilities of the patient reported by Funnell (1983) with the well-preserved comprehension skills of the patient described by Patterson (1982). PALPA includes a number of other semantic processing tasks which can be tested both in written and spoken word versions. Perhaps the most important task apart from that of word–picture matching is the synonym judgement task. Here the patient is required to judge whether pairs of words are closely related in meaning (e.g. *marriage/wedding* vs. *marriage/ocean*). An important feature of the task is that it also manipulates imageability; half of the pairs are high in imageability, half are low (e.g. *marriage/wedding* vs. *safety/security*). Deep dyslexic reading is particularly affected by imageability, and so they show particular difficulty in the items that are low in imageability.

Word production tasks

It is important to realise that, while some acquired reading disorders are relatively pure disorders of *reading* (e.g. pure alexia/letter-by-letter reading), others integrally involve other components of the language system (e.g. word pronunciation). A disorder affecting access to word phonology might be manifest as deep dyslexia if sub-lexical reading is abolished, or surface dyslexia if sub-lexical reading can be maintained, but it will also affect word retrieval in other contexts such as picture naming and repetition. In assessing reading disorders it is also necessary to compare performance on a variety of tasks (we have seen this already with respect to assessing both written and auditory word comprehension). Performance on reading aloud should always be compared with performance on other 'output' tasks such as picture naming and repetition. The PALPA tasks explicitly allow this, and also allow performance to be compared using the same materials, so that only the mode of response differs.

This almost concludes my whistle-stop tour around current knowledge about normal reading (or at least reading of single words), major types of acquired reading disorder and cognitive assessment. Cognitive models, even relatively simple schemes such as that illustrated in Figure 12.1, can produce detailed predictions which may lead to effective assessment, diagnosis and treatment (although the relationship between cognitive assessment and rehabilitation is highly complex; see Howard and Patterson, 1989; Wilson and Patterson, 1990). Before I finish, however, I would like to stress that the role of clinical judgement should not be underestimated here. Acquired disorders of reading may stem from damage to the processes of reading themselves, or they may be secondary to more general perceptual or linguistic difficulties. Clinical judgement can provide useful information about whether the patient's difficulties are confined to reading, or reflect a broader impairment, even before targeted assessment tasks are carried out. For example, careful attention to whether the patient makes appropriate eye movements when asked to examine a picture can give an initial indication about general perceptual and attentional abilities such as scanning and orienting. This can be backed up by using simple tests, such as asking the patient to follow the point of a pencil as it is moved smoothly by the examiner into both left and right sides of space (Riddoch and Humphreys, 1994). Similarly, observing the quality of the patient's speech (and writing) when asked to describe the same picture can indicate whether the patient may have linguistic difficulties not limited to reading. Clinical judgement can indicate where to begin cognitive assessment, but that is when the work really begins.

ACKNOWLEDGEMENT

During the writing of this chapter, the author was supported by a Wellcome University Award.

REFERENCES

Allport, D.A. (1985). Distributed memory, modular subsystems and dysphasia. In S. Newman and R. Epstein (eds), *Current Perspectives in Dysphasia*. Edinburgh: Churchill Livingstone.

Allport, D.A. and Funnell, E. (1981). Components of the mental lexicon. *Philosophical Transactions of the Royal Society of London*, Series B, 295, 397–410.

Arguin, M. and Bub, D.N. (1994). Pure alexia: attempted rehabilitation and its implications for interpretation of the deficit. *Brain and Language*, 47, 233–68.

Baxter, D.M. and Warrington, E.K. (1983). Neglect dysgraphia. *Journal of Neurology, Neurosurgery and Psychiatry*, 46, 1073–8.

Beauvois, M-F. and Derouesne, J. (1979). Phonological alexia: three dissociations. *Journal of Neurology, Neurosurgery and Psychiatry*, 42, 1115–24.

Behrmann, M. and McLeod, J. (1995). Rehabilitation for pure alexia: efficacy of therapy and implications for models of normal word recognition. *Neuropsychological Rehabilitation*, 5, 149–80.

Behrmann, M. and Shallice, T. (1995). Pure alexia: a nonspatial visual disorder affecting letter activation. *Cognitive Neuropsychology*, 12, 409–54.

Behrmann, M., Black, S.E. and Bub, D.N. (1990). The evolution of pure alexia: a longitudinal study of recovery. *Brain and Language*, 39, 405–27.

Berndt, R.S. and Mitchum, C.C. (1994). Approaches to the rehabilitation of 'phonological assembly': elaborating the model of non-lexical reading. In M.J. Riddoch and G.W. Humphreys (eds), *Cognitive Neuropsychology and Cognitive Rehabilitation*. Hove, Sussex: Lawrence Erlbaum.

Bouma, A. (1971). Serial position curves for the identification of letter strings in visual half-field studies. *Journal of Clinical and Experimental Neuropsychology*, 9, 22.

Bub, D.N., Arguin, M. and Lecours, A.R. (1993). Jules Dejerine and his interpretation of pure alexia. *Brain and Language*, 45, 531–59.

Bub, D.N., Cancelliere, A. and Kertesz, A. (1986). Whole-word and analytic translation of spelling to sound in a non-semantic reader. In K.E. Patterson, J.C.

Marshall and M. Coltheart (eds), *Surface Dyslexia: Neuropsychological and Cognitive Studies of Phonological Reading*. Hove, Sussex: Lawrence Erlbaum.

Byng, S. and Coltheart, M. (1986). Aphasia therapy research: methodological requirements and illustrative results. In E. Hjelmquist and L.G. Nilsson (eds), *Communication and Handicap*. North Holland: Elsevier.

Caplan, D. (1995). PAL: Psycholinguistic Assessments of Language. In R. Mapou and J. Spector (eds), *Assessment of Cognitive Function*. New York: Plenum Press.

Caramazza, A. and Hillis, A.E. (1990). Where do semantic errors come from? *Cortex*, 26, 95–122.

Coltheart, M. (1981). Disorders of reading and their implications for models of normal reading. *Visible Language*, 15, 245–86.

Coltheart M. and Byng S. (1989) A treatment for surface dyslexia. In X. Seron and G. Deloche (eds), *Cognitive Approaches in Neuropsychological Rehabilitation*. London: Lawrence Erlbaum.

Coltheart, M., Masterson, J., Byng, S., Prior, M. and Riddoch, M.J. (1983). Surface dyslexia. *Quarterly Journal of Experimental Psychology*, 35, 469–95.

Dejerine, J. (1892). Contribution a l'étude anatomo-pathologique et clinique des différentes variétés de cécité-verbale. *Memoires Societe Biologique*, 4, 61–90.

DePartz, M.P. (1986). Re-education of a deep dyslexic patient: rationale of the method and results. *Cognitive Neuropsychology*, 3, 149–77.

Ellis, A.W., Flude, B. and Young, A.W. (1987). 'Neglect dyslexia' and the early visual processing of letters in words and nonwords. *Cognitive Neuropsychology*, 4, 439–64.

Franklin, S.E.,Turner, J. and Ellis, A.W. (1992). *The ADA Comprehension Battery*. University of York, UK.

Friedrich, F.J., Walker, J.A. and Posner, M.I. (1985). Effects of parietal lesions on visual matching: implications for reading errors. *Cognitive Neuropsychology*, 2, 253–64.

Funnell, E. (1983). Phonological processes in reading: new evidence from acquired dyslexia. *British Journal of Psychology*, 74, 159–80.

Funnell, E. (1987). Morphological errors in deep dyslexia: a case of mistaken identity? *Quarterly Journal of Experimental Psychology*, 39A, 497–539.

Goldblum, M-C. (1986). Word comprehension in surface dyslexia. In K.E. Patterson, J.C. Marshall and M. Coltheart (eds), *Surface Dyslexia: Neuropsychological and Cognitive Studies of Phonological Reading*. Hove, Sussex: Lawrence Erlbaum.

Goodglass, H. and Kaplan, E. (1983). *Assessment of Aphasia and Related Disorders*. Philadelphia: Lea and Febiger.

Harley, T.A. (1995). *The Psychology of Language: From Data to Theory*. Hove, Sussex: Lawrence Erlbaum.

Hillis, A.E., Rapp, B.C., Romani, C. and Caramazza, A. (1990). Selective impairment of semantics in lexical processing. *Cognitive Neuropsychology*, 7, 191–244.

Howard, D. and Patterson, K.E. (1989). Models for therapy. In X. Seron and G. Deloche (eds), *Cognitive Approaches in Neuropsychological Rehabilitation*. London: Lawrence Erlbaum.

Kay, J. and Hanley, J.R. (1991). Simultaneous form perception and serial letter recognition in a case of letter-by-letter reading. *Cognitive Neuropsychology*, 249–73.

Kay, J. and Patterson, K.E. (1986) Routes to meaning in surface dyslexia. In K.E. Patterson, J.C. Marshall and M. Coltheart (eds), *Surface Dyslexia: Neuropsychological and Cognitive Studies of Phonological Reading*. Hove, Sussex: Lawrence Erlbaum.

Kay, J., Lesser, R. and Coltheart, M. (1992). *Psycholinguistic Assessments of Language Processing in Aphasia* (PALPA). Hove, Sussex: Lawrence Erlbaum.

Kay, J., Lesser, R. and Coltheart, M. (1996). *PALPA: The Proof of the Pudding is in the Eating*. Hove, Sussex: Lawrence Erlbaum.

Kertesz, A. (1979). *Aphasia and Associated Disorders*. New York: Grune & Stratton.

McClelland, J.L. (1976). Preliminary letter identification in perception of words and letters. *Journal of Experimental Psychology: Human Perception and Performance*, 2, 80–91.

Margolin, D.I., Marcel, A.J. and Carlson, N.R. (1985). Common mechanisms in dysnomia and post-semantic surface dyslexia. In K.E. Patterson, J.C. Marshall and M. Coltheart (eds) *Surface Dyslexia: Neuropsychological and Cognitive Studies of Phonological Reading*. Hove, Sussex: Lawrence Erlbaum.

Marshall, J.C. and Newcombe, F. (1966). Syntactic and semantic errors in paralexia. *Neuropsychologia*, 4, 169–76.

Marshall, J.C. and Newcombe, F. (1973). Patterns of paralexia: a psycholinguistic approach. *Journal of Psycholinguistic Research*, 2, 175–99.

Mitchum, C.C. and Berndt, R.S. (1991). Diagnosis and treatment of 'phonological assembly' in acquired dyslexia: an illustration of the cognitive neuropsychological approach. *Journal of Neurolinguistics*, 6, 103–37.

Morton, J. and Patterson, K. (1980). A new attempt at an interpretation, or, an attempt at a new interpretation. In M. Coltheart, K. Patterson and J.C. Marshall (eds), *Deep Dyslexia*. London: Routledge & Kegan Paul.

Moyer, S. (1979). Rehabilitation of alexia: a case study. *Cortex*, 15, 139–44.

Nelson, H.E. and O'Connell, A. (1978). Dementia: the estimation of premorbid levels using the new adult reading test. *Cortex*, 14, 234–44.

Newcombe, F. and Marshall, J.C. (1985). Reading and writing by letter sounds. In K.E. Patterson, J.C. Marshall and M. Coltheart (eds), (1986) *Surface Dyslexia: Neuropsychological and Cognitive Studies of Phonological Reading*. Hove, Sussex: Lawrence Erlbaum.

Nickels, L. (1992). The autocue – self-generated phonemic cues in the treatment of a disorder of reading and naming. *Cognitive Neuropsychology*, 9, 155–82.

Nitzberg Lott, S., Friedman, R.B. and Linebaugh, C. (1994). Rationale and efficacy of a tactile-kinaesthetic treatment for alexia. *Aphasiology*, 8, 181–95.

Patterson, K.E. (1981). Neuropsychological approaches to the study of reading. *British Journal of Psychology*, 72, 151–74.

Patterson, K.E. (1982). The relation between reading and phonological coding: further neuropsychological observations. In A.W. Ellis (ed.), *Normality and Pathology in Cognitive Functions*. London: Academic Press.

Patterson, K.E. (1994). Reading, writing and rehabilitation: a reckoning. In M.J. Riddoch and G.W. Humphreys (eds), *Cognitive Neuropsychology and Cognitive Rehabilitation*. Hove, Sussex: Lawrence Erlbaum.

Patterson, K.E. and Hodges, J.R. (1992). Deterioration of word meaning: implications for surface dyslexia. *Neuropsychologia*, 30, 1025–40.

Patterson, K.E. and Kay, J. (1982). Letter-by-letter reading: psychological descriptions of a neurological syndrome. *Quarterly Journal of Experimental Psychology*, 34A, 411–41.

Patterson, K.E., Marshall, J.C. and Coltheart, M. (1986). *Surface Dyslexia: Neuropsychological and Cognitive Studies of Phonological Reading*. Hove, Sussex: Lawrence Erlbaum.

Rapp, B.C. and Caramazza, A. (1991). Spatially determined deficits in letter and word processing. *Cognitive Neuropsychology*, 8, 275–311.

Riddoch, M.J. and Humphreys, G.W. (1994). Towards an understanding of neglect. In M.J. Riddoch and G.W. Humphreys (eds), *Cognitive Neuropsychology and Cognitive Rehabilitation*. Hove, Sussex: Lawrence Erlbaum.

Schwartz, M.F., Saffran, E. and Marin, O.S.M. (1980). Fractionating the reading process in dementia: evidence for word specific print-to-sound associations. In

M. Coltheart, K.E. Patterson and J.C. Marshall (eds), *Deep Dyslexia*. London: Routledge & Kegan Paul.

Shallice, T. and Coughlan, A.K. (1980). Modality specific word comprehension deficits in deep dyslexia. *Journal of Neurology, Neurosurgery and Psychiatry*, 43, 866–72.

Shallice, T. and McCarthy, R. (1985). Phonological reading: from patterns of impairment to possible procedure. In K.E. Patterson, J.C. Marshall and M. Coltheart (eds), *Surface Dyslexia: Neuropsychological and Cognitive Studies of Phonological Reading*. Hove, Sussex: Lawrence Erlbaum.

Shallice, T. and Warrington, E.K. (1980). Single and multiple component syndromes. In M. Coltheart, K.E. Patterson and J.C. Marshall (eds), *Deep Dyslexia*. London: Routledge & Kegan Paul.

Shalliice, T., Warrington, E. and McCarthy, R. (1983). Reading without semantics. *Quarterly Journal of Experimental Psychology*, 35A, 111–38.

Temple, C. and Newcombe, F. (1986). Surface dyslexia: variations within a syndrome. In K.E. Patterson, J.C. Marshall and M. Coltheart (eds), *Surface Dyslexia: Neuropsychological and Cognitive Studies of Phonological Reading*. Hove, Sussex: Lawrence Erlbaum.

Warrington, E.K. and Shallice, T. (1980). Word-form dyslexia. *Brain*, 103, 99–112

Wilson, B.A. and Patterson, K.E. (1990). Rehabilitation for cognitive impairment: does cognitive psychology apply? *Applied Cognitive Psychology*, 4, 247–60.

Woodcock, R.W. and Johnson, M.B. (1987). *Woodcock–Johnson Psycho-Educational Battery*. Allen, TX: DLM Teaching Resources.

13 Computer-based assessment of reading

Chris Singleton

INTRODUCTION

We have reached a watershed in the history of psychological and educational assessment. It is hard to see how conventional assessment methods could be further improved – in effect, they have reached the zenith of their development. In a relatively short time, however, they are likely to be usurped by computerised assessment as swiftly as the electronic calculator banished tables of logarithms from the classroom (and for very similar reasons). The rationale for this view derives from the particular advantages that computer-based testing has over conventional methods. The purpose of this chapter, therefore, is first to outline the nature and advantages of computer-based assessment techniques and to explain why it is at this particular moment in history that such an advancement should take place. I will then go on to consider some of the critical problems concerning how computer-based approaches to assessment can be shown to have equivalence with conventional methods of assessment. Current research on computer-based assessment of reading and dyslexia will be critically reviewed. Finally, I will address the integration of screening and computer-based assessment approaches and evaluate the prospects for more effective and practical screening procedures that can be computer-based.

Computer-based assessment systems are steadily becoming more widespread in industry and business on an international scale. To a more limited extent they are employed in further and higher education, especially in the United States, but they are only just beginning to be used in primary and secondary education. In 1994 the National Council for Educational Technology reported on the use of, and prospects for, computer-assisted assessment in education in the UK (NCET, 1994). A wide range of approaches was identified, with the majority falling into two main categories: recording and reporting of pupil or student results, and 'paper-less' examinations. A national survey reported significant advantages of such approaches, including savings of staff time, greater objectivity and easier analysis of results, although disadvantages were noted, the main one being the need for special training of teachers. Nevertheless, despite its currently small beginnings, the indications are that there will be a dramatic growth in computer-based assessment methods throughout education during the next decade. 'Why now?' you may ask. The history of computing is replete with examples of exaggerated predictions. Machine intelligence has proved to be a much more difficult nut to crack than many distinguished authorities ever imagined (McCorduck, 1979; Simon and Newell, 1958), and we are still patiently awaiting those diligent robots which, according to the 'experts' of thirty years ago or more, should by now have arrived in all our homes and be attending to our every need (Evans, 1979). On the other hand, the history of computing also testifies to the enormous potential that has been overlooked or even disregarded by the experts, and particularly so by those who have been hidebound by years of conformity to one paradigm. A compelling illustration of this effect was the early failure to appreciate the potential of the personal computer and its associated software, which was a major embarrassment for the leaders of the mainframe computer industry. Nor was the enormous potential and growth of industrial robots generally anticipated by those same gurus who had confidently prophesied robots in the home. And how many computing experts foresaw the recent explosive growth of the Internet?

However, the prediction of rapid growth in computer-based assessment methods in education over the next decade is not comparable with the prophecies regarding robots and artificial intelligence, which were theoretically inadequate extrapolations from the early capabilities of the technology. Rather, it is based on the fact that the technology necessary to deliver and meet the requirements of computer-based assessment in education is already in existence, and the theoretical and methodological framework for computer-based assessment has been well established for several years. What until very recently has been the missing link is that the hardware required for an effective implementation of the computer-based approach to assessment has not generally been available in places of education. In order to realise the full advantages of the computer-based approach, multimedia hardware of comparatively high specification is required to run the software. It has only been of late that large numbers of schools and colleges have acquired such hardware. A critical mass of hardware is now in the education system, and the educational ethos has assimilated the central role which computers play in society in general and learning in particular. Teachers have been able to develop a reasonable degree of confidence in working with computers. In consequence, teachers are now willing, as well as able, to exploit the considerable power of the technology for the purposes of assessment. As the realisation of this dawns on test publishers, teachers and psychologists are likely to be confronted with a proliferating range of computer-based tests. Although these tests may look very attractive, not all may be up to scratch in psychometric terms, and all professionals would be wise to maintain a critical eye when deciding what to buy and use.

Most of the computer-based tests currently used in industry and business are simply on-screen equivalents of paper-based forms. The most common types are text-based multiple-choice tests of knowledge in specific domains, such as accounting, financial management, computing and electronics (Guildford Educational Services, 1993). Computer-based assessment of personality and aptitude is also increasingly being used in the fields of personnel selection and management training, but again, these methods are predominantly text-based (Bartram, 1994). The main advantage of such systems over conventional methods of assessment is that they can be extremely labour-saving and can enable tests to be delivered by personnel who do not have to be trained to such a high level. Computerised assessment methods can usually be administered more speedily than conventional tests and because scoring is automatic, the results can be immediately available. Consequently, computerised tests are especially suitable for self-assessment, for situations in which large numbers of people have to be assessed quickly, and for situations in which professionally trained assessors are not available. The type of tests used in industry and business will not be reviewed here, because they are of little relevance to computer-based assessment of reading. However, they do raise an important issue which must be addressed, namely that of equivalence of computer-based assessment devices with conventional (usually paper-based) forms.

EQUIVALENCE OF COMPUTER-BASED TESTS WITH CONVENTIONAL FORMS

The issue of equivalence with conventional forms is central to the conversion of existing tests to computer-delivered format which, in fact, has been the predominant type of computer-based assessment to date. This problem was one of three critical issues identified in a comprehensive review of computerised assessment by Bartram (1994), the other two key issues being the development of adaptive testing methods, and the use of computers to generate interpretative reports. While untimed multiple-choice tests may be minimally affected by the computerised format, timed tests may well show significant differences from the original version. Tests of 'maximum performance', i.e. attainment, ability and aptitude tests, are the ones most likely to show an impact of computerisation on test scores. Subjects may perform better – or worse – on the computerised version than on the paper-based version. Problems of equivalence have been encountered in translating a number of existing tests to computer (e.g. Dimock and Cormier, 1991; French and Beaumont, 1990; Martin and Wilcox, 1989), but some successes have been reported (e.g. with the *Peabody Picture Vocabulary Test* – see Maguire *et al.*, 1991). The issue of test equivalence is especially critical in cases in which the speed of the subject's response is an integral part of the test. Time constraints in paper-based tests are partly a function of the time it takes to write or mark the answers. It is often quicker and easier for the testee to respond on a computer by clicking with a mouse or even touching a touch-screen. On the other hand, reading text on a screen can be more difficult for some people than reading paper-based materials, and this could be a significant factor for the design of computerised reading tests. Although this may not be a major problem for tests in which there is not a great deal of text involved (e.g. tests of word recognition or sentence reading) it will almost certainly have to be taken into account in comprehension assessment. In the latter case, a solution may be to have the text which is to be read and understood printed in conventional format, while the test questions are delivered and scored by the computer. Publishers currently contemplating the computerisation of existing reading tests will need to address such matters. Nor will it be sufficient to demonstrate equivalence in a generic sense – just as a redesign of a paper-based test calls for a re-standardisation, so too will computerisation require evidence of both equivalence to the original form as well as re-standardisation where necessary. (For discussion of these issues see Bartram, 1989; Bartram *et al.* 1987, and Federico, 1991.)

Test equivalence can be affected by the testee's attitudes to computer-based assessment. Some people may react negatively to taking a test on a computer, while others may find it less intimidating than conventional assessment. A study by Singleton *et al.* (1995), which examined the feasibility of computerised assessment of reading, found that while children who were good readers did not mind taking a paper-based test and, indeed, many enjoyed the experience, less able readers often find conventional assessment threatening and many display reluctance to participate. They view it as yet another situation in which their failure will become manifest. By contrast, however, the poor readers did not object to, and mostly preferred, a computer-based form of the same test. The computer was not seen as threatening at all. Hence computer-based assessment, in addition to many other advantages, may prove to be more humane than conventional assessment.

ADAPTIVE TESTING

The capability of delivering adaptive tests is one of the principal advantages of the computer in the field of assessment. In principle, the term 'adaptive testing' refers to any technique which modifies the nature of the test in response to the performance of the test taker. In practice, however, it has most typically been applied to tests which use *Item Response Theory* (Hambleton and Swaminathan, 1985). Paper-based tests are *static* instruments, fixed in their item content, item order and duration. By contrast, computer-based assessment can be *dynamic*. Since the computer can score performance at the same time as item presentation, it can modify the test accordingly, tailoring it to the capabilities of the testee much more effectively than has ever been possible before. As well as being able to give results immediately, computer-based tests can also use the power of the technology to the full so that test items can include speech and sound, animation, etc. Conventional tests can be very crude instruments in which much of the time a testee's abilities are not being assessed with great precision. For part of the time the testee may be attempting items that are far too easy (which will be boring), while at other times the test items may be far too difficult (which will be frustrating and discouraging). In an adaptive test the testee can be moved swiftly to that zone of the test which will most efficiently discriminate his or her capabilities, and some test items can be omitted altogether, thus avoiding the necessity for lengthy (and redundant) assessment using items which are either too easy or far too difficult. Consequently, testing can be shorter, more reliable and more efficient. The same test may be different for each testee, as the computer selects items from a test item bank, the difficulty of which have been precisely calculated beforehand (for reviews of item-based adaptive testing, see Reckase, 1989; Wainer *et al.*, 1990). The savings in testing time are beneficial both for the testee (who feels less pressurised) and the tester. Olsen (1990) compared paper-based and computer-administered school achievement and assessment tests with computerised adaptive tests. The computer-based non-adaptive version took 50% to 75% of the time taken to administer the conventional version, while the testing time for the adaptive version was only 25% of the time taken with the paper-based version. Such savings in educational assessment are considerable and could far outweigh any disadvantages of transferring from conventional methods to computer-based methods.

COMPUTER-GENERATED REPORTS

To date, the use of computers to generate interpretative reports has been largely restricted to assessment in clinical psychology and personality (Bartram, 1994; Moreland, 1991). However, this approach will ultimately be of relevance to educational psychologists, who spend a great deal of their professional time writing reports based on assessment of children. It might also have a relevance for the computerisation of diagnostic reading tests, where interpretation can be complex and time-consuming for the teacher. There are two mains ways to create a computerised test interpretation program. The first involves studying in depth the means by which human 'experts' carry out this task, charting the sequence of decision processes and then simulating this on the computer, checking the computer's judgements against human interpretations of the same data. The second involves the use of a 'neural net', a program for pattern recognition which simulates the networks of neuronal connections in the brain. The neural net is first given data which have already been classified by a human expert, and the system learns to recognise the patterns in this, progressively adjusting the weightings which it assigns to various 'nodes' or decision processes. After sufficient training, the net is tested on new data, and the judgements it makes are compared with those of an independent human expert. The outcome of both these different methods can be called an *expert system*. The chief difference between the two is that in the former we can understand how the computer arrives at its decisions (because the relevant algorithms are incorporated into the program), while in the latter we have no real idea how the computer carries out the task, only that its conclusions are more or less the same as the human expert. Some things are more amenable to neural networking than others. For these reasons, it would be tempting to suppose that the former type of expert system would always be preferred, since we can have more confidence in something we can understand. However, 'experts' cannot always specify exactly *how* they arrive at any given judgement, so the algorithms derived may be inadequate to create an effective expert system. This method can also take a long time, whereas if the problem is one which is suited to neural networking, a satisfactory expert system can often be generated quite quickly. Although the *implications* of computerised test interpretation will be considered below, the *mechanics* of the process will not be elaborated any further, because this would require technical discussion of the design, implementation, validity and reliability of different types of expert systems, which is beyond the scope of this volume. (For reviews of the psychology of expert systems and neural networks, see Hoffman, 1994; Rich and Knight, 1991.)

COMPUTER-SPECIFIC ASSESSMENT TECHNIQUES

It has largely been expediency and the desire for *quantitative* improvements in test delivery that have driven the development of the first generation of computer-based tests. The outcome has been tests that are demonstrably faster, easier to administer and more efficient. The next generation of computer-based tests is likely to centre on *qualitative* improvements in test design, which enable the assessment of abilities and characteristics that have not been satisfactorily measurable by conventional means. Such tests will be designed specifically for the computer, utilising features that are not available to designers of paper-based tests or other conventional assessment instruments. In this context the term 'computer-specific' does not imply simply that the test has never appeared in paper-based or other conventional format, but rather that the design and implementation of the test is such that it could *never* be properly or accurately replicated in paper-based or conventional format. Such a test might use sound, animated graphics, measure the testee's reaction times or motor coordination in response to different items, or use an interactive task in which the nature, rate and sequence of responses can be interpreted diagnostically. Of the range of computerised tests already developed, however, only a very small proportion have been designed specifically for the computer. It is not difficult to see why. While conversion of conventional tests to computerised format presents undeniable problems, the challenge to the creators of computer-specific tests is a far greater one of harnessing the power of the technology to do much more than could ever be done with paper-based methods. Having done so, the computer-based test still has to be validated and standardised like any other acceptable psychometric instrument.

Progress towards generic computer-specific assessment techniques is being made by the exploitation of multimedia-authoring packages, often in conjunction with an assessment-authoring package such as *Question Mark Designer*. Most notably, this approach has been adopted within some branches of higher education (see Bull, 1994; Dempster, 1994; Stephens, 1994). *Question Mark Designer* enables a lecturer or tutor to create objective computer-delivered tests which can incorporate text, graphics (still or animated), sound and video. Answers can be in many different formats, including multiple choice, multiple response, explanation and graphical 'hot-spot' (e.g. a point on a diagram which can be clicked on by use of a mouse). Scoring is automatic wherever possible and tests can be delivered via a network. Such systems are very flexible, and since the questions are of the tutor's own making they can be closely tailored to the learning needs of the students and/or course being taught. They are especially useful for self-assessment by students who wish to monitor their own progress in a subject, and although a great deal of work must be devoted to the creation of a test, the assessment of large numbers of students via networked machines can be labour saving (Peel and Rowe, 1995). However, this approach has yet to make a significant impact within higher education in the UK, although computer-based approaches to teaching and learning (as opposed to assessment) are rapidly gaining the interest of academic staff (Percival *et al.*, 1995; Strang *et al.*, 1995). Perhaps the major disadvantage of these systems at the present time is the considerable investment of academic time which is necessary to create an individualised test. With progressive modularisation of courses in higher education, however, we are likely very soon to see the development of standardised computer-delivered multimedia assessment systems as part of the whole teaching and learning package marketed by publishers. These can be used for personal monitoring of progress as well as for summative assessment.

In general, the most significant assessment initiatives which involve a greater degree of computer-specificity have emanated from applied cognitive psychology. Examples of such initiatives include the assessment of cognitive deterioration in the elderly using computer simulation of everyday learning and memory tasks (Larrabee and Crook, 1989); computerised tests of perception, concentration, general intelligence, reaction time and coordination for assessing pilot and driver aptitude (Schuhfried,

1990); dynamic spatial reasoning assessment (Pellegrino and Hunt, 1989); assessment of psychomotor coordination and complex information management for the purposes of pilot selection (Bartram and Dale, 1991), and computerised assessment of cognitive skills in young children for predicting learning problems (Singleton *et al.*, 1996). The development of virtual reality systems and other improvements in user-interface design will undoubtedly extend this already widening vista of assessment possibilities for psychology and education (Booth, 1991). However, as Kyllonen (1991) pointed out, we know comparatively little about abilities that may be measured by techniques that lie outside conventional assessment formats.

COMPUTERISED ASSESSMENT OF READING

Computers are now extensively used at school and at home to assist in the development of reading in a wide variety of ways. 'Talking books', in which the computer reads a story to the child and the child is able to click on any unfamiliar words in order to hear them again, are increasingly popular, especially as a way of stimulating young children's interest in books and reading. Reading 'adventure' software, in which the child has to understand the text and solve problems in order to proceed with the story are beneficial in developing the reading comprehension skills of older children. Programs which provide structured practice for learning phonic skills and for improving speed and fluency of word recognition and spelling have been shown to be particularly useful for children with dyslexia or other learning difficulties. Word processing with speech feedback focuses the child's attention on word structure and helps him or her to recognise errors. (For reviews see Day, 1993; Hawkridge and Vincent, 1992; Singleton, 1991a, 1994a, 1994b; Singleton and Hutchins, in press). However, although the technology is being enthusiastically exploited as a tool for teaching and learning there has as yet been comparatively little exploration of the computer as a tool for *assessing* or *monitoring* reading progress.

In 1994 the National Council for Educational Technology funded a total of nineteen pilot projects on computerised assessment, recording and reporting, of which three involved the assessment of reading (NCET, 1995). NCET also funded a major project to trial *Integrated Learning Systems* (ILS) in the UK over the period 1994–5. Although an ILS is essentially a large-scale computer-based 'drill-and-practice' approach to teaching English and mathematics, it necessarily incorporates careful assessment and monitoring of student progress, and consequently has important implications for the future development of computerised assessment of reading.

The first of the three NCET projects involving reading concerned a computerised version of the ALBSU (Adult Literacy and Basic Skills) paper-based test. This is a fairly simple instrument which comprises tests of reading comprehension and basic numeracy, and which is often used for assessment of students entering further education in the UK. Although fairly speedy to administer (twenty minutes per group) its disadvantage is that it tends to absorb a lot of staff time in marking. No significant differences were found in students' reactions between the paper test and the computerised version, but further work would be necessary to generalise the results beyond the small sample used in this study. Nevertheless, the savings in staff time make such a computerised test very attractive (NCET, 1995; Wass and Hamp, in press).

The second NCET project focused on a suite of adaptive tests called *Accuplacer* (College Board, 1995), which has been widely used over the past ten years for university and college selection in the USA. These tests are sometimes referred to as CPTs (Computerised Placement Tests). *Accuplacer* includes tests of reading comprehension, sentence skills, basic English proficiency, arithmetic, algebra and higher mathematics. The on-screen presentation is text-based, but each question a student answers correctly leads to a more difficult question, and each item answered incorrectly is followed by an easier item. The item bank comprises 2200 questions, with a fifteen-to-one item-to-question ratio. In 1995 twenty-two UK institutions participated in pilot trails, which included comparison with the much simpler ALBSU paper-based test described above. Although detailed results were not published, the outcome of the pilot was said to be encouraging and a larger scale evaluation with over 1000 students is under development. Recent surveys by ALBSU indicate that as many as 40% of entrants to further education lack the skills in English required to complete their courses successfully. This type of computerised assessment can readily be administered to large groups of students using networked computer facilities, and provides instant availability of results. Hence it is regarded as particularly useful where there are open enrolment policies in further education and where it is essential not only to ensure that students enter courses at the right level but also that appropriate support is accurately targeted (NCET, 1995).

The last of the three reading-based NCET projects examined the feasibility of computerised reading assessment with a sample of 263 children aged 7 to 10 years (NCET, 1995; Singleton *et al.*, 1995). A pilot computerised version of a new test of reading comprehension was compared with conventional paper-based assessments. The computer-based test, which used colourful graphics and sound, was found to be easier to administer and was successful in discriminating children within different categories of reading skill. Children found the computer-based test more interesting than the written tests and showed higher levels of motivation with the computerised forms. The authors summarise the principal advantages of computerised reading assessment as: greater precision in presenting assessment tasks; greater accuracy in measuring responses; greater objectivity of assessment; greater attractiveness to children; savings on paper, storage and cost of test booklets, and immediate availability of results. Furthermore, if the technology was fully exploited, the technique offers the possibility of diagnostic assessment of reading, which would be much easier for teachers to administer than conventional diagnostic reading assessment methods. Although teachers acknowledge that diagnostic tests of reading are potentially of enormous value, they are currently avoided because of the considerable amounts of time involved not only in mastering and delivering such tests, but also in analysing and interpreting the results (Ames, 1980). Computerisation of diagnostic tests of reading (and spelling) could therefore result in a resurgence of interest in and use of such tests.

An *Integrated Learning System* (ILS) is a term that may be applied to any large adaptive software package which includes curricular materials, procedures for maintaining student records and an online management system. The materials could be related to any aspect of the curriculum, but to date, most have concentrated on mathematics and English. Materials have to fulfil tutorial, practice and assessment functions for students over a wide range of abilities. The student record system must control the learning route each student takes, keep a record of achievements and provide the teacher with diagnostic reports. The online management system must provide menu access to learning materials at different levels and immediate feedback on progress, with individualised work plans for students. Although some ILS programs are available as stand-alone versions which can be used on one computer, most are designed to run on a network of several machines in which the file server holds the content, the student records and the management system, and orchestrates the administration for a number of students simultaneously (Glossop, in press). Although such systems are primarily for the purposes of delivering curriculum content, they inevitably involve assessment and monitoring of student progress in order to chart an appropriate path through practice items for each individual student and to give useful feedback to the teacher. A variety of reports of varying degrees of sophistication may be obtained from the system, including information on student performance against predetermined targets. Reports can focus on individual student performance, and may highlight particular skills which are causing problems. This can alert the teacher to take some remedial action. Reports can also provide information about the progress of groups of students, including student gains in achievement level over a number of sessions.

The ILS approach has achieved some popularity in the USA and Canada, and during the period 1993 to 1995 was trialled in a total of twenty-three UK schools in a project coordinated by the National Council for Educational Technology (NCET, 1996). The schools included primary, secondary and special schools. Two different packages were trialled:

SuccessMaker (an American program marketed in the UK by RM Learning Systems) and *Global Mathematics and English* (a British program marketed by Systems Integrated Research). The chief difference between the two systems is that in the former the computer automatically moves children forward in their learning, whereas in the latter the teacher is required to set the path. The idea is that each child should spend a short but regular amount of time on the ILS (say half-an-hour each day). The results of the trials were mixed, and should be interpreted with caution as there were methodological weaknesses in the study and much of the evaluation was qualitative rather than quantitative. Technical problems made it difficult for some schools to give the ILS a proper trial. Nevertheless, promising gains in mathematical skills were shown by most, but not all, of the schools. The results for English skills were less clear. In the majority of schools there were no significant improvements in reading over an eighteen-month period, but in a few schools there were impressive gains. Much seems to depend on the way in which the system is used and the quality of teacher supervision and intervention. Benefits for underachieving pupils and those with special educational needs were noted. However, teachers who have been involved with trialling ILS seem on the whole to be convinced that learning is enhanced, while stressing that the role of the teacher is vital. They report that use of the ILS gives them more time and information to support individuals in the learning process, and that pupils show increased motivation, time on task and concentration levels (Glossop, in press).

The success, or otherwise, of ILS impinges not only on the potential of technology in learning, but also on the role of *assessment* in good teaching. Efficient learning involves a subtle combination of two complementary types of experience: on the one hand, a *repetition* of activities in order to sharpen skills and to consolidate understanding, and on the other hand, introduction of *new* concepts and techniques which, although they may be understood by the student, will have to be well rehearsed and practised before they are fully assimilated. In good teaching, the decision when to move a student on to new material in the curriculum requires an evaluation by the teacher (or the computer) of the student's existing levels of understanding and skills in the subject. Hence the process of *assessment* is an unavoidable and integral part of any teaching activity, be it teaching a child to read or any other aspect of education. Whether the computer can, in certain circumstances, and to some extent, do this better (or as well as) the teacher is an extremely important issue, and more research is essential.

COMPUTER-BASED ASSESSMENT OF DYSLEXIA

Singleton (1987, 1988) outlined a framework for the early diagnosis of dyslexia, based an assessment of underlying cognitive deficits. Although

Inouye and Sorenson (1985) were among the first to appreciate the potential of the computer for providing more accurate profiles of such deficits, it was Seymour (1986) who was the first to demonstrate the feasibility of computer-based assessment techniques in dyslexia. Seymour used two types of tasks (vocalisation tasks and decision tasks) in which the computer was employed not only to generate the experimental stimuli but also to record the performance of the child. In the vocalisation tasks, single words and nonwords were presented and the subject was asked to read them aloud. Measures of vocal reaction time (using a voice-operated switch) as well as accuracy and error type were taken. The decision tasks involved judgements about visual, lexical or semantic properties of stimuli, signalled by a Yes/No key-press response. Again, measures of accuracy and reaction time were recorded. A purpose of this study had been to provide evidence for different types of dyslexia and although the data did not fully support this, it did demonstrate the value of the computer in identifying specific impairments of individuals with dyslexia.

Hoien and Lundberg (1989) reported on a study in which a computer-based test battery discriminated between the cognitive profiles of two 15-year-old boys with dyslexia. The tasks involved oral reading, lexical decision, rhyme detection, letter categorisation, visual analysis, naming and semantic categorisation. One boy, who had succeeded in reaching a degree of literacy despite serious phonological deficits, was shown by the computer analysis to have some orthographic competence which to some extent had compensated for his other deficits. The other boy was discovered to have more proficient phonological capacity but was nevertheless a very poor reader because he was unable to develop any orthographic representations, so his reading was slow and laborious and this seriously affected his comprehension.

Researchers investigating the visual, auditory and cognitive processes which underpin reading are increasingly turning to the computer to deliver stimuli and record the subject's responses, although investigators sometimes have to use non-standard additions to the hardware, such as a 'voice key' – which can assist in timing the subject's responses accurately. However, where any skill has been found susceptible to computerised measurement in the research laboratory, it is not a large step to the development of assessment instruments which may find a wider use. One example in which this is already happening is the investigations into the nature of non-linguistic auditory temporal processing deficits in children with reading and language difficulties carried out by Tallal and her co-workers (e.g. Tallal *et al.*, 1985; Tallal *et al.*, 1993). A further example has been the creation of tests in conjunction with computerised hemisphere-specific training (HSP training) in Denmark. The principle of HSP training is to direct reading activities to either the right or left hemisphere (via the left or right visual field) in the attempt to remedy what are alleged to be hemisphere-specific weaknesses in subtypes of dyslexia (Bakker and

Vinke, 1985). The HSP test is a computerised system that can calculate relative speeds of reading when words are displayed separately to the right and left visual fields. A version using shapes rather than words, is employed for younger children who have yet to begin reading (Moller-Sorensen, 1994; Moller-Sorensen and Moller-Neilsen, 1991).

Fawcett and Nicolson (1994) explored the practicalities of an early screening system which combines items from conventional psychometric tests with a number of simple computerised items, including simple and choice reaction time, rapid naming, paired-associate learning, articulation rate, nonword repetition, phonological discrimination and rhyming. These authors argue that the computer-based approach provides 'the opportunity for constructing a new generation of psychometric tests, more sensitive than traditional tests and more easily administered, thus de-skilling the administration requirement, and enabling low-cost screening for dyslexia (and other problems)' (Fawcett *et al.*, 1993, p. 489–90).

Singleton (1991b) created a program for assessing impairments in associative memory which incorporated the systematic variation of many relevant parameters, including storage capacity, speed of information assimilation (encoding) and delay between presentation and recall. Results of exploratory studies with children between the ages of 8 and 14 indicated that those with dyslexia were significantly impaired in comparison to controls on all three of the above parameters (Singleton, 1994a). This approach was subsequently developed in a longitudinal study carried out by Singleton and Thomas (1994a). Twenty-seven computerised tests of various cognitive skills were devised, including visual and verbal memory, sequencing, phonological awareness, naming speed, auditory discrimination and visual-perceptual analysis. These tests, which are in the form of games with colourful graphics, animation and high-quality digitised speech, were administered to a representative sample of 400 children aged 5 years in twenty-four different schools, and the children's literacy and numeracy development was monitored by means of a wide range of conventional standardised tests over the next four years. In addition, verbal, nonverbal and general intelligence was assessed. Correlational and discriminant function analyses were carried out on the data when the children were aged 8 years. The highest correlations between the computerised tests at five years and reading ability at age 8 were in auditory sequential working memory ($r = 0.56$), phonological awareness (rhyming) ($r = 0.52$), auditory discrimination ($r = 0.44$) and visual sequential memory ($r = 0.39$). Phonic skills at age 8 also correlated significantly with these measures, with the highest correlation coefficient being 0.73 for the computerised test of auditory discrimination (Singleton and Thomas, 1994b). Discriminant function analysis indicated very favourable results. Two groups were composed: those children who attained scores of less than one standard deviation below the mean, and those above this score on the *British Ability Scales* Word Recognition Test. The overall prediction rate was found to be 96%, with a false negative rate of 16.7% and a false positive rate of only 2.3%, both of which are within acceptable limits (Singleton, 1995a). The authors selected the eight computerised tests which gave the most satisfactory results and these were consolidated in a software package incorporating a pupil registration system and facility for on-screen profiling and print-out of results, which has recently been published (Singleton *et al.*, 1996). This system, now known as *CoPS 1* (Cognitive Profiling System) is designed for use with children in the age range 4 to 8 years and has been provisionally standardised in school trials in three local education author-ities, with a large-scale national standardisation in progress.

The main purpose of CoPS 1 is to provide an early screening system which is attractive to young children and which teachers can use easily to discover children's cognitive strengths and weaknesses that are likely to affect their literacy development. This information can then be used to frame teaching methods which are appropriate to individual needs, and to target training activities more effectively. The test is therefore of poten-tial benefit to all children, not simply those with dyslexia (Singleton, 1995a, in press). Young children find these computer tests highly enjoyable, which overcomes many of the inherent difficulties experienced when trying to assess cognitive skills at this age. For example, the rhyming test which is used to assess phonological awareness does not place any undesirable memory load on the child (as it does in the traditional Bryant and Bradley tasks) because the pictures are on the screen for the child to refer to. Further modules are under development: these provide computer-based assessment of reading, spelling, number skills, verbal and nonverbal reasoning, and fine motor coordination, which will enhance the applica-bility of the suite for baseline assessment. A particular attraction of this approach is that the tests can be easily translated into other languages, and a Swedish-language version is currently undergoing national trials in Sweden. The possibilities for using CoPS 1 for assessment of young children in UK schools for whom English is not their first language is also being studied (Singleton *et al.*, 1996).

Computer-based screening for dyslexia in higher education

In recent years there has been a dramatic increase in the numbers of students in higher education in the UK requiring assessment for suspected dyslexia (Singleton, 1995c, 1996). Formal assessment requires the admin-istration of a complex variety of tests and procedures which can be very time-consuming (Closs *et al.*, 1996; McLoughlin *et al.*, 1994). The dearth of reading tests that are suitable for use with adults has been criticised by Singleton (1994b) and the lack of suitably qualified personnel to carry out such assessments is also a major cause for concern. Even among educa-tional psychologists, few are experienced in the assessment of adults and in the evaluation of how various literacy problems may affect a student's studies at higher education level. The possibilities for computer-based screening or more detailed assessment of dyslexia in adults are now being seriously investigated. Nicolson *et al.* (1992) reported on a feasibility study for adult dyslexia screening, the recommendations of which were for a two-stage process, the first stage being a computer-based screening system, the second stage being follow-up by more conventional psychological assessment. Zdzienski (1996) has devised a computerised test for dyslexia assessment in adults which was partly modelled on the *Scholastic Abilities Test for Adults* (a conventional test) used in the USA. To the basic test components of verbal and nonverbal intelligence, reading vocabulary and comprehension, writing composition and mechanics, and mathematics, Zdzienski added tests of various cognitive abilities relevant to the diagnosis of dyslexia, such as auditory and visual memory. The main application of this self-administered program is envisaged in screening self-referrals for dyslexia assessment at higher education level. However, if students are subsequently found to have dyslexia and wish to apply for a Disabled Student's Allowance which will assist them in financing equipment and extra support, they will still need an assessment by an educational psychologist. No comparative data or measures of predictive validity of Zdzienski's test have been published to date. Nevertheless, based on evaluations of the original conventional tests from which the computerised form was derived, Zdzienski (in press) concluded that the computerised approach is 'likely to be a valid method for the identification of students with learning difficulties both of a dyslexic and more general nature. . . . It would enable group and individual assessments to be efficiently carried out in terms of cost and time allocations'. She also argues that the student profiles obtained would assist in the design of appropriate strategies for improving study skills.

Zdzienski's test, which in its computer form has yet to be published, is fairly complex and the whole suite would take a considerable amount of time to work through. However, since it is self-administered, the time factor does not represent a major administrative burden, although it may have more significant implications where hardware resources are limited. By contrast, a much simpler computerised self-administered program for dyslexia assessment in adults is reported by McLean (in press). This system takes about thirty minutes to administer and is totally confidential to the user. It covers a range of activities including spelling, proof-reading, digit span and knowledge of phonology, all of which are areas which typically present problems for adults with dyslexia. Feedback given to the students indicates whether they would benefit from further assessment or support with tasks involving reading and writing. The designers see the particular advantages of such a system being the facility for precise control of time and presentation of stimuli, and the accurate measurement of response times. The latter can be an important consideration in the case of people with dyslexia who may perform adequately but will generally take longer than non-dyslexics to complete certain tasks. Again, the predictive validity and reliability of this instrument has yet to be established, but the attraction of a system which is non-threatening, confidential, and can provide instant and useful feedback to the student and tutor is undeniable, especially in view of current concerns about dyslexia in higher education (Singleton, in press).

CONCLUSIONS

Are we to conclude that the computer holds all the cards for future progress in the assessment of reading and reading-related skills? It certainly appears that conventional assessment has advanced as far as paper-based methods will allow. Newly published tests of reading are not radically different from tests that were developed twenty, or even thirty, years ago. In many cases, they are simply revised versions of tried-and-tested instruments which have become popular with teachers and psychologists. The pictures are improved, the vocabulary updated, the texts made more interesting for today's youngsters. Perhaps they have been better standardised. But they still have to be administered by hand and scored by hand. And they do not tell us anything new. In contrast to that, what has the computer got to offer? The answer is: a great deal. In the first place, computer-based tests can be much more attractive, especially to children. They can even be fun. Use of colour and animation can help to sustain the child's interest in the task, which can enhance the reliability of the instrument. Second, not only are computers more precise and objective in their measurements, they can also measure supplementary parameters such as response time for individual items, or number of rereadings of a text, which are potentially very important in the appraisal of reading skills but which would be extremely difficult to accomplish reliably by conventional means. They can assess the cognitive abilities which underpin reading and give a prediction of likelihood of the child encountering difficulties in reading at a later date, so that early preventive action may be taken. Third, computerised assessment can be labour saving for the teacher, a feature which becomes progressively more significant as test complexity increases. Mastering the skills of administering a complex test in conventional form, such as a diagnostic reading test or a multiplex early screening instrument, demands considerable time and effort, and the test itself will require a substantial expenditure of time to carry out, score and interpret. Computers offer a realistic solution to the accuracy/complexity dilemma which confronts those trying to develop effective screening tests or baseline assessment instruments, i.e. ones that can give worthwhile information while at the same time being easy to administer. If the computer could generate an interpretative report for a diagnostic reading test then teachers may well develop a renewed enthusiasm for such tests. What is also likely is that learning support teachers, who often play a peripatetic role in the education service, would welcome assessment programs on portable computers that could be carried from school to school and used when testing individual children who are failing in reading. Finally, computerised tests can be adaptive, which decreases testing time significantly and makes testing more efficient and agreeable for the testee.

However, computerised assessment is not without its disadvantages and its limitations (NCET, 1994), nor even its dangers, as Groth-Marnat and Schumaker (1989) and Bartram (1994) have cautioned. The computer may create an undeserved impression of objectivity and accuracy, because people have come to expect such standards from the technology. Hence computer tests that are of unproven validity and reliability may gain an acceptance that is scientifically unjustified. Obviously, schools and other educational establishments will have to possess computer hardware that is suitable for the tests which are being delivered. Complex tests demand hardware with relatively high specifications, and computerised screening of pupils or students would require appropriate hardware resources. Increasingly, networked computer facilities are being seen as the solution, but although institutions of further and higher education are mostly well equipped with up-to-date technology and secondary schools are not far behind, primary schools are relatively deprived where networked computer equipment is concerned.

Despite impressive technological advancement, there are some things that computers still do not do particularly well, or at least, not well enough for the purposes of assessment. Speech recognition or 'voice-input' systems have developed remarkably in recent years, and are now widely used in business and education for dictating straight into word processors (Litterick, in press). Such applications have obvious utility in reading assessment, because, in principle, the child could simply read the words (e.g. of a single-word recognition test) into the computer, and the computer would then score the reading performance. In practice, however, the technology is not yet quite up to this. Voice input systems still generate a fair number of errors (i.e. misinterpreted words or complete failures of interpretation), even with accomplished users of the system. Consider, for example, the sentence: 'We'll meet at the weekend and I'll buy you a coat', which could be interpreted by a voice-input system as 'Wheel meat hat the weak end and isle by ewe a goat'! Error rates are even higher if the computer has not already had substantial training to recognise the user's voice and speech patterns. Although these pitfalls will usually be outweighed by the benefits conveyed by such a system for rapid word processing by an experienced user who can readily detect and correct errors (although touch-typing might be better), they would undoubtedly be the downfall of any program designed for reading assessment. The system would certainly be far too unreliable to be of use. Furthermore, the voice-recognition system could not at the moment distinguish between reading errors which indicated gross inadequacy of phonic analysis and those which represented only slight phonic lapses, differences which would have particularly important implications for diagnosis and teaching. Hence, it must be admitted that detailed diagnostic evaluation of lexical and phonic skills – for example, those which may be employed in miscue analysis or in the reading of nonwords – are for the moment outside the scope of computerised assessment. Unquestionably, however, the technology will continue to evolve at an accelerating rate, and the capabilities required for complex diagnostic assessment of reading by computer will be available sooner or later. When it comes, or even before then, we will be forced to reconsider the role of the human 'expert' in assessment. The assessor may be relegated to the role of mere technician, or perhaps eliminated altogether, the latter scenario carrying with it the additional danger of computerised tests being available for use by unqualified people. It would be foolish not to consider the wider implications of all this. If computers are in future going to interpret (as well as deliver) tests, what need have we of highly qualified (and expensive) professionals who hitherto have been the 'experts' on psychological and educational assessment?

REFERENCES

Ames, T. (1980). *Teach Yourself to Diagnose Reading Problems*. Windsor, Berks: NFER-Nelson.
Bakker, D.J. and Vinke, J. (1985). Effects of hemisphere-specific stimulation on brain activity and reading in dyslexics. *Journal of Clinical and Developmental Neuropsychology*, 7, 505–25.
Bartram, D. (1989). Computer-based assessment. In P. Herriot (ed.), *Handbook of Assessment in Organisations*. London: Wiley.
Bartram, D. (1994). Computer-based assessment. *International Review of Industrial and Organizational Psychology*, 9, 31–69.
Bartram, D. and Dale, H.C.A. (1991). Validation of the Micropat battery of pilot aptitude tests. In P.L. Dann, S.H. Irvine and J.M. Collins (eds), *Advances in Computer-Based Human Assessment*. Dordrecht, Netherlands: Kluwer Academic Publishers.
Bartram, D., Beaumont, J.G., Cornford, T., Dann, P.L. and Wilson, S.L. (1987). Recommendations for the design of software for computer-based assessment – summary statement. *Bulletin of the British Psychological Society*, 40, 86–7.
Booth, J. (1991). The key to valid computer-based testing: the user interface. *European Review of Applied Psychology*, 41, 281–93.
Bull, J. (1994). Computer-based assessment: some issues for consideration. *Active Learning*, 1, 18–21.
Closs, A., Lannen, S. and Reid, G. (1996). Dyslexia in further and higher education – a framework for practice. In G. Reid (ed.), *Dimensions of Dyslexia*. Edinburgh: Moray House Publications.
College Board (1995). *Accuplacer 5.0 for Windows*. New York: College Entrance Examination Board.
Day, J. (1993). *A Software Guide for Specific Learning Difficulties*. Coventry: NCET.
Dempster, J. A. (1994). Question mark designer for Windows. *Active Learning*, 1, 47–50.
Dimock, P.H. and Cormier, P. (1991). The effects of format differences and

computer experience on performance and anxiety on a computer-administered test. *Measurement and Evaluation in Counselling and Development*, 24, 119–26.

Evans, C. (1979). *The Mighty Micro*. London: Gollancz.

Fawcett, A.J. and Nicolson, R. (1994). Computer-based diagnosis of dyslexia. In C.H. Singleton (ed.), *Computers and Dyslexia. Educational Applications of New Technology*. Hull: Dyslexia Computer Resource Centre, University of Hull.

Fawcett, A.J., Pickering, S. and Nicolson, R.I. (1993). Development of the DEST test for the early screening for dyslexia. In S.F. Wright and R. Groner (eds), *Facets of Dyslexia and its Remediation*. Amsterdam: Elsevier Science Publishers BV.

Federico, P-A. (1991). Measuring recognition performance using computer-based and paper-based methods. *Behavior Research Methods, Instruments and Computers*, 23, 341–7.

French, C. and Beaumont, J.G. (1990). A clinical study of the automated assessment of intelligence by the Mill Hill Vocabulary Test and the Standard Progressive Matrices test. *Journal of Clinical Psychology*, 46, 129–40.

Glossop, G. (in press). Integrated learning systems. In C.H. Singleton and J. Hutchins (eds), *Computer Support for Children with Dyslexia*. Hull: Dyslexia Computer Resource Centre, University of Hull.

Groth-Marnat, G. and Schumaker, J. (1989). Computer-based psychological testing: issues and guidelines. *American Journal of Orthopsychiatry*, 59, 257–63.

Guildford Education Services (1993). *Directory of Computer Assisted Assessment Products and Services*. London: Employment Department.

Hambleton, R.K. and Swaminathan, H. (1985). *Item Response Theory: Principles and Applications*. Boston: Kluwer-Nijhoff.

Hawkridge, D. and Vincent, T. (1992). *Learning Difficulties and Computers. Access to the Curriculum*. London: Jessica Kingsley Publishers.

Hoffman, R.R. (1994) *The Psychology Of Expertise*. Hillsdale, NJ: Erlbaum.

Hoien, T. and Lundberg, I. (1989). A strategy for assessing problems in word recognition among dyslexics. *Scandinavian Journal of Educational Research*, 33, 185–201.

Inouye, D.K. and Sorenson, M.R., (1985). Profiles of dyslexia: the computer as an instrument of vision. In D.B. Gray and J.K. Kavanagh (eds), *Biobehavioural Measures of Dyslexia*. Parkton, Maryland: York Press.

Kyllonen, P.C. (1991). Principles for creating a computerized test battery. *Intelligence*, 15, 1–15.

Larrabee, G.L. and Crook, T.H. (1989). Dimensions of everyday memory in age-associated memory impairment. *Psychological Assessment*, 1, 92–7

Litterick, I. (in press) Computer speech systems for adult dyslexics. In C.H. Singleton and J. Hutchins (eds) *Computer Support for Adults with Dyslexia*. Hull: Dyslexia Computer Resource Centre, University of Hull.

McCorduck, P. (1979). *Machines Who Think*. New York: Freeman.

McLean, B. (in press). Assessment and screening of dyslexia in further and higher education: how the computer can help. In C.H. Singleton and J. Hutchins (eds) *Computer Support for Adults with Dyslexia*. Hull: Dyslexia Computer Resource Centre, University of Hull.

McLoughlin, D., Fitzgibbon, G. and Young, V. (1994). *Adult Dyslexia: Assessment, Counselling and Training*. London: Whurr.

Maguire, K.B., Knobel, M.-L.M., Knobel, B.L. and Sedlacek, L.G. (1991). Computer-adapted PPVT-R: a comparison between standards and modified versions within an elementary school population. *Psychology in the Schools*, 28, 199–205.

Martin, T.A. and Wilcox, K.L. (1989). Hypercard administration of a block-design task. *Behavior Research Methods, Instruments and Computers*, 21, 312–15.

Moller-Sorensen, T. (1994). Hemisphere-specific computer assisted reading training. In C.H. Singleton (ed.) *Computers and Dyslexia: Educational Applications
of New Technology*. Hull: Dyslexia Computer Resource Centre, University of
Hull.

Moller-Sorensen, T. and Moller-Neilsen, M.M. (1991). *Hemisphere Specific Reading
Training and Visual HSP-test*. Sonderborg, Denmark: MN-Data.

Moreland, K.L. (1991). Assessment of validity in computer-based test interpretations. In T.B. Gutkin and S.L.Wise (eds) *The Computer and the Decision-making
Process*. Hillsdale, NJ: Erlbaum.

NCET (1994). *Using IT for Assessment – Going Forward*. Coventry: National
Council for Educational Technology.

NCET (1995). *Using IT for Assessment – Case Studies Reports*. Coventry: National
Council for Educational Technology.

NCET (1996). *Integrated Learning Systems. A Report of Phase II of the Pilot
Evaluation of ILS in the UK*. Coventry: National Council for Educational
Technology.

Nicolson, R.I., Fawcett, A.J. and Miles, T.R., (1992). *Adult Dyslexia Screening
Feasibility Study* (Report to the Employment Department). Sheffield: University
of Sheffield.

Olsen, J.B. (1990). Applying computerized adaptive testing in schools.
Measurement and Evaluation in Counselling and Development, 23, 31–8.

Peel, A. and Rowe, G. (1995). Computer-aided assessment through hypermedia.
In W. Strang, V.B. Simpson and D. Slater (eds), *Hypermedia at Work: Practice
and Theory in Higher Education*. Canterbury: University of Kent.

Pellegrino, J.W. and Hunt, E.B. (1989). Computer-controlled assessment of static
and dynamic spatial reasoning. In R.F. Dillon and J.W. Pellegrino (eds), *Testing:
Theoretical and Applied Perspectives*. New York: Praeger.

Percival, F., Land, R. and Edgar-Nevill, D. (eds) (1995). *Computer Assisted and
Open Access Education*. London: Kogan Page.

Reckase, M.D. (1989). Adaptive testing: the evolution of a good idea. *Educational
Measurement: Issues and Practice*, 8, 11–16.

Rich, E. and Knight, K. (1991). *Artificial Intelligence*. New York: McGraw-Hill.

Schuhfried, G. (1990). Progress in computer-aided testing. In E. Farmer (ed.),
Human Resource Management in Aviation. Aldershot: Avebury Technical
Academic Publishing Group.

Seymour, P.H.K. (1986). *Cognitive Analysis of Dyslexia*. London: Routledge &
Kegan Paul.

Simon, H.A. and Newell, A. (1958). Heuristic problem solving: the next advance
in operations research. *Operations Research*, 6, 1–10.

Singleton, C.H. (1987). Dyslexia and cognitive models of reading. *Support for
Learning*, 2, 47–56.

Singleton, C.H. (1988). The early diagnosis of developmental dyslexia. *Support for
Learning*, 3, 108–21.

Singleton, C.H. (ed.) (1991a). *Computers and Literacy Skills*. Hull: Dyslexia
Computer Resource Centre, University of Hull.

Singleton, C.H. (1991b). Computer applications in the diagnosis and assessment
of cognitive deficits in dyslexia. In Singleton, C.H. (ed.), *Computers and Literacy
Skills*. Hull: Dyslexia Computer Resource Centre, University of Hull.

Singleton, C.H. (1994a). Computer applications in the identification and remediation of dyslexia. In D. Wray (ed.), *Literacy and Computers: Insights from
Research*. Widnes: United Kingdom Reading Association.

Singleton, C.H. (ed.) (1994b) *Computers and Dyslexia: Educational Applications of
New Technology*. Hull: Dyslexia Computer Resource Centre, University of Hull.

Singleton, C.H. (1994c). Issues in the diagnosis and assessment of dyslexia in

Higher Education. *Proceedings of the International Conference on Dyslexia in Higher Education.* Plymouth: University of Plymouth.

Singleton, C.H. (1995a). *Computerised Cognitive Profiling and Early Diagnosis of Dyslexia.* Paper presented to the British Psychological Society Conference, London.

Singleton, C.H. (1995b). Assessing individuality. *Interactive*, 2, 34–5, and 3, 46–7.

Singleton, C.H. (1995c). Dyslexia in Higher Education. *Dyslexia Contact*, 14, 7–9.

Singleton, C.H. (1996a) Dyslexia in higher education: issues for policy and practice. In C. Stephens (ed.), *Proceedings of the Conference on Dyslexic Students in Higher Education.* Huddersfield: Skill and the University of Huddersfield.

Singleton, C.H. (1996b). Computerised screening for dyslexia. In G. Reid (ed.) *Dimensions of Dyslexia*, Vol 1. Edinburgh: Moray House Publications.

Singleton, C.H. (in press) Adults with dyslexia – liberation by technology? In C.H. Singleton and J. Hutchins (eds), *Computer Support for Adults with Dyslexia.* Hull: Dyslexia Computer Resource Centre, University of Hull.

Singleton, C.H. and Hutchins, J. (eds) (in press). *Computer Support for Children with Dyslexia.* Hull: Dyslexia Computer Resource Centre, University of Hull.

Singleton, C.H. and Thomas, K.V. (1994a). Computerised screening for dyslexia. In C.H. Singleton (ed.) *Computers and Dyslexia. Educational Applications of New Technology.* Hull: Dyslexia Computer Resource Centre, University of Hull.

Singleton, C.H. and Thomas, K.V. (1994b). *The Creation and Evaluation of a Suite of Computer Software for the Early Identification of Dyslexia* (Final Project Report). Hull: Dyslexia Computer Resource Centre, University of Hull.

Singleton, C.H., Horne, J. and Vincent, D. (1995). *Implementation of a Computer-based System for Diagnostic Assessment of Reading.* (Final Report to the National Council for Educational Technology.) Hull: Dyslexia Computer Resource Centre, University of Hull.

Singleton, C.H., Thomas, K.V. and Leedale, R.C. (1996). *CoPS 1 Cognitive Profiling System.* Nottingham: Chameleon Educational Systems Ltd.

Singleton, C.H., Thomas, K.V., Leedale, R.C. and Horne, J.K. (in press). Computerised screening and assessment of dyslexia. In C.H. Singleton and J. Hutchins (eds) *Computer Support for Children with Dyslexia.* Hull: Dyslexia Computer Resource Centre, University of Hull.

Stephens, D. (1994). Using computer-assisted assessment: time saver or sophisticated distraction? *Active Learning*, 1, 11–15.

Strang, W., Simpson, V.B. and Slater, D. (eds) (1995). *Hypermedia at Work: Practice and Theory in Higher Education.* Canterbury: University of Kent.

Tallal, P., Miller, S. and Fitch, R.H. (1993). Neurobiological basis of speech: a case for the pre-eminence of temporal processing. *Annals of New York Academy of Sciences*, 682, 27–47.

Tallal, P., Stark, R.E. and Mellits, D. (1985). The relationship between auditory temporal analysis and receptive language development: evidence from studies of developmental language disorder. *Neuropsychologia*, 23, 527–34.

Wainer, H., Dorans, N.J., Flaugher, R., Green, B.F., Mislevy, R.J., Steinberg, L. and Thissen, D. (1990). *Computerized Adaptive Testing: A Primer.* Hillsdale, NJ: Lawrence Erlbaum.

Wass, K. and Hamp, R. (in press). A computerised version of the ALBSU screening test for reading and maths. In C.H. Singleton and J. Hutchins (eds) *Computer Support for Adults with Dyslexia.* Hull: Dyslexia Computer Resource Centre, University of Hull.

Zdzienski, D. (1996). Computerised self-assessment for dyslexic students in Higher Education. In C. Stephens (ed.), *Proceedings of the Conference on Dyslexic Students in Higher Education.* Huddersfield: Skill and the University of Huddersfield.

278   *Chris Singleton*

Zdzienski, D. (in press). A computerised assessment package for dyslexia at higher education level. In C.H. Singleton and J. Hutchins (eds) *Computer Support for Adults with Dyslexia*. Hull: Dyslexia Computer Resource Centre, University of Hull.

14 The legal aspects of the assessment of literacy and writing difficulties

John Friel

INTRODUCTION

The law was largely a matter of deduction and educated guesswork from other areas of professional practice until 29 June 1995, when the House of Lords clearly defined the liability of professionals in this area. Psychologists in private practice, independent schools, teachers acting privately as specialist teachers and advisory teachers in the independent sector are all providing a service. They worked, whether they knew it or not, under fairly clearly defined legal guidelines, which were relatively easy to discern due to a law of contract. It is true to say that the law of negligence concerning those in the independent sector could have been described as less obvious, but as they provided a contractual service, deductions could be drawn from others providing similar services such as private medical care. There was little doubt that they were subject to liability. For those involved in statutory assessments under the Education Acts, the statute provided guidance as to the task but not as to professional standards. There was no clear guidance on liability.

However, in relation to cases which actually came before the courts, apart from the more obvious type of case involving claims for school fees, there was little litigation in this area. This position is likely to change in the future.

For those working in the public sector, the situation was different from the private sector. Psychologists, specialist advisory teachers working with local education authorities, those staff working within school in the equivalent role, together with education officers, who interpreted advice, were thought by some to be subject to the same liability as the private sector. There was, as in the independent sector, no clear law on this issue, and opinion was divided as to whether those working in the state sector were liable in negligence other than for physical injury due to breach of duty. As with all local authority employees, there is no question of contract; the law of negligence therefore governs their position.

To escape liability, those working within the state sector would have had to show that they were an exception to the normal legal principles, due to the fact that there could be no question but that the private sector would be liable in cases of negligence or breach of contract.

The debate in this field was decided by the House of Lords, who also considered the position of social workers, and similar specialists, including psychologists advising in Children Act cases, where there is a necessity to intervene to protect the child. In a series of five cases – two Children Act and three Education Act cases – the House of Lords clearly set the standards and defined the law in this area.

None the less, the issues of liability and negligence, for those who work with children with difficulties and assess their needs, produces considerable controversy. In the first instance, in the High Court, Mr Justice Otton (now Lord Justice Otton) in an unreported judgment, struck out the two lead cases, *E (a minor) -v- Dorset* and *Christmas -v- Hampshire County Council* on the basis that no such claim was sustainable. The two Children Act cases reported, although heard in the High Court after the judgment of Mr Justice Otton, went to the Court of Appeal first, and, by a majority of two to one, on the issue of common law and negligence, the Court of Appeal dismissed the cases largely on the basis of the reasoning of Mr Justice Otton (reported in *(1994) 2 Weekly Law Reports*, p. 334).

When the education cases came to the Court of Appeal, they were joined by a third case: *Christmas -v- Bromley*. All were reported as *E (a minor) -v- Dorset County Council ((1994) 3 Weekly Law Reports, p. 853)*. All three cases succeeded in the Court of Appeal or issue of common law negligence unanimously. In the House of Lords, all three education cases again succeeded unanimously. They were reported as a series of cases entitled *X (minors) -v- Bedfordshire County Council and Others ((1993), 3 Weekly Law Reports*, p. 153). In his dissenting judgment in the Children Act cases in the Court of Appeal, the Master of the Rolls, Sir Thomas Bingham, was overruled by two very senior Lord Justices, who followed the reasoning of Mr Justice Otton in the earlier education cases. It can be seen that there was considerable controversy in the Higher Courts over this issue. Indeed, although the House of Lords indicated that educational psychologists were liable in negligence, and by parity of reasoning education officers who implement their advice, they extended this category to headteachers of schools who were responsible for children who were failing or under-performing, and teachers who gave specialist advice. However, the implications of the House of Lords opinion, particularly in the *Christmas* case, the second of the three conjoined education cases, is wider than the actual claims made in all three cases before the House of Lords.

The Court of Appeal based its reasoning on a medical comparison, and the comparison with private schools. This comparison with medical practice had previously been adopted in cases of statements of special educational needs *R -v- Secretary of State ex parte 'E' (1992) FLR 377*. In the Court of Appeal, the education cases were argued before the Court Master of the Rolls, Sir Thomas Bingham, Lord Justice Evans and Lord Justice Rose. In oral exchanges they considered it likely that if the standard of education provided in a private school was not reasonably fit for its purpose, a contractual test, an action was available to the child's parents.

This view appears to be the main basis for the opinion of the House of Lords delivered in detail by Lord Browne-Wilkinson in the case of *Christmas -v- Hampshire County Council ((1994) 3 Weekly Law Reports 153, pp. 196H-199B).* He pointed out that 'the education of the pupil is the very purpose for which the child goes to the school. The Headteacher being responsible for the school, himself comes under a duty of care to exercise the reasonable skills of the Headteacher in relation to such educational needs.' The claim before the House of Lords in the *Dorset* and *Christmas* cases were both based on traditional negligence claims, which founded the existence of special educational needs rooted in a discernible physical origin or an identifiable and recognised illness of a psychiatric origin. Thus, for example, in the *Dorset* case, it was made clear that dyslexia or specific learning difficulties had their origins based on psychological defects in the brain. Therefore, there was no difference in the role of specialists in this area from those offering treatment at a hospital or a doctor's surgery.

For example, where a person presents to hospital staff as a result of brain damage at birth or a road accident, it is immaterial that the condition arises either from problems the person was born with, or problems experienced as a result of accident or injury. The hospital staff hold themselves to be experienced in remediating the condition so far as it is possible to do so on the basis of the current knowledge and facilities available to the profession.

The House of Lords has not fully addressed the issue as to whether educational needs which arise from other issues that are not discernible by psychiatric illness, physical origin, or some later accident or injury can found an action in negligence. However, for those assessing literacy learning difficulties, the cases where it will be difficult to show an origin of this type will be rare and the law is now relatively clear.

The implications of the judgment are that it is possible a claim can be extended for education that is so bad it is not fit for its purpose in contractual terms. For those who work in the public sector, a claim that it is negligently delivered remains open. Were such an extension to take place, in my view, it would extend the potential area of liability for those working in this field very considerably. However, by equating professionals in this field and those in the health service, the House of Lords has afforded considerable protection to those professionals. I will discuss this aspect in more detail below.

THE POSITION IN NEGLIGENCE

The law in this field is the same for all those providing professional services education, whether in the public or the independent sector. Although this book is about assessment and provision for those with literacy-related difficulties, the law is exactly the same for all children and young persons with special educational needs. The law in this field extends to educational psychologists, education officers (a category that would include those who work for further education funding councils and, for that matter, within universities), teachers who provide specialist advice, whether with specialist qualifications or simply by the exercise of their experience, and headteachers. The implications of the judgment of the House of Lords are in fact more extensive.

The liability of the headteacher is on the basis that he or she is responsible for the school and comes under a duty to exercise the reasonable skills of a head in relation to such educational needs.

> If it comes to the attention of the Headmaster that a pupil is under-performing, he does owe a duty to take such steps as a reasonable teacher would consider appropriate to try to deal with such under-performance. To hold that in such circumstances, the Headteacher could properly ignore the matter and make no attempt to deal with it would fly in the face, not only of society's expectations of what a school will provide, but also of the fine traditions of the teaching profession itself.
>
> Lord Browne-Wilkinson, p. 198E–F in the *House of Lords X (minors) and Others -v- Bedfordshire and Others* (the actual title of the case is very long and is therefore reproduced in short form (see *(1995) 3 Weekly Law Reports p. 153 supra*).

If the school does not identify the child with special needs, where the matter is not brought to the headteacher's attention, and if the failure to identify the child as under-performing and failing is due to negligence of the organisation of the school, or to negligence of a class teacher or a number of teachers, then the headteacher will not escape liability.

This reasoning of course has considerable implications particularly for education officers, but even more so for psychologists. It is advisable for all those who come in from outside, particularly from a local authority, or those in the independent sector who are advising on the child in a school, to carefully check the facts brought to their attention and to ascertain the true position. If mistakes have been made, if information is wrong, due to a previous negligent error or omission, this will of course affect later professional opinions.

VICARIOUS LIABILITY

The judgment in the House of Lords was based on the principle of vicarious liability in the public sector and the independent sector. Psychologists, education officers, all in the teaching profession, are normally employed, and it will be their employers, whether a local authority or institution, who will be the subject of an action. For those in the independent sector, particularly for educational psychologists operating their own service or who are part of such a service, and specialist teachers in the same position, there is a clear need to ensure that insurance cover is available and has been taken out. Teaching and administrative staff in the private sector are governed by the same principle of vicarious liability, and it will be their employers against whom an action is brought.

THE DUTY OF CARE

The imposition of a duty of care in the field of education is based solely on the common-law duty of care. In the *Dorset* case, Lord Browne-Wilkinson said, 'Psychologists (including educational psychologists) hold themselves out as having special skills and they are, in my judgment, like any other professional bound to possess such skills and to exercise them carefully. Of course, the test in *Bolam -v- The Friern Hospital Management Committee ((1957) 1 Weekly Law Reports, p. 582)* will apply to them.' This test means that psychologists are only bound to exercise the ordinary skill of a competent psychologist. If they can show that they acted in accordance with the accepted views of a reputable psychologist at the relevant time, they will have discharged the duty of care even if some psychologists would have adopted a different view. It was pointed out by the Lords that the advice on the treatment of dyslexia had advanced considerably in recent years, and this may be an important factor in proving liability. Therefore, as long as psychologists work in accordance with an acceptable body of opinion in the profession, they will normally be exempt from liability if that is the only issue.

However, it should be noted that in a leading case on this issue, a medical negligence case, *Sidaway (1985) Appeal Cases p. 871*, the House of Lords expressly reserved the issue as to whether a reputable body of opinion would be regarded by the courts as unreasonable. There have been cases where a failure to make adequate provision for educational needs was due to lack of funds, despite the fact that the statutory duty is that the law requires provision to be reasonably appropriate irrespective of cost. This would mean that a body of opinion which takes this approach would not have been reasonable, even if respectable, if it failed to advise adequate provision in these circumstances. A decision by a psychologist which is related to cost may in some cases be in conflict with his or her own duty. The fact that there is a body of opinion may not be sufficient to justify the decision, if a provision is not adequate or appropriate due to cost issues.

The field of educational psychology has not been subject to such clear-cut rules as medicine, with which the House of Lords now equates it.

There are alleged cases of psychologists accepting employers' orders or
bowing to pressure to change their professional advice. In such cases, the
courts may not be prepared to allow a psychologist to escape liability.
Psychologists exercise a higher degree of professional skill for the purposes
of legal liability than do teachers.

This was defined in the House of Lords in three education cases *supra*
as being the following question in the case of teachers:

> The question therefore is whether the headmaster of any school
> whether private or public or a teaching adviser, is under a duty to his
> pupils to exercise care and skill in advising on their educational needs?

It is accepted that a school and teachers at that school are under a duty
to safeguard the physical well-being of a pupil (see *Van Oppen -v- Clerk
to the Charity Trustees ((1990) 1 Weekly Law Reports, p. 235)*. The House
of Lords extended this principle to cover the advice given to and remediation of those pupils with special educational needs. In the passage
quoted above, Lord Browne-Wilkinson held that a headteacher was bound
to exercise a duty of care. In the case of an advisory teacher brought in
to advise on the educational needs of the specific pupil, if such a teacher
knows that his advice will be communicated to the pupil's parents, the
teacher must proceed on the basis that they will rely on that advice.
Therefore, in giving such advice, a teacher owes a duty to the child to
exercise the care and skill of a reasonably competent advisory teacher.
The teaching profession therefore falls within the same category.

The standard of care for teachers

The headteacher and an advisory teacher are only bound to exercise the
skill and care of a reasonable headteacher and advisory teacher. The test
in the *Bolam* case set out above which applies in cases of educational psychologists will also apply to the teaching profession, namely whether the
advice and views might have been entertained and given by reasonably
competent members of the teaching profession. Clearly, such teachers are
not under any duty to exercise a higher degree of skill such as that of an
educational psychologist. If their views on dyslexia are reasonable, held on
the date by a responsible body of educational thinking, in the same way as
psychologists would escape liability, so will teachers, even if they are wrong.

On a practical basis, liability is likely to be proved in cases which involve
maladministration, namely doing nothing or doing what is needed far too
late when the needs of the child are known or providing for the needs
inadequately, either ignoring clear evidence as to the greater extent of the
needs, failing to act, or deliberately taking the decision not to act. In such
cases, professionals will not escape liability simply because they might
have another view available, where no such view was ever consulted or
applied. Further, in some ways, it is also possible that in the long run the

independent sector, because of its constituency, could face as many claims
as the public sector.

The position in contract

The law of contract has no application in the public sector. Those working
within the public sector are not subject to liability in contract. Their
contract is with their employer. For those working within schools, particularly headteachers and advisory teachers, the House of Lords equated
the position within the independent sector and within the state sector as
being exactly the same for the law of negligence. It is a useful guide to
the duty and contract. An independent school and all those working
in the independent sector will certainly be expected to provide advice in
this area that is reasonably fit for its purpose. Where there is specialist
provision, the provision must also be reasonably fit for its purpose and
delivered by those who are competently qualified either through experience or qualification to deliver such provision, in a manner that is efficient
and fit for its purpose.

The main implication for the independent sector for those in teaching
is that it would be wise and expedient to have views checked by a competent independent professional, normally an educational psychologist. This
would in any event mirror the public sector which is under such a statutory
duty, and would be an appropriate move by those working in the independent sector.

The position of the independent educational psychologist and independent advisory teacher is dependent on the contract that they will have
with the parent. In practice, such contracts are often governed by the
absence of anything in writing or, alternatively, the absence of anything
relevant to the task in hand. As a result of the House of Lords judgment,
it can be said that psychologists exercise a higher degree of professional
care and skill than members of the teaching profession and are to be
treated as skilled professionals, to a degree of skill and ability which is
equated to that of the medical profession. The law will imply into a
contract a term that all psychologists will exercise a reasonable degree of
care and skill to the appropriate professional standard.

Second, the advice given must be fit for its purpose. This term of the
contract is well established as a matter of law and it is in fact trite law.
Experience in dealing with children with special needs has shown however
that reports of independent psychologists do not in fact always provide
advice fit for the purpose, as they do not deal with all the issues.

If the referral is from a school, it is highly unlikely that the school will
simply want a diagnosis of the child's needs but will also seek advice on
the provision to meet those needs. In the same way, if a parent consults
a psychologist, he or she will expect not only a diagnosis but advice on
provision. The law will imply such a term into such a situation. The advice

needs to be fit for the purpose which governs the consultation between the psychologist and the child's parents. Psychologists therefore ought to bear in mind that failure to advise on provision adequately will be capable of a claim in the law of contract and they will be expected to provide their advice competently to a high degree of care and skill. This means that, for example, where a child is entitled to a statement, as some are within the state sector, that the psychologist may be in breach of a contract or negligent in failing to advise the parent to seek an assessment by statute for a statement. The report must therefore deal with the basis of the advice sought by the parent on behalf of the child or young person. If it does not do so, the advice will be in breach of contract. Those who do not wish to become involved in certain issues concerning the 1993 Education Act, its procedures and the appeal procedures, would be well advised to make this quite clear prior to any assessment in their literature and in any contract that exists.

STATUTORY DUTIES – THE ASSESSMENT PROCEDURE

The 1981 Act introduced a statutory assessment procedure for children with special educational needs. As part of this assessment procedure, the authority must obtain educational and psychological advice. Currently, the statutory procedures are set out in Statutory Instrument Number 1047 of 1994, the Special Educational Needs Assessment Regulations. The standard of such advice is exactly the same as the standard set out above in relation to the law of negligence and contract.

In the statutory system, the one additional issue that arises is the issue of consultation under Regulation 6 for psychologists. The Regulation provides that where a psychologist has reason to believe he or she should consult another psychologist or any person who has relevant advice, this should be done before his or her advice is given. It has to be noted that this duty is placed on the public sector educational psychologist. An educational psychologist working independently would be well advised to obtain the parents' permission as a term of the contract to carry out such a consultation. However, if no such term exists, and the request relates to matters that are entirely confidential, it is only the parent who can give permission for a response to the consultation, as the information is confidential and cannot be disclosed without permission. Equally, it may be no longer practical or appropriate for an educational psychologist in the private sector to act in such consultation, if they are not further consulted or have been effectively abandoned by the client. This is an important statutory provision for psychologists in practice to bear in mind, and in this respect their legal duty differs from other professionals.

STATUTORY SYSTEM – GENERAL CONSIDERATIONS

The 1993 Education Act replaced the 1991 Education Act which governed the assessment of children with special educational needs. This clearly covers children with reading and literacy difficulties. The law in this area obviously covers all children with special needs and is not confined to children with reading and literacy difficulties. The statutory system provides for the identification assessment and provision for children with special needs including those with literacy difficulties. The system deals with the most severe problems by way of a statement of special educational needs made under the provisions of Section 168 of the 1993 Education Act. However, estimates vary as to how many children should be the subject of a statement. The majority of children with difficulties will not be the subject of a statement and will be catered for in the ordinary school with remedial education appropriate to the child's needs (see *R -v- Secretary of State ex parte Lashford ((1988) 1 Family Law Reports, p. 26)*).

The 1993 Education Act introduced a Code of Practice under Section 157 of the Act. The Code of Practice provides for the assessment of children with special needs from Stages 1–5, Stage 5 being children with statements, and Stage 4 being the statutory assessment. The first three stages provide for increasingly complex forms of intervention in the ordinary school. It is not the aim of this chapter to go into detail on the Code of Practice. The statute provides that local education authorities and all those working to the Code shall have regard to the Code. Regard to is a legal term of art and does not mean apply rigidly or that the Code is the equivalent of the law. It is however evidence of national practice, and of what is considered to be good practice. A departure from its practice is of course permissible so long as the departure provides for a reasonable alternative. For a detailed consideration of the Code, see Friel (Chapter 5). The Code of Practice provides evidence of what is the test for a reasonable body of teachers or psychologists. Standards will not fall below the contents of the Code.

For those children who require a statutory assessment, in the words of statute, 'if it is necessary', thereafter educational advice is sought upon the child's special educational needs, and psychological advice is sought on the child. In all cases, the standards of the advice and the professional requirements were set by the Court of Appeal in *R -v- Secretary of State for Education ex parte 'E' ((1992) Family Law Reports*, p. 377). A statement was held by the Court of Appeal to be the equivalent of a medical diagnosis and prescription. Therefore, all those performing their duties under the statutory system, not only where there is a statutory assessment but also under the Code of Practice, need to carry out the assessment on the basis of diagnosing the special educational needs, and prescribing the appropriate provision.

The existence of a statutory Code of Practice will certainly have an effect in relation to whether the national standards are being appropriately applied. This therefore has a bearing on the law of negligence, and indeed on the contractual duties of psychologists and all other specialists. It therefore interlinks with the common law.

REFERENCES

Friel, J. (1997) *Children with Special Needs, Assessment Law and Practice* (4th edn). London: Jessica Kingsley.

Friel, J. and Hay, D. (1996) *Special Educational Needs and the Law*. London: Sweet & Maxwell.

Test reviews

THE BANGOR DYSLEXIA TEST
(FORMERLY THE DYSLEXIA TEST)

Test author   T.R. Miles.

Purpose   The instrument is offered as a way of advancing understanding of an individual's learning difficulties. It is *not* intended as a 'means of definitive diagnosis' (Manual, p.1, 1983b).

Participant population   7 to 18 years, excluding pupils 'of limited ability'.

Administration time   The test is untimed but can take about 40 minutes to administer.

Materials   Manual (7 pp.) and subject's record booklet (4 pp.).

Structure and administration   The skills tested are:

1 Left–right (body parts)
2 Repeating polysyllabic words
3 Subtraction
4 Tables
5 Months forwards

6 Months reversed
7 Digits forwards
8 Digits reversed
9 b-d confusion
10 Familial incidence

The test is individually administered.

Scoring and interpretation   Using both quantified responses and qualitative judgements, the test items are scored and the results of each section coded as either 'dyslexia positive', 'dyslexia negative' or 'zero' (ambiguous). Adjustments are indicated to allow for certain maturational effects. It is suggested that after having used 'the test a few times you may prefer to rely on your overall impression rather than on the subject's precise score. Good sense is more important than numerical impression' (loc. cit.). The importance of 'incongruities' in performance on the sub-tests are seen as crucial in deciding whether an individual has, has not, or has partial dyslexia. The psychological significance of the particular patterns of incongruities is determined by the particular case.

Technical details   After extensive clinical and empirical work, the Dyslexia Test was first published in 1983. An account of it was published in *Dyslexia: The Pattern of Difficulties* (Miles, 1983a). A second edition appeared ten years later (Miles, 1993). Greek, German and Japanese versions of the *Bangor Dyslexia Test* are presented. Technical details of the items and the construction and validation of the instrument are not presented in the manual. The details can be found in Miles (1983a, 1993).

An early review suggested that considerable further development work was required if the potential of Miles' approach was to be capitalised upon (Pumfrey, 1985). Subsequent research has provided support for the theoretical position adopted by Miles. Small-scale studies from Britain are reported as confirming the ability of the test to discriminate between pupils with or without dyslexia (Miles, 1993).

Standardisation The test cannot be considered as standardised. The items comprising the test were developed over time using data collected between 1972 and 1978 from 291 subjects of whom 223 'could be regarded as pure or typical cases of dyslexia' (Miles, 1983a, p.26).

Reliability Evidence as to the reliability of the test is not given in the manual. For such information as bears on these issues one must consult the books (reliability is not specifically listed in their indices). Because of the clinical and cumulative nature of Miles' work, its presentation differs from most other books on the construction and validation of a screening instrument.

Validity Although the items comprising the test are theoretically linked via verbal labelling theory, the term 'validity' does not appear in the indices to either the first or second edition of Miles' book. Despite this, much clinical and some empirical evidence of validity is provided.

Evaluation The appeal to many practitioners of this relatively short screening test is considerable. Anyone wishing to use the *Bangor Dyslexia Test* is advised to read Miles' books before doing so. The manual rightly notes that the test should be used as part of a wider assessment and 'not a means of definitive diagnosis'.

Country of origin UK

Publisher LDA, Duke Street, Wisbech, Cambridge, PE13 2AE

References

Miles, T.R. (1983a). *Dyslexia: The Pattern of Difficulties*. London: Whurr.
Miles, T.R. (1983b). *The Bangor Dyslexia Test*. LDA: Wisbech.
Miles, T.R. (1993). *Dyslexia: The Pattern of Difficulties*. London: Whurr (2nd edn).
Pumfrey, P.D. (1985). *Reading: Tests and Assessment Techniques*. London: Hodder and Stoughton (2nd edn).

Peter D. Pumfrey

BASIC SKILLS TESTS

Test authors   Pauline Smith and Chris Whetton.

Purpose   This test covers basic skills in reading, writing and numeracy. The reading test is a naturalistic one involving reading a newspaper. The purpose of this reading comprehension test is to provide an assessment of functional literacy.

Participant population   Fifth-formers through to adults whose literacy skills are at a functional level.

Administration time   30 minutes.

Materials   Specially designed newspaper *The Shelley Gazette*, question-and-answer booklet.

Structure and administration   The reading section of these tests (there are also tests of writing and numeracy) measures comprehension at a 'basic skills' or functional level. It consists of a specially prepared newspaper. It is designed for group administration but can be given individually, either timed or untimed. Examinees are asked to read the newspaper and write their answers to the questions in the test booklet. Responses can be given verbally when writing and spelling skills are limited.

Scoring and interpretation   Scoring is based on answers to questions being right or wrong but some flexibility is allowed. One point is allocated to each correct response. It is a normed test and raw scores are converted to centiles using tables provided.

Standardisation   Normative data are based on two UK samples: 1538 fifth-form students from schools stratified by geographical area, school type and school size. The second sample consists of 336 YTS trainees.

Reliability   KR2 internal consistency reliability coefficients for the school sample are quoted as being in the range 0.81 to 0.89 and for the YTS sample as 0.87 to 0.93.

Validity   The authors indicate that feedback from people included in the normative samples suggested high face validity. Criterion-related validity is based on the meeting of 'adequacy levels' derived from the opinions of a panel of five people, two representing the publishers of the test, a personnel officer, someone from an FE college and a training officer from a YTS scheme. The standard set was for clerical work and minimum 'adequacy levels' for this type of occupation.

Evaluation   This test does have good face validity. Reading a newspaper is a 'real' reading task. It is, however, only useful in determining whether someone can meet 'adequate standards'. It is of little or no diagnostic value.

Country of Origin   UK

Publisher   NFER-Nelson, Windsor (1988)

David McLoughlin

BRITISH ABILITY SCALES (BAS II) SPELLING SCALE

Test author   Colin D. Elliott.

Purpose   The scale is intended to provide accurate age norms for correctness of spelling and to allow scores to be compared with those from other tests in the British Ability Scales (BAS II) battery. It is also intended to provide diagnostic information concerning the use of phonetic and non-phonetic spelling strategies. Phonetic strategies are said to be auditory-sequential attempts at 'mapping the constituent sounds (phonemes) in spoken words on to single letters or groups of letters (graphemes) in written words', whereas non-phonetic strategies are rather loosely described as 'visual' or 'holistic'.

Participant population   The test is suitable for anyone with spelling attainment in the range defined by averagely performing children and young people aged 5–18 years.

Administration time   5–20 minutes.

Materials   BAS II test manuals, record booklet, worksheet, pencil and eraser.

Structure and administration   Items for the spelling scale were drawn from many sources and differ in word length and vocabulary level as well as exemplifying a range of spelling 'rules'. At the upper end of the test there is a deliberate attempt to assess spelling rather than vocabulary knowledge through the inclusion of such words as 'thoroughly' and 'definite'. The full scale contains 75 items, but not all are administered, as the first step is to establish an individual's basal level. Testing is discontinued after eight failures in a block of ten items.

For each item the word is first spoken in isolation, then in a sentence and then again in isolation. Pauses are made before and after the illustrative sentence, and the target word is slightly stressed in each sentence. The participant is encouraged to read each word after writing it and to make changes as required. With difficult words the child is encouraged to guess.

Scoring and interpretation   A raw score total is worked out according to rules that refer to basal and ceiling levels. This score is then turned into an age-independent Ability Score. Using the appropriate tables, the Ability Score may be converted into a standard score (mean = 100, standard deviation = 15), T-score (mean = 50, standard deviation = 10), percentile point and Spelling Age. As standard errors of measurement are provided for Ability Scores, it is also possible to determine within what range of Spelling Ages, centiles or T-scores the individual's true score can reasonably be expected to lie.

Space is provided in the Record Booklet for spelling errors to be categorised according to the following BAS II diagnostic system, which is explained in Appendix B of the Administration and Scoring Manual:

pre-spelling errors   semi-phonetic errors
major non-phonetic errors   basic phonetic errors
non-phonetic order errors   plausible phonetic errors

Criteria for each of these categories are provided, with illustrative examples. The important caveat is made that the system should be used only to generate hypotheses, not as a definitive analysis. This reviewer suggests that the same tentative approach should be applied to the apparently arbitrary statement that errors revealing reliance on non-phonetic strategies *always* involve the omission of phonemes or contain some letters out of sequence. Is it not the case that the *addition* of graphemes may also reveal a reliance on non-phonetic strategies?

The user can make statistical comparisons between Spelling and General Cognitive Ability and between Spelling and the Special Non-verbal Composite score, which is thought to be more appropriate where there are certain problems with expressive language. However, at the time of writing, no published tables are available to allow the user to evaluate a given difference between Spelling and Word Reading scores in terms of frequency and statistical significance. As a result of the present reviewer bringing this to the publisher's attention it is expected that these tables will in due course be provided.

Technical details

Standardisation   Norms for the Spelling Scale were obtained as part of the 1995 standardisation of the BAS II cognitive and achievement test battery. This was carried out with a nationally representative sample of some 1400 children who were either in mainstream education or who had completed it. Separate norms for boys and girls are not provided and the issue of possible gender-related attainment differences is not raised in the test manuals.

Reliability   The internal consistency reliability coefficients of Ability Scores for different age groups vary between 0.84 and 0.92. The standard errors of measurement indicate that at Key Stages 1 and 3, the chances are 19/20 that an individual's true Spelling Age lies within a range from about six months above to six months below the obtained Spelling Age, while at Key Stage 2 (7–11 years) this range may be as little as two months above and below the obtained score. The test–retest stability coefficient for a sample of 40 pupils aged 5–14 years is encouragingly high at 0.97. These figures indicate that the Scale is one of the most reliable on the market. However, the manual does not address the important issues of inter-scorer reliability and profile stability in relation to the BAS II system of error analysis.

Validity   Construct validity is claimed in relation to the models of spelling development put forward by Frith (1985) and by Gentry (1982). Single-word spelling tests are well-established as an efficient way of assessing spelling in isolation from the many factors involved in continuous writing. However, when compared with other graded spelling tests, the BAS Spelling Scale has a higher proportion of short words with relatively uncommon spelling patterns in the first half of the test, and hardly any words with regularly-spelt short vowels. This, together with the fact that the first 40 items include only two words of more than one syllable, means that in relation to the words actually used by primary-aged children, the Scale lacks face validity. However, in the upper ranges of the test there is an attempt to ensure that the Scale assesses spelling competence with longer words that most individuals will use and understand. Here, the main source of difficulty again lies in coping with more difficult spelling patterns, such as those found in small families of words and those used to represent neutral vowel sounds. 'Friend' is the only 'one-off' irregularly-spelt word in the whole test.

Elliott reports a correlation coefficient of only 0.63 between the BAS II Spelling Scale and the spelling test which forms part of the WORD battery. There is clearly a need to provide further evidence of test validity, in studies using other spelling tests as well as children's spelling in writing samples.

Evaluation   The Spelling Scale has some advantages and some disadvantages when compared with other individual and group tests of spelling. It is certainly useful to be able to compare spelling attainment with cognitive ability measures on scales which are known to have a common metric. However, the individual diagnostic assessment of spelling is hard to justify in terms of the best use of professional time by a psychologist, even if the overall measure is highly reliable. Insufficient evidence of concurrent and criterion-related validity has been provided and it is unfortunate that there are no parallel forms of the Scale. Psychologists may well regard the scale as a useful research tool and will look out for studies that relate assessment to intervention. The BAS II diagnostic system appears to be well thought out, although it needs further research and development. Apart from its use in the Spelling Scale, this scheme could well be applied to errors made on other tests and dictations or collected from pupils' written work.

Country of origin   UK.

Publisher   NFER-Nelson, Windsor (1996).

References

Frith, U. (1985) Beneath the surface of developmental dyslexia. In Patterson, K.E., Marshall, J.C. and Coltheart, M. (eds), *Surface Dyslexia: Neuropsychological and Cognitive Studies of Phonological Reading*. Hillsdale, N.J.: Lawrence Erlbaum.
Gentry, R. (1982) An analysis of developmental spelling in GNYS AT WRK. *The Reading Teacher*, 36, 192–200.

David V. Moseley

BRITISH ABILITY SCALES (BAS) WORD READING TEST

Test author   Colin D. Elliot.

Purpose   To obtain a measure of reading ability within the process of retrieval and application of knowledge abilities. Abilities, centiles and a reading age are obtained.

Participant population   Norms available for children aged 5 years to 14 years 5 months.

Administration time   Variable depending on reading ability. In practice, a maximum of 10 minutes.

Material   Card with list of 90 graded words in rows of five.

Structure and administration   This is a typical graded word reading test. Children are presented with a list of words which become more difficult to read on each successive row (and smaller in text). The child reads the word out loud with general encouragement but no specific help or prompting. Words are read until either five or ten successive errors are made, depending on whether the shortened or full version of the test is given.

Scoring and interpretation   The number of words read correctly is added up. Tables provided convert this raw score to an ability, and thus into a centile and T-score. Tables to convert ability to reading age scores are also given. Discrepancy tables are provided to evaluate the reading score being statistically significantly poorer than any other ability in the BAS.

Standardisation   This was based on 3435 children from all over the UK. The technical manual gives a detailed breakdown of age groups, gender, region and so on.

Reliability   The internal reliability is very good at 0.98 and the test-retest reliability on the alternative forms is 0.97.

Validity   The intercorrelations of the word reading with other BAS sub-tests are given. Word reading correlated at 0.85 with COP (classroom observation procedure), and 0.86 with the young group reading test. Data are given on studies on children with dyslexia, hearing impaired children and others.

Evaluation   The BAS word reading is an up-to-date, simple, quick and reliable measure of word reading. Particularly useful if the facility to compare the score, statistically, with scores on other BAS sub-tests. One can therefore say, for example, that a given child's score on reading is significantly poorer than verbal reasoning or word definitions. My own experience suggests that there is a good correlation with Neale Accuracy.

One disconcerting feature, however, is that ceiling, for example, from raw score 80–87 gives a three-year rise in reading age 11 years 4 months to 14 years 5 months), whereas raw score 50–70 gives a rise of nineteen months (7 years 7 months to 9 years 2 months). Care should be taken in ceiling level interpretation, as one or two words can make a great deal of difference and children do vary from day to day!

Country of origin   UK.

Publisher   NFER-Nelson, Windsor (1992).

Michael Thomson

THE DIAGNOSTIC GRID AND THE DIAGNOSTIC DICTATIONS IN 'SPELLING IN CONTEXT'

Authors   Margaret Peters and Brigid Smith.

Purpose   The diagnostic grid is intended to assist teachers to look analytically at children's spelling and handwriting. It is seen both as a class screening procedure and as a means of assessing the progress of children needing special help.

Participant population   The dictation passages are intended for children aged 7–11 years, but may be used with others if the difficulty level is judged to be appropriate.

Administration time   Each dictation passage takes 5–10 minutes.

Materials   Writing samples or paper and pencil for the dictation passages. Chapters 5 and 6 of *Spelling in Context* (Peters and Smith 1993).

Structure and administration   The dictation passages have a steep gradient of difficulty in terms of vocabulary, word length and sentence structure, with the fourth passage appearing more appropriate in terms of readability for the secondary than for the primary age range. Each passage contains a small number of commonly misspelt high-frequency words (about 5% of the total). The passages are read slowly, phrase by phrase, and the teacher makes sure that an attempt is made for every word. After dictation the passage is reread slowly, to give an opportunity for self-correction.

Scoring and interpretation   Each misspelt word is entered in the grid in one of four columns: plausible and readable, plausible and unreadable, invented and random. Examples of misspellings involving unacceptable handwriting, including perseverations (or repetitions) and reversals are listed separately. In terms of Gentry's model of developmental stages, random spellings are said to be 'pre-phonetic' (and at National Curriculum Level 1), invented spellings are 'phonetic' (National Curriculum Level 2) and plausible spellings are 'transitional' (National Curriculum Level 3). The allocation of misspellings to categories is acknowledged to be subjective, but the overall pattern is said to 'show at a glance'. A preponderance of misspellings in any one of the three main categories (random, invented and plausible) indicates the child's level. However, at all levels the recommendations are the same: (1) identify common letter strings within words; (2) learn spellings by the look-cover-write-check method, relying on 'how the words *look* rather than how they *sound*'. Detailed allocation of errors to subtypes such as doubling, omission, insertion or transposition of letters is said to be a waste of time and to have no implications for teaching.

Technical details A table is provided to support the vocabulary grading of the words in the four dictation passages. It is claimed that the first two passages are made up of familiar vocabulary for young children, whereas passages 3 and 4 are more challenging and contain some words which children may have heard but have probably never attempted to write.

Standardisation Not applicable.

Reliability No data provided.

Validity This is a criterion-referenced assessment tool. Data provided in an earlier version of the instrument suggested that dictation passages 2–4 increase in spelling difficulty in steps of approximately one year, but with a tendency for each level to include an increasing proportion of harder words (reaching 25% in the last passage). While these harder words may generate misspellings for analysis, there is certainly an under-representation of commonly misspelt high-frequency words in the passages. Moreover, the validity of the underlying developmental model is open to question (Seymour and Evans, 1994) as is the view that phonological skills somehow develop without explicit teaching (see Upward, 1995). The authors place an overriding emphasis on visual memory, which appears strange in view of the finding by Lennox and Siegel (1994) that poor spellers aged 8–10 years rely on visual memory skills to spell difficult words, whereas good spellers spell phonologically.

Evaluation The *Diagnostic Grid* does not live up to its title. When using the dictation passages, the teacher already has to know the approximate level of pupil performance. The recording of errors is a highly subjective procedure and adds little to what is already known about performance level. More importantly, no clearly different courses of action are suggested for different kinds of profile. 'Look-cover-write-check' is the universal prescription.

The question as to how the difficulty of the writing task interacts with the assignment of errors to categories is not addressed by the authors. The examples provided to illustrate how the grid should be used include one dictation passage where 65/100 words are misspelt. It is not surprising in this case (where the passage is clearly far too difficult) that the 'random' column has the highest number of entries. It would be unwise, however, to conclude that this pupil's spelling would be at a pre-phonetic NC Level 1 stage in more appropriate writing tasks.

Country of origin UK.

Publisher NFER-Nelson, Windsor (1993).

References

Lennox, C. and Siegel, L.S. (1994). The role of phonological and orthographic processes in learning to spell. In G.D.A. Brown and N.C. Ellis (eds), *Handbook of Spelling*. Chichester: Wiley.

Peters, M.L. and Smith, B. (1993). *Spelling in Context*. Windsor: NFER-Nelson.

Scymour, P.H.K. and Evans, H.M. (1994). Sources of constraint and individual variations in normal and impaired spelling. In G.D.A. Brown and N.C. Ellis (eds), *Handbook of Spelling*. Chichester: Wiley.

Upward, C. (1995). Review of Brigid Smith's *Teaching Spelling*. *Language and Literacy News*, 17, 7–8.

David V. Moseley

DIAGNOSTIC SPELLING TEST

Test authors   Denis Vincent and Jenny Claydon.

Purpose   This instrument was designed for the identification and diagnosis of spelling difficulty at Key Stage 2. It can be used with groups as a global measure to assess progress over time, as two equivalent forms are provided for the first six sub-tests. For diagnostic assessment a qualitative approach to sub-test analysis is recommended.

Participant population   Norms are provided for primary school pupils aged between 7 years 8 months and 11 years 8 months, but a ceiling effect for able spellers is present in Year 6.

Administration time   45–55 minutes.

Materials   Test manual, pupil response booklets, pencil(s) and paper for the dictation test.

Structure and administration   The first six sub-tests exist in two forms (A and B), but the spelling self-concept and dictation sub-tests do not. There is a practice item for each sub-test.

Test 1 is a sentence-reading task in which the child has to select one of a pair of homophones (e.g. A fishing rod is no use without a reel/real). Help can be provided with the reading if required.

Test 2 also involves sentence reading, but requires the pupil to write in a missing word, given the initial letter and a picture clue. The missing words are all high-frequency nouns of between five and nine letters.

Test 3 is a proof-reading task in which the child has to find and correct five errors in a passage of 52 words.

Test 4 presents initial letters, pictures and relevant letter strings repeated in a word group as clues to 'spelling by analogy'.

Test 5 is a multiple-choice task where the child has to select a nonsense word that 'looks most like an English word'.

Test 6 is a speeded word-recognition task in dictionary form with between eight and twelve distractors per item.

Test 7 is a self-rating scale with items like 'My spelling is rather poor' which are read aloud by the teacher.

The supplementary dictation passage is read once at normal speed and then dictated in phrases, repeating each phrase three times.

When the Diagnostic Spelling Test is administered to groups, precautions against copying are needed. The teacher does not allow discussion between children but may provide help with reading test items, such as the sentences in Tests 1 and 2.

Scoring and interpretation The total score for Tests 1–6 is added to the dictation score out of 10 to obtain a raw score total. The conversion tables provide standard scores according to age in years and completed months. A 'spelling age' can be derived by finding the age at which the raw score in question corresponds to a standard score of 100. Some guidance is given regarding the identification of strengths and weaknesses, and it is suggested that poor performance in a particular sub-test indicates the need to develop certain skills. For example, a low score on Test 1 (homophones) is said to indicate the need to develop a more precise visual approach to spelling and a poor performance in Test 5 indicates the need for conscious study of the composition of words.

Technical details

Standardisation The *Diagnostic Spelling Test* was standardised on 4236 children in a nationally representative sample of schools. Separate norms for boys and girls are not provided, although girls were found to score significantly higher.

Reliability Internal consistency reliability for tests 1–6 combined (55 items in all) is excellent (0.95), but the spelling self-concept measure of 10 items is understandably less reliable and can yield discrepant results (same-day test-retest r = 0.72). No information is provided concerning the reliability of the following individual tests: homophones, common words, proof-reading, letter strings, nonsense words and dictionary use. The correlation coefficient between forms A and B for tests 1–6 combined is high at r = 0.95. The dictation test yielded a high split-half reliability coefficient (0.96).

Validity Evidence is presented that Tests 1–6 both separately and in combination are a valid measure of spelling competence as indicated by spelling performance in the dictation test and in other school work including free writing. These validity coefficients are in the range 0.51–0.88. Test 2 (common words) and Test 4 (letter strings) yield the highest corre-lations with these criteria. Test 7 (self-concept) appears to be of relatively low validity, with coefficients in the range 0.31–0.47. Factorial validity is demonstrated by the high loadings of Tests 1–6 and the dictation test on a single common factor accounting for approximately 70% of the variance between sub-tests.

Evaluation The *Diagnostic Spelling Test* provides a useful range of tech-niques for assessing spelling, some of which go beyond informal classroom assessment. Of these the dictation passage, the spelling of common words and the letter strings test appear to be the most valid. Both dictionary use and proof-reading play a part in producing a well-spelled piece of writing, but the tasks provided here can only be a starting point for assessment. The question has to be asked as to how far the test is truly diagnostic. It does not readily provide a basis for analysis of different types of misspelling as there may well be too few errors for reliable differentiation. Considerable effort could be expended in profile analysis when apparent strengths and weaknesses may be no more than random fluctuations. If the test provides no more than a global measure of spelling accuracy, it is rather cumbersome for the purpose. However, it does serve the useful function of informing the teacher's thinking about how children can be helped to improve their spelling.

Country of origin   UK.

Publisher   NFER-Nelson, Windsor (1982).

David Moseley

DYSLEXIA SCREENING INSTRUMENT (DSI)

Test authors K.B. Coon, M.M. Waguespack and M.J. Polk.

Purpose The DSI is designed for use in schools as 'a starting point for identifying students at risk for dyslexia' (Manual, p.3). It is designed to help teachers in the USA obtain the evidence required in relation to legislation concerning students with dyslexia. The instrument claims to be efficient and non-intrusive.

Participant population The DSI can be used to screen students aged between 6 to 21 years. The rating scale discriminates between students who have, or do not have, dyslexia. It can be used as an initial screening instrument with groups and individuals.

Administration time Rated and scored in less than 60 seconds.

Materials These consist of: a manual (33 pp.); teacher rating forms containing 33 items (2 pp.); computer software for scoring and tests (3.5" and 5.25" diskettes). An IBM compatible computer is also required with DOS version 3.0 or higher, and a printer.

Structure and administration The DSI consists of a 33-item rating scale to be completed by a teacher. Each of the items in the scale is rated by the teacher on a 5-point scale. A rating of 1 signifies 'Never exhibits' and one of 5 indicates 'Always exhibits' the behaviour specified in the item. It is essential that the teacher carrying out the rating should have 'worked directly with the student for at least six weeks' (Manual, p.3). No more than three of the statements can be left blank without invalidating the scoring.

Scoring and interpretation Using a computer, the student's ratings are analysed via the scoring program software. The program can be run from either floppy disc or hard drive. The end result includes a summary. This can provide student's name, identification, date of rating, grade, school, rater's name, rater's title, etc. Then comes a classification of the student: Passed (not dyslexic); Failed (dyslexic); Inconclusive; or Cannot be scored. In addition, the ratings given by the teacher on each item can be viewed, stored and printed out as required.

Technical details The DSI measures a cluster of behavioural characteristics associated with dyslexia. It discriminates between students who have, or have not, been classified as having dyslexia.

Based on a review of the literature, a pool of some 70 statements was identified. Teachers experienced in work with students with dyslexia sorted the items for their importance as indices of dyslexia. The result was that

42 of the original items were retained. Additional experts in the diagnosis of dyslexia considered these remaining items and added further ones. Other items were deleted where overlaps existed. The total of items that remained was 43.

Standardisation From a population of 60,699 students attending 97 schools in a metropolitan school district, rating forms were collected from 386 students in the age range 5 years 10 months to 21 years 4 months. Of these 172 were elementary school students and 314 were from the secondary sector, and of these, 103 were participating in a dyslexia alleviation programme. (One is surprised at such an apparently low incidence of dyslexias on a special programme, unless the sample was only a subset of such students in the school district.) These students were of 'average intellectual ability' and were significantly underachieving.

Discriminant function analysis is often used to determine the best weighted combination of a set of item scores to maximise the differences between groups. It is used to increase the accuracy with which students are classified. Using this technique, actual group membership was compared with the predicted group membership, as indicated by the 43-item rating scale. A refined scale of 33 items was retained. Separate analyses were carried out for primary and secondary school students.

Given that a student has to be classified into one of two groups, the posterior probability shows the likelihood that the student belongs to an appropriate group. The posterior probability level was set at 95%. If this stringent criterion is not met, the screening is deemed 'inconclusive'.

Reliability This was assessed by internal consistency reliability and the standard errors of measurement for both primary and secondary samples, respectively. The former were 0.99 and 0.98; the latter 0.28 and 0.42.

Inter-rater reliability was checked using 27 elementary and 29 secondary school students deemed to be at risk because of dyslexia. At the primary school level, inter-rater correlation was $r = 0.96$ and the agreement on classification, 100%. At the secondary level the figures were $r = 0.91$ and agreement = 97%.

Validity Content validity of the items comprising the scale is claimed. Construct validity was based on the initial discriminant function analyses. Out of 172 primary school students and 214 in the secondary sample, 169 and 211, respectively, were correctly classified. Predictive validity on the ability of the rating scale to predict a diagnosis of dyslexia was carried with two small samples ($N = 34$ and $N = 9$).

An additional three-stage screening study is also reported with a population of 762 primary and secondary school students who had never been referred for testing. The DSI, when used in conjunction with other measures including academic attainments and cognitive ability, demonstrated the value of the DSI as a screening instrument. Of the 762 students in the study, 4.7% were found to have dyslexia.

Evaluation The potential of 'expert systems' and computer technology for valid and efficient assessment and diagnosis is considerable. The authors are to be congratulated on their aspirations and the mechanics of their system.

Dyslexia is a complex and variable syndrome, rather than a discrete condition. In my view, there is neither an unequivocal conceptual consensus concerning its nature nor empirical consensus as to its identification. The diagnosis of children as having dyslexia is notoriously problematic (Pumfrey and Reason, 1992). The discriminant analyses build on already identified groups. How confident are we that this initial classification has been adequately done, even though guidelines exist? False positives and false negatives remain ever-present threats to the validity of any assessment procedure. In addition, when one examines the 33 items of the DSI, one sees a set of items that will almost certainly distinguish between students of low, average and high attainments in reading and in other academic subjects, irrespective of general ability.

Personally, I would have preferred a more technical manual in which the various analyses were presented in greater detail and the decision making for the acceptance and rejection of items made explicit.

One would have expected the possibility of indicating different *types* of dyslexia to have been explored and, if found, possibly indicated in a screening procedure. As the authors themselves point out, decisions based on rating scales have many limitations, but can be used to advantage in conjunction with other assessments. Despite the reservations indicated above, colleagues in this and other countries could, to advantage, explore the validity and develop further the utility of this particular approach to initial screening.

Country of origin USA.

Publisher Psychological Corporation (1996).

References

Coon, K.B., Waguespack, M.M. and Polk, M.J. (1994). *Dyslexia Screening Instrument*. San Antonio: The Psychological Corporation.

Dykman, R.A. and Ackerman, P.T. (1991). Attention deficit disorder and specific reading disability: separate but often overlapping disorders. *Journal of Learning Disabilities*, 24, 96–103.

Pumfrey, P.D. and Reason, R. (1992). *Specific Learning Difficulties (Dyslexia): Challenges and Responses*. London: Routledge (5th impression, 1995).

Peter D. Pumfrey

LONDON READING TEST

Test Author   Neil Hagues.

Purpose   This is a reading comprehension test, which mainly uses the cloze technique, that can be given to groups of children or to a whole class. The child needs to be able to have basic word-reading skills and to be able to generate the appropriate word in the gaps in the text. In addition, the child will need to have appropriate skills in verbal reasoning, vocabulary and writing. This is a reading comprehension test originally designed by teachers, inspectors and researchers of the old Inner London Education Authority. It enabled information on reading skills to be provided for pupils transferring to secondary schools. There has been a recent standardisation, so the test is still up to date.

Participant population   Children between 9 years 7 months to 12 years 2 months, depending on Forms D and E, which have slight variations in age range.

Administration time   Untimed, 15 to 30 minutes for the practice test and 30 to 60 minutes for the main test, as maximum times. In practice, average readers will probably take less than 30 minutes for the main test.

Materials   A single sheet for the practice test, a booklet for the main test and a manual. The booklets are completed by the children and the summary scoring is worked out on the front page of the booklet.

Structure and administration   Forms D and E are the latest standardised forms. The passages were written to be interesting and suitable for a social and ethnically mixed population. The test is untimed and the practice test should be given in a separate session before the main test. The purpose of the practice session is to familiarise the pupils with the cloze procedure, which has its own specific features, such as only one word in the gap, no contractions (e.g. *he's*), gap length does not give a clue to word length, there is often more than one possible answer.

The main test is allocated one hour to be completed by the whole class or group. This consists of three passages. The first two use the cloze technique as already described, but the third is a complete passage followed by questions. The child has to write answers after each question in the long gap provided. The children are told that they should work through all the passages until they finish. The manual suggests that they should be encouraged to check their answers when they reach the end.

Structure and administration   Marking keys are provided with several suggestions for each cloze gap. 'Drain, gap, hole, *and so on*' were appropriate first correct answers in the first gap in the first passage of Form E! Words incorrectly spelled, but recognisably correct are acceptable. Careful explanations are given for some of the underlying statistics with a teacher readership in mind. Given the age of the child and the total raw score, the standardised score, percentile rank and confidence band can be looked up. For children with reading difficulties an examination of their answers in the cloze passages can offer insights into whether the children provided answers which were syntactically or semantically appropriate. This could indicate that the problem is more a limited grasp of English language than a problem in basic reading skills.

Standardisation Despite its name the test was standardised not just in London, but was also based on a random sample of the national register of maintained schools in England. This resulted in testing a proportionally stratified sample of 3428 pupils in 1992. The actual sample ranged from 10 years 6 months to 11 years 6 months, so the young and old extremes of ages in the tables are based on extrapolations. An inner London sample of a massive 19,845 children tested in 1989 is given in a table of separate norms.

Reliability Internal consistencies were 0.91 and 0.93, respectively for the national and London samples.

Evaluation This is a test provided for the specific purpose of giving teachers a test instrument to assess reading comprehension skills at the point of transfer to secondary schools. These children entering secondary schools should not only be able to read individual words, they need other reading skills as well. This test in a limited way is testing those skills such as the ability to use reading to extract information and to make inferences about the text. It is a useful coarse first filter, in the sense that those who pass through satisfactorily should be able to cope at the secondary level. However, there will be some children who will not have these skills. A small proportion of these could find the prospect of this test too daunting and teachers will presumably be sensitive to other tests that would be more suitable for their particular needs. This is because the London test is not tailored so that there is a fast exit for those who are struggling beyond their level. Children who perform poorly on the London test would need to be looked at in more detail, and depending on outcome, a programme of training might need to be devised.

Country of origin UK.

Publisher NFER-Nelson, Windsor (1993).

John R. Beech

MACMILLAN INDIVIDUAL READING ANALYSIS (MIRA)

Test author Denis Vincent and Michael de la Mare.

Purpose This is a test of oral reading ability for infant and junior school-aged children, designed primarily to assess reading accuracy, although reading comprehension skill is also measured. The test can be used to determine the performance level of children with reading difficulties. Diagnostic assessment of their particular difficulties can also be conducted and their short-term progress monitored. In addition, the test can be used as an annual measure of reading development for mainstream infant and young junior school-aged children.

Participant population Children between 5 years 6 months and 10 years.

Administration time Untimed, approximately 5 to 15 minutes.

Materials The complete pack contains a reading booklet, which has three parallel forms of the test, and packs of individual record sheets for each form. There are also two manuals: the administration manual, which contains the basic information necessary to administer and score the test and the teacher's guide, which provides additional details about diagnostic assessment and the development of the test.

Structure and administration Children read aloud a series of texts that are graded in difficulty. The texts include examples of narrative and expository forms (at differing levels across the three forms) and each is accompanied by pictures. The test administrator is not permitted to correct or supply misread or unknown words. Once a prescribed number of errors in a particular passage have been made the child is encouraged to finish that passage, but subsequent texts are not attempted. A number of comprehension questions assessing both literal and inferential information are asked after each passage is read. These questions are asked regardless of the number of errors made during reading. A miscue analysis can be conducted for diagnostic purposes and a qualitative evaluation of reading strategies can also be completed if desired.

Scoring and interpretation Two types of score, for both reading accuracy and comprehension, are provided for each of the three forms. Standardised scores for top year infants (6–7 year olds) are given. These scores can be used to follow a child's progress within this age group, in particular to monitor the effects of a remediation programme. Age-equivalent scores, from approximately 5 years to 10 years 10 months (slight variation according to the particular form used), are also provided. These scores are given as an age range with a mid-point. However, the authors note that comprehension scores are only intended as a 'rough check' of this ability and that a discrepancy of less than 18 months between accuracy and comprehension scores should be interpreted cautiously. In addition to these quantitative measures, diagnostic miscue analysis and qualitative evaluation of both accuracy and comprehension behaviours, designed to provide an evaluation of the strategies and cues used during oral reading, can be conducted. Clear and detailed instructions on all methods of scoring and their interpretation are provided in the manuals, including worked examples of the miscue analysis.

Standardisation The test has been standardised, by teachers, on two different populations for the two different intended uses mentioned above. First, a cohort of between 1144 and 1296 top year infant children were administered each of the three forms of the test (absence etc. meant that full data were not available for all three forms). A two-to three-month time interval elapsed between each form. This sample was used to assess short-term progress in reading. For the second standardisation, a sample of between 1072 and 1097 children received each of the three forms. Children between the ages of 6 years 1 month and 10 years 1 month took part in this process and these data were used to produce the age-equivalent scores.

Reliability Inter-form reliability of the test was assessed by computing the correlations between the scores obtained for each form in the second standardisation process. The correlations across the three forms were all 0.97 for accuracy and 0.89 for comprehension.

Evaluation The test appears simple to administer, enabling the user to obtain a quick yet reliable measure of a child's reading accuracy level. Teachers of children with reading difficulties may find the optional miscue analysis and reading strategy observations particularly helpful if they wish to pinpoint a child's specific needs and design remediation programmes to suit the individual. The inclusion of very simple passages in each form enables the assessment of the oral reading of children who are just beginning to read continuous prose and this feature is one of the main differences between this test and the *New Macmillan Reading Analysis* (Vincent and de la Mare, 1985). The other main difference is the norm data, which enable progress to be assessed. These are both useful modifications. However, in my view, aspects of the test such as the 'no-help' rule, constrain the assessment of comprehension skill and the limitations of this measure are rightly noted by the test authors. Thus, although this test will be useful for those interested in assessing reading accuracy, it will not provide a reliable indicator of comprehension skill: those requiring an accurate assessment of this skill would need to use a different test.

Country of origin UK.

Publisher Macmillan Education Ltd, London (1989 – record sheets and reading booklet, 1990 – teacher's guide and manual).

Kate Cain

THE NEALE ANALYSIS OF READING ABILITY – REVISED

Test author   Marie D. Neale (British adaptation and standardisation by Una Christophers and Chris Whetton).

Purpose   The Neale Analysis is designed to test rate, accuracy and comprehension of oral reading, and there is a set of supplementary tests for diagnostic assessments. The test can be used to assess reading progress, and can also be used to obtain diagnostic observations of an individual's reading.

Participant population   Children aged between 6 and 12 years.

Administration time   Individually administered: time depends on the reading ability of the child (about 5-20 minutes).

Materials   The manual contains information about the development, administration and scoring of the test. The reader contains the test materials (a series of graded narratives) in three colour-coded sections: Form 1, Form 2 and Diagnostic Tutor Form. The individual record sheets are for recording a running analysis of errors on each passage, answers to comprehension questions, and the time taken to read the passage. A demonstration cassette is also provided to help test users to familiarise themselves with the procedure for administering the test.

Structure and administration   Children read out loud a series of texts that increase in difficulty, beginning with a practice passage. Each text is accompanied by a picture. If a child misreads or will not attempt a word, that word is supplied for them so that, by the end of a text, all the words will have been correctly identified. Once a specified number of errors have been made in a passage, testing is discontinued, on the assumption that subsequent passages would be too difficult for the child. Following each passage, a number of questions are asked to assess comprehension. The child is asked these questions, regardless of the number of errors made during reading. A miscue analysis of the child's errors can also be recorded for diagnostic purposes, and their reading rate recorded.

Scoring and interpretation   Instructions are provided for deriving the accuracy, rate and comprehension raw scores, with the help of extensive guidelines for what constitutes an acceptable answer to each of the comprehension questions. Tables are given for conversion of the raw scores to standardised scores of three types: percentile ranks, stanines and age equivalents. The Diagnostic Tutor is an additional (but not standardised) form, and there are a number of suggestions for its use as a diagnostic tool. Also included are supplementary diagnostic tests of letter naming, sound discrimination, auditory discrimination and blending, and spelling.

Standardisation   The British Standardisation took place on a total sample of 1760 children (998 on Form 1 and 762 on Form 2), and was administered by teachers.

Reliability The assessments of stability (test-retest reliability) and internal consistency of the test are both high, except that the reliability coefficients for rate and accuracy in the youngest age band seem to depend crucially on the order in which the forms are administered.

Validity The test's validity is discussed under three categories: content-related, criterion-related and construct-related. *The Neale Analysis – Revised* probably fares better than most reading tests in terms of construct validity, since reading the test passages and answering questions about them with an adult is not too far from everyday reading activities. Evidence for criterion-related validity is, unfortunately, drawn from old data from the original *Neale Analysis*, except that some of the Australian sample were tested on both the *Neale Analysis – Revised* and the *Schonell Graded Word Reading Test*. Correlations between the two tests (particularly Neale accuracy) were very high. In terms of construct validity, the *Neale Analysis – Revised* has been demonstrated to discriminate clearly between groups of children known to differ in reading ability.

One worry about the validity of this test is that there is a persistent sex bias on one of the forms for the youngest age band. On Form 2 (but not Form 1) girls outperform boys in the 6 years to 6 years 11 months age band, both on the accuracy and comprehension measures. Stothard and Hulme (1991) have replicated this bias. In addition, these authors point out that the comprehension questions are not appropriately graded on Form 2: in a study, Stothard and Hulme showed that children performed highly significantly better on the level 6 than on the level 5 comprehension questions.

Evaluation The *Neale Analysis* has a number of attractive properties. Not only does it enable the teacher or psychologist to assess word reading and comprehension skill to some extent independently, but it also includes other diagnostic procedures. The revised version of the *Neale Analysis* maintains the general format and aims of the original, but with modernised stories (the milkman's horse has at last been put out to grass!) and presentation. The parallel forms allow for retesting while avoiding practice effects on the passages. However, in light of the points made above concerning the problems with Form 2, it seems that Form 1 is likely to be a better measure of reading skills (Form 1 was also standardised on a larger sample).

Country of origin Australia (with British Standardisation).

Publisher NFER-Nelson 1989.

Reference

Stothard, S. and Hulme, C. (1991). A note of caution concerning the Neale Analysis of Reading Ability (Revised). *British Journal of Educational Psychology*, 61, 226–9.

Jane V. Oakhill

NEW READING ANALYSIS

Test authors   Denis Vincent and Michael de la Mare.

Purpose   This is a test of oral reading ability and comprehension. It can help in the diagnosis of reading difficulties and in reading progress in the early junior years.

Participant population   Children aged between 7 and 9 years and older poor readers of equivalent reading range.

Administration time   Untimed, approximately 10 to 15 minutes.

Materials   These consist of a test manual, a reading booklet and record sheets for the three parallel forms A, B and C of the test.

Structure and administration   The important features of the administration of this test are: that the reader reads the passage aloud; that when asked questions, the reader is allowed to look back quickly at the passage; that no help is forthcoming on difficult words, and that the reader is allowed to look briefly at each passage before reading it. There are six passages graded in difficulty with an accompanying picture on the left-hand side. Questions are asked after each passage is read. The test stops when the reader makes sixteen or more reading errors in any one of the first five passages. However, the current passage should be completed and the comprehension questions answered, even if it is the last passage read by the child. The final passage does not have a cut-off rule. The questions are testing the literal text and the ability to make inferences. If the reader directly quotes text, the tester has to probe further to find out whether the meaning has been grasped. Extensive rereading of the passage is discouraged after each question by only allowing the child about 10 seconds to answer. The reading aloud of the child is scored in terms of accuracy, but other aspects can be noted as well. These are the reading errors (or miscues) and other aspects of reading behaviour, such as omissions or hesitations.

Scoring and interpretation   The test provides scores for oral reading accuracy and reading comprehension. Age equivalent scores for accuracy range from 6 years 5 months to 12 years 4 months, with slight discrepancies between the three parallel forms. Similarly, reading comprehension ranges from 5 years 8 months to 13 years. Any particular score provides a range of age equivalence, for instance, a score of 29 is given as equivalent to 7 years 2 months to 8 years 3 months in reading accuracy. These ages are within the 95% confidence bands. The reading errors and a miscue analysis are treated in detail in the manual.

Standardisation A total of 600 children ranging from age 7 years 5 months to 12 years 7 months were tested in 1984 in order to obtain age norms, using the primary reading test as a benchmark test to determine average reading performance. This method of analysis unfortunately precluded the calculation of standard scores.

Reliability The intercorrelations between the three parallel forms ranged between 0.91 to 0.94 for accuracy and 0.76 to 0.83 for comprehension. Thus the accuracy component is highly reliable but the comprehension test produces less consistent performance. Internal consistencies (Kuder-Richardson, KR-20) were calculated on smaller subsets of data, three from each form of the test. The test compilers give an impression of disappointment that these were not as high as would be hoped, perhaps due to inconsistencies in applications between the field workers. During training from recordings of children reading there was evidence of underestimation of reading aloud errors. This implies that some of the more vigilant scorers would produce more pessimistic assessments of reading performance.

Evaluation This test is similar in structure to the Neale test and the *MacMillan Individual Reading Analysis* with the main difference being that in the Neale a reading error or omission is corrected or supplied compared with the Vincent and de la Mare tests. See Kate Cain's discussion of the possible problems this might involve in her review of the *MacMillan Individual Reading Analysis*, the other Vincent and de la Mare test. *The New Reading Analysis* generally has many of the advantages of the Neale in providing an assessment of accuracy and comprehension.

I personally dislike the use of reading age bands in this particular test. While this may help to give an impression of the imprecision of such a measure, the provision of a mid-point age would have been preferable, with separate tables for confidence intervals. A minor quibble is that *The New Reading Analysis*, formerly known as *The New Macmillan Reading Analysis*, still retains the initials NMRA in the manual, which is not even acronymic – especially if one has a cold.

Country of origin UK.

Publisher NFER-Nelson (1985).

John R. Beech

PARALLEL SPELLING TESTS

Test author Dennis Young.

Purpose These tests provide objective individual and group measures of spelling competence in a task where the many interacting factors involved in prose writing play no part. The item bank approach allows for a large number of equivalent tests to be generated, which means that practice effects are minimised if the *Parallel Spelling Tests* are used to evaluate progress over short periods. Another use of the tests is to provide a starting point for individual exploratory testing of linguistic patterns on which teaching programmes can be based.

Participant population Anyone with spelling attainment in the range defined by averagely performing children aged between 6 and 15 years.

Administration time 15–20 minutes.

Materials Test manual, paper and pencil(s).

Structure and administration Test A has an item bank of 276 words and Test B 300 words. The source of 90% of the words used is a study of the spoken vocabulary of young children (Burroughs, 1957). According to age, between 34 and 50 items are presented, using Test A up to Year 4 and Test B at and above Year 4. Items are selected in pairs from the banks, taking at each successive level one of six pairs at random or according to a predetermined rule.

The test is suitable for both individual and group administration. When groups are tested, precautions against copying are taken by separating children if necessary. For each item, the number of the item and the word are dictated, an illustrative sentence is read, and the word is repeated. Slow and clear diction is used, avoiding exaggerated 'spelling' pronunciations which provide extra clues. Sufficient time (up to 30 seconds per item) is allowed for slow writers, but not enough to allow several attempts to be made.

Scoring and interpretation Using a check-list of correct answers, all items are marked and the total correct determined. A correct sequence of letters is marked as correct, despite individual letter problems involving orientation or letter formation. Such problems are resolved by asking children to read back the letters they have written. The raw scores may be converted into spelling ages and, given the child's age in years and completed months, into standard scores using the appropriate table of norms.

It is not recommended that a detailed error analysis should be undertaken unless further exploratory testing is undertaken in order to find out whether a particular error is a chance event or indicates a lack of familiarity with a structure or spelling pattern. Attempts to categorise errors as auditory or visual or to derive separate error scores for regular and irregular words are thought to be arbitrary and subjective.

Technical details

Standardisation The main standardisation samples consisted of 1981 children for Test A and 1923 children for Test B. In addition, calibration methods were used with two further samples to extend the norms upwards and downwards by approximately one year. The junior school samples were drawn from nineteen schools known to be representative of national standards. Separate norms for boys and girls are not provided, but the superiority of the girls is said to decline from 5 standard score points in Years 1 and 2 to 1½ points in Year 6.

Reliability Scores from non-overlapping parallel versions of Test A given to 88 7 year olds correlated very highly ($r = 0.93$), as did parallel versions of Test B given to 100 10 year olds ($r = 0.94$). Similar results are reported for eleven subsamples in which different presenters were used for test and re-test. The standard errors of measurement show that the chances are 19/20 that an individual's true spelling age lies within a range from about one year above to one year below the obtained spelling age. With children of infant school age, this range is less: plus or minus six months.

Validity The test has excellent concurrent validity ($r = 0.91$–0.92) when compared with other graded word spelling tests (Vernon, Schonell and Daniels and Diack). Predictive validity in three mixed ability classes over a one-year period was found to be very high ($r = 0.92$).

Evaluation The *Parallel Spelling Tests* are easy to administer, once the principle of selecting items from the banks is understood. Marking is straightforward and practical suggestions for achieving accuracy and speeding this up are provided in the manual. They provide a highly reliable tool for measuring progress in spelling and have the considerable advantage that the vocabulary used is likely to be familiar to most children. They achieve their stated aim of establishing the limits of pupils' spelling skills in a situation where attention is focused on spelling alone. Because they cover a wide range of age and ability they provide an excellent means of tracking progress over long periods across Key Stages 1–3. They are also well suited to identifying individuals with specific spelling difficulties if the scores are compared with other measures of attainment and intelligence as suggested in the manual. The author may be over-cautious in advising against all diagnostic interpretation, but correctly sees this instrument as adding useful additional information to help the teacher or psychologist understand what help children need to improve their spelling and written expression.

Country of origin   UK.

Publisher   Hodder & Stoughton, London (1983).

Reference

Burroughs, G.E.R. (1957). *A Study of the Vocabulary of Young Children*. London: Oliver & Boyd.

David V. Moseley

PROGRESS IN ENGLISH 8–13

Test authors   Anne Kispal, Neil Hagues and Graham Ruddock.

Purpose   This series of six tests is intended to provide individual and group information about performance in a range of editing and reading tasks. Spelling, punctuation and written grammar are tested by correction and production tasks, while reading comprehension is assessed largely by gap-filling exercises with an emphasis on the meanings of words and phrases. Age-appropriate guidelines for assessing children's writing are also provided in each test manual, using the following headings: purpose and organisation, grammar, style, spelling, handwriting, and presentation.

As there is a different Progress in English test for each year group, the progress of individuals and groups can be measured at annual intervals.

Participant population   Children aged 7–13+ years who are able to read the material for themselves.

Administration time   Not timed but takes about an hour.

Materials   Test manual, test booklets, pens or pencils.

Structure and administration   Each test booklet contains four or five separate exercises, with their own instructions. The pace of administration is that of the slowest pupil and a 'filler' activity is recommended between exercises. The number of assessed items per exercise may be as low as 4, but the total number per booklet ranges from 42 items for 8 year olds to 59 items for 13 year olds. Exercises 1 and 2 (the editing tasks) require the correction of spelling, grammatical and stylistic errors. For 8 year olds in Exercise 1 only, the passage is read aloud by the teacher. The remaining exercises are based on a starter passage of several paragraphs and involve a range of comprehension skills and (in Exercise 4) a further requirement for correct spelling. The teacher reads the passage aloud only for the 8 and 9 year olds, but even for these age groups a considerable amount of unsupported reading is necessary. In Exercises 3 and 4 the passage is rewritten in shorter forms, with gaps to be filled in, given initial letters or synonym prompts. In Exercise 5, which deals with the meaning of stylistic elements such as idiomatic expressions and figurative language, open-ended responses are required.

Scoring and interpretation   One mark is awarded for each correct response. Correct spelling is essential in Exercises 1 and 4, while grammatical accuracy is essential in Exercise 2. The marking key makes it clear which common errors are unacceptable, but markers are advised to read the passages and to use their judgement in marking Exercises 3–5. Raw score totals are then converted into standard scores and into percentile ranks using the appropriate tables.

In interpreting the results it is important to realise that about 40% of the items in each test require correct spelling. The other major variable which determines performance is reading for meaning. Punctuation and awareness of standard English are also assessed, but by relatively few items. The items with the highest discrimination value tend to be longer words and more demanding vocabulary items which are hard to read or to spell.

Technical details

Standardisation   Each test was standardised on a sample of more than 2300 pupils attending schools randomly selected from the register of maintained and independent schools in the UK. However, pupils with severe reading difficulties were excluded from the standardisation and neither the manuals nor the technical supplement state how this was done nor how many such pupils there were in each year group.

Reliability   Each test is highly reliable, with Kuder-Richardson internal consistency coefficients of 0.93 or 0.94. Test-retest reliability over a one-week period is of the same order, with coefficients in the range 0.89–0.95. Clear guidance is given concerning the use of 90% confidence bands at all points on the scale. What is not made explicit is that if 95% confidence bands are used, they extend to a 20–24 month range in terms of attainment age.

Test users are encouraged to use adjacent tests in the series in order to evaluate pupil progress over a year. This is done by referring to a calibration table, for which reliability data are presented only in terms of an imprecise 'normal range'. It is surprising that we are not told how closely related adjacent tests proved to be. In the absence of more precise information, apparent gains and losses by individuals rather than class groups should be viewed with extreme caution.

Validity   Content validity is established by reference to National Curriculum statements. No information is available on concurrent or predictive validity.

Evaluation   The format of these tests is attractive and in some ways innovative. The authors have avoided gender or cultural bias and have produced a global measure of some important skill-based and knowledge-based aspects of English. However, reading and spelling, rather than the understanding and use of spoken language, are the main areas sampled, so children with specific learning difficulties in the area of literacy have little chance to demonstrate their abilities. Bilingual children may also find the tests difficult. The readability levels of the passages are such that at least half of each age group will find it difficult to extract the full meaning.

Although a wide range of skills is covered, the tests have not been designed to produce a profile of strengths and weaknesses. However, there is potential if not a need for separate scores for 'mechanical' and meaning-based aspects to be derived, and for spelling competence to be isolated as a separate component.

Country of origin UK.

Publisher NFER-Nelson, Windsor (1994).

David V. Moseley

SPADAFORE DIAGNOSTIC READING TEST (SDRT)

Test author Gerald J. Spadafore

Purpose This is a test of single-word reading, prose reading, reading comprehension and listening comprehension which can be used for diagnostic purposes. It has a wide age span.

Participant population From children starting school to adults.

Administration time 30 to 60 minutes.

Materials A manual, book containing all the stimulus materials, record forms.

Structure and administration This is a very comprehensive package consisting of four sub-tests which assess word recognition, oral reading and comprehension, silent reading comprehension, and listening comprehension. The word recognition test(s) consists of twenty words listed on a page; there are twelve pages, one for each grade from first to the adult level. Oral reading is measured by having the participants read a passage; they are then asked questions about the content to measure oral comprehension. Silent comprehension is measured by asking participants to read a passage silently and they are then asked questions; there is a time limit for each passage. Listening comprehension involves the examiner reading a passage aloud and then asking participants questions about the text.

Scoring and interpretation Criterion referenced. Performance is evaluated in terms of independent, instructional and frustration reading and comprehension levels. Using these criteria allows for two administrative procedures. The first provides for the identification of the students' ability at their present grade level. The second allows the examiner to determine the highest grade level where the student shows adequate performance in each of the areas assessed. A system for analysing oral reading errors in also provided for those who use the test for diagnostic purposes. Information is also provided that ties performance to reading literacy levels and their associated vocational alternatives. This is especially useful in interpreting the performance of older students.

Standardisation Criterion referenced. Forty-five students were used to evaluate the word reading test, 110 to evaluate the comprehension tests.

Reliability The author reports test-retest correlation coefficients of between 0.95 and 0.99 for the different sub-tests. Information from a study of inter-tester reliability for error analysis is also presented and interpreted as being sufficient to indicate that 'the procedure outlined for error analysis is effective'.

Validity Concurrent validity for word recognition was based on comparison with the *Wide Range Achievement Test* (WRAT), and yielded a correlation of 0.95. for the comprehension sub-tests comparisons were made with the *Woodcock Reading Mastery Tests* (WRMT). Correlations were as follows: oral reading comprehension 0.84; silent reading comprehension 0.81; listening comprehension 0.86.

Evaluation This is a very thorough test in that it covers all aspects of reading. Confining lists of words to twenty and presenting short passages of one per page means that is it not threatening, particularly for older, poor readers. It is particularly useful for older readers with its rating of professional, technical, vocational and functional levels. Criterion referencing avoids some of the problems presented by using an American test in other countries, although American spellings do abound.

Country of origin USA.

Publisher Academic Therapy Publications, Novato, California (1983).

References

Jastak, J. and Jastak S. (1978). *The Wide Range Achievement Test.* Wilmington, DE: Jastak Assessment Systems.
Woodcock, R. (1973). *Woodcock Reading Mastery Tests.* Circle Pines, MN: American Guidance Service.

David McLoughlin

SUFFOLK READING SCALE

Test author Fred Hagley.

Purpose This is a group-administered test of general reading ability, with comparable tests for a wide age range.

Participant population Ages 6-12 years.

Administration time About 40 minutes (20 minutes' working time).

Materials Teacher's guide and test booklets at three ability levels, with two parallel forms at each level. All test items are of the multiple-choice sentence completion type. The child is required to select one word (from a choice of five) to fit the sentence context.

Structure and administration The test is designed for administration to groups of children. There are a number of practice items, followed by the test items which increase in difficulty. Testing terminates after 20 minutes.

Scoring and interpretation The tests can be scored by hand (a key is provided) or, in the case of Level 3, can be scored through the NFER-Nelson Computer Scoring Service. Tables are provided for conversion of the raw scores to standarised scores, percentile ranks and age equivalents (for which 90% confidence limits are provided). The age-equivalent scores can also be used to indicate reading texts suitable for children at different levels of ability. However, since this test was first published in 1987, and so many new reading materials have been produced since then, these guidelines are now of doubtful use.

Standardisation The scale was standardised at a national level, on a total sample of 38,625 children: about 5000 in each of six primary age groups, and 4000 in each of two secondary age groups.

Reliability The test-retest, parallel form and internal consistency estimates of reliability were all high, indicating that the scale is internally consistent, that it is stable from one test session to another, and that the parallel forms are closely related.

Validity Teachers' estimates of children's reading ability were used to assess the validity of the test in the primary range. The correlations between teachers' estimates and performance on the Suffolk Scale were high.

Evaluation This test provides an easy-to-administer assessment of general reading ability. It spans a wide age-range, and the parallel forms at each level can be used to prevent copying during group testing, and for retesting.

Country of origin UK.

Publisher NFER-Nelson (1987).

Jane V. Oakhill

WECHSLER OBJECTIVE READING DIMENSIONS (BASIC READING AND READING COMPREHENSION SUB-TESTS)

Test authors John Rust, Susan Golombok and Geoff Trickey.

Purpose The test aims to assess competencies in three areas: basic reading, spelling, and reading comprehension. These assessments can be used together to give an overall assessment of competence, or can be administered separately. In addition, the test is linked with WISC-III. In this way, discrepancies between reading achievement and ability can be assessed.

Participant population Children between 6 and 16 years.

Administration time All three sub-tests take about 20 minutes. The reading sub-tests take between 8 and 20 minutes, depending on the age of the child.

Materials The test stimuli for the basic reading and reading comprehension sub-tests are attractively presented in a coloured book. The basic reading sub-test is concerned with phonetic and word analysis, and word recognition. Tasks are presented in order of increasing difficulty. The first items require the child to select a word that begins or ends with the same sound or sounds as the name of a picture that accompanies the words. The picture name is spoken for the child. In the next few items, the child selects the word that names an accompanying picture, and finally the most difficult items require the child to read words aloud. The reading comprehension sub-test comprises a series of printed passages, with orally presented questions. The first eight test items are single sentences each accompanied by a picture, whereas later items are longer texts and are not illustrated. The child can choose to read aloud or silently, and is not helped with any words he or she does not know. The test manual contains details of the procedures for testing and scoring. The record form has pages for each sub-test, with a removable sheet for the spelling sub-test, and a summary page.

Structure and administration It is suggested that the tests are administered in a set order but, in particular, that the child's performance on the basic reading sub-test should be used to determine whether or not the child should be administered the reading comprehension test. For both reading sub-tests there are three different starting points depending on the age of the child, and testing is discontinued after a specified number of failures. Precise guidelines are given for prompting and querying, and there are detailed instructions for dealing with children who start other than on the first level, but who fail some initial items.

Scoring and interpretation   Test responses need to be scored as the test is administered. The basic reading sub-test is readily scored, but the reading comprehension sub-test is more subjective. The manual provides information on common correct and incorrect responses, and the record form is clearly laid out so as to facilitate administration and scoring. The raw scores can be converted to age-equivalent scores, which span an age range of four months. There are also instructions for using the sub-test standard scores to calculate confidence intervals, percentile ranks, stanine equivalents, and WISC-III scaled score equivalents.

Standardisation   Two standardisation samples were used: a US sample of 4252 children (about 300 to 350 in each of eleven age bands), and a UK validation sample of 794 children. The test was developed for use with both British and American children, so there are only minor differences between the US and UK versions of the test. In the US sample, a sub-set of the children was also administered the WISC-III (about 100 in each age band), or the WPPS1-R or WAIS-R in the case of the youngest and oldest groups.

Reliability   Data on the split-half reliability, test/retest stability and inter-rater agreement on the basic reading and reading comprehension sub-tests showed high levels of reliability.

Validity   Studies of WORD, including content-, construct- and criterion-related evidence of validity, indicate that the word sub-tests are measuring the constructs they were designed to measure. In addition, comparison of performance on the WORD with that on other comparable tests indicates that performance aligns well, and that performance on the WORD is within the expected range.

Evaluation   This is an attractively presented and easy to administer test. Its main disadvantage is that it is time-consuming to administer, so is probably not suitable for routine assessment of children's ability. However, the wealth of information provided by the test makes it highly suitable for children who are referred because of reading problems, and for the selection of populations of children for research.

Country of origin   UK.

Publisher   Harcourt Brace Jovanovich (1976).

Jane V. Oakhill

THE WIDE RANGE ASSESSMENT OF MEMORY AND LEARNING

Test authors David Sheslow and Wayne Adams.

Purpose Not directly a test of reading, this individually administered battery addresses memory skills acknowledged to be implicated in reading. Three scales (verbal, visual and learning) comprise three sub-tests each; all nine scaled scores (mean 10, SD 3) combine into a general memory index. (After the first four tests WRAML may be discontinued and a memory screening index obtained.) Five of the sub-tests offer a *delayed* version with which immediate scores may be compared.

Participant population Children aged from 5 years to 15 years 11 months.

Administration time Screening from 10–15 minutes; entire WRAML 45–60 minutes.

Materials As with other cognitive tests, verbal learning materials are mostly printed in manual and record form. Visual materials include cards, easels, pictures and tray. Pencil drawing is required on one test (design memory).

Structure and administration Unless screening only is required, the nine sub-tests are administered in sequence, with five *delayed* versions if required. One (only) of the nine sub-tests may be omitted and the scores pro-rated.

Scoring and interpretation Scoring rules with exact criteria are clearly supplied on the record form and in the manual. Raw scores convert into 'Wechsler' scaled scores ranging from 1–19 and the sums of these give index standard scores. For tests of delayed recall, difference scores may be evaluated normatively and assigned to categories of bright average, average, low average, borderline or atypical.

Standardisation A sample of 2363 individuals in twenty-one age groups, with 110 to 119 in each group, was tested at half-year intervals up to age 13; at year intervals at age 14–15, and at two-year intervals at age 16–17. US census criteria from 1980 were used to prescribe proportions of participants by sex, race, region and metropolitan/non-metropolitan residence. A random sub-sample of 226 individuals was analysed for SES characteristics (parental occupation); chi-square goodness of fit was satisfactory.

Reliability Coefficient alpha for all four composites ranged from 0.90 to 0.96; lowest median value for the nine sub-tests was 0.78 (verbal learning);

all others fell within 0.80–0.90. Test-retest reliability was determined for a sample of 87 individuals and yielded stability coefficients of 0.84 (general memory index), 0.82 (verbal memory), 0.61 (visual memory) and 0.81 (learning). SEMs for the nine sub-tests are never more than 1.3 scaled score points and for the indexes 4.7 standard score points.

Validity   Many assumptions about the nature of memory were made for the purpose of devising an innovative test. Concurrent validity studies used the McCarthy Memory Index (with which general memory correlated 0.72, verbal memory 0.90, but visual memory 0.48 and learning 0.10) and the SB-IV short-term memory (correlations all above 0.62). For ages 16–17, correlations with the *Wechsler Memory Scale – Revised* are reported: here correlations are all *below* 0.63. Moderate relationships with WISC-R FSIQ emerged (highest correlation 0.558 with general memory index). Following principal components analyses, three convenient factors are described, of which the visual memory factor receives most consistent support; the verbal memory factor attracts only immediate repetition tasks; and the learning factor acquires a mainly verbal character from the other verbal tasks.

Evaluation   This is an ingenious attempt to devise a battery in which a minimum of prior learning is assumed (though verbal learning inevitably draws on longer-term stores (Hulme *et al.*, 1995). Instead, immediate and delayed memory storage and retrieval, along with multi-trial learning, are surveyed across sensory modes. Preliminary factor analyses by the authors show the inevitable segregation into verbal and visuospatial dimensions, with a large *g* component. However, immediate verbal memory tests, of a kind central to reading, show a stubborn independence. Two of these, sentence memory and number/letter memory (in spite of the inclusion of the three-syllable *w* among the latter's items) are welcome additions to classic Wechsler, DAS and WJ-R versions. Indeed, WRAML is the *only* version of a span task to mix numbers and letters: stimuli are delivered slowly (one per sec.) and are repeated forwards only. Sound symbol is another promising task of paired associate learning conjoining visual symbols with syllables; the latter, however, rather like visual-auditory learning (WJ-R) and rebus learning (KAIT), lend themselves to verbal associations and mnemonics.

Country of origin   USA.

Publisher   Jastak Associates, Wilmington, Delaware (1990).

References

Hulme, C., Roodenrys, S., Brown, G. and Mercer, R. (1995). The role of long-term
  memory mechanisms in memory span. *British Journal of Psychology*, 86, 527–36.
Martin Turner

WRAT-3: WIDE RANGE ACHIEVEMENT TEST

Test author   Gary S. Wilkinson.

Purpose   As far as the reading and spelling components are concerned, this test is notable for the great range of ages it caters for. The reading part tests ability to read single-words out of context, while the spelling test involves writing single-words, with a sentence context provided.

Participant population   Children and adults.

Administration time   10 minutes for reading only.

Materials   Manual, card with lists of words, score sheet. There are alternate forms, blue or tan, for re-test purposes.

Structure and administration   The WRAT-3 is the latest version of the test, replacing WRAT-R. The reading component is just a single letter and word reading test; fifteen letters and forty-two words graded in order of difficulty are presented to the examinee on a card and they are asked to read them aloud.

Scoring and interpretation
One point for each letter or word that is correct. Raw scores can be converted to standard scores, centile rankings and American grade norms.

Standardisation   This was based on a stratified, representative sample of 5000 individuals from forty-nine American states.

Reliability   Correlation quotients for internal consistency range from 0.85 to 0.95. Consistency between the two reading forms is cited as being between 0.87 and 0.99. Re-test reliability coefficients range from 0.91 to 0.98. This is a high standard of reliability.

Validity   Rasch statistics for item separation are placed as high as 1, suggesting very high content validity.

Evaluation   The WRAT -3 reading test is just a measure of word recognition or decoding skill. It does have the advantage of providing scores across the age span but its presentation is poor. The adult with reading difficulties might find the sight of forty-two words, ranging from 'in' to 'terpsichorean' rather daunting. However, they would exit long before this point is reached. It could still be subject to the criticism Spreen and Strauss (1991) levelled at WRAT-R, that is, it is too specific to American curricula for use in other countries.

Country of Origin   USA.

Publisher   Jastak Associates, Delaware (1993).

Reference

Spreen, O., Strauss, E. (1991). *A Compendium of Neuropsychological Tests.* NY:
    OUP.

David McLoughlin

THE WOODCOCK READING MASTERY TESTS – REVISED

Test author   Richard W. Woodcock.

Purpose   The test is designed to provide individual assessments of skill across all the main components of reading ability. To this end the battery includes a test of nonword reading, one of single-word identification, three tests of comprehension at the single-word level (synonyms, antonyms and analogies) and a further test of passage comprehension. In addition, one (Form G) of the two parallel forms (G and H) contains two tests for younger pupils. The first, Visual-Auditory learning, a test of *fluid* ability reproduced in full from the *Woodcock–Johnson Psycho-Educational Battery – Revised* (WJ-R; Woodcock and Johnson, 1989, 1990), surveys the child's learning of unfamiliar pictorial forms (rebuses) to which linguistic meanings are attached. The second, Letter Identification, requires the child to give names or sounds of single letters in varying fonts and typefaces. (A supplementary check-list of *all* lower- and upper-case letters in *one* typeface is provided.)

Participant population   Individuals aged between 5 and 75 years.

Administration time   20–30 minutes.

Materials   An easel presents stimulus items to the participant, while on the reverse side, facing the examiner, are detailed instructions for administration and criteria for scoring. The manual provides full norms; scoring software is available.

Structure and administration   The sub-tests may be used selectively and two parallel forms are provided to permit reassessment following an intervention. Only one component, the test of word comprehension, requires the administration of three parts. No test or element within any test is timed. Starting and stopping points within tests permit longer, and hence more reliable, scales to be used: for instance, Word Identification consists of 106 items. Only the 'basic skills' pair (Word Identification and Word Attack) require reading aloud. Older and more able students are likely to need longer administration times on the later items of Passage Comprehension as complexity seems to be a necessary feature of tests of comprehension.

Scoring and interpretation   Each of the four tests (Word Identification, Word Attack, Word Comprehension, Passage Comprehension) yields standard and percentile scores, with age and grade equivalents. These combine, further, into composite scores with higher associated reliability: a basic skills cluster and a comprehension cluster. Finally a total reading cluster summarises all four measures. The resulting profile isolates reading skills from phonological decoding, through reading of (and reasoning with) single words, to integrated silent reading for meaning of complex passages. Adults and younger children may be assessed and, for the latter, supplementary tests are provided, as mentioned. Aptitude/achievement discrepancies may be evaluated in relation to assumed or observed correlations (word reading normally correlates with IQ at about 0.6). The 1983–5 USA norms are provided throughout and these are likely to be acceptable in Britain except for children in the 5–7 year age group, who in the UK are expected to achieve more at an earlier stage. Abilities and difficulties in decoding and comprehension may be contrasted in a way potentially of diagnostic significance (Turner, 1995). A renorming exercise is currently in progress with this test.

Standardisation   6089 subjects were tested between November 1983 and November 1985. Drawn from 60 geographically diverse communities, these were representative of the US population, according to census data from 1980–3, on variables of region, community size, sex, race and ethnic origin; the college sample (n = 1023) was representative in addition in terms of public and private institution and length of course; and the other adults (n = 865) in terms of length of education and occupational status and type.

Reliability   Split-half reliabilities are reported on eleven possible measures, five of them composites, for seven age bands. Median correlation (*rs*) range is from 0.84 (letter identification) to 0.98 (total reading full scale). Seven of the eleven are at 0.90 or above. When Forms G and H are combined, greater precision is achieved: median correlation (*rs*) range is from 0.94 to 0.99.

Validity   Open-ended or free-response items enhance the content validity of these tests. Their elaborate diagnostic apparatus ensures they are closely linked to reading curricula. Intercorrelations with the (unrevised) Woodcock–Johnson reading tests are offered as evidence of concurrent validity. These are similar tests (only Word Comprehension has no direct equivalent in WJ) and for sample *n*s of 33–122 the total reading composite achieves correlation ranges with its equivalent of 0.85–0.91; Passage Comprehension of 0.55–0.71; Word Attack of 0.64–0.90; and Word Identification of 0.69–0.83. Correlations of the unrevised (1973) WRMT with the Iowa, PIAT and WRAT tests of reading are also given and these range from 0.78 to 0.92 for sample sizes of 40 to 86.

Evaluation   This battery usefully investigates more aspects of reading than any other. Only the ability to read connected text aloud with interpretive prosody is omitted. The rebus learning test, Visual-Auditory Learning, gives a neat demonstration of how symbolic equivalents of whole words may often be learned quite easily, thus isolating the alphabetic component in initial reading as the cause of trouble. Perhaps the *verbal reasoning* aspects of word comprehension are of less interest, especially to psychologists used to performing a fuller analysis of these aspects of verbal learning. But the contrast between word and nonword reading is hardly possible outside this battery and the author's related WJ-R; the latter's more recent and streamlined versions of these tests are restricted, however, to users with psychologist qualifications.

Country of origin USA.

Publisher American Guidance Service, Circle Pines, Minnesota, USA (1987).

References

Turner, M. (1995). Assessing reading: layers and levels. *Dyslexia Review*, 7(1), 15–19.
Woodcock, R.W. and Johnson, M.B. (1989, 1990). *Woodcock–Johnson Psycho-Educational Battery – Revised*. Allen, Texas: DLM.

Martin Turner

THE DIFFERENTIAL ABILITY SCALES (DAS) WORD READING TEST

Test author   Colin D. Elliott.

Purpose   This 90-item conventional test of word recognition evaluates the ability to recognise and pronounce out-of-context words of increasing difficulty. Like its predecessor, *Word Reading* in *the British Ability Scales* (BAS, Elliott *et al.*, 1979, 1983), with which it shares overlapping item content, it belongs within a full child psychological assessment battery and, together with companion tests of achievement in spelling and basic number skills, is fully co-normed with all other scales so as to permit use of regression techniques to generate expectancies, and to identify and evaluate discrepancies.

Participant population   *The Differential Ability Scales* (DAS) covers individuals aged from 2 years 6 months to 17 years 11 months. Word reading is normed on individuals within the range 5 years to 17 years 11 months, unlike the BAS equivalent which terminates at 14 years 5 months.

Administration time   Normally under 5 minutes.

Materials   A card with stimulus items is provided with the DAS.

Structure and administration   Words are listed and read aloud in rows. Precise pronunciation criteria are provided in the record form. Alternative starting points, together with discontinuation criteria, reduce further the time needed to give the test.

Scoring and interpretation   Number correct within each of the alternative sets is related to *ability* (Rasch) score equivalents given in the record form. The manual then lists *standard score* equivalents of these (together with percentiles, age and grade equivalents) which may be compared with the scores expected. Full instructions are provided for both *simple difference* and *prediction* methods (the latter are to be preferred). However, some information, missing from the record form, must be retrieved, not from the manual, but from the accompanying technical handbook (Elliott, 1990).

Standardisation   A sample group of 3475 children in the US aged 2 years 6 months to 17 years 11 months was given the DAS during 1987–9. Sample targets were updated in accordance with March 1988 census data. Stratification variables achieved included (in interaction) age, sex, race, parent education (as SES proxy), region and community size. Ethnic minority, pre-school enrolment and special education category variables were given additional consideration.

Reliability To take account of starting and decision point rules, the DAS uses item response theory as well as coefficient alpha procedures for estimating reliability. Internal reliabilities for word reading fall below 0.90 only at ages 16–17 when 'the Word Reading test is less accurate for high-achieving examinees' (Elliott, 1990, p. 303n). The median internal reliability coefficient is 0.92 and the mean SEM in points of T-score is 4.11 (in the primary years it tends to be 3–4 points). Test-retest reliabilities of 0.93–0.97 are given for sample sizes of 79–121.

Validity Concurrent validity data are reported (Elliott, 1990, pp. 245–54) for Word Reading with BASIS (Basic Achievement Skills Individual Screener) Reading (0.64 at age 11, n = 157 and 0.79 at age 7, n = 198), K-TEA decoding (0.79) and Comprehension (0.80) at ages 7–11 (n = 29), WRMT-R Word Identification (0.84) at ages 8–11 (n = 100), at least four group-administered tests of reading and other achievement and also school grades.

Evaluation Word reading is a highly serviceable and versatile word recognition measure of a conventional kind, whose special power derives from the regression apparatus of the DAS, with which it is included. Experience suggests that a comparable UK-normed test should be used for the 5–7 age group, since US norms will flatter British children at this early stage. Thereafter it is precise and reliable, if a little hard on older pupils of high or low reading ability. With only 90 items for an age range of thirteen years, it is, if anything, over-efficient.

Country of origin USA.

Publisher Harcourt Brace Jovanovitch/The Psychological Corporation, New York and San Antonio (1990).

References

Elliott, C.D. (1990). *Differential Ability Scales: Introductory and Technical Handbook*. New York: Harcourt Brace Jovanovitch, The Psychological Corporation.
Elliott, C.D., Murray, D.J. and Pearson, L.S. (1979, 1983). *The British Ability Scales*. Windsor, Berks: NFER-Nelson.

Martin Turner

WORD (WECHSLER OBJECTIVE READING DIMENSIONS): SPELLING

Test author   David Wechsler.

Purpose   To provide a norm-referenced assessment of spelling attainment suitable for profile analysis, monitoring of individual progress and comparison with intellectual abilities.

Participant population   The test is suitable for anyone with spelling attainment in the range defined by average performance of children aged between 5 and 17 years.

Administration time   5–10 minutes.

Materials   Test manual, record form, pencil and eraser.

Structure and administration   The words were selected so as to include words commonly used in children's writing as well as to reflect a vocabulary gradient. A balance of regular and irregular spellings is included as well as fourteen homonyms. Items with an ethnic or gender bias were removed in the process of test development. In the published test there are 50 items and four different starting points according to age. The first six items sample single-letter knowledge and the rest assess the spelling of words. It is necessary to achieve a baseline of five consecutively correct responses and the test is discontinued after six successive failures.

For each test item the word is first spoken in isolation, then in a sentence and then again in isolation. Pauses are made before and after the illustrative sentence. For the first six items the tester moves on if the child does not respond within 10 seconds and for the remaining items 15 seconds is allowed. The child is allowed as much time as desired to complete a response once a start has been made. The responses are written in numbered boxes.

Scoring and interpretation   It is stated that illegible handwriting should not influence scoring and that the child should be asked to spell ambiguous responses aloud as an aid to marking. If more than one attempt is made, the last one is normally scored. The raw score can be converted into a spelling age and into standard scores and percentile ranks. As the spelling test was not intended to be a diagnostic instrument, nothing is said about the significance of homonym misspellings or about other types of error.

The WORD test battery also includes basic reading and reading comprehension measures. Users may wish to compare spelling with reading scores, especially in older children where there may be a specific difficulty with spelling, but not with reading. Tables D1 and D2 in the manual enable the user to evaluate the significance level and frequency of such differences.

The use of discrepancy analysis (comparing spelling with IQ) is dealt with in some detail. Tables are provided that allow this to be done (1) by the simple-difference method, and (2) by the predicted achievement method. Caution in interpretation is urged with regard to ceiling and floor effects and it is recommended that many other factors should be considered before the diagnostic category of 'specific learning difficulty' be applied.

Technical details

Standardisation The UK validation sample consisted of 794 pupils and was nationally representative in terms of geographic region and socio-economic status. There were some differences in the ordering of item-difficulty between the US and UK samples, and the WORD test uses the UK ordering.

Reliability Split-half reliability coefficients for the different age groups averaged 0.92. The standard errors of measurement show that the test is most reliable in the middle and upper primary years. An American test-retest study yielded an average stability coefficient of 0.94. However, when raw scores are converted into spelling ages it is seen that above an attainment age of 11 years the test has a true score range of up to five years (at the 95% confidence level). This is because only one or two words are equivalent to a year of progress.

Validity Correlations with other individual and group spelling tests are moderate to high. For individual tests the following validity coefficients are reported: *Basic Achievement Skills Individual Screener* (BASIS) 0.88, *Kaufman Test of Educational Achievement* 0.73, *Wide Range Achievement Test – Revised* (WRAT-R) spelling 0.84, *Differential Ability Scales Spelling* sub-test 0.86.

Evaluation The WORD spelling test has some serious limitations. It does not have alternative forms and particularly at the secondary stage it is not sufficiently fine-grained to be useful as a measure of individual progress. With a steep gradient of difficulty and a discontinuation rule of six consecutive misspellings it does not provide sufficient misspellings for meaningful error analysis. For this reason it is of questionable value that homonyms and irregularly spelt words are identified on the record form, especially as some of the latter could be classified as regular (e.g. things, apparently, absence, excitement, prestigious and conscientious).

On the positive side, the WORD test battery offers objective discrepancy analysis based on the US standardisation. The predicted achievement method provides a useful tool for the educational psychologist if, as recommended, it is used in conjunction with other measures. Here it is preferable to use verbal IQ as the basis for predicting spelling, since across the age range in the UK standardisation, spelling and performance IQ tended to have less than 10% of variance in common.

The manual contains much important technical information but is rather lengthy and cannot be seen as a model of easy access for the busy professional.

Country of origin   United States, with UK norms.

Publisher   The Psychological Corporation, London (1993).

David V. Moseley

WORD RECOGNITION AND PHONIC SKILLS (WRAPS)

Test authors   Clifford Carver and David Moseley.

Purpose   This is a word recognition test for early readers which also provides a profile of strengths and weaknesses in phonics. The manual is clearly written for teachers and suggests that it could be useful for large-scale assessments as it can be administered in a group setting. It can monitor progress during the early reading years; it could be useful for diagnostic teaching and it could be used with older slower readers. The diagnostic element concentrates on letter identities, letter sequence and word-building skills.

Participant population   Readers from 4 to 7 years; the age equivalents reach 8 years.

Administration time   Untimed, usually 15 to 30 minutes.

Materials   A booklet for each child, a test manual and scoring keys to use as overlays.

Structure and administration   Each question consists of several items, such as *knees, orange, ranger, treat,* and *arange.* The tester for this particular question says: 'ORANGE that we eat.' The correct response is for the child to underline the word *orange.* It is designed to be given to a whole class and is untimed. If younger children are tested the presence of an assistant and working in smaller groups is recommended. The children are encouraged to try each item and to guess if necessary. Instructions are given to abandon the test if there is any sign of distress during the first 10 items. There is a blank page inside the front cover where a picture may be drawn instead. The test begins with a practice item which is used to establish the correct procedure for completing the rest of the 50 test items. The items are generally organised in order of difficulty.

Scoring and interpretation   The scoring templates provide the correct answers. Reading ages can be looked up from the resulting total score. There are four diagnostic categories: consonant grapheme, vowel grapheme, letter order and shortening (fewer letters) for the incorrect choice of items. Tables of norms for these miscue categories for eight levels of ability in word recognition are provided in the manual. The manual provides teaching suggestions to help children with each of the four types of weakness in reading.

Standardisation   The original test was Carver's *Word Recognition Test* (1970) which was derived from 300 test items. In the current version 2 items replaced items that appeared to be dated. The new and old items were compared in a study of 229 children.

Reliability   This was tested on 148 children. Split-half reliability was 0.95 and Kuder-Richardson (KR-20) was 0.98; both these consistencies are excellent.

Validity   For 440 children in the UK tested in 1993 the correlation between Young's *Group Reading Test* and WRaPS was 0.87. Validation has so far only concentrated on word tests involving reading aloud single words of increasing difficulty. The validity of the diagnostic elements needs to be checked against other tests of phonic ability such as in nonword reading and the Bradley and Bryant (1983) rhyming test.

Evaluation   This is a test aimed at beginning readers that has a diagnostic element. It may prove slightly problematic for children who are poor at listening to English as they have to clearly understand the words being spoken and match these to one of the items before them. There could also be a problem in keeping track of the current question for weaker children, to which the manual alerts the tester.

One problem for a recognition test of this nature is how to handle correction for guessing. There are five or six alternatives to choose from per question, which means the chances of getting the correct item by chance are either 0.20 or 0.17. This puts the baseline of chance at between 8.5 to 10 items and if a child scored at this level this would put reading age equivalence at about 5 years or below. Accordingly this should not be a problem, but one is occasionally going to get an inflated erroneous score, by the laws of probability.

It would be useful in the next edition of the manual to have tables of standard scores, percentiles and confidence intervals.

The test has in its title 'phonic skills' and the diagnostic element of phonic skills appears to be really useful. However, there does need to be further research to determine if abnormal problems in all these four areas (e.g. consonant grapheme confusions) causally determine future problems in reading. As knowledge of phonics improves reading prospects (see Chapter 6), the likelihood is that positive connections would be found. One use for the test would be after a course of phonic training to see whether the child had learned to apply his or her phonic skills.

Country of origin   Canada, but UK norms.

Publisher   Hodder & Stoughton (1994).

Reference

Bradley, L. and Bryant, P. (1983). Categorising sounds and learning to read: a causal connection. *Nature*, 301, 419–21.

John R. Beech

Name index

Aaron, P.G. 61–2, 226, 230
Adams, W. 327–8
Ajzen, I. 163
Alston, J. 207, 209
Ames, T. 30, 40
Anderson, R.C. 187
Arnold, H. 39
Avons, S.E. 149
Awaida, M. 88, 148, 150–1, 153, 155

Baddeley, A.D. 145, 150–1
Badian, N.A. 88–9
Baker, C. 226, 230
Baker, L. 183
Ballard, P.B. 49
Bartram, D. 259, 273
Beaucham, G.R. 111
Beauvois, M.-F. 244
Beck, I.L. *et al.* 187
Beech, J.R. 3, 11, 50, 88, 148, 150–1, 153, 155
Behrmann, M. 242–3
Bell-Gredler, M.E. 172
Bennett, N. *et al.* 38
Bentin, S. *et al.* 190
Bentote, P. *et al.* 218
Berndt, R.S. 246
Biemiller, A. 230
Bingham, Sir Thomas 280–1
Birnbaum, M.H. 111
Blatchford, P. 84
Boder, E. 36–7, 61, 92, 108, 116, 204, 214–16
Boote, R. 86–7, 208
Bowey, J.A. 179
Bradley, L.L. 6, 62, 88–9, 126, 135–7, 139–40, 270, 340
Brember, I. 167–8
Brooks, G. *et al.* 57

Brooks, P. 205
Brown, A.L. 230–2
Brown, G.D.A. 205
Browne-Wilkinson, Lord 281–4
Bruck, M. 211
Bryans, T. 16–17, 69, 76, 79
Bryant, B.R. *et al.* 229
Bryant, P.E. 6, 88–9, 126, 129, 135–6, 137–40, 270, 340
Bryant, P.E. *et al.* 136–7, 138–9
Bub, D.N. *et al.* 242
Byng, S. 244

Cain, K. 191–3, 315
Caplan, D. 247
Carlisle, J.F. 196
Carnine, D. *et al.* 62
Carpenter, P.A. 184, 194
Carroll, J.B. 195
Carver, C. 218, 339–40
Castle, M. 172
Cato, V. 55, 56
Catts, H.W. 89
Chall, Jeanne 50
Chapman, J.W. *et al.* 63
Christophers, U. 312–13
Clarke, A. 214
Clarke, A.D.B. 67
Clay, M.M. 86
Claydon, J. 302–4
Cline, T. 84
Coles, M. 28
Colthcart, M. 128–30, 244, 247
Conner, C. 82
Connor, C. 29
Conoly, J.C. 166
Coon, K.B. 305–7
Cooper, M. *et al.* 40
Cornwall, K. 71

Subject index

attitudes to teaching of reading
166–7; and computerised assessment
257–8, 267; and diagnostic testing
37–8; and 'edumetric' approach 28,
31–2; and liability and negligence
280–1, 282, 283–5; and planning
58–9; and psychometric testing 2–3,
10, 22, 27, 29, 30–1; as researcher
29; and screening accuracy 75–6,
77–8, 93; and screening practicality
79–80, 89, 94; and standards of care
284–5; and teaching of spelling 205;
see also expectation
teacher training: and assessment
practices 166; and differentiation 94;
and teaching of reading 55
teaching: and causes of reading
problems 1, 4, 52; structured 50–1
*Teaching and Learning of Language
and Literacy* 55
*Test of Word Recognition and Phonic
Skills* 218
testing, and cultural bias 5, 227
tests: accuracy 75–7; and acquired
impairment 247–53; adaptive 260–1,
265, 273; for adults 18, 227, 270;
cognitive 59–60, 102; comprehension
9, 176–7, 195–7, 230, **331–3**;
computerised 23, 93–4, 258–9,
262–3, 265–6, 269–70, 273–4;
diagnostic 27, 36–40, 153, 176–7,
195–6, 197, 214, 217, 219, 261, 266;
for dyslexia 92–3, 153, **289–90**;
eyesight 104, 105, 106–9, 115–16,
118–20; general ability 59;
hemisphere-specific 269;
letter-recognition 86, 93, 155; of
memory 144–5, 147–8, 154, 184,
327–8; nonword 6, 8–9, 61, 62,
136–7, 148, 150–1, 152–3, 155, 331;
passage-reading 60; phoneme
substitution 127; phonological
awareness 127–32, 134–5, 140,
147–8, 185; picture-based 35, 75,
178, 251, 259; placement 58–9; for
poor reading 12, 20, 37, 59–61;
prose 228, 230; reading
comprehension 34, 41, 53, 60,
308–9; reading speed 9–10, 208,
230, *231*, 269; reviews **289–340**;
sentence-completion 33, 52, 53, 60;
sentence-reading 60; single word 7,
9, 11, 12, 60, 86–7, 214, 227–8, 230,
273, **295**, **322–3**, **331**, **334–5**, **339–40**;

spelling 11, 57, 62, 204, 213–17, *215*,
294–6, **299–300**, **302–4**, **316–18**,
329–30, **336–8**; standardised 14–15,
16–17, 28–9, 40, 41–3, 57–8, 165–6,
214, 225, 291:
  and test reviews 292, 297, 303,
  308, 311, 313, 315, 317, 320, 322,
  324, 326, 327, 329, 332, 334, 337,
  339–40;
vocabulary 188; word-order 189; *see
also* assessment; diagnosis; screening
training: and comprehension skills
185, 190–1; computerised 21; for
diagnostic screening 39–40;
handwriting 209; hemisphere-specific
(HSP) 268–9; longitudinal studies
133–6, 185–6; and memory 156;
phonological awareness 6–9, 133–6,
140, 156; sound categorisation
135–6, 139–40; training studies 185,
190–1; vocabulary 187
truancy 21
type size, and visual problems 103

validity: and baseline assessment 84;
concurrent 12, 93, 296, 317, 323,
328, 332, 335; construct 12, 295, 306,
313, 326; content 12, 306, 313, 320,
326, 329, 332; criterion-related 12,
216, 292, 300, 313, 326; face 12, 72,
93, 216, 229, 292–3, 295; factorial
303; predictive 72, 77–8, 80, 85,
92–3, 95, 271–2, 306, 317; of SATs
measurements 22, 82; and testing
11, 12, 291, 297, 303, 324, 337, 340
verbal efficiency theory 50
vergence problems 104, 107–8, 110,
116–17
vision 7, 88, 102–21, 132; acuity
and refractive error 104–5, 120;
aids 103; and behavioral optometry
110–11; binocular 106–8, 119,
120; and cause of reading failure
118, 121; and dyslexia 102, 105,
107–11, 115–18, 120; and eye
movements 10, 61, 103, 109–10,
111, 117, 120; higher visual
processing 116; linkage of visual
correlates 116–18; Meares-Irlen
Syndrome 111–14, 118; and
ocular dominance 106, 108–9,
120; and screening 118–20;
transient visual sub-system deficit
114–15, 116–18, 121; treatment

Indexes compiled by Meg Davies